Zanzibar Was a Country

THE CALIFORNIA WORLD HISTORY LIBRARY
Edited by Edmund Burke III, Kenneth Pomeranz, and Patricia Seed

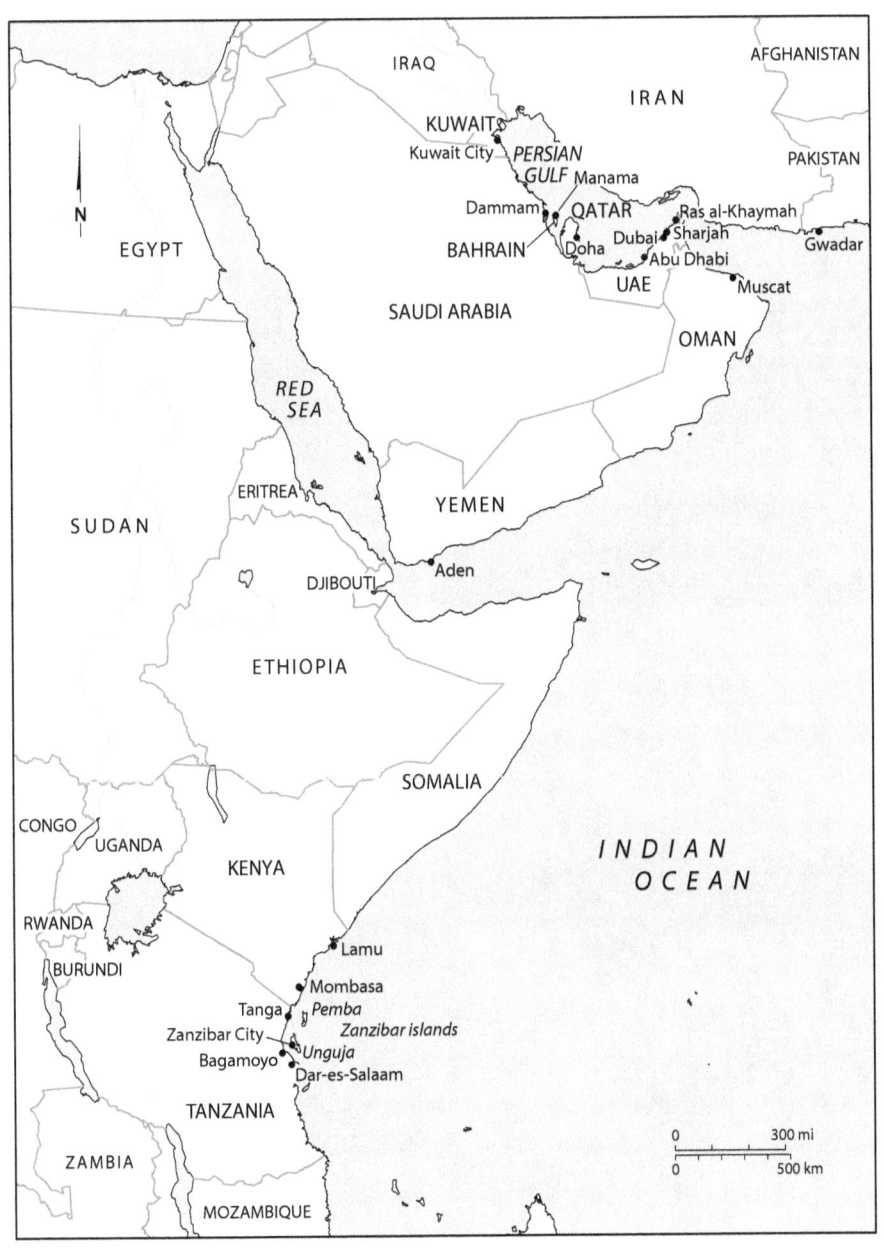

The western Indian Ocean in 1971. Map created by Bill Nelson.

Zanzibar Was a Country

EXILE AND CITIZENSHIP BETWEEN
EAST AFRICA AND THE GULF

Nathaniel Mathews

UNIVERSITY OF CALIFORNIA PRESS

The publisher and the University of California Press Foundation gratefully acknowledge the generous support of the Constance and William Withey Endowment Fund in History and Music.

University of California Press
Oakland, California

© 2024 by Nathaniel Mathews

Library of Congress Cataloging-in-Publication Data

Names: Mathews, Nathaniel, 1981– author.
Title: Zanzibar was a country : exile and citizenship between East Africa and the Gulf / Nathaniel Mathews.
Other titles: California world history library ; 32.
Description: Oakland, California : University of California Press, [2024] | Series: California world history library ; 32 | Includes bibliographical references and index.
Identifiers: LCCN 2023041746 (print) | LCCN 2023041747 (ebook) | ISBN 9780520394520 (cloth) | ISBN 9780520400702 (paperback) | ISBN 9780520394537 (epub)
Subjects: LCSH: Swahili-speaking peoples—Oman—History. | Swahili-speaking peoples—Tanzania—Zanzibar—Migrations—History. | Nationalism—Tanzania—Zanzibar. | Oman—Emigration and immigration—History. | Zanzibar—History—Revolution, 1964.
Classification: LCC DS219.S93 M38 2024 (print) | LCC DS219.S93 (ebook) | DDC 967.8/104—dc23/eng/20231214
LC record available at https://lccn.loc.gov/2023041746
LC ebook record available at https://lccn.loc.gov/2023041747

33 32 31 30 29 28 27 26 25 24
10 9 8 7 6 5 4 3 2 1

CONTENTS

Acknowledgments ix
List of Abbreviations xv

Introduction: Diaspora, Development, and National
Citizenship in the Indian Ocean 1

PART ONE
BELONGING IN ZANZIBAR

1 · Immigration, Exogenous Origins, and the Politics
of Citizenship in Zanzibar, 1957–1963 31

2 · Violence and Emigration in the Zanzibar
Revolution, 1964–1965 52

PART TWO
BELONGING IN DIASPORA

3 · "On Behalf of Zanzibaris Abroad": The Zanzibar Organization
and Postcolonial Tanzanian Politics, 1964–1985 77

4 · Zanzibari Diaspora Communities in the
Arabian Gulf, 1964–1977 103

PART THREE
BELONGING IN OMAN

5 · Return Migration from East Africa and the Politics
of Citizenship in Oman, 1970–2020 133

6 · Transregional Relations, Omani Heritage, and a Vernacular
   Historiography of Zanzibar, 1990–2020 158

       Conclusion 185

        Notes 191
      Bibliography 283
        Index 329

ACKNOWLEDGMENTS

To my partner, Shalini, thank you for your love and support. Mom and Dad, I was probably able to write this because of my weekly chapter summary Bible studies growing up, so I hope you like it. To my brothers, Ben, Joel, and Luke, I love you. To the Mbuvi family and their Kenyan friends—my interest in East Africa came about because of your hospitality.

First among my teachers is Tony Norman, and I am grateful for the many hours I spent in his remarkable library, and our extensive in-depth conversations on history, philosophy, and politics. The primary historian whose research has shaped this book is my PhD adviser Jonathon Glassman, who mentored me as a graduate student and has sharpened the writing and reasoning of this entire project from its inception, in the most generous of ways. I am deeply grateful to him for his faith in me as a scholar and a thinker, without which I would not have succeeded. I am also deeply indebted to my other major instructor in African history, Dr. David Schoenbrun. Professor Schoenbrun did much to shape my understanding about methods for thinking and writing about the ancient African past and instilled in me an appreciation for slow, deliberative, and systematic thinking.

This book is a product of lifelong learning from various extraordinary teachers who helped prepare me with the ability to do a complicated multiyear research project. I am grateful to my University High school history teachers: William Sutton, Chris Butler, Barb Wysocki, and Henry Kamerling for introducing me to historical thought and writing. My journalism teacher Dave Porecca taught me a lot about the art of non-fiction. In Clarksdale and Farrell and Sherard, MS, my thanks to Dorothy and Rev. Walter Jenkins, the late Rev. Carl Thomas, and the New Covenant Missionary Baptist Church family. In Atlanta, thanks to the extended community around the Open Door: Ed Loring and the late Murphy Davis, Hannah, Dick and Gladys Rustay, Amy Vosburg-Casey, Sara Jane Toering, Alan Jenkins, and James Walker. At Lincoln University, Dr. Lenetta Lee, William Garcia, Nosakhere Griffin-El, Dr. Zizwe Poe, and Dr. Todd Herring were influential on my thinking and development. Thank you to the brilliant Sherod Smallman for an enduring friendship made that year.

At Howard University, thank you to Mwalimu Lyabaya for facilitating multiple opportunities for me to study Swahili in Tanzania. Thank you, Dr. Edna Medford at Howard University, for creating avenues to share my historical research as a history major. Thank you, dearly departed Dr. Mark Mack, for decolonizing my thinking on race. Thank you to the late Dr. Ayo Langley for enduring me as an undergraduate in a graduate seminar. My friends from undergrad days in the Howard history department have remained a source of insight, mirth, and mutual support. Thank you especially to Nathalie Pierre and Christine Clarke, fellow history educators, and to Masake Kane for many philosophical conversations over the years. My travel to Africa began with a small group to South Africa coordinated by Dr. Greg Carr and Dean Barbara Griffin at Howard University. The other students on that trip were very influential on my thinking at the time. Thank you to the late Fatima Yasin for lessons in Swahili. For Arabic language, Katya Hildeshem taught me the Arabic alphabet. Terence Potter, Ragy Mikaael, and Lynn Whitcomb tried to get me to understand modern standard Arabic. My Arabic teachers at Qasid Insitute grounded me in Arabic grammar, especially Ustadh Abdul-Rahman and Ustadh Yusuf. Lessons at the Diwan of the Royal Court in Muscat, Oman, through the help of Mohamed al-Wohaibi, were also invaluable. Mohamed al-Shuali also offered additional tutoring. Dr. Moulay Ali Bouanani also assisted me in translation of certain passages.

My old colleagues at AGA in Washington, D.C., were incredibly supportive as I began the initial experiences and travels that would lead to this project, especially Christina Sames, Kate Miller, Nneka Assing, and Juanita Spence. Thank you to the DC Graduate chapter of Groove Phi Groove, especially Karl Berry and Bernie Gordon, Jeff, JB, and Omar. Thank you to Simone Jacobson for enduring friendship and many great conversations on writing, art, and culture.

At Georgetown, thank you to John McNeill, Judith Tucker, John Tutino, John Voll, and Aparna Vaidik for strengthening my writing and opening the doors to the PhD. Thank you to my MAGIC colleagues, most especially to Graham Pitts and Enass Khansa for their friendship and support. Thank you to Nicole Shivers at the Smithsonian made it possible for me to publish my research early on with the National Museum of African Art. Thank you also to Vivian Lusweti, my Swahili instructor.

A Boren Fellowship allowed me to go to Oman for the first time in 2007. That time was made particularly special because of the help of Dr. Elizabeth Langston, who worked with Farouk Barwani and other SIT officials to make homestays available in Muscat for American students. My homestay led to my longest lasting relationship in Oman, with a family who adopted me as part of their extended family unit. I owe so much to the extraordinary hospitality and friendship of Hamoud, Jamila, Ruqaya, Dida, Said, Ahmed, and Lamk, and the extended Lamky family, and everything I was able to accomplish with this research began with our conversations at family gatherings.

In Chicago, at Northwestern University, other professors in the history, anthropology, religion, and African American studies departments made a deep impression on my thinking: Carl Petry, Kristen Stilt, Rajeev Kinra, Melissa Macauley, Robert Launay, Ruediger Seesemann, Muhammad Sani Umar, and the late Richard Iton. A very special thank you to various graduate school colleagues who helped me navigate the African history doctoral program: Andreana Prichard, Emily Callaci, Rahma Bavelaar, Yaari Felber-Seligman. Rahma Bavelaar, Zahida Sherman, Rachel Taylor, Christopher Muhoozi, and Pamela Khanakwa. Also, thanks to Will Caldwell, Ryan Hilliard, Mohannned al-Natour, Raeven Jimenez, Nicholas Smith, Tahir Abdullah, Khairunissa Mohamedali, Moses Khisa, Nurhaizatul Jamil, Nikki Yeboah, Mona Oraby, Hassan Ndzovu, and Jared Rodriguez. Susan Hall and Annerys Cano were great support in the history department. Substantial portions of this work were written at the former Zanzibar Coffee Shop on Bryn Mawr Avenue in Chicago. Ife Carruthers and the friends of Carruthers Center for Inner-City Studies provided me a platform to talk about African history to students at Northeastern Illinois University.

In Zanzibar, to the current and former staff of the Zanzibar National Archives, especially to Sheikh Omar Khamis and Maalim Salim, gratitude for your kindness, your integrity, and your tireless work to preserve Zanzibar's history inside and outside the archives. Mr. Fuad in the search room was also a great help. Thanks also to Said al-Gheithy, who read an early draft; to Ahmed Gurnah for his advice; and to Sauda Barwani and

Ritter Samson for permission to use key sources and for critical feedback. I received valuable support and assistance from Sandra Staudacher, the late Erich Meffert (RIP), Saada Meffert, Faroque Abdela, Helen Peaks, Ummie-Hamoudha Aley Hamid, Amir Mohamed, and Amanda Lichtenstein. I wish my former Stone Town neighbors in Hurumzi all the best, especially Bi Chiku, Maryam and family, and Fahad (Faby), wherever you are.

In Dar-es-Salaam, my thanks to Dotto Luhigo, and Shomari Shija. Dr. Mohamed Bakari at the University of Dar-es-Salaam facilitated access to the library there during a brief stay. Thank you to my Swahili teachers, including Rose Mwangalifu, Wende Mponzi, and Alden Mutembei. Thank you to Ian Tarimo, Gwamaka Mwabuka, and Alphonce Haule for their friendship.

Steve Hill helped me write a Fulbright application to get to Oman in 2012–2013. Dr. Ibrahim Soghayroun facilitated my Fulbright research there. Michael Henderson introduced me to many people in Muscat. Thank you to Abdallah, Sinda, and family, who have been friends and helped facilitate my time in Muscat over the years. Dr. Mohamed Moqadam was also an invaluable support in 2012–2013, as was Mohamed al-Mahrooqi. Batool Baqer and Erin Hart were also a tremendous support during my Fulbright. Also in Muscat, special thanks to Tom Griep, Ali Zefeiti, Laila, Martin, Samira Abdul-Karim, Maryam, Seif and Mo, Koola, Sabriya, Mami, Jamal, Sara, Majda, Sultan, Hamid, Mohsin, Shamis, Hilal, Kim, Muhammad al-Rahbi, Dr. Harith Ghassany, Nasser al-Riyami, Professor Ibrahim Noor, Dr. Nafla al-Kharusi, Dr. Samir al-Adawi, Abdulhakim al-Maamiry, the late Muhammad Ali Muhsin, Gussai Hamror, Muhammad al-Riyami, Heather Saenz, and Mayuko Okawa, who were extraordinarily generous with their time and gave many great suggestions and facilitated connections that enriched this book.

Thank you to the archivists without whom this project would not have been possible: Fabrizio Bensi at the International Red Cross in Geneva, Heather Faulkner and Iordanis Ronganakis at the UNHCR archives in Geneva, and Stephen Noble at the British Red Cross in London. Thank you to the staff of the Charles Young Research Library and the Omani National Archives. Thank you to the interlibrary loan specialists at Northwestern University and SUNY Binghamton, who provided me with access to countless hundreds of rare and hard-to-obtain books.

Across the United States and Anglophone academic community, thank you to my colleagues Hisham Aidi, Marc Lynch, Scott Reese, Thomas

"Dodie" McDow, James Brennan, Jeremy Prestholdt, Amal Ghazal, Valerie Hoffman, Nancy Um, Wendell Marsh, Kimberly Wortmann, Devin Smart, Amir Syed, Hollian Wint, Yacine Addoun, Ahmed al-Maazmi, Toivo Asheeke, Mwenda Ntarangwi, Syed Mustafa Ali, Greg Childs, Neelika Jayawardene, Hafsa Kanjwal, Erin Pettigrew, Saarah Jappie, Khaled Mohamed, Amidu Sanni, Mauro Nobili, and Terje Ostebo.

At SUNY Binghamton, I am fortunate to have the support of a great group of departmental colleagues in Africana studies. Elikem Nyamuame's friendship has enriched my life immeasurably. I am especially grateful to Michael West. Moulay Ali Bounanani helped me with several key Arabic testimonies. Lisa Norris and Kaitlyn Bailey made the work I do possible with their dedication and sincerity. My department chair, Dr. Titilayo Okoror, made it possible for me to go on fellowship to write.

Alexandra Moore at Binghamton University helped convene a workshop on the manuscript, where I received valuable feedback. Thank you also to colleagues in the History Department: Anne Bailey, Wendy Wall, Elisa Camiscioli, Heather Welland, Yi Wang, Leigh Ann Wheeler, Heather DeHaan, Arnab Dey, and Kent Schull.

To my students in Africana studies, especially to those in my Health and Healing in Africa, Africans in the Indian Ocean, and African History Since 1800 courses, and to Jessica, Dale, Ayesha, Jade, Nyantwig, Deanna, Emery, Ifeoma, Jawan, Brianna, Shanayah, Khadija, and Vanessa—I have learned a lot from you all.

Thank you to those who read or gave critical feedback on all or part of the manuscript: Yanqiu Zheng, Jamal Bradley, Justino Rodriguez, Kimberly Wortmann, Mona Oraby, Ricardo Laremont, Marie-Aude Fouéré, James Brennan, Nkiru Nzegwu, John Cheng, Said al-Gheithy, Noora Lori, Nathalie Koenings, Gary Burgess, J. E. Peterson, Hisham Aidi, Jonathan AC Brown, Mandana Limbert, Calvin Allen Jr., and Moulay Ali Bouanani. Fahad Bishara has been a tremendous encouragement and offered critical insight into this book at every stage. Ricardo Laremont performed an invaluable service by closely reading the manuscript through twice and offering comments and suggestions. The three anonymous reviewers from University of California Press also improved the book immeasurably. It was a pleasure to work with Niels Hooper, who believed in this book even before it was complete.

Financially, this project was completed with external support from the Fulbright program, from the Institute of Advanced Studies at SUNY

Binghamton, and from the Oman Studies Centre in Berlin. My gratitude goes to Joachim Duester, founder and director of the Centre, for his support of and interest in this project. The initial draft of this book was completed during a short stay at Zentrum Modern Orient in Berlin. I am grateful to members of the "Swahili Baraza" group who commented on a presentation of this research (especially Ritter Samson, Sauda Barwani, and Farouk Topan), as well as to the larger ZMO community, especially Kai Kresse, Ulrike Freitag, Katrin Bromber. Jacob Nerenberg, and Kadara Swaleh. The Zanzibar stamps in the cover art are used by the kind permission of Adam Gaiser. If I have forgotten any names, I ask forgiveness for my absentmindedness.

I thank The Creator for allowing me to complete this project. May the next generation rectify any mistakes or errors therein.

ABBREVIATIONS

ASP	Afro-Shirazi Party
ASU	Afro-Shirazi Union
BRC	British Red Cross
CCM	Chama Cha Mapinduzi
CO	Colonial Office (documents before 1966); Commonwealth Office (documents after 1966)
CRO	Commonwealth Relations Office
EAMWS	East African Muslim Welfare Society
FCO	Foreign and Commonwealth Office
FO	Foreign Office (also FRO)
FZV	*Free Zanzibar Voice*
GCC	Gulf Cooperation Council
ICRC	International Committee of the Red Cross
IMF	International Monetary Fund
KP	Kharusi Papers (archive of Ahmed Seif Kharusi)
ONA	Omani National Archives
PAFMECA	Pan-African Freedom Movement of East and Central Africa
PDO	Petroleum Development Oman
SQU	Sultan Qaboos University
TANU	Tanganyikan African National Union
TNA	The National Archives (UK)
UAE	United Arab Emirates

UN	United Nations
UNHCR	United Nations High Commission on Refugees
ZA	Zanzibar Association
ZNA	Zanzibar National Archives
ZNP	Zanzibar Nationalist Party (Hizbu)
ZO	Zanzibar Organization
ZPPP	Zanzibar and Pemba People's Party
ZRC	Zanzibar Red Cross

Introduction

DIASPORA, DEVELOPMENT, AND NATIONAL
CITIZENSHIP IN THE INDIAN OCEAN

HABIBA AL-HINAI WAS FIVE YEARS OLD in 1970, when she was smuggled out of Zanzibar for fear she would be recruited into the government's revolutionary youth organization, or perhaps forcibly betrothed to a top party official. These were the paranoid years of revolutionary consolidation on the islands, and many Zanzibaris lived in fear of falling afoul of the new leadership. On the choppy channel between Unguja and the Tanzanian mainland, al-Hinai and her brother Hamed hunched down in the bottom of the boat for seventeen hours, hidden under an old tarp. They were smuggled offshore opposite the Tanzanian town of Tanga and made their way on foot to the Tanzanian capital, Dar-es-Salaam. There they hid again, in their aunt's house, as Zanzibari security forces alert to their escape combed the city looking for them and other undocumented Zanzibaris.[1]

Back on the islands, members of the Revolutionary Council then arrested al-Hinai's paternal grandmother, placed her in solitary confinement, and used her ignorance against her by telling her that her son had been arrested and would be executed and her two grandchildren had been drowned at sea while escaping. She remained in solitary confinement for four months without knowing the truth that they had successfully escaped. Al-Hinai's mother later successfully escaped to join Habiba's father in Dar-es-Salaam. As a result of her subterfuge, her mother's family was ignorant of her whereabouts. Al-Hinai's maternal grandfather was arrested and accused of financing the mother's escape.[2]

Related in her 2012 memoir, *ʿĀʾidūn min Ḥaitha al-Ḥulm* (Return from the land of dreams), al-Hinai's childhood memories offer a rare historical account of a tumultuous era of migration, exile, and statelessness in the aftermath of the 1964 Zanzibar revolution, the signature causal event of Zanzibar's modern transition to nation-statehood. Mere weeks after the national independence of the Sultanate of Zanzibar and Pemba in December 1963, the government was overthrown in what many in the community refer to as "inqilāb al-dammawi" (a bloody revolution). The Zanzibar revolution from its beginnings was shrouded in mystery, conspiracy, and alleged horrors. Memories of the revolution have relevance to the status of post-imperial citizenship, to the political union that created modern Tanzania, and to the broader history of relations between Africa and the Arab world.[3]

This book focuses on the significance of these memories for transformations in national citizenship after the revolution in relation to what Nienke Boer has called "how sentiment functions in the formation of displaced identities."[4] A community of fifty thousand Arab Zanzibaris in 1963 was reduced through killing and forced migration to a community of twelve to fifteen thousand by the end of 1964.[5] Due to the violent displacement they experienced or witnessed during and after the revolution (often later leading to their decision to emigrate from Zanzibar), exiles and émigrés experienced the Zanzibar revolution as a profoundly personal cultural trauma.[6] The fact that some Zanzibari Arab youth participated in the revolution, and that many perpetrators were known by their victims, made the trauma more difficult to absorb.[7] The revolution dispersed Zanzibari family networks around the world, among Dubai, Muscat, Portsmouth, London, Nairobi, Dar-es-Salaam, and other cities.[8] Al-Hinai's account refers to the events as a "nakba," as do others.[9] A letter by Zanzibari exiles in Tripoli, Libya, referred to what happened to Zanzibar as "maafa ya nchi yetu, watu wetu, na dini wetu" (a great disaster for our nation, our people, and our religion).[10] As this book will show, their violent expulsion from the island helps to explain why many exiles and émigrés from Zanzibar eagerly embraced a fundamentally ethnic conception of citizenship in the Omani homeland they adopted after 1970.[11]

The book broadly argues for the value of placing experiences in diaspora at the center of the meaning of decolonization and nationalism and insists on the enduring significance of older transregional relations between East Africa and southern Arabia for shaping postcolonial belonging.[12] As Charles Tilly noted four decades ago, nation-state boundaries do not "mark the limits of interpersonal networks, shared beliefs, mutual obligations, systems of production, etc."[13] The subjects of this book are a socio-cultural legacy of three kinds of diasporic phenomena over their history in the Indian Ocean world: historical diasporas from antiquity to the Middle Ages, modern diasporas from the seventeenth century, and "incipient diasporas" since World War II.[14] The book's focus is the last of these phenomena.

In the context of evolutionist and developmental assumptions after World War II, the "nation concept" as well as autochthony became important for thinking about the boundaries and limits of the political community. Popular expectations of restive citizenries shaped what governing leaders deemed necessary or possible to do to shape the nation as an instrument of development. Debates over post–World War II citizenship in Indian Ocean states often centered on the meanings of indigeneity and led to demands for the removal of nonnational foreigners deemed to be exploiting the national population.[15] Not only imperial logics but the internal evolution of democracy within the new nation-states influenced these demands by tying them to the integrity of national membership. The new arrangements produced territorial displacements, contestations of belonging from below, and state attempts to resolve a number of difficult legal and cultural dilemmas associated with the new regime of national citizenship. From the late 1940s through the 1970s, a number of micro-migration events accompanied national consolidation, as states articulated a homogenous vision of their new national identity and formalized documentation requirements for entry, exit, and residence.[16]

The greatest demographic impact of border thinking occurred in South Asia, with the independence of India and Pakistan and the accompanying acts of mass violence and migration. Majoritarian thinking shaped ethnic prejudice against diaspora communities. In Malaysia, ethnic Chinese became targets of popular suspicion. In Hyderabad, the Zanzibari Hadhramis around the Nizam's court faced down popular pogroms against Muslims.[17] In Tanganyika, nationalism provided a platform for grievances against those involved in overseas trade and export sectors, who were predominantly South Asians.[18] In Uganda and Kenya, South Asian minorities were also challenged by the xenophobic edge of nationalism wielded by nationalist ideologues.[19] In Zanzibar, ethnic minorities, especially Arabs and South Asians, were violently coerced into migrating from the state.

The term *diaspora* often better describes an existential condition than it does a unified community. Those forced to migrate from their homes in this period suffered traumatic ruptures of communal ties that changed their presentation of self. As Earl Lewis noted, "Relational differentials in power maximize the likelihood that certain forms of the self-dominate at certain times."[20] In addition to different passports, social class, generational differences, ascriptions of race and ethnicity, sociolinguistic practices, and gender affected how communities fractured by forced migration negotiated belonging to the nation.

Diaspora groups of the Indian Ocean world, whose migrations within the region predated the era of national citizenship, were uniquely affected by nationalism and nation formation: "the creation of homogenous polities through coercive leveling."[21] They developed diverse attitudes to the formalization of territorial citizenship rules, as well as to the contours of the imagined community of the nation.[22] Some East African coastal residents advocated for a separate "coastal" nation-state, based on their putatively unique culture.[23] South Asian Muslim minorities on the coast saw Muslim universalism as the basis of a nonracial nationalist alternative to both Arabocentrism and African nationalism.[24] A few radical intellectuals and activists refused the very notion of "homeland elsewhere" and de-diasporized, submerging themselves in local liberation struggles.[25] Many ordinary members of diaspora groups tried to negotiate forms of dual citizenship just as they had navigated "the bills and decrees of the colonial empires."[26] While their assertions of indigeneity or national belonging were sometimes distrusted by other citizens, their efforts to retain (as a form of social insurance) multiple passports or multiple rights of residence seemed to confirm to some their "antinational" motivation.[27]

Swahili-speaking Zanzibar Arabs of Omani descent were among a number of groups who underwent a massive structural transformation in their collective subjectivity from the 1950s to the 1970s, as a result of decolonization.[28] The book explores their national belonging claims and how these have impacted their historical memory, with special focus on the transregional impact of a nationalist idea: Zanzibar as a sovereign country. As a result of the 1964 revolution, they carried Zanzibar nationalist ideas into the diaspora, eventually to inform and contribute to modern Omani citizenship after 1970.[29] Their experiences of displacement and the shift in national citizenship they undertook demonstrate the importance of a dialectic between subjective and ascriptive identity to comparative histories of state and nation.[30] In effect, the experience of denationalization in the revolution compelled the exiles to instrumentalize primordial descent claims, embracing a more explicitly ethnic claim to citizenship as an Omani diaspora returning to their ancestral homeland.

The Afro-Arab idea of "Zanzibar as a country" has had a significant influence on the politics of citizenship in three locations: the territorial homeland of Zanzibar, the diaspora to the Gulf and United Kingdom, and the ethnic homeland of Oman in the Indian Ocean.[31]

CITIZENSHIP, DIASPORA, AND THE DEVELOPMENTAL STATE

The expansions of the political entitlement of citizenship and its vestment in the sovereign nation-state were the fundamental political transformation of the twentieth century in most of Africa and Asia. The vicennial period of mass national independence (1950–1970) was a globally transformative change (affecting around 750 million people) when most of Africa and Asia made a transition from large multinational empires to territorially independent states.[32] Citizenship as a status denoting membership in a national territory obtained new importance from 1950 to 1970 as a measure of value, status, protection, and belonging.[33] Between 1940 and 1965, twenty-five new states emerged in Africa alone, most during the heady years of 1960–1963.[34] In the Gulf, beginning with Kuwait, the minor states of the Trucial coast all gained independence from the British from 1961 to 1971.[35] Though Oman had no formal decolonization process and remained under a British sphere of influence, it was recognized before the United Nations as a member of the community of nations in the early 1970s.[36] Overall membership in the international body of nations grew from 32 at the end of World War 1 to 147 by 1976.[37]

What was the meaning of the citizenship obtained through national independence and imperial withdrawal? For those invested in the idea of developmental nation-building, national independence was the gateway to a process of the collective progress of the national citizenry toward greater prosperity together, transcending past conflicts.[38] For the masses it was not primarily the abstract idea of "belonging" to the "nation" that attracted them to citizenship, but rather the promise of economic development and an improved standard of living for them and their offspring.[39] Delivering this progress was seen as depending on management of the national economy, especially a smooth transition to a state revenue model dependent on export-led growth.[40] While late colonial development was offered through metropolitan loans to finance local investment in social welfare, postcolonial development depended more exclusively on territorial exports, which has remained the economic basis of most postcolonial states in Africa and Asia (the export of cloves remains Zanzibar's largest single revenue source).

Though the new nations broke with metropolitan political rule, and although policymakers debated the precise mix of state intervention necessary to facilitate an economic transition, the new nations did not substantially break with the basic fiscal imperatives of the previous state administration or the economic processes essential to its constitution.[41] Modern postimperial citizenship emerged in an international regime of development and inherited conceptions of rule from previous colonial administrations.[42] Ideologically, development remained a common grammar between socialist and capitalist models of the state after independence, broadly shared even between otherwise disparate monarchical and republican, socialist, and capitalist models.[43] Thus the phrase "developmental state" is often used to describe this new/old citizenship-granting and economy-managing territorial institution, in contrast to "post-colonial state."[44]

The world economy grew rapidly from 1950 to 1970, aiding the transition to a postimperial world and sparking optimism about the possibilities of state development.[45] The period marked a profound shift in the economic basis of Indian Ocean societies. The regional economy of the basin shifted away from a primary emphasis on mercantile networks to the technical exploitation of hydrocarbons.[46] Jeremy Prestholdt argued that as a result Indian Ocean societies "became increasingly unmoored from the ocean itself."[47]

A profound material disparity in a single territorial resource shaped the horizon of what was possible for any given development policy to accomplish and fundamentally shaped the unequal value of different national citizenships in this era. An accident of ancient history gave certain regions of the Indian Ocean world vast deposits of petroleum, a product incapable of synthetic duplication and crucial to the growth of the modern global economy after World War II. The different outcomes in processes of development in Indian Ocean states were driven by this key material difference, more than they were by modes of rule (monarchy or democracy) or distinct ideologies (capitalism or communism). Because petroleum is essential to modern industry, not uniformly distributed, and incapable of synthetic duplication, petroleum-producing countries could, unlike agricultural commodity producers, exert more control over its price in international markets.[48]

Petroleum wealth altered the relations between Gulf Arab societies and the rest of the Indian Ocean countries, including those in East Africa. Before petroleum, there was almost no wage-earning economy in the Gulf states, and most food and raw materials had to be imported from India and Iran.[49] Wealth enabled most Gulf national economies to essentially skip the process of industrial diversification, plow industrial investment into petroleum extraction, and transform into service-oriented economies.[50] With their low population density and limited or contested histories of state building, this resource helped consolidate the hegemony of Gulf states over their citizens and legitimated forms of autocratic and dynastic rule that were otherwise being challenged across the societies of the Indian Ocean.[51] Gulf state elites legitimated themselves by redistributed petroleum wealth to the national citizenry while relying on an imported labor force with limited rights of belonging and residence.[52] The demands for popular sovereignty heard elsewhere in the African and Asian world could thus be pushed off, often indefinitely, as long as the existing citizenry's territorial indigeneity (usually demonstrated through existing patronage networks) was secure employment or a substantial social welfare benefit.[53]

Coastal communities from non-oil-producing East African states became increasingly oriented around migration to petroleum-producing states, as remittances from wage labor came to constitute an additional and significant national revenue source in many East African countries. Esmond Bradley Martin observed that from 1960 to 1975 more "illegal" immigrants immigrated to the petroleum-producing Gulf states "than the total number of Africans who were brought as slaves from East Africa to Arabia, Persia and India for the entire 19th century."[54] This created social tensions between what Ali Mazrui called "underpopulated but very rich Islamically traditionalist countries and more populous, more secular and less endowed Muslim countries on the other."[55]

Returnees from East Africa to Oman are part of this broader story of transformation in Afro-Arab relations caused by the emergence of petroleum economies and the migration of East Africans to the Gulf. Oman faced a profound deficit among its citizens at the beginning of this era in the technical aspects of state development, which included the construction of basic infrastructure and the creation of modern ministries.[56] The unsettled climate of citizenship in Zanzibar made available to the Omani developmental state a class of professionals, many of whom were former civil servants from the islands or had substantial secondary and higher education in Africa. Many of the proponents and pioneers of a "Zanzibari" territorial ethnicity on the islands during the 1950s were refugees from the mid-1960s and embraced an ethnic conception of citizenship in their adopted Omani homeland by the 1970s.

OMANI MUWALLADŪN ON THE EAST COAST OF AFRICA, FIRST CENTURY CE THROUGH 1890

The emerging world of state borders and national citizens was already " transversed by older geographies ... created by the movement of people, cultures, and ideas."[57] In the case of the Indian Ocean these geographies date back to antiquity.[58] Arab migration to East Africa likely dates to the first century CE, before the Swahili language had begun to more noticeably diverge from its parent protolanguage, Sabaki, and well before the advent of Islam.[59] As recent DNA analysis indicates, Persian Gulf men intermarried with local elites to produce an elite who likely spoke Persian, Arabic, and/or Swahili.[60] Through these marriage patterns Arab and Persian migrants became culturally closer to the "Zanj" (the antique and generic Arabo-Persian term for the darker-skinned peoples of East Africa), with whom they already had commercial and political relations.[61] The offspring of their intermarriages were darkened and became bilingual, strengthening their lineage and aiding their exercise of local authority.[62] Certain Arab clans later became well established on the islands off the Swahili coast during periods of religious warfare in the Islamic caliphate (eighth through twelfth centuries CE).[63] Rather than creating Swahili civilization sui generis through migration, the majority of Arab migrants assimilated into and influenced an existing urban Muslim milieu on the coast.[64] As a result of these processes occurring repeatedly over half a millennium, we have plenty of evidence allowing us to hypothesize that many Arab migrants between the ninth and fifteenth centuries, if they did not eventually return to southern Arabia, became part of the Swahili-speaking Muslim milieu of the coastal towns, retaining Arabic for ritual purposes of prayer and reading Quran, practicing a hierarchic bilingualism, and retaining a self-conception derived from their paternal ancestry in Oman or Yemen.[65] Enseng Ho has referred to Hadhramis born in non-Arab countries to non-Arab mothers as *muwalladūn*; this designation is also apt for similar Omani and Yemeni dynamics on the East African coast.[66] Arab identity in East Africa was permeable in specific ways, even when the wealthy Omani muwalladūn clans in Zanzibar and Mombasa became more "caste-like" in their marriage and association practices.[67]

Oman had historically been divided between the coast, a region more connected to the secular world of Indian Ocean trade, and the mountainous interior, the seat of the historic Imamate, a unique nonhereditary form of Ibadi Muslim governance. The Ibadis were a dissident "sect" of Islam who recognized only the first two caliphs as "Imams" of the Muslim community. The Ibadis generally rejected a hereditary approach to leadership succession but eschewed the violent and sectarian approach of other secessionist sects like the Khawārij (a more extreme set of dissidents prepared to shed the blood of other Muslims for deviant beliefs). Ibadis instead emphasized the importance of shura (consultation) for electing a ruler.[68] Ibadis were initially persecuted by the caliphate leadership and the belief system only survived in certain regions of North Africa, and in Oman. Among the Omani Ibadis the Imamate ideal underwent periods of decline and renaissance between the seventh and seventeenth centuries.

In 1624, a ruler from the al-Ya'araba tribe, Nasir bin Murshid reclaimed the title of Imam. Oman's political influence in East Africa originated in this early modern period of national renaissance under the al-Ya'araba. Nasir's successor, Sultan bin Saif I, succeeded in driving out the Portuguese from Oman in 1650 and sent fleets to attack them in East Africa and India. In the late seventeenth century, a Muslim delegation from East Africa sailed to Muscat to invite Imam Saif bin Sultan al-Ya'araba I (1692–1711) to assist them in their attempt to expel the Portuguese presence at Fort Jesus, Mombasa. The Imam's naval forces were successful in that venture from 1696 to 1698 and subsequently retained a local garrison, which grew into a governance structure that eventually developed into a dynastic form of rule by an Omani clan, the al-Mazrui.

In cities governed by an Omani representative, conflicts between the new Omani governor and local elites led to back channels seeking Portuguese assistance in overthrowing the new Omani suzerainty.[69] But although the al-Ya'araba Imams appointed governors over certain East African cities like Mombasa in the eighteenth century, there was no lasting unified sovereignty over the East African coast established at the time. By the early eighteenth century Oman was engulfed in civil war between two rival tribal factions (1719–1749), and in 1739 the sixth Imam of the al-Ya'araba, Saif bin Sultan II, invited the Persians to Oman to assist him in wars against challengers to his rule. Rule over Mombasa became a point of contention again in the 1740s, after a new dynasty came to power in Oman under Ahmed bin Said al-Busaidi, who became the acknowledged Imam of the whole country after expelling the Persians.[70] Imam Ahmed, who developed the maritime capabilities of the state, also claimed the Imamate over parts of coastal East Africa. He would be the last titleholder of "Imam" in the Busaidi dynasty, as the increasing commercial influences of the Indian Ocean trading economy wrought a rift between governance at Muscat and that of the interior. Ahmed's son Said ruled as Imam in the interior, while his grandson Hamad moved the capital to Muscat. Hamad and subsequent Busaidi rulers would take the title of Seyyid.[71]

Ahmed's grandson Said bin Sultan was still a young man when his father died. "Seyyid Said," as he became known, won hegemony over Oman through strong political alliances with his father's family forged by his paternal aunt Seyyida Moza bint Ahmed, who helped him achieve victory over a scheming regent.[72] Seyyid Said became highly significant to the history of the Swahili coast after his first military expedition to Mombasa in 1828, his intention to make Zanzibar his capital in 1832, his conquest of Mombasa from the Mazrui in 1837, and the permanent move of his family to Zanzibar in 1840.[73]

For the next six decades, Seyyid Said and his Zanzibar-born descendants ruled over a dynastic state with its seat in Zanzibar's two islands, Unguja and Pemba. Seyyid Said became famous for encouraging the mass cultivation of the clove tree on the islands. Tree seedlings were brought to Zanzibar either at the end of the eighteenth or the beginning of the nineteenth centuries from Reunion or Mauritius (where they had recently been introduced from Indonesia), and Seyyid Said encouraged their cultivation on land grants given to his supporters and worked by slave labor.[74] The sultan's main capital was the more populous Unguja, while a substantial portion of state agricultural exports was derived from Pemba to the northeast. The "state" under Seyyid Said was more of a loose juridical and commercial network, regulating land disputes and sales while also leasing the right to the islands' custom receipts to a Gujarati commercial family firm.[75] Zanzibar's center as a trading entrepot for products from the interior stimulated a broader commercial transformation already underway in the region by the late eighteenth century, in which mainlanders brought ivory, gold, slaves, and animal skins to the coast and the islands for trade.[76]

Omani Arabs migrated freely to the islands in the nineteenth century, either as clients and kin of the wealthiest landowners, soldiers in coastal garrisons, or traders eager to join the caravan trade on the mainland.[77] Often the first Omani migrant to go to East Africa remitted his wealth back to family members in Oman's interior, in the form of building a family house in his natal village. Among Omani clans in nineteenth-century East Africa arose subtle but significant hierarchies of wealth and status, based in part on length of settlement in the region.[78] The most important Omani clan in eighteenth- and nineteenth-century African history was probably the al-Hirth, individuals from whose related clans (al-Barwani, al-Miskery, al-Marhuby) were extremely important to politics, culture, and society on the coast.[79] They predominated among the landed elites of Zanzibar, and the Busaidi dynasts frequently negotiated with their powerful clan heads to maintain rule over Zanzibar. Other prominent elites were drawn from the Ghafiri tribal section, which included al-Riyami and al-Mugheiry clans. The al-Kharusi and al-Lamky clans were also predominant among this landed elite.

Later-arriving migrants from Oman, mainly from the eastern interior, and with less capital than the early settlers, were more likely to risk their livelihood on the more dangerous trading expeditions into the interior, and many settled permanently in the African interior instead of Zanzibar.[80] Some of these traders also converted their clients and helped introduce Islam into interior polities like Buganda.[81] Many locally born East African Arabs also avidly participated in the caravan trade. The muwalladūn grandson of a coastal-born Afro-Arab, Hamed Muhammad al-Murjebi ran one of the most successful trading expedition firms in all of nineteenth-century East Africa.[82] This was also during a period when free African merchants from Unyamwezi and "Yao-land" traveled in increasing numbers to coastal cities like Bagamoyo and Dar-es-Salaam to trade.[83] There were appreciable numbers of Baluchi mercenaries serving in the sultan's military or in private militias in the interior, as well as merchants from Gujarat, Kachchh, and Hadhramaut involved in financing the trade.[84] Many of these imperial and commercial entrepreneurs also traded in slaves. By the mid-nineteenth century, traders were bringing them from farther in the East African interior and retaining them for work on clove, coconut, and grain plantations on the coast or the islands.

An autonomous domain of the political acting to reshape society was never carved out by the Busaidi rulers as it was by the later iterations of the British and German colonial states who colonized the coast. Though they installed local representatives of their rule, the limited power of the Omani elites meant they were largely constrained to act within codes of political conduct that had long shaped coastal society. The argument that coastal values made some kind of fundamental transition from "uungwana" (a locally based coastal ideal) to "ustaarabu" (an Arab-based value system) has been overdrawn and frequently misunderstood.[85] A better way to see the ideological transition is to understand that through Busaidi rule, "Ibadism struck deeper roots there."[86] As a result, Zanzibar became the center of a cosmopolitan intellectual exchange between Sunnism, Ibadism, and Shiism.[87]

After Seyyid Said's death in 1856, his empire's sovereignty underwent a division by which the two "rims" of the empire were detached from each other. British intervention into a Busaidi succession dispute produced the Canning Award (1861), in which Zanzibar and Oman were split into separate states to be ruled by Seyyid Said's offspring.[88] The award further specified an annual subsidy to be paid by the ruler of Zanzibar to the ruler of Oman.[89] The award was initially used by Zanzibar's rulers after Said to facilitate the loyalty of their Omani counterpart, and during the twentieth century it was often paid by the British government of India as a reward for an Omani ruler's loyalty.[90] Oman at the time was viewed as a poor marginal backwater in the eyes of British rulers, useful only as a security buffer for Britain's colonies in India.[91]

Zanzibar, on the other hand, remained East Africa's foremost commercial center, and its agricultural exports experienced steady demand throughout the nineteenth century.[92] Under Bargash bin Said (1870–1888), Zanzibar became the center of a Muslim intellectual renaissance, spurred by the importation of a printing press and the printing of classic Ibadi texts in the early 1880s.[93] From the early decades of the nineteenth century through the 1870s, British power in Zanzibar grew with a succession of British consuls who essentially forced the end of the slave trade by treaties with Zanzibar's sultans.[94] After 1890, the Busaidi dynasty in Zanzibar was invested with a limited form of sovereignty under a British protectorate. British policy in the Zanzibar protectorate left the figure of the sultan symbolically intact and deemed the landed families of the island essential to the agricultural productivity of the state.[95] Slavery was eventually outlawed in 1897, without breaking up the largest agricultural estates.[96] Poorer Omanis continued to migrate to Zanzibar in the first few decades of the twentieth century, along with many mainlanders attracted by relatively high wages in the protectorate. Despite the new cash nexus, wage labor could not meet the demand for skilled pickers, and landowners gave former slaves various kinds of stakes in the land to retain their labor at harvest time.[97]

THE DEVELOPMENTAL STATE IN ZANZIBAR
AND THE MAKING OF THE AFRO-ARABS, 1890–1954

Unguja and Pemba in the 1950s were unique in Africa as a whole, in that Arabs made up to as much as 20 percent of their total population, the second largest proportionally among Arab communities in Africa south of the Sahara.[98] However, their minority status differed dramatically between the islands. According to the 1948 census, Arabs were just under 10 percent of Unguja's population and over one-quarter of Pemba's.[99] Though Arabs were overrepresented at the top of colonial government administration and among large landowners, only a minority of the total Arab population on either island was in the latter category.[100] Many were small landowners, and there were substantial numbers of Arabs in nonagricultural occupations like petty trading, food selling, or transport. These latter Arabs were by and large recent immigrants from Oman or Hadhramaut, distinguished from locally born Afro-Arabs by status, language, and education.[101]

The descendants of Omani muwalladūn were some of the earliest Arab adopters of elite colonial education.[102] Unlike Omani immigrants to Zanzibar, they took up territorial nationalism and embraced a new territorial ethnicity—Zanzibari—by the mid-twentieth century.[103] They are referred to here as *Afro-Arab*, signifying both their ethnically and linguistically mixed heritage and a more overt political desire among numbers of them to unify and integrate the civilizational, racial, and ethnic discourses of pan-Africanism and pan-Arabism around a common goal of national territorial independence for Zanzibar.

The first Arabs to embrace anticolonial nationalism in Zanzibar were born in the last decades of the nineteenth and first decade of the twentieth centuries, and not all of them were muwalladūn; in fact, many were born in Oman and only later chose to make their home in Zanzibar. Their nationalism was not primarily territorially oriented, and some of them viewed Oman as the homeland.[104] They were the first to grow to adulthood under the British protectorate government (est. 1890), though they had not yet been integrated into colonial educational institutions. As a literate elite, they were oriented primarily toward issues, connected to intellectual currents of pan-Arabism, pan-Ibadism, and Salafism, and exchanged poetry with each other.[105] In contrast to the later secular turn of territorial nationalists, their nationalism was tinged by a highly religious dimension, continuing the work of the nineteenth-century Islamic renaissance in Zanzibar, especially with regard to raising the educational level of coastal Muslims under colonial rule.[106] The members of this generation were early advocates for limited rights under British colonial rule through ethnic associations, of which the Arab Association (formed in 1901 and registered in 1922) was by far the most prominent.[107] They saw Zanzibar as an extension of an "Arab-Muslim" cultural and religious ecumene and saw secularization as a serious generational problem.[108] They were active in the journalistic sphere in Zanzibar, founding three important Arabic-English newspapers: *al-Najah*, *al-Nahda*, and *al-Falaq*.[109] They were more peripatetic than the more territorially oriented nationalists of the 1950s, aided by the growth of imperial transportation networks of steamships.[110] *Al-Falaq*'s editor Sheikh Hashil Rashid Al-Miskery traveled regularly between Oman and Zanzibar during the 1930s and 1940s, while Muhammad al-Barwani wrote of his travels throughout Egypt and the Levant.[111]

In Zanzibar, the first colonially educated generation came from middle- and upper-class muwalladūn families who resided in adjoining urban neighborhoods on the western end of Unguja in linked households with ties to other urban town dwellers, usually from the town's landowning and merchant classes.[112] The most significant difference between the previous generation and a new generation born after World War I was the impact of their colonial education. Educated Zanzibaris of this generation have more in common with similar metropolitan educated and nationalist sympathetic elites in Ghana and Nigeria of the time than they do with their traditionally educated fathers and grandfathers or their lower-class contemporaries in Oman who migrated to Zanzibar. Proximity to the colonial state through its bureaucratic or educational institutions meant that certain social groups under the Zanzibar protectorate imbibed the state's later developmentalist credos and aspirations, which they often tried to integrate within the civilizational framework of the earlier generation.[113] The generation born on the islands between World War I and 1930 was the first to be educated in government schools and the first to be educated primarily in Swahili and English (beginning in 1923). Its members were the primary beneficiaries of a late colonial shift to a developmental model as a legitimation tool.[114]

This generation was exemplified by individuals whose names will appear throughout the book, including Shaaban Saleh al-Farsy (b. 1914), Hilal Muhammad Ali al-Barwani (b. 1916), Ali Muhsin al-Barwani (b. 1919), Saud Ahmed al-Busaidi (b. 1920), Aman Thani (b. 1927), Issa Nasser al-Ismaily (b. 1927), Ahmed Hamoud al-Maamiry (b. 1928), and Samira Salim Seif al-Maamiry (b. 1923).[115] Among this cohort also was Zanzibar's most prominent socialist intellectual of the twentieth century, Abdulrahman Mohamed Babu (b. 1924).[116] Despite their ideological differences, all of these individuals exemplify the rise of a new self-conscious expression of territorial ethnicity in nationalist politics, characterized by muwalladūn ancestry, local birth in Zanzibar, the primacy of Swahili and English in language, and the embrace of nationalism as a secular and progressive force.

Many from this generation obtained their higher education at Britain's flagship African colonial university at Makerere University in Uganda.[117] Others went to Cairo and imbibed nationalist ideas from watching the struggle in Egypt against the British.[118] The Afro-Arabs of Zanzibar were also some of the first Muslim women in East Africa to send their daughters for higher education. Their return and their subsequent employment as teachers helped break down resistance among more conservative Muslim families to women's higher education. Thus from among the Afro-Arabs came Zanzibar's first woman doctor, Dr. Fatma bint Saada Nassor Lamky.[119]

The colonial government in Zanzibar visualized these individuals as those best placed to "Zanzibarize" the civil service in preparation for local rule and development.[120] Through university education abroad and through junior positions in the civil service, this generation of Afro-Arabs became some of the most highly educated colonial subjects of their era.[121] The educated Afro-Arabs internalized the ideal of "progress" and saw more muscular state intervention as necessary and desirable to enhance and develop "society" in the fields of education and health.[122] Attending secular schools for the first time, they developed social and political attitudes more radical than those of their socially conservative parents.[123] Many were sympathetic to the progressive ideals and future orientation of a secular anticolonial nationalist territorial identity, as it represented a battle against the paternalist racism of some colonial officials and an assertion of a form of noncivilizational belonging, based around the idea of progress and bringing together different social classes and ethnicities in a common project.[124] For many ethnic minorities coming of age after World War II, as Prasenjit Duara has phrased it, "internal sovereignty was a promise of equal citizenship."[125]

The new graduates returned to Zanzibar in the late 1940s and early 1950s, and many began working for the protectorate government.[126] Afro-Arabs who later became important in Oman's post-1970 government were appointed as district commissioners and immigration officers in Zanzibar after World War II, including Muhammad Said Abdullah al-Barwani, Saud Ahmed al-Busaidi, Issa Nasser al-Ismaily, and Ahmed Seif Kharusi.[127] Others, like Ahmed Hamoud al-Maamiry (Maalim Ahmed Hamoud) and Samira Salim Seif al-Maamiry, began serving as primary and secondary schoolteachers from this time.[128] Makerere University graduate Said Shaksy served in multiple capacities, including as a member of the Naturalisation Advisory Committee processing applicants for Zanzibar nationality.[129]

Between 1945 and 1954, a new more militant spirit in Zanzibar's Arab Association led its leaders to embrace demands for radical democracy in the form of common roll elections. In 1954 Ahmed Lamky, one of the nationalist-sympathizing, Cairo-educated Zanzibari youth, wrote a series of articles in *al-Falaq* opposing racial representation in the colonial government.[130] Lamky and others from the younger generation pushed their elders to advocate that members of the Legislative Council be elected from an electoral roll made up of Zanzibar "nationals," a proposal opposed by the Indian and African Associations.[131] The campaign was not without intracommunal and generational tensions. After one Arab elder, Sultan Ahmed al-Mugheiry, a former assistant superintendent of police and unofficial member of the Legislative Council, refused to go along with an Arab Association–sponsored legislative boycott, he was stabbed outside his home, admitted to the hospital, and later discovered there and stabbed to death by the same assailant. Ten members of the Arab Association were also charged with sedition by the colonial government. While they embraced the recommendation of a British official that the phrase "Arab state" should be abandoned in the quest for democracy in Zanzibar, Zanzibar's nationalists militantly rejected British temporizing around common roll elections.[132]

Lamky also formed the Zanzibar National Union in 1952, the precursor to Zanzibar's first nationalist political party, the Zanzibar Nationalist Party (ZNP), formed in 1955.[133] Representatives of the ZNP increasingly tried to link with other nationalist movements in Africa and Asia; they attended the Afro-Asian People's Solidarity Conference in Cairo, Egypt, at the end of 1957.[134] ZNP intelligentsia also sought to make populist inroads with Africans by occasionally appealing to anti-Indian sentiment, and later by inventing a narrative of the party's origins in a 1951 protest by rural farmers against cattle inoculation (a protest that most elite and middle-class nationalists had decried as backward at the time).[135]

Another generation of Afro-Arabs whose names appear throughout this book were born in the late 1930s and early 1940s (e.g., Ahmed Ali Ahmed al-Riyami, b. 1940; Hamoud al-Marhuby, b. 1944; Salim Rashid, b. 1941; Salim Ahmed Salim al-Riyami, b. 1942; Bi Ubwa Amour Zahor al-Ismaily, b. 1938; and Seif Sharif Hamad, b. 1943). They came of age with increasing nationalist agitation and social protest across Britain's and France's African and Middle East dominions.[136] Some of them became part of the first generation of Zanzibari students to receive higher education in communist bloc countries, and many were sympathetic to socialist student groups while studying in the colonial metropole.

Socialism was seen by many nationalists as the best ideology to transcend divides of class and ethnicity in national territories. It thus became important to members of the ZNP whose greatest liability was its popular association as a vehicle of Arab domination. How the Afro-Arab nationalist leadership would deal with this challenge would define the character of nationalist debates in Zanzibar from the early 1950s through Zanzibar's 1963 independence. Socialist sympathizing members of the younger generation were more sensitive to this dynamic than their elders running the ZNP.[137] A young Afro-Arab Salim Hamdan, a technician for the radio broadcast system, Sauti ya Unguja, worked closely at a young age with activists in KANU at the height of Mau Mau.[138] Many other young Afro-Arabs gravitated toward Abdulrahman Mohamed Babu's socialist Umma Party. The influence of nationalist ideas reached even politically sensitive youth studying outside Zanzibar in Cairo and Great Britain.[139]

Though they formed social clubs and joined radical social groups, few of these middle-class urban youth had any deep roots among the African working classes. The gap between the territorial nationalist vision of Zanzibar's elites and the popular imagination of the island's working classes was revealed during a 1948 dockworkers strike on Unguja (influenced by a similar strike in Mombasa in 1947), which threatened to become a more general labor stoppage and became the basis for militant demands for workers' rights among Zanzibar's African working classes, many of whom had mainland roots.[140] Zanzibar's Afro-Arabs sought to make common cause with the laboring classes through trade unions and student and youth associations (Federation of Progressive Trade Unions, Youth's Own Union, the Young African Social Union, the Zanzibar Youth and Students Union, and the Zanzibar Youth Union).[141] At the same time, the 1951 formation of a parallel youth organization by African civil servants, and the founding of a newspaper, *Afrika Kwetu*, signaled a new self-consciously African ethnic militancy and attempt to shape the debate around nationalism in the image of an asserted "African" majority.[142] Many Africans felt that the highly educated Afro-Arabs espousing nationalism had been beneficiaries of education and development at the expense of Africans.[143]

REVOLUTION AND EXILE: THE AFRO-ARABS IN DIASPORA

Mere weeks after Zanzibar's formal independence celebration in December 1963, an independent state led by members of the ZNP was overthrown in a revolution. In the early morning hours of January 12, 1964, an attack was launched on the police station in Ziwani, some three kilometers east of Zanzibar City, by John Okello, a Ugandan resident of Zanzibar, leading a band of paramilitaries who had trained secretly in the rural areas of Unguja. Approximately a week of "mopping up" and violent consolidation operations occurred targeting Arabs and other supporters of the ZNP on both Unguja and Pemba. During the extended pogrom between one and three thousand people were killed, some fifteen hundred ended up in hospital, and thousands were detained on Prison Island or remanded to camps and detention centers around the island.

The demography and timing of Arab emigration from Zanzibar after the pogrom was class stratified and helped determine the politicized character of exile. In Zanzibar, the term *Manga* was used to indicate someone with ethnic or tribal descent in Oman, an Arab but not "indigenous" or locally born in Zanzibar.[144] Manga in Zanzibar typically worked in rural areas as intermediaries between agricultural producers and exporters.[145] These poorer migrants from Zanzibar's countryside were the worst victimized by the violence and some of the first to leave—sent on Red Cross ships and government-sponsored dhows to Oman. UNHCR officials estimated that between January and June 1964, 3,549 "Arabs [had] left in dhows or other vessels for Oman and Muscat."[146] In total, at least 4,600 Arabs left Zanzibar from February 1, 1964 to January 1965, with assistance from the Red Cross and United Nations High Commission on Refugees (UNHCR), not counting those who made private arrangements to leave.

In April 1964 a "union" was formed between Zanzibar and mainland Tanganyika, and a new country, Tanzania, was created. The Union's structure dictated that Tanganyikan president Julius Nyerere would become president of Tanzania, while the president of revolutionary Zanzibar,

Abeid Karume, would take the position of vice president of Tanzania.[147] The Union's formation has been the subject of intense debate over the last five decades, since it was negotiated in secret between the two leaders and never popularly ratified.[148] Its formation was not the result of an overarching anticommunist conspiracy, nor was it an American-led plot. It should be seen for the instrumental value it held at the time to both leaders. Karume was able to gain access to mainland resources for consolidating his rule internally against radicals in government by giving them ministerial portfolios on the mainland, while Nyerere burnished his continental and international credentials as a progressive pan-African statesman.[149] The Union was meant also to be the precursor to the formation of the East African Federation between Kenya, Tanzania, and Uganda, a project that broke down soon after the Union was formed.[150] In practice the Union repositioned Zanzibar from a sovereign state to what Godfrey Baldacchino has called a "subnational island jurisdiction."[151] It also decisively influenced the possibility of Zanzibari exiles obtaining citizenship abroad, especially in the United Kingdom, since to do so they had to demonstrate evidence of their prior nationality. Though Tanzanian citizenship was relatively liberal and based on prior birth in the territory, many exiles were unable to obtain Tanzanian nationality through petition based on prior birth and residence in Zanzibar, because after the revolution Karume decreed that anyone who had left the islands in the two months after the revolution would be denied the right to citizenship.[152] In Zanzibar, those who remained behind after the revolution faced difficulties due to their citizenship documents being destroyed or lost in the violence and looting of January 12–14, 1964.[153]

Most Afro-Arabs did not leave Zanzibar immediately after the revolution, except for a handful personally loyal to the sultan in Portsmouth, United Kingdom. Extensive family ties often led them to stay in Zanzibar for months or years after 1964.[154] Some Afro-Arabs became stranded in Zanzibar after August 1965, when it became impossible to leave the island legally without permission, and island residents were asked to surrender their passports to the authorities. In 1966, all Zanzibaris were required to have an identity card, but no legal requirements for citizenship were ever formalized, and the cards become a weapon to punish political enemies.[155] The dilemma between kinship ties and the desire to emigrate is evident in Habiba al-Hinai's memoir. Habiba's mother initially refused to escape from Pemba, because she was pregnant with her seventh child, Hafez, and because her grandfather was in the hospital.[156] When Habiba's mother expressed a desire to leave, she was opposed by many of her older family members, who wanted her to stay in Zanzibar. As a result, she kept her 1971 escape plan secret from her family.[157]

The privileges of mobility afforded by nationality also became evident during the upheaval. Members of a mixed Arab-English family with a British parent were taken to England by the Red Cross, while the Arab siblings of a previous marriage remained in Zanzibar until after Karume's assassination.[158] Generational shifts within families are evident in the divergent trajectories of those who stayed behind and those who left. "Hamoud" was an Afro-Arab member of the Umma Party who had trained in Cuba, fought for African liberation in Mozambique, and died in Zanzibar, fighting to be recognized as a Zanzibari. His grandfather had been born in Oman and had three brothers from Ibra in the poor mountainous Omani interior who left and came back to East Africa and, at some point in the nineteenth century, settled permanently in Zanzibar. Hamoud's son "Said" migrated to Portsmouth in March 1964 after the revolution. In 1974, Said's uncle (Hamoud's brother) came to Portsmouth to give Said an Omani passport. Said waited six years before coming to Oman in 1980, where he still lives.[159]

Many exiled Afro-Arabs did not disavow their Zanzibari national identity even after their displacement and even after they assumed Omani nationality in the 1970s.[160] Ali Muhsin Al-Barwani, in his assessments of politics in Zanzibar, argued the deciding factor in nationality was birth or choice; birth in Zanzibar made him a Zanzibari, above other cultural relations, rather than anything else. He repudiated the discourse of autochthony and indigeneity, which he regarded as having contributed to the political upheavals in Zanzibar. Zanzibari exile Ahmed Seif Kharusi (1911–1986) continued to edit a newspaper sharing letters from Zanzibar, accounts of illegal imprisonment and torture, and political analysis of Tanzanian state policy. The *Free Zanzibar Voice* represented itself as the voice of the oppressed masses in Zanzibar and positioned the Zanzibari exiles as the righteous victims of a hijacked decolonization process characterized by external conspiracy against a vulnerable state.[161] The newspaper subjected state leadership in Tanzania, especially Zanzibar's president Abeid Karume and Tanzania's president Julius Nyerere, to withering critique.[162] In a 1973 editorial in the *Free Zanzibar Voice*, the writer (most likely Ali Muhsin al-Barwani) expressed the essence of the Afro-Arab appeal to a nonracial territorial Zanzibari identity: "*By virtue of her history, her geographic position, and her cultural heritage, Zanzibar belongs to the Afro-Arab world. To reject either side is like rejecting a parent* and can only result in injury to the country's psyche. There are many countries which have these double... links and have managed to integrate them completely.... [I]t is about time we were proud of BOTH sides of our national identity."[163] Significantly, some Afro-Arabs in exile adopted the nisba, al-Zanjibāri in correspondence, as an expression of their commitment to this nationalist vision in exile.

Complex ideological tensions developed between the exiled Afro-Arab intelligentsia and their offspring scattered in diaspora communities. Some from the younger generations saw their parents' dream of an anticolonial homeland in Zanzibar as a failed project. The tensions originated with the mixed birthplace of family members, with one or two children born in Zanzibar and subsequent children born in the Gulf or the United Kingdom. The older ones struggled to find educational and employment opportunities outside of Zanzibar.[164] Some let their hopes alight on a more pragmatic and less sacrificial vision of the future in which they obtained a permanent national status elsewhere.[165] To them, the primary debt owed was not to the nation as such, but to kin back in Zanzibar. As one interviewee put it, "All the Arab Zanzibaris who left at that time that was their intention: to have a good job, to earn something, I send it home. Because the parents were there, the children were there, the sisters the brothers.... This when we left Zanzibar, our duty our responsibility was to look after our parents and ourselves. So, politics was out of the question.... [M]any people that I know, their job was to live, to survive."[166] The Zanzibaris in diaspora focused their initial energies on regularizing their residence, obtaining regular employment, and pursuing higher education. They sought broader horizons in areas where they might put their training and education to use. A community organization formed by the Zanzibaris in exile, the Zanzibar Association (ZA), represented the communal needs of Zanzibar's diaspora communities in the Gulf, mediating between state leadership, British officials, UNHCR officials, and new migrants.

THE APPEAL OF OMAN'S DEVELOPMENTAL STATE TO ZANZIBAR'S AFRO-ARAB EXILES

With the surveillance power of the developmental state, national citizens became more efficiently subject to ideological, political, and educational interventions to shape national consciousness and national loyalty.[167]

Managing the new states while reforming their governance and delivering on developmental expectations was intensely difficult. The new state leadership expected to command as their predecessors had done, and in many states there was a period of undemocratic state consolidation broadly similar to the autocratic rule that preceded it.[168] The stakes of achieving national unity and controlling patronage in the state activated and irritated majority-minority dynamics and sometimes aggravated violence.[169] By the 1970s indebtedness, unfavorable trade balances, and stagnant economic growth had begun to aggravate these tensions, causing political instability in many East African nations.[170] From 1973 the price of industrial imports went up because of the Organization of the Petroleum Exporting Countries (OPEC) embargo against countries supporting Israel.[171] The increasingly indebted state governments of non-oil-producing countries faced declining prices for exports as well.[172] These difficulties meant declining state revenues, combined with increasing levels of authoritarian surveillance; many states in the Global South seemed to get poorer and less free at the same time.[173]

The Gulf development model and its appeal to displaced Zanzibaris must also be understood in this context. The economic success of the Gulf monarchies by the early 1970s seemed to promise to the exiled Zanzibaris an alternative form of development that was invulnerable to internal and external subversion by opposing ideological forces and could also guarantee a more "developed" style of life and future opportunities for descendants. The largesse of Gulf governments and the ability to access routes to consultation without democracy made free speech and expansive civil liberties seem like misguided ideas to some.

In 1964, petroleum was discovered in commercial quantities in the Sultanate of Oman.[174] Oman was still basically a poor country at this time, with a gross national product (GNP) per capita of ~$400.[175] It was challenged by antimonarchical trends in the region from the mid-1950s all the way through the mid-1970s. The Omani ruler Said bin Taimur was the first Omani sultan to have a modern colonial education (at Mayo College in India). He began as an energetic reformer and was aware of the role of external funding for development in creating relationships of dependency and indebtedness.[176] After 1957 he defined the political charter of a developmental state over the entire territory of Oman with British technical and military assistance, including the building of several modern schools.[177] With British military support, Said interfered in the Sultanate's historically contested sovereignty with the Imamate in the Omani interior, defeating the nascent Imamate government and forcing its leaders into exile.[178] He intended to use petroleum revenues to inaugurate development plans including offices, hospitals, schools, roads, and communications, "until modern projects spread over the whole of the Sultanate, to each area according to its needs."[179]

Said bin Taimur was reluctant to draw on the educated Omani diaspora, represented for instance by the Omani National Union and its publication *Sawt 'Uman* (Voice of Oman), and even turned down scholarship offers for Omani students to study in Kuwait.[180] A second Imamate uprising in 1957 was crushed with British assistance, although acts of sabotage by Imamate supporters against the regime continued into the late 1960s, causing concern about Said bin Taimur's ability to rise to the challenge of providing development at a fast enough rate to forestall more radical alternatives to the British-backed sultan. A 1963 nationalist uprising in the south in Dhofar further eroded confidence in Said. Two years later, Said was overthrown and replaced with his son, in a palace coup engineered by top British officials unhappy at the pace of change. Because of British power and influence in the state, and as a result of integration of petroleum rents into Omani state revenues, an autocratic model of an Omani state as a "sultanate" became entrenched, countering republican trends in the broader region.[181] Petroleum legitimized this autocratic model of the developmental state in ways that made its citizenship a more tangible material benefit than it was in many democratic states.[182]

From 1964 to 1977, petroleum accounted for over 90 percent of Oman's revenue.[183] Oman began intensive spending of petroleum revenues only after 1970, when OPEC countries first succeeded in setting the international price of petroleum.[184] The petroleum market had by that time been transformed from a buyers' to a sellers' commodity, and Oman reaped this benefit of earlier advocacy while also remaining closely attached to its British patron.[185] Petroleum revenue funded the state's ambitious development plans, and the price increase allowed it to purchase a controlling stake in the state oil company.[186] The doubling of petroleum prices during 1979–1980 helped further fuel the boom.[187] Despite the 1986 petroleum price slump, Oman's petroleum exports and low citizen population guaranteed that an advanced capitalist "standard" of living, equivalent to the most luxurious areas of the first world, could be maintained in urban Muscat. As a result of oil wealth, Omani citizenship became for the first time an internationally attractive material benefit of protection and patronage.[188]

Conscious of the shifting economic conditions of Gulf societies, Zanzibaris in exiles made strategic claims on Omani nationality. For instance, in 1970 two Zanzibar-born refugees living in Dammam, Saudi Arabia, wrote a letter to the United Nations High Commissioner on Refugees to protest the recent expulsions of members of their community from Saudi Arabia.[189] The signatories to the UN letter were concerned with the framing of their denial of asylum as being due to their being "Zanzibari" refugees. Instead, they argued, by virtue of their exile from Zanzibar and their Omani ancestry, they had "technically ceased to be Zanzibaris" and "had been granted the privilege to settle here as Omanis and not as Zanzibaris or refugees from Zanzibar."[190] Not yet Omani citizens, the refugees were deliberately portraying Oman as their homeland. Zanzibar was a country, but it existed no more in the form they had once imagined themselves to be part of.

Afro-Arabs from Zanzibar played key roles as ethnic returnees in the Omani developmental state.[191] Exiled Zanzibaris who could claim a current Omani relative as kin or who claimed a more distant paternal ancestor in Oman began a process of transforming themselves into citizens of Oman, assimilating into the social conception of Omani national belonging. But the influence between Omani-imagined national community and the diaspora was not one-sided. The social world the Zanzibaris were trying to become a part of in Oman was not a "stable fixed point of reference to which the newcomers 'adapt.'"[192] Rather, Oman itself was in flux throughout this period, and the returnees fundamentally shaped the character of national citizenship there as they had in Zanzibar. They imprinted the national project with their uniquely urban Afropolitan Swahili coast culture, creating a Swahili-speaking subculture in modern Muscat.[193] Their educational background, their shared experiences of exile, and their sociolinguistic identity are what continue to mark them as a group with a unique history within Omani national heritage. They were especially instrumental in infusing the Omani heritage concept with an emphasis on cultural mixing through intermarriage, a reflection of their muwalladūn ancestry.

OMANI-ZANZIBARIS AND THE VERNACULAR HISTORIOGRAPHY OF ZANZIBAR

National citizenship in Oman didn't obliterate the symbolic importance of Zanzibar as a nation to the returnees. In fact, Omani national citizenship was a necessary pre-condition for their multidirectional memory of Zanzibar to be codified into published narratives. Like similar kinds of community historians in the wake of political upheaval elsewhere, a subset of Zanzibari intellectuals remained over the decades since 1964 preoccupied with the meaning and impact of the revolution.[194] The acquisition of Omani citizenship largely domesticated a revanchist tendency that had persisted in exile. After 1990 there reemerged a transnational space articulating relations between the Swahili coast, the interlacustrine region of East Africa, and the Arab world, which provided new opportunities for the former exiles (now Omani citizens) to visit Zanzibar.[195] Between 1994 and 2014, the memory of Zanzibar as an independent nation-state and the significance of its revolution were increasingly openly discussed among Omani-Zanzibaris in the lead-up to the fiftieth anniversary of the revolution, at the same time that Zanzibar's past was appropriated as part of Oman's cultural heritage in the Indian Ocean world. This expansion of publications about Zanzibar from different sources within the Omani national context provides an opportunity to examine the influence of shifting political conditions on the living memory of the Zanzibar revolution, its transformation into historical narrative, and the reception of these narratives by different national publics.[196] Authors in this historiography confronted and debated individual and community experiences and sought to educate the next generation in Oman and Zanzibar. Their novels, autobiographies, and works of history in Swahili, Arabic, and English are sites of "multi-directional memory," a "fragmented form of commemoration that cannot be contained within the traditional nation-state format of memory studies."[197] They deal with topics that do not have a place in official Omani heritage publications nor in official celebrations of Omani cultural heritage in Zanzibar. They are multidirectional insofar as they point to the old homeland of Zanzibar, while not being authored from that location.

Ali Muhsin's memoir, *Conflict and Harmony in Zanzibar*, was the most significant early work and is a cornerstone of this historiography. It was published in English in 1997, with a 2004 Swahili translation done by the author and a 2010 Arabic translation.[198] Representations and interpretations of the revolution also occurred in self-published memoirs by Shaaban Saleh Farsy (1994), Hamoud Marhuby (2017), and Hashil S. Hashil (2018); popular histories like Nasser al-Riyami's, *Zinjibar: Shakhsiyāt wa Aḥdāth* (2009) and Harith Ghassany's *Kwa Heri Ukoloni, Kwa Heri Uhuru!* (2010); political commentary like Ibrahim Noor Shariff's *Tanzania na Propaganda za*

Udini (2014); biographies like Asya al-Bualy's of Fatima Jinja (2010), Gary Burgess's of Ali Sultan Issa al-Ismaily and Seif Sharif Hamad (2009), and Zuhura Yunus's of Bi Ubwa Amour (2021); and historical fiction like Salem ben Nasser al Ismaily and Richard Tzudiker's *The Sultanate of Zanzibar* (2014). The production of this vernacular historiography has also involved the work of translating these works between Swahili, Arabic, and English.

Development is on the move in Zanzibar at the beginning of the twenty-first century's second decade. New buildings and new roads have transformed parts of the urban landscape. Descendants of Zanzibaris who fled the island in the 1960s visit old family homes in Stone Town, have built new vacation homes on the island's east coast, and patronize religious schools and mosques on the island.[199] As Omani citizens, they continue to assert a coresponsibility for the development of Zanzibar and to engage with the Zanzibar government's outreach to the "Zanzibar diaspora."[200] Many of their East African kin are today "status non-citizens" in Oman.[201] There is a mutual influence between national regimes of citizenship and diaspora populations in the modern era. Exploring the multidirectional memories of the latter in relation to transformations in the former reveals ongoing contentious debates about the boundaries of national citizenship in the Indian Ocean and the shifting fortunes of muwalladūn lineages from an age of empire to an age of development and beyond.

CHAPTER OUTLINE

The book proceeds in three parts. The first part deals primarily with struggles for national belonging in modern Zanzibar. Chapter 1 argues that Zanzibar's electoral transition to an independent state between 1957 and 1963 was stymied by nativist contradictions generated by the very mechanisms meant to generate popular sovereignty. Chapter 2 deals with the aftermath of the Zanzibar revolution, the controversies about its violence, and the crisis of statelessness that followed. Latter-day memories provide eyewitness testimony of the revolution and provide a contextual understanding of post-1964 relief operations in Zanzibar, which transported thousands of Manga Arabs off the islands and to Oman.

The second part of the book deals with Zanzibaris in exile. Chapter 3 explores the politics of diaspora for the Zanzibar nationalist generation through the *Free Zanzibar Voice* and the Zanzibar Organization and their critiques of governance in Zanzibar and Tanzania after the revolution. Chapter 4 explores escapes from Zanzibar from the late 1960s to the late 1970s and provides archival "snapshots" of Zanzibari communal life in the various cities of the Gulf, especially Dubai. There is a noticeable ideological shift among Zanzibari communities living in the Gulf as they reject the irredentist vision of some exiles and embrace an apolitical turn, with a more pragmatic focus on education and employment.

The third and final part of the book examines Zanzibari belonging in relation to Omani national citizenship. Chapter 5 explores the "return migration" of the Zanzibari diaspora to Oman at the beginning of the state's modern regime of national citizenship. The returnee experience of Omani citizenship is characterized by a deeply affective relationship to Sultan Qaboos, returnees' presence in many white-collar and technocratic careers, and their experience of otherness based on not speaking Arabic fluently. Chapter 6 relates how Zanzibaris in Oman, spurred by global and regional developments after 1990, returned to Zanzibar and began writing about the Omani empire, slavery, anticolonial politics, and revolution in Zanzibar. These processes of turning multisited memory into narrative in a new homeland constituted a vernacular historiography, a multifocal historical corpus through which readers may discern the agency of individual authors as well as the shared agendas, arguments, and anxieties of writers "within" several different kinds of community, including the nation.

PART ONE

Belonging in Zanzibar

ONE

Immigration, Exogenous Origins, and the Politics of Citizenship in Zanzibar, 1957–1963

ON THE SURFACE, the elections held in Zanzibar in 1957–1963 to prepare the ground for national independence were models of popular electoral participation. The British opened up the franchise to women in 1959, lowered the voting age from twenty-five to eighteen, removed property qualifications, and reduced the residency requirement to one year.[1] In the July 8–15, 1963, election, 98 percent of the electorate voted, over one-half of the total population.[2] The overwhelming majority of voters were locally born.[3] Zanzibar had a competitive and engaged public sphere during this time as well, with nearly two dozen publications competing for readers' attention.[4] In spite of this, the British singularly failed to install a Westminster style parliamentary democracy on the islands.[5]

Why did the electoral transition attempted by the British in the late 1950s and early 1960s in Zanzibar fail to facilitate sustainable political power sharing?[6] The failure of the 1963 Sultanate of Zanzibar and Pemba, a UN-recognized independent state, is a puzzle much discussed by historians, anthropologists, and political scientists. Many authors have hastily attributed its failure to the legacy of slavery. Jonathon Glassman has argued that the revolution is inextricable from the emergence of developmentalist ideas on the islands that brought political tensions into public life in Zanzibar.[7] Though it is false to say, as British officials in 1961 claimed, that political conflict beginning in 1957 divided a peaceful, unified island, there is no doubt that the electoral process embarked on from the mid-1950s heightened the future political stakes of existing inequalities.[8] There can also be no doubt that the accelerated pursuit of the political kingdom by large sectors of Zanzibar's society brought politics into every single realm of civic life, in ways unprecedented in the island's history. Social and economic tensions previously embedded in largely unspoken and unwritten social codes of deference emerged into public life as sites of contentious politics.[9] The question of who was more representative of popular sovereignty was increasingly understood by both sides to hinge on who had "more" supporters. As Michael Lofchie observed, "Party and racial conflict [became] practically synonymous."[10] Electoral competition elevated the material stakes of elections and politicized everyday life, from shopping at certain stores to the apparati of citizenship migration control and the census. Spiraling rhetoric between political rivals threatened to, and eventually did, spill over into violent action.

Though the slow pace of colonial reforms and the conservative mandate of the protectorate government generally impeded either the stable transition from protectorate to constitutional monarchy or the successful transition to a republican form of government, the failure of the electoral process was not merely the direct result of the "divide and rule" policies of the British, but was an expression of deeper political divides endemic to the transition from indigenous vertical sovereignties (many of them originally "empires" under dynastic rule) to modern nation-states based in the popular will, expressed at an individual level through universal adult franchise and equality between citizens.[11]

The rising prices for cloves throughout most of the 1950s had brought optimism in Zanzibar that the broadening of social participation and its attendant rising expectations could be managed by a general increase in overall economic prosperity.[12] At its 1963 independence celebrations, the Sultanate of Zanzibar and Pemba had the third highest per capita income in sub-Saharan Africa, next to Ghana and South Africa.[13] But the question of independence, instead of unifying the colonized around national development, raised the reality of the antagonistic "collective" interests of categories of ethnicity like Arab and African, "wenyeji" (natives) and "wageni" (foreigners), and "wazanzibari" (Zanzibaris) and "wabara" (mainlanders), and prevented unification behind a form of territorial citizenship.[14] The contentions between these interests were also linked to debates about modernization and representation in a democratic polity, including the right to freedom from foreign political subjugation as the basis for development.[15]

The coherence and integrity of elections are typically deemed to be an important indicator of the health and stability of a democratic state because they are trusted as a reliable indicator of the popular will. In the devolution of power from imperial metropole to nation-state, this trust requires the existence of some sort of basic technologies of bureaucratic registration to distinguish citizens with the right to vote from foreigners who lack that right. The nationalist intelligentsia of Zanzibar did not entirely refuse the notion of indigeneity but repurposed it around territorial birth.[16] The politics of exogenous origin were thus brought out into the open by more banal processes of registering voters and determining eligibility for election candidates. Controversies over exogenous origins and political registration in Zanzibar's late-colonial elections contributed to the racialization of nationalist thought.

DEMOCRATIC REPRESENTATION, ETHNIC RELATIONS, AND INDIGENEITY IN COLONIAL ZANZIBAR

Successful democratic transitions to popular sovereignty are usually slow, halting, and contingent affairs, with many pitfalls. A state's governance form must have already gained broader acceptance and acquiescence within "civil society" and the broader culture to achieve political legitimacy.[17] Both elites and the masses were skeptical of the idea for different reasons. For many elites who had carved out niches within imperial hierarchies, anti-colonial nationalism was a chimerical promise that would unleash subterranean currents of discontent against their relative socioeconomic position and thus stymie their own limited self-determination under colonial rule. In the lead-up to national independence many business and economic elites in East Africa were skeptical of the argument about majority rule bringing prosperity for all.[18] A few wealthy coastal Arabs in Tanganyika even joined the white-settler-dominated United Tanganyika Party in the lead-up to independence.[19] The Arab Association in Zanzibar was initially opposed to common roll elections.[20]

The rapid demand for total independence of Zanzibar was first made fifty years after the protectorate's establishment by Arab nationalists educated in both traditional and colonial contexts. They demanded the reestablishment of the territorial independence of Zanzibar in the late 1940s, and development was key to the broader appeal of their vision among the Zanzibar masses. According to an estimate made by Muhsin al-Kindi, 76 percent of Zanzibar newspaper *al-Falaq*'s articles between 1931 and 1963 dealt with some aspect of nationalist political discourse. The most important demand by its editors was for the expansion of the scientific and industrial arts, as well as further development of basic services in education, health, and transportation.[21]

What consultative government there was in colonial Zanzibar took place largely with the landed muwalladūn elites closest to the sultan. Power came to be vested first in British consuls and then British "residents." Their relationships with local Arab elites were formalized through the Protectorate Council established in 1914.[22] There were some attempts at very limited reform after World War I; in 1926 an Executive Council and a Legislative Council were established. The latter was headed by the British resident and had seventeen members.[23] Most real policy functions remained vested in the Executive Council headed by the sultan.[24] Notably neither body was elected; both still had only nominated and appointed members, mainly representatives from the Arab and Indian communities.[25] After World War II, members of Zanzibar's appointed Legislative Council increasingly pressed for the direct election of unofficial members.[26]

By the 1950s in their East African colonies the British, partly influenced by the enormous expense of suppressing anticolonial rebellion in Kenya, sought to blunt popular discontent through the political process by increasing direct representation in the colonial legislatures.[27] In Zanzibar, the British had planned to open the franchise to all British Protected Persons. Arab Association representatives, including its vice president Seif Hamoud, vigorously opposed this proposal, insisting that only Zanzibar nationals should be able to vote, a status they defined by being a subject of the sultan, rather than by permanent residency.[28]

The African working classes of Zanzibar, also working from expectations of the need for development, interpreted the British colonial protectorate in Zanzibar in a completely different manner from the Arab nationalists. The leadership of the African Association was opposed to immediate independence, as they felt it would entrench the social and economic power of the muwalladūn elite. To its older members the development of the island's African population depended on continued British protection from exploitation, so as to raise the educational standard of the overall community. They interpreted this protection as holding at bay the return of Arab colonial rule over the islands. Members of the African Association thus opposed opening the franchise; their newspaper, *Afrika Kwetu*, argued in 1951 that it would be better for Africans to continue to be directly nominated by the association and regarded nationality status as following from the logic of African indigeneity.[29] The African Association opposed the appointment of Ameir Tajo and Ali Sharif Musa to Zanzibar's Legislative Council, objecting to them as unrepresentative of Africans as they were "Shirazis" of exogenous "Asiatic origin."[30]

The attitudes of the African Association symbolized the fractious and tense meaning of Shirazi and its situatedness between Africanity and indigeneity in the context of the islands' debates over popular sovereignty. The term, which references a city in Iran named Shiraz, has a more specific local meaning in Zanzibar. In reality, the link to Persian ancestors, though now genetically substantiated in the broader population, was attenuated in terms of living lineal connections; the Shirazi of Zanzibar were more closely linked with other coastal African Muslim peoples of long residence.[31] Before the mass settlement of Omani Arabs, they had been loosely governed through village elders and several different independent rulers, including a number of queens and a ruler called the Mwinyi Mkuu.[32] Moreover, Shirazi was a permeable ethnicity; one could acculturate oneself to village life and the Muslim religion and become "part" of them, as many "Swahili" did between 1924 and 1932.[33] One Shirazi group from Unguja, the Wahadimu, had the most contentious relations with the Arabs of all Shirazi groups, largely as a result of the nineteenth-century conversion of some of their communal lands in Unguja into the freehold property of large Omani landowners, thereby confining them to the less fertile land on the eastern side of the island over the course of the early to mid-nineteenth century.[34] In the early twentieth century, the term *Shirazi* was also appropriated in Zanzibar into individual projects of ethnogenesis, culminating in the formation of a project for collective representation of Shirazis in the Shirazi Association, founded in 1940. But members of the African Association in Zanzibar decried those who continued to think of themselves as Shirazi, rather than African, until the brokerage of a union between the two associations and the formation of that union into a nationalist political party, the Afro-Shirazi Party (ASP).[35]

IMMIGRATION AND REGISTRATION IN ZANZIBAR, 1890–1960

The derivation of eligibility to vote from citizenship status proved through local residence in Zanzibar was where electoral procedure confronted the politics of exogenous origins. The late colonial democratic transition in Zanzibar came with greater state reliance on new and emerging technologies of mass social surveillance of territorial residents, distinguishing citizens from immigrants. The force of these new sites of contradiction is related to the increasing force of positive law in Zanzibar's legal order since the early to mid nineteenth century, defining extraterritorial relations of European powers.[36] Colonial rule in Zanzibar changed the populace's understanding of the protected sultanate's sovereignty by transforming the state's procedures for establishing legalized residence in the territory. By the late nineteenth century, state systems of migration control were overwhelmed by the massive increase in movement of people, in part stimulated by revolutions in transportation that lowered the risk of travel while making it more affordable for the masses. The passport was a paper originally meant to bring order to the allegedly unruly dynamics of travel and immigration by colonial subjects in the early twentieth-century British Empire. In the words of Engseng Ho, "The relation of photograph to face, the similarity between image and visage, engraves person onto paper and establishes a connection of metonymy with the bearer, while the text inscribes the name of that person in the country of which he or she, is thereby made a part."[37] The passport symbolizes a right to travel under the protection of a specific nation-state.

However, many people in East Africa traveled to Zanzibar without a passport until the 1950s. Mobilizing immigrant labor to pick cloves was of paramount importance to the fiscal success of the colonial state in Zanzibar. In the 1920s and 1930s the state was still committed to propping up the largest landowners, which was in part the purpose of the formation of the Clove Growers Association in 1927, whose role was to serve as a kind of insurance for the largest clove producers.[38] As a result of the need for labor to be available for clove harvesting, the protectorate government in Zanzibar had not required a passport from a person considered to be "an African of a tribe indigenous to Uganda, Kenya, Tanganyika and Zanzibar."[39] Letters between various protectorate officials argued about the need to keep regulations lax so as not to disrupt the immigrant labor on which Zanzibar's economy depended, and to control immigration that disrupted public order.[40]

Regulation of migration from other nodes of Britain's Indian Ocean empire preceded regulation of migration from the African mainland. By 1911, all passengers (aside subjects of the sultan of Muscat) "traveling in a native vessel" were required to obtain a passport.[41] World War I further entrenched the legal status of the passport as official proof of the national status of its holder.[42] Colonial governmental authorities asserted the right to deny entry to any passenger without a passport on the big steamships, creating a dilemma for shipping companies, who, unlike their dhow predecessors, were strongly linked to and dependent on colonial authority for guarantees on immigration.[43]

Passage on a dhow continued to be the main way that Arabs from the Gulf entered the Zanzibar protectorate, even in the era of steamship travel. Trading was exemplary of the kind of Indian Ocean translocal residence and circular migration common across the Afro-Asian maritime world. The typical pattern for Arabian dhows was to leave by September, go to India to trade, and then make their way around the Gulf and the northern Swahili coast, arriving in Unguja in January and February. They would stay for several months on the coast and coastal islands of East Africa. The trade brought mangrove poles and grain to Arabia, in exchange for dates, dried fish, salt, and luxury items. One could also book passage on the trading dhows.

Dhow captains were not subject to the same regulation as steamship captains.[44] Their economic margins were also far lower. The British government's main preoccupation regarding Arab immigration during the 1930s and 1940s was indigence of passengers, the risk of their becoming dependent on the protectorate government, and the cost of repatriating them to Oman.

British officials blamed a 1939 migration crisis on the Clove Growers Association decision in 1937 to hire the Manga as clove-buying agents. Although the practice had since been discontinued, many Manga had returned to Oman flush with profits from their venture. In 1939 and in several years preceding, crops in Oman had failed due to drought. Lured by the promise of profits in Zanzibar, Manga often took dhows there to earn money to support their families in Oman. In 1939, 70 percent of the thirty-five hundred migrants to Unguja during the dhow season remained after the end of trading season. They lived mostly outside Stone Town in Ngambo, where they borrowed money to obtain a shop license or trade in dry goods. Some also picked cloves on the larger estates in Pemba, along with mainlanders who had migrated there for this temporary work. In 1940, the Deportation Decree attempted to clarify the status of these tangled immigration statuses.[45] Arab migrants incurred the envy and fear of some settled Zanzibaris and even other migrants, and were at times regarded as a dangerous nuisance by the colonial administration and associated with criminality and fighting. According to the British resident, the government agreed "that the problem is to maintain the long established and traditional contact between the Arabs of Zanzibar and Oman, whilst keeping out the riff-raff who are menace here and thrive principally as receivers of stolen agricultural produce."[46]

Though a nationality decree had existed since 1941 in Zanzibar, and though revisions of the immigration and naturalization laws followed on the end of World War II, a major legal reconfiguration of nationality in Zanzibar occurred after passage of the British Nationality Act of 1948, a law with significant implications for deriving nationality from local residence status. The law made those who were formerly British subjects "Citizens of the United Kingdom and Colonies" or citizens of a specific Commonwealth country under that country's citizenship act. Commonwealth citizens now had to apply to their home countries for passports, to retain their citizenship, and those previously coming under the status of British Protected Person saw that status eliminated.[47] Translocal Arab migrants came under the newly formulated immigration controls stemming from the new local definition of belonging; the 1948 Immigration (Control of Arabs from Southern Arabian States) Regulations that attempted to distinguish "Arabs from Southern Arabian States" from local Arabs who were subjects of the sultan of Zanzibar. This was made more difficult because some Arabs moved between Muscat and East Africa carrying colonial identity documents from mainland territories like Tanganyika. Many Arab immigrants voluntarily embraced Zanzibar nationality in the late 1940s up until the early 1960s, as a result. There were also cases of individuals born in Zanzibar, whose fathers had left Zanzibar for India or Arabia, claiming a local status on the islands.[48]

A new 1952 Nationality Decree in Zanzibar updated the previous law to formalize eligibility for citizenship through local birth.[49] The decree reflected relatively progressive assumptions of birthright citizenship, and it formalized links between territorial birth, subject status, and the national passport.[50] The decree announced that every person born in Zanzibar after its propagation would be recognized as a Zanzibar subject by birth. Additionally, after three years of continuous residence in the "Dominions of the Sultan," anyone born outside could claim resident status and apply for status as a naturalized Zanzibari.[51]

Throughout the early 1950s, Africans continued to be able to immigrate to Zanzibar without a passport, although there were abortive attempts by British officials to provide a form of unofficial documentation for African permanent residents of Zanzibar to visit family on the mainland.[52] By the mid-1950s this began to change, as a result of political upheaval in neighboring Kenya, which helped spur immigration restrictions targeting non–East Africans, as well as Kikuyu, Embu and Meru tribes. The restrictions also prohibited Arabs, Comorians and "alien Africans" from entering the Protectorate "by posing as East Africans."[53]

Though long-term residents of Zanzibar, mainland-origin Africans often lacked documentation of local birth, necessary to register to vote. Birth certificates cost applicants; they were required to pay a fee to have one issued if they were not already in possession of it.[54] Yet some could not afford the 35 shillings it cost to obtain this document or were not informed of its urgency, to say nothing of the naturalization and certificate fees. Mainland migrants were disadvantaged by illiteracy in English and their lack of patronage ties to the island's elite. Documents from Pemba indicate that many mainland Africans who entered without a permit, often in the service of a particular employer who would also act as patron, faced difficulties with the new regime of documentation.[55] Being unable to produce documents proving local birth led to contestations over the admissibility of oral evidence for citizenship claims. For instance, Bibi Msinionee from Pemba was married to a Tanganyikan man and went to live with her husband in Tanganyika using the free system of movement provided by colonial authorities before Tanganyika became independent. When she tried to come back to Pemba to see her parents, the Tanganyika government did not issue her a passport, as it considered her a Zanzibar subject. She was allowed provisional landing in Zanzibar and then asked to produce evidence that she was a citizen of Zanzibar. But her birth, like the birth of many Africans in Zanzibar, was not registered, so she only managed to get an affidavit from the local *sheha* (a local office of consultative government), who knew the parents of the lady and vouched for her. The affidavit was not accepted, and she was threatened with deportation unless she produced an original birth certificate. The district officer in Pemba reported that this situation was quite common among ordinary Zanzibaris, and that a new system had to be put in place to avoid disenfranchising such people.[56]

The racial stakes of citizenship and disenfranchisement are evident from newspaper editorials and correspondence in the Zanzibar archives. In a May 14, 1958, editorial in *al-Falaq* the writer criticized the government for continuing to allow mainland Africans to enter Zanzibar without the obligation of having passports. The editor compared the issue of African immigration to Zanzibar with the flow of West Indians to Britain, suggesting that Zanzibar's cultural identity would be swamped by such migration.[57] At the urging of ZNP and Zanzibar and Pemba People's Party (ZPPP) supporters, the colonial government investigated the matter of illegal immigration to Pemba in the early 1960s and concluded it was not a serious issue and that legal immigrants far outweighed illegal ones.[58] The complaints were responding to a suspicion that naturalization was a political tool to reshape Zanzibar's demography by opening the door for fraudulent citizens to vote. These individuals felt more immigration surveillance was necessary to preserve the integrity of national citizenship. In 1956 some elites of Pemba requested the government to do something to address the illegal immigration of Africans from the mainland. The letter requested that legislation be introduced so that no person, regardless of race or tribe, would be allowed to enter the Protectorate without a passport.[59] In the pro-ZNP newspaper *Adal Insaf*, one writer insisted that the government not permit anyone to register as a voter without first showing both a birth certificate and a certificate of naturalization.[60]

Abdulla Rashid, a district commissioner in Pemba, had little pity for those who were unable to bureaucratically prove their Zanzibar nationality: "Whilst I appreciate the difficulties experienced by Zanzibar nationals who are on the mainland and are not in possession of documentary proof of their nationality to satisfy the Immigration Authorities when they return to the Protectorate . . . the Registration of Births Decree was passed a long time ago, but these people (or their parents) did not see its value and declined to take advantage of it, with the result that their children now suffer." Rashid considered that many people in Zanzibar had obtained fraudulent naturalization certificates and that "because of the lack of strict ruling regarding proof of place of birth, many people have registered who have no right to vote."[61]

Meanwhile, the difficulties placed in the way of mainlanders' naturalizing aroused indignation among Zanzibar's Africans, expressed in some of the newspapers of the time. In November 1959 a front-page article in *Agozi* complained that thousands of Arabs were "buying" citizenship on Unguja.[62] In February 1960 an editorial in *Sauti ya Afro Shirazi* complained that many Africans had sacrificed themselves in World War II and had long considered themselves citizens of "Mtukufu Bwana Seyyid" (the sultan), only to be told now that "in seeking for themselves freedom and development" they were "wageni" (foreigners).[63] Similar sentiments appeared two years later in the pages of *Afrika Kwetu*.[64]

ELECTORAL POLITICS, IMMIGRATION, AND VISIONS OF CITIZENSHIP IN ZANZIBAR

Only six of twelve seats on the Legislative Council, all previously nominated positions, were in contention during Zanzibar's first election in 1957.[65] The election was contested by two main parties. With help from Julius Nyerere, head of the Tanganyikan African National Union headquartered in nearby Dar-es-Salaam, Abeid Karume, head of Zanzibar's African Association, had managed to unite it with the Shirazi Association, forming the Afro-Shirazi Union.[66] The ASU (later the Afro-Shirazi Party, ASP) was in favor of delaying independence until Zanzibar's Africans had reached a level of development more equal to other island communities (for instance by increasing African representation in the civil service).[67] Though the ASP was neither well organized nor had as many resources as the ZNP, and as a result had far less access to the machinery of state, it did have the ability to promote its ideas in a public sphere where it would be guaranteed a hearing, and its potential sympathetic constituency was much larger than the ZNP's and could count on mainland support. It also had covert support from the island's wealthy Indian creditors, who were anxious to weaken the power of the landed Arab elites.[68]

The ASP leadership's conception of the nation was more popular but practically narrower than the ZNP's and stemmed from the broad ideological currents present within the original African Association. ASU members saw the ZNP leadership as non-African exploiters attempting to protect anachronistic privileges of sovereignty gained under colonial rule.[69] They perceived the ZNP as seeking anti-African self-rule and as wanting to remove mainlanders from Zanzibar.[70] Like Southeast Asian nationalists' rhetoric about Chinese nationals, the ASU leadership initially grafted anticommunism onto this long-standing distrust of Arabs.[71] ASP Youth League members challenged this anticommunist stance while affirming its anti-Arabism. Increasing African landownership through redistribution of land owned by the Arab elite was central to the party's vision.[72] In pro-ASP rhetoric in Zanzibar's newspapers, underdevelopment was linked to the region's past in slavery, and the fault was laid at the feet of minority ethnicities, especially Arabs, and their desire to preserve "feudal" relationships with Africans.[73] "Arab slavery" discourse provided the ideological glue holding together the fragile coalition between the African and Shirazi Associations, and it became a seductive pretext for the more extreme displays of ethnic chauvinism and resentment by some ASP intellectuals.[74]

In contrast to the ASP, the ZNP's call was for immediate independence. The ZNP leadership was drawn from the ranks of the island's middle and upper classes, and the party had considerably more resources than the ASP.[75] Though forbidden to become politically active, most Afro-Arabs who had entered the colonial civil service were influenced to covertly help mobilize for the ZNP. Their political platform asserted that popular sovereignty was "natural," inclusive, and universally rooted in an already existing relationship to a precolonial sovereignty symbolized by the monarchy.[76] Leaders assumed that common religion and language organically tied them to ordinary islanders. Like "creole nationalists" in Latin America, they argued their local intermarriage and acculturation had made them "sons of the soil" in Zanzibar.[77] Most were social democrats. While the younger nationalists may have cherished socialist ideals, their elders ultimately regarded individual private property as needing to be protected under the law.[78] They favored civic nationality as a progressive force to overcome racial identities; they later instructed their followers to answer "Zanzibari" to the March 1958 census question about race, origin, or ancestry.[79]

Younger ZNP leadership was internationalist, pan-Africanist, and more socialist in policy orientation than their rivals. Despite the social progressivism of many members of the party, it came up against the paradox of popular sovereignty as it debated the need for immigration and birthright restrictions to ensure the integrity of democratic elections. While religious tolerance was trumpeted and colonial nativism criticized among Zanzibar's Afro-Arab nationalists, immigration from the mainland especially was perceived by many of them as an existential threat to the cultural and political integrity of the state.[80] ZNP rhetoric even portrayed the ASP as a straightforward instrument of mainland Christian domination.[81]

Before the 1957 election commenced, a significant legal controversy occurred that defined the hostile relationship between Zanzibar's two rival parties and entangled the issue of immigration with that of race. At issue was legitimate versus illegitimate claims to national citizenship and representation, based on the immigration of oneself and one's parents. One of the party's key supporters, Ali Ahmed al-Riyami, sued Abeid Karume, the leader of the Afro-Shirazi Union-cum-Party, on charges that he was ineligible to stand for elections, as he was not a citizen of Zanzibar.[82] The charges were patently politically motivated. To ZNP supporters, some of ASP leader Abeid Karume's stump speeches were a form of vile, racially divisive, and norm-trespassing behavior of the ideals of anticolonial unity, and he needed to be put in his place. Even though many of the Afro-Arab elites knew Karume very well and retained good relations with him throughout the time of politics, others trespassed on well-established norms of Zanzibari social life in their eagerness to see him discredited.[83]

Lurking behind the accusation of being a false national was the assumption that Karume was the offspring of laborers, possibly former slaves from the mainland, who had come to Zanzibar to work on elite plantations.[84] The case thus raised the material inequalities between putative citizens. Karume came from the same class and status as many of those born in Zanzibar without a birth certificate. Whether he had been born in Zanzibar or not, he had deep roots in the working classes of the urban area of Ngambo, "Swahilini" as it is called today.[85]

On May 20, 1957, according to Thabit Kombo, "Hizbu (ZNP) sent Sh. Riyami, who knew Karume very well, to the courthouse to testify that Karume was not born in Zanzibar." At the trial Karume produced a passport showing his Zanzibar citizenship and that he was born in August 1905 in Koani Mudiria, South Unguja.[86] He claimed he had attended elementary school at Mwera in Zanzibar.[87] According to Kombo, al-Riyami, age thirty-seven, had improbably claimed to have seen Karume, age fifty-two, being carried by his mother on the mainland.[88] Riyami lost in a June 11, 1957, decision and was held liable for all the court fees, which were eventually paid by the ZNP.

The court case made Karume a cause célèbre among the island's African masses. As a result of how Karume's trial was conducted, it became possible to interpret the lawsuit as the desperate gamble by foreign Arab exploiters attempting to protect anachronistic privileges of sovereignty gained under colonial rule. More extreme partisans took the lawsuit as Arab plotting designed to implement their desire to re-enslave the islands' Africans.[89] At the same time, the ASP's inflammatory racial rhetoric and ties to mainland parties made it possible for the opposing ZNP to see ASP as trespassing on the limits of legitimate political discourse and acting illegally to encourage voting of noncitizens.[90]

In the 1957 election, only approximately 36,000 (11.9%) of the total population of 300,000 determined the election results.[91] In overall votes, the ASU was a clear winner, getting 21,632 votes to the ZNP's 7,761, plus 5,968 for candidates of the Indian, Muslim, or Comorian associations. The

ASU/ASP's plurality in the popular vote was a whopping 61.2 percent. As a result, they won five seats out of the six contested, despite not contesting in Pemba, while the ZNP won zero. To the ASP leadership, this was a clear sign of the impending end of Arab hegemony in Zanzibar.[92]

Voter naturalization became a further politicized issue in 1958 and 1959. After their failure in the 1957 election, the ZNP held mass naturalization drives to drive up the numbers of their supporters. Abdulrahman Mohamed Babu was an instrumental factor in the success of the ZNP's popular mobilization campaign. There was a sudden and rapid increase in naturalization applications between 1957 and 1961.[93] The expansion of ZNP's electoral base in the 1958 and 1961 elections came through naturalization drives among the approximately four thousand immigrants from Muscat reported in the 1958 census. In the last two months of 1959, officials reported as many naturalization applications submitted as had been received since the decree came into effect, often up to fifty per day.[94] By and large those who naturalized were ZNP supporters encouraged to do so by the party. The ASP did not embark on a similar campaign; far fewer ASP supporters legally naturalized themselves as citizens.[95] Clearly some were troubled by the links between naturalization and electoral mobilization; one British official felt compelled to send a memo to the attorney genera, stating that "naturalization means allegiance to His Highness and citizenship—not just a device to obtain extra votes."[96]

From 1959, the ZNP sought to curb what they saw as voter roll inflation by the ASP by checking for procedural abnormalities in the system of naturalizing citizens and by using their limited power within the colonial state to urge more restrictive enforcement of immigration regulations.[97] Enforcement was complicated by the political rivalry between different villages; some Zanzibaris alleged that politically sympathetic villages had been ignoring the landing of non-Zanzibaris at night. At the time, British officials found no evidence of extensive illegal entry, although they did acknowledge there had been some unlawful landings.

Beginning in September 1958, a newly formed pan-African body in the region, the Pan-African Freedom Movement of East and Central Africa (PAFMECA), attempted to mediate the deepening conflict between the parties in the interest of anticolonial unity.[98] The ASP's participation in the PAFMECA agreement caused dissension among ASP leadership, particularly from the more radical members of the Youth League.[99] The ASP underwent a crisis at the end of 1959 in which its Pemba Shirazi membership became split on the "race" question in the ASP's official platform.[100] As the ASP weakened, the ZNP made efforts at genuine electoral mobilization under the dynamic leadership of its general secretary, Abdulrahman Babu.[101]

The fragile unity brokered between the parties by PAFMECA lasted fifteen months before breaking down. Colonial officials in Zanzibar, anxious over the deepening conflict, asked a colonial officer named Hilary Blood to come to Zanzibar and make recommendations for reforming the electoral sector to resolve the parties' political impasse. The 1960 Blood report recommended the creation of twenty-one electoral districts. ZNP leadership rejected Blood's conclusion and burned his report publicly.[102] The political impasse deepened, and the planned July 1960 election was eventually postponed.[103] Political campaigning was thus continuous on the islands from early 1960 until the election of June 1961. In 1960, during this long contentious election campaign, the popular, long-reigning Sultan Khalifa bin Harub died and was replaced by his less popular son, who died in 1963 before independence.[104] Sultan Khalifa was replaced by his far less popular offspring at a time of deep and entrenched political divisions. Initially, ASP party heads did not publicly or inherently object to the monarchy; in a 1960 communiqué, they affirmed that the sultan of Zanzibar "is our head of state, above and outside politics" and accepted that "the present dynasty should be safeguarded and guaranteed."[105] Even some intellectual ideologues of the ASP clearly respected Sultan Khalifa bin Harub for his seniority and ability to stand above politics.[106] But to some younger anticolonial radicals the sultans were symbols of an old "feudal" order, adding further fuel to the fire of existing antipathies to exogenous origins.[107]

THE ELECTIONS OF JANUARY AND JUNE 1961

Eventually the parties agreed to the terms for another election, in which the voting age would be lowered to twenty-one and women were to be given the vote.[108] Though sixty-five thousand voters were added to the rolls by these reforms, as well as by registration and naturalization drives, the eligible electorate was still only 28.6 percent of the total population. A third party, the ZPPP, a splinter group formed in 1959 from former Pemba Shirazis upset with the "racial" turn of the ASP, also contested the elections.[109] In the January 1961 election, the ZNP performed strongly compared to previous elections, while still not winning an outright majority; the share of the vote obtained by the ZPPP was split by its internal fracture, with some members embracing the ZNP and others the ASP. In this election the ASP candidates won 36,698 votes, the ZNP candidates won 32,724 votes, and 15,541 votes went to the newly formed ZPPP. Although ASP won more seats than the ZNP, ten to nine, the three ZPPP seats first swung to the ZNP, before splitting and deadlocking each party at eleven seats apiece.[110] The election was seen as vindication by both sides. The radicals within the ASP regarded their victory in the popular vote as further proof of the perfidy of the colonial system, which was an obstacle to the genuine realization of popular sovereignty. ZNP members were elated; they had organized and had made substantial inroads into Zanzibar's African majority significant enough to form an independent government with ZPPP support. Some in the ASP leadership, noticing the substantial inroads ZNP leaders had made into the electorate, suspected illegal voting or other forms of fraud.[111]

Another election was set for June 1, 1961, with largely the same districts as in January, with an additional seat in Pemba. Some 30 percent of the islands' total population was eligible to vote. Over 99 percent of registered voters cast votes, surely a record in terms of mass political mobilization. The ASP candidates won a plurality of all votes cast (50.6%). However, with twenty-three seats up for election, the ASP and ZNP won an equal number of seats (ten each), while the ZPPP again won three seats. Trouble began early on, with rumors about voter fraud prompting acts of mass intimidation that escalated into stone throwing and then out-and-out street warfare between the parties.[112] The intensity of the electoral competition, alongside rumors about prevention of voting and illegal voting, triggered a violent pogrom that led to the death of sixty-eight people and the injury of nearly four hundred others. Nearly three thousand persons were rendered refugees.[113] In the wake of this inconclusive election and its accompanying criminal violence, both parties nursed skyrocketing levels of bitterness toward their opponents, making the likelihood of peaceful power sharing completely remote.[114]

The sovereignty of the nearby Kenya coast also became a sensitive issue at this time. The Kenya coast had been considered a part of the sultan's domains, rented out to the colonial government of Kenya; the coast was even originally organized into a separate "Seyyidie" province within Kenya.[115] In the late 1950s there was a movement for this region to become its own independent state or to accede to Zanzibar. Called "Mwambao," its association with Kenya's white settler community discredited it in the eyes of Kenya's dominant anticolonial parties while also uncomfortably associating ZNP leadership with the specter of white settler domination.[116] As the ZNP distanced themselves from the movement in an effort to avoid alienating anticolonial nationalists in Kenya, the new Tanganyikan president Julius Nyerere was stating his opinion that sultanic rule in Zanzibar invited regional insecurity because of its ties to the Arab and Muslim world.[117]

ZANZIBAR'S INDEPENDENCE OF 1963

Another election was called for July 1963. The stakes of this election were greater than in previous elections (which were about representation in the Legislative Council); British authorities decided in June 1962 that they would hand over power to the winner of the next election. Over 51.6 percent% of the total population was eligible to vote, and over 99 percent of the electorate again participated. Before this election, the charismatic Babu resigned from the party and founded a new political grouping, the Umma Party, with membership largely drawn from the younger generation of urban Zanzibaris.[118] Babu became an anticolonial cause célèbre in 1962 after being jailed on charges of sedition by the colonial state. After serving an eighteen-month sentence, he emerged from prison in August 1962 and demanded the ZNP run more African candidates in a number of "safe" seats to exhibit the ZNP's commitment to multiracial democracy, a proposal the party leadership refused.[119] Babu believed that the ZNP had become dominated by the more "conservative" elements of its membership: Ali Muhsin, Ahmed Lamky, Muhammad Salim al-Barwani (Jinja), Ahmed Seif Kharusi, and Ali Ahmed al-Riyami.[120] His ambitions stoked by the support he had received upon his release from prison, he set out to counter this influence by building bridges to ASP Youth League leaders like Abdullah Kassim Hanga.[121] Both the ZNP and the ASP saw an increasingly sharp divide between their more radical and more conservative wings, with the former ready to resort to armed struggle in concert with global examples of anticolonial insurgency in Kenya, Algeria, and Vietnam.[122] Some Youth League members had formed their own covert plans for an armed uprising against the sultan in alliance with mainland colleagues.[123]

In the July 1963 election, the ASP again won a majority of all votes cast, over 87,000 of 163,511 (54%).[124] But the number of seats each party won remained close: thirteen for the ASP and twelve for the ZNP. The Shirazi vote was evenly split between the ZNP and ASP because of Pemba's Shirazi vote largely going to the ZPPP. Again, the ZPPP played the spoiler role and "gave" their seats to the ZNP to form a government. After the rejection by ZNP-ZPPP leadership of the possibility of the ASP being part of a national government, ASP leadership was divided over whether to enter the government as a loyal opposition or to pursue political power through other means.[125] The ZNP and ZPPP leadership thus formed the government that was to take power from the British without ASP participation. Whether this was an active omission by the victorious parties' leadership or a desire blocked by more militant ASP members, it meant that the final transition to national independence was a divisive affair, further aggravated by the death of Zanzibar's first "constitutional monarch," Abdullah, and the succession of his son Jamshid.[126]

From July 1963 to December 1963, things seemed outwardly calm on the islands. A September 1963 constitutional conference in London laid down the details of the power handover from the British. The victorious ZNP leadership did not act with restraint or modesty in victory. They imposed new limits on opposition political parties and took other steps that assumed their cultural base among the masses was stronger than the election results showed.[127] Economic challenges—rising unemployment and cutting of social services—followed on a precipitous drop in the price of cloves in the early 1960s.[128] Subsequent firings of mainlanders from the police force gave further strength to ASP frustrations.[129] In December 1963, the first independent government of Zanzibar celebrated its independence; it was a somewhat somber affair. Critics derided Zanzibar's December 10, 1963, independence from British rule as "uhuru wa Waarabu," or "freedom for Arabs."[130] Several weeks later, the ZNP-led government was overthrown.

CONCLUSION: WHY DID THE 1963 INDEPENDENT STATE OF ZANZIBAR FAIL?

The reasons for the lack of success in transitioning the nineteenth-century sultanate sovereignty into an independent constitutional monarchy are multiple and comprehensible, rather than shrouded in an overarching external conspiracy (chapters 3 and 6 explore these conspiracy theories in greater detail). They are divided into first long-term and then short-term causes. First, precolonial vertical state sovereignty in Zanzibar was minimalist, not broadly rooted in popular social consent. Popular sovereignty, based on the idea of national development, would have produced a decisive break with the past of vertical sovereignty, even if the ZNP had managed to hold onto power after independence. The precolonial economic foundations of state revenue and its slavery-dependent labor relations were left only partially reformed by colonial rule. Colonial rule's ambiguous goals trapped Zanzibar in a stagnant and conservative socioeconomic order. Transition to popular sovereignty exposed the deep traces of material inequality left by the previous economic system, and these inequalities contributed to resentment that the electoral process was rigged toward the powerful and would re-enslave Zanzibar's Africans. Zanzibar's relatively small size as an island nation often aggravated these problems.

In the short term, colonial officials did not anticipate the vibrancy of the expanded civil society that arose because of reforms that aimed to institute popular democratic rule in Zanzibar.[131] Anticolonialism's immediate goals were interpreted differently by the two rival parties the ASP and the ZNP, but they were also interpreted differently by generations and education levels within the party. In the short term, electoral democracy produced internal dissension between different groups, classes, and parties claiming the islands as sovereign political space, which electoral mechanisms were unable to resolve. Each party resorted to forms of blatant ethnic chauvinism and stoked racialized fears of being "swamped" by the other.[132] In Michael Lofchie's words, "they misunderstood and misinterpreted each other's parties to a degree which made mutual accommodation impossible."[133]

Second, the dependence of popular democracy on an infrastructure of citizenship raised fatal contradictions between that ethos and the need to circumscribe the franchise through bureaucratic surveillance distinguishing citizen from noncitizen. Popular sovereignty as aspirational discourse produced xenophobic rhetoric about fitness for national membership and led to competing discourses of national autochthony. The ZNP's bungled prosecution of ASP leader Abeid Karume was representative of the party's general tone deafness on immigration, and it alienated many voters with mainland roots. The victorious ZNP leadership continued to exhibit arrogance and shortsightedness in resolving this issue, for instance by firing immigrants on the police force and passing a number of laws essentially criminalizing political protest.[134] They also underestimated how vulnerable they would be once British military protection was withdrawn.[135] In imagining that their opponents were mostly illegal immigrants, rather than citizens of Zanzibar, they vastly overestimated the security of their own position after independence; this led them to reject the possibility of being gracious in victory and forming a national government.[136] Moreover, the ballot box was viewed in almost purely instrumental terms; elections were less an expression of the consensual norms of Zanzibari political culture than the most direct lawful means to achieve political power.[137] Militant ASP members, after being frustrated at the ballot box, saw the bullet as the only feasible alternative. Through an audacious display of military decisiveness, they and John Okello's insurgents gifted the state to Karume and the Revolutionary Council. But they also destroyed the possibility of a democratic modus vivendi in Zanzibar for a generation, entrenching an autocratic dictatorship that ended up sending several Revolutionary Council members to the firing squad.

The final short-term factor was the weakness of Zanzibar's monarchy at the end of empire. At a moment when the institution of monarchy was being challenged by radical currents of popular democracy, Zanzibar's most popular and longest serving ruler, Seyyid Khalifa, died; the throne was inherited by his younger son, and then on the eve of independence, by his grandson. The young constitutional monarch of Zanzibar, Jamshid, was placed in an unenviable and explosive situation and was not equal to the admittedly monumental task of standing above the growing tide of partisanship on the islands. The political weakness of the monarchy and its decayed roots in popular social life symbolized the larger decay of the political position of the island's Arab oligarchy.[138] Their weakness prevented Zanzibar's vertical sovereignty from serving as the ideological foundation for an independent postcolonial island state in Zanzibar or resolving the deep electoral impasse between Zanzibar's two main parties.

Different choices by party leadership in this period could have led to a different and more stable outcome in Zanzibar, even given the inevitability of a violent uprising. Proportional representation instead of single-member districts would have allowed the ASP to take its overall electoral majority into power more peacefully.[139] The victorious ZNP leadership could have had more forethought about power sharing in the wake of their bitter electoral debate with their political rivals in the ASP. They could have left the police force alone instead of firing many mainlanders. Harith Ghassany also stresses that it was a mistake for the ZNP leadership to continue to rely on British military security.[140] The ethnicization and polarization of electoral politics and the political stalemate of each election combined to produce a significant number of Zanzibaris as well as their mainland neighbors ready to conspire to use violence to achieve political goals frustrated by procedural democracy. But this could have been countered and contained by bipartisan gestures and back channels among different elements of each party's leadership. Instead, all parties seemed to have plunged themselves headlong into violent conspiracies. This violence would spiral out of control and reverberate not only in the lives of its exiled victims (chapter 2) but in the paranoid and often arbitrary policies of the post-1964 regime that replaced the 1963 elected government (chapter 3). Questions of citizenship became acute for many Zanzibaris in the wake of violent experience.

TWO

Violence and Emigration in the Zanzibar Revolution, 1964–1965

THE MOST CONTESTED CHAPTER in Zanzibar's modern history, even more so than the six years of the "time of politics," was the overthrow of the 1963 constitutional monarchy on January 12, 1964. What made it particularly notorious was the brief but widespread violation of neighborly codes of conduct, essentially turning what could have been a brief putsch overthrowing the sultan into an intense racial pogrom of several days, mainly directed against Arabs, but also against those perceived to be supporters of the "minority government" of the ZNP, including many Pembans. The racial discourse of 1957–1963 made this transgressive violence against neighbors and political rivals appear necessary to some. As competing forms of nationalism politicized exogenous origins, ethnic others could be imagined as guilty perpetrators.[1] Rumors turned "everyday patterns, sounds, into signs of impending violence."[2] Partisans successfully persuaded themselves that their crimes, "the transgressive behavior of the pogrom," were for the greater good.[3]

In this chapter the immediate aftermath of the revolution is considered in two chronologies: the four days of revolutionary upheaval, January 12–16, and the six to twelve months following.[4] Oral history narratives collected decades later from eyewitnesses are used as a window into quotidian experiences of violence during the revolution.[5] Despite their limitations, as sources they are undoubtedly superior to the existing audiovisual narratives around which analysis has sometimes been built, including a racist snuff film made by two Italians to cynically parody decolonization.[6] Use is also made in this chapter of the UNHCR archives in Geneva; the International Committee of the Red Cross (ICRC) archives in Geneva; the British Red Cross (BRC) archives in London; and the Zanzibar, Omani, and UK National Archives.

This chapter demonstrates the character of the revolution's violence and the class character of mass emigration from Zanzibar in 1964 and 1965.[7] The dehumanizing racial rhetoric of the previous seven years ironically impacted those marginal to the immediate political events. The descendants of the island's largest landowners were not the revolution's main victims, despite its ostensibly "antifeudal" character. Instead, poorer immigrant Arabs (the Manga discussed in the previous chapter) were racially targeted, and the majority of the displaced and stateless after the revolution were from this community. Their experiences during the revolution have barely been included as part of the narrative of the revolution itself.[8]

The violence of the events in January 1964 was greater than simple acts of revenge against political opponents and more widespread than simply murder, involving "life force atrocities" like assault, rape, and arson.[9] Violence in the rural areas of Unguja rendered Manga displaced persons and led UNHCR officials to debate their status as refugees. Their relief was then taken on by the Red Cross, which also worked with the UNHCR, and the Zanzibar and Omani governments, to arrange repatriation of thousands of these individuals to Oman. As UNHCR records show, at least some of the subsequent voyages out of Zanzibar (particularly the government-sponsored April 1964 dhow voyages) ought to be considered forced migration events.[10]

The former Umma revolutionary Ali Sultan Issa compared the revolution to a kind of secular judgment day and downplayed the violence by implying that its victims were simply bad neighbors: "It was a day of reckoning, based on how you had treated your fellow human being. If you were a good Muslim, you had no fears. If you lived nicely with your neighbors, you were all right. If not, then some people might have a grudge against you, and when they got the upper hand, they could be nasty. There were some Arabs hidden in African homes, so it all depended on how you had lived with your neighbors."[11] Oral testimony makes it difficult to accept Ali Sultan's contention that the revolution was merely isolated acts of revenge against notorious and misbehaving bad neighbors.[12] Such justifications were already part of a post hoc attempt to control the explanation and interpretation of the events of the revolution by radicals interested in portraying it as a politically necessary move toward socialism.[13]

The suddenness of the Zanzibar revolution created intense and unresolved interpretive confusion about the origins of the revolution for many decades. The exact relations among all these people and plots is still a subject of intense debate and has often been obscured by extravagant and opportunistic claims and conspiracies about external subversion.[14] Many claimed to see the hidden hand of Babu in the revolution.[15] The presence of Cuban-educated Umma leaders in the streets in the early hours of the revolution led to false charges that Cuban mercenaries were behind the events.

Some doubted that John Okello, the public face of the revolution in its early days, could have planned such a daring and audacious maneuver.[16] One of Harith Ghassany's interviewees even claimed that John Okello was merely a front used by the real revolutionaries to divert any potential anger to Uganda instead of Tanganyika.[17] Moreover, Okello himself was an untrustworthy narrator, presenting the revolution solely as his personal initiative. A "Committee of 14" led by Seif Bakari claimed they had recruited Okello.[18] The ASP leadership even erased Okello from the official narrative of the revolution, which they presented as a centralized plan by themselves.[19] The Tanganyikan foreign minister, Oscar Kambona, and ASP leader Abdullah Kassim Hanga had close links, and Kambona had attempted to build up the power and capacity of the ASP for armed struggle.[20] Babu and Hanga had similar talks. However many of those directly involved in the aforementioned military training dispute that anyone in Umma had foreknowledge of their revolutionary plans.[21] The insurgents similarly deny foreknowledge by the main ASP leadership: Abeid Karume, Aboud Jumbe, and Thabit Kombo.[22]

Ghassany's book contains an interview with the late Victor Mkello, in which he claimed to have directed approximately five hundred Makonde laborers at a camp called Sakura outside of Tanga to mobilize for the revolution, with assistance from Oscar Kambona.[23] One of Ghassany's interviewees claimed that Kambona and Hanga informed Nyerere that they were able to overthrow the Zanzibar government at any time.[24] Another Ghassany interviewee, J. J. Mchingama, claimed he was part of a militia being trained by Karume at Shimo la Mungu. Issa Kibwana claimed that Karume was in direct charge of the revolution.[25] Both Mchingama and Kibwana denied any knowledge that Makonde laborers or other non-ASP outsiders played a role in the revolution, with Mchingama adding that he nevertheless does not rule out the possibility.[26] The veracity of these accounts is contested by former Umma Party members. In a 2014 interview, Salim Rashid, a former Umma Party member, dismissed the idea totally. In another 2014 interview, Tanzanian president Jakaya Kikwete publicly denied the role of outsiders/mainlanders in the Zanzibar revolution.[27]

There were in Zanzibar multiple parties willing to resort to an armed uprising against an elected government, and many politically active mainlanders were willing to assist them because of the broader political climate in the region. We cannot rule out mainlander influence on the revolution, but it is important to note that the term *invasion* is a rhetorical gloss on what are a complex set of associations between revolutionaries in Zanzibar and their supporters outside.

CHARACTER OF VIOLENCE DURING THE REVOLUTION

A major difficulty in characterizing the violence as genocide is the wide disparity in reporting 1964 deaths and casualties.[28] The semi-coerced migration from Zanzibar of many of the survivors meant that casualty numbers and emigration numbers were conflated in some estimates. A notorious Umma Party member and revolutionary, Ali Sultan Issa, estimated that in the days after January 12, "one-third of the Arabs in Unguja were killed or forced into immediate exile."[29] His interviewer, G. Thomas Burgess, argued that this was likely bombast. It is similarly difficult to credit Okello's apocalyptic figure of over twenty thousand, related in his memoir, but easy to see that inflating casualties helped confirm for Okello the significance of his actions and the imagined persona he had adopted as dispenser of violent justice. The official estimate by the revolutionary government, communicated in a press communiqué of March 12, 1964, was far lower than Okello's or Issa's estimates: 17 dead, 347 casualties, and 30 people still in the hospital.[30] A more accurate estimate comes from one of the Zanzibar hospital's surgeons, who stated that 1,000 killed was a reasonable estimate. He further reported that 470 wounded people had been admitted to the hospital at the time.[31] The BRC files on the subject cite various numbers, including 200 hospitalized and 3,000 killed.[32] Irregular warfare between ZNP and ASP supporters claimed more than a few lives, including many Africans. But most of those targeted in the pogrom were innocent Arab civilians.

Estimates of casualties in the revolution serve different ideological purposes, depending on one's position within the events.[33] Postcolonial Tanzanian historiography has tended to downplay the scope of the revolution's transgressive violence. Radicals in Zanzibar justified the violence in class terms as a spontaneous "lumpen" uprising that they "guided" into a revolution. Meanwhile, the Arab exiles, influenced by the traumas of the experience and desiring to place the issue before an often-fickle Western public, characterized the violence as a "genocide."[34]

Both perspectives are severely limited. We still know very little about the perpetrators of the mass violence of January 12–14, 1964. An accurate account of all those killed is obscured by the tendency to inflate casualty numbers to increase the gravity of the situation and draw international attention to the issue. There is no evidence that the killings, horrific as they were, amounted to a systematic plan for elimination, the sin qua non of genocide.[35] Latter-day oral testimonies show, as do interviews with perpetrators, that the violence had an irregular character and rarely proceeded from centralized instructions for violent elimination.[36] Jonathon Glassman calls it a pogrom, which seems an apt term, since the violence in Zanzibar was more of a discrete, one-off event than an organized, multistep process.[37]

In the hours and days of violence following the morning of January 12, large numbers of the island's Arab families were marched to Raha Leo, a large, open ground outside of town, where they were confined for several days. This does seem to have saved many people who would otherwise have been killed in the countryside. Most former government ministers surrendered voluntarily. Ali Muhsin was roughed up and brought into Raha Leo. Okello pressured Thabit Kombo and Karume to punish certain Manga detainees who had defended themselves and killed his men, which both men refused to do.[38]

Who were those who committed the killings, and why did they do so? Testimony of victims shows a widespread perception that the bands who committed the atrocities were strangers. Most of the killings were not directly ordered by ASP leadership, even if members of the mob had organizational ties to Okello, Hanga, and others.[39] The more extreme members of a faction often coerced reluctant individuals to participate.[40] Local criminal gangs were among participants, for instance the black-shirt-and-pants-wearing "Tupendane," originally mobilized by Karume in the 1961 elections and the June 1961 riots.[41] Another group was recruited from plantation workers (Manamba) and had a dominant mainland membership component. It was connected to the efforts of Victor Mkello and claimed covert sponsorship and support from Kambona and Nyerere.[42] Many participants had been living in Zanzibar for five, ten, or fifteen years prior to the revolution. Among Ghassany's interviewees, Issa Kibwana emphasized the complexity of the designation "invasion": "Mainlanders didn't come to make the revolution, the originally came for those sultans (maSultani) to tend cloves. . . . [W]hen the revolution came, they participated."[43] For some interviewees the mainland identity of the killers was fundamentally a moral question, as they asserted the absolute impossibility of any of the killers being "Zanzibari."[44] A Zanzibar-born interviewee became animated on this point, insisting that "there was no way in hell Zanzibaris could have done those killings. Zanzibaris are too religious to do such things. I am 100% sure that the people who did the killings were from the mainland and had no religion."[45]

The killings followed on orders to intimidate and thus neutralize perceived political foot soldiers of the defeated ZNP, especially Manga Arab immigrants from Oman, in rural villages in central Zanzibar, especially Bumbwini, Nungwe, and Bububu; certain neighborhoods of Ngambo; and only rarely Stone Town.[46] Issa Kibwana described a situation in which revolutionary leaders like Said Natepe distributed weapons to poor country people, "the hungry" ("wenye hamaki"), and instructed their holders to go to places on Unguja where there was known to be heavily armed Arab resistance. There they would engage in killings, enacting a displaced revenge against the "ethnic kin" of those who had previously harassed them or their associates.[47] Ghassany's anonymous interviewee relates the way they proceeded with the pogrom: "We went around Unguja farm by farm. In the group there were people with their own private grudges: 'Here is an Arab,' and three, four, or five Makonde would disembark there. Now, you know the cruelty of that individual, he just goes and enters inside. . . . [H]e doesn't consult with anyone. If there is a panga, he is instructed to use the panga."[48] Many times the assailants raped and assaulted women affiliated with the ZNP.[49] What began as a mopping-up operation quickly got out of individual leaders' control, until it became a mob. The mob opened the main prison and even killed some ASP supporters and others of mainland origin.[50] Large swathes of the countryside were devastated by these armed partisans. Revolutionary activities to pacify Pemba with these gangs began the morning of January 13; similar kinds of killings were conducted there, though not on the scale of what occurred at Unguja.[51]

The mob violence was quickly curtailed by the new leadership. According to Issa Kibwana, Karume stood up at Raha Leo and urged supporters not to kill any more people in the rural areas and to return the distributed weapons.[52] Karume further ordered protection of certain elite Arab families with whom he had close ties.[53] Umma Party members also seemed to have in certain cases intervened to try to halt the violence. A force of mainland policemen from the Police Field Force, sent by Nyerere, also helped to quell the mobs.[54]

Regarding motivation, Glassman's discussion of the violence argues that rumor and coercion helped to create a "violent subjectivity," an attitude that the killings were necessary, for either ideological or social reasons.[55] As Glassman showed, the consciousness of many violent actors had been shaped by the xenophobic discourses of the previous decade and further radicalized by rumors and gossip. Testimony by revolutionaries indicates that the days of violence were perceived as a communal payback for individual incidents of Arab injustice and prejudice. Okello, for instance, worked for several Arabs on the mainland and felt he was poorly treated.[56] J. J. Mchingama stated that he was motivated to violence by what he had observed of Arab-African relations when he arrived in Unguja in 1953. He observed an elderly Nyasa-origin man and woman, both former slaves, living on the plantation of their former masters, where they were made to do arduous daily work. When the elderly man was gored by a boar, he was harassed by Arab landowners for shirking work, and his wife had to cover the work. In another case, an Arab landowner demanded a tax in kind of five rice bushels from squatters who did not have it. This same Arab's uncle appropriated several antelope that Mchingama had killed on the land, taking the meat and leaving Mchingama with the legs.[57] But while some killings were motivated by either a general or a specific desire for revenge, others seem to have been criminally opportunistic, more for personal material gain than out of revenge against a particular person.[58]

FIRST- AND SECONDHAND NARRATIVES OF THE POGROM

The traumatic events of the revolution are still rarely talked about publicly among victims in Zanzibar, and only privately in Oman. Both anthropologist Kjersti Larsen and historian Gary Burgess noted that for fear of repercussions, people have only recently begun to speak openly about events that occurred during the revolution; Burgess observed that their stories survived in "in storytelling and private performances."[59] Many Zanzibari exiles in Muscat were still reluctant to talk about the days of the revolution. One significant exception was "Salim." He was recently retired and reflecting on a unique and exceptional life as the first "native" Omani oil well driller; he was profiled in *Petroleum Development Oman*'s fortieth anniversary issue. His narrative in that issue began in Bahla after his family's emigration from Zanzibar, omitting the seven years he spent in Zanzibar growing up. The oral account he related added the crucial details of his time in the aftermath of the Zanzibar revolution and was anchored in specific details only someone locally familiar with Zanzibar could know.[60]

On the morning of January 13, 1964, "Salim" and sixteen members of his family confronted a mob outside their home. The men called for his father and uncle to come outside the compound, along with their families. One man from the neighborhood, a disabled man named Rajab who used to beg for food from Salim's father, called out "mpe chuma" (give him the bullet/metal), and Salim heard a shot ring out and watched his father fall to the ground. His uncle tried to run away to the family car fifty meters away and was shot in the back. The remaining family members were herded into a Bedford truck and taken to Raha Leo. Salim's father died a few minutes after being shot; his uncle remained writhing in pain the entire day of the January 13 and was, according to Salim, beaten by several groups of assailants as he lay there, before dying that evening. The family were kept for five or six days at Raha Leo before being released. They promptly went to Salim's stepmother's relative's house nearby.[61] The violence and its resulting displacement eventually prompted the emigration of Salim and his family from Zanzibar.

Other interviewees in Oman revealed deep wounds carried from childhood, of a dream deferred and dashed by the social dynamics of the revolution. "Sharifa" spoke from her latter day-perspective, remembering events that occurred when she was fourteen or fifteen. "We went through a difficult time both during the election time and the revolution time. The revolution took place in 1964, my grandfather was killed. He was killed because he was sheltering Arabs. We were taken to the town—Raha Leo. Later, we were taken to Pemba to stay with the brothers of my grandfather. They were forcing people in Unguja to come out of the houses and bow to them." Later in her interview she related that her parents sent her to Burundi to be married instead of allowing her to continue going to school in Zanzibar for higher study, out of their fear that she would be forced into marriages with revolutionary state officials. "When I got married, I was 16,

I did not finish secondary school.... [T]his was the time of forced marriages in Zanzibar. My parents decided to marry me off to prevent forced marriage. At that time, we had no choice.... [W]hatever the parents said you had to follow them." She hated being in Burundi, as it reminded her of the dashed hopes she had had as a young woman for a professional career:

> I went there hoping to continue my studies, but I was not able to continue my studies. The first four years I was just crying. I was good at school and wanted to continue my studies. I have forgiven them, but it hurt me. Till I had my third child I was thinking when I would go to school.[62]

Sharifa's older relative was less willing to talk about her life. Beaming, with a broad smile, she claimed she didn't know anything and had no story to tell. Polite attempts at encouragement did not prompt her to break her silence. Her family said she was heartbroken at being absent from Zanzibar during the revolution and not being able to pay her respects to her father and others who were killed in the massacres. She had been married off in Burundi at a young age, even before the revolution.[63]

The late Issa Nasser al-Ismaily survived the revolution. But the revolutionaries burned his father's home to the ground and shot Issa's father. Issa's grandmother died from smoke inhalation a few days later.[64] Issa wrote to British resident George Mooring on March 27, 1964. In this letter Issa relates to Mooring the killing of his father; the throwing of his corpse into a nearby well; and the detention of his mother, siblings, and nephews and nieces:

> He was attacked by an armed gang at this house in shamba on Sunday Jan 12, 1964, and was shot on the head in the presence of my mother, my young sister and the children of my elder sister.... My mother and the children were taken into town and were thrown into a camp at Raha Leo for a week without food or anything to eat.[65]

Other narratives come from a collection of oral histories and narrated events about Ibadi Muslims in Zanzibar, *Hikāyāt wa Riwāyāt al-Ibādhiyya fī Zanjibār*. This remarkable book contained some eyewitness accounts of the Zanzibar revolution.[66] The al-Rawahi family were a prominent family of Ibadi scholars in Zanzibar; many of them had served as Ibadi qadis of the sultans of Zanzibar.[67] Issa, Hilal, Said, Hamoud, Ali, and Muhammad were all brothers. Hamoud was the first to be born, in 1914, followed by Said in 1916. Said and Hamoud naturalized as Zanzibar citizens in 1948, a right they were entitled to by virtue of their birth in Zanzibar to parents born in Oman who had resided continuously in Zanzibar. In their naturalization application, they listed their occupation as "landlord"; the particulars of the registration indicate they owned three "shambas" (farms) and a "a large stone house in partnership."[68] This big house was in Kiponda Zanzibar, a neighborhood in northeast Stone Town abutting N'gambo, and it was central to the narrative as a place of refuge during the pogrom. In the book, each brother relates his story in turn. Issa Salim al-Rawahi describes the first day of the revolution: "We own a small house and a big one, and the big one is like a fortress [the house in Kiponda]. In the morning [of January 12], I heard shooting, so I ran out of the small house into the big one, and we locked the doors."

The brothers settled in to listen to the radio, as Okello began to broadcast alarming warnings of impending violence and demanding unconditional obedience to his demands. As the seriousness of the situation dawned on the brothers, they battened down the house: "We stayed there [in the house] until morning. The radio was announcing: 'Those who don't open will see their doors battered down by grenades.'" Issa notes that the house served as a partial deterrent to the mob: "The cars drove past the big house while we were watching them, but they didn't dare get near because they knew there were guns in there." Others were not so lucky and were caught by the mob: "There was a man named Yahya who had two children, 15 and 16; he left them and went to his shop. I asked him, 'where are you going?' He said, 'to the shop.' And I said, 'What for? I have left my house with more things in it than what is in your shop. So don't go!' But he insisted on going, so he got killed at the shop. And there were three Omanis who didn't come into our house and were all killed."

The story takes an interesting turn on the morning of January 13, revealing the key role of intermediaries not only as guides but as negotiators brokering the peaceful surrender of the al-Rawahi brothers to Raha Leo: "While we were looking down from the house, we saw an African man we knew, and who was ordering us to come down. We asked two of our youths to go and find out what he wanted while we stayed in. He said, 'We want your safety. It would be better if we took you to your country. Don't stay here.' Indeed, it was better, for we were almost killed."

Surrendering themselves upon the advice of this man, the brothers were carried unmolested to a detainment point at a school near the island's radio station, where they were detained outside with other relatives. The al-Rawahi brothers were then imprisoned, along with other men of Omani origin, while women were released to return to their homes. The personal intervention of Zanzibar's new president, Abeid Karume, facilitated the release of the al-Rawahi brothers and their families during May Day Eve amnesties, in which the last of some 2,228 detainees from the revolution were released.[69] Two dhows put out to sea that same day, carrying refugees; anywhere between 1,350 and 1,750 refugees from Zanzibar arrived in Oman during May.[70] As he walked down the line choosing detainees to release from prison, Karume argued at that time that their detention was for their own protection: "When he got to someone he wanted to release from prison, he'd put his hand on his chest and push him back. And before he freed us all (those he'd chosen) he said, 'we put you in prison for your safety, only to preserve you from being killed.'"[71]

The story of the al-Rawahi brothers shows that many lives were actively preserved by revolutionary leadership in ways inconsistent with a planned elimination event. Good relations with Karume were the thing that saved them from a potentially forcible dispossession and permanent displacement from their homes. Though the revolution facilitated his rise to power, Karume himself was relatively conservative in his attitude and actively tried to disassociate himself from its violent lawlessness. The al-Rawahi brothers acknowledge that "he valued and respected us" and that his protection saved their house from being pillaged. But they also show the lens through which they and many other Arabs of their time viewed him: they do not refer to him as President Karume, or Sheikh Karume, but as a former porter.

Issa's brother Hilal relates that "three Africans," strangers to him, demanded they vacate their house, now that it was the government's property:

> And when the coup took place, as we were sitting in the house, three Africans came and said to Badr, son of my brother Hamoud, "This house belongs to the government, and we want it vacant by tomorrow morning." And they put a paper on the door. We asked, "where shall we go? And we have women and children?" He answered, "go into the street." The police came and tore off the paper, then they went and brought the three men who had put the paper on the door. They told them in our presence not to approach the house ever. I left Zanzibar and will not return to it, Inshallah, because I hated it after what had happened in it.[72]

Issa and his brothers immediately left Zanzibar upon their release and went to Mombasa, where many refugees from Zanzibar had gathered, fleeing the revolution. Muhammad Salim al-Rawahi, also imprisoned, went to Saudi Arabia, where he received asylum before settling permanently in Oman.[73]

Not everyone was able to call on Karume's personal protection. Two stark stories of the transgressive violence of the revolution's first days show the specific targeting of Arab men to be killed. The first is an interview with Umm Saif bint Ahmed al-Fahdiyya. It captures a common dynamic wherein scared families fled to larger houses that could be more adequately fortified against a mob. Umm Saif and her husband were engaged in preparations for Ramadan, a holy month in which violence is historically forbidden, when her husband observed things that impressed on him the urgency of events:

> We were waiting the month of Ramadan and my husband brought in dates for the month of Ramadan and went out. Shortly after, he returned and made the children get into the house. I had three children, of whom the eldest was ten years old. I asked him (my husband) what was going on, he said, "They have come." We left our home and went to a certain Muslim al-Aufi's house. He was one of the biggest arms dealers/merchants, and he owned a big house. When we entered the house, we found it full of Omani men, women and children who were escaping the killings.

Unfortunately the house did not protect Umm Saif and her family and was overrun by the mob. Her account telescopes the killing of her husband and middle son with the later death by starvation of her youngest son:

> After a while, crowds of Africans came and knocked but no one opened, so they shot at a window and its glass shattered. They entered from above the house and battered the door, the roof collapsed over our heads. I saw my husband being killed and so was one of my sons who was almost ten years old. As for my baby son, he died of hunger as there was no food to give him, and I was left with only my eldest son.[74]

Another story in this collection was told to the grandchildren of Ziyana Hamad Nasir Al-Salimiyya:

> I was in our farm at Tongoo, feeding some sheep, when about a hundred well-armed revolutionaries approached. They asked about my children and my husband and about the money we had.... There was no time for dribbling, quibbling, or eluding, as the "storm" ("āṣifat al-inqilāb") of the revolution was at its beginning. And the pillaging was at its peak all over Zanzibar.

The revolutionaries were clearly more interested in the men in the community, while criminal elements among the mob seemed motivated by the potential for looting:

> They asked, "Where are your husband and your children?" I told them where they were, and they went after them. My husband [the interviewer's grandfather] Yaarub Majid Sulaiman al-Saifi, had been suffering from fever for days. They threw him with his sons Badr and Hilal into a very high military truck, the way you would toss a ball ("mithlumā turmā al-kura"). Then they tore the house upside down, damaging and destroying furniture, and ended up by the clothes, searching for money, scattering everything on the floor.

Before leaving, they searched al-Salimiyya against the wall, with her back to them. She said, "I was expecting in those moments to be shot in the head, and I uttered the shahādatain" [the double declaration of Muslim faith: "There is no God but God/Muhammad is his messenger"].[75]

PROTECTION FROM THE MOB: STORIES OF HEROIC PERSONAL INTERVENTION

Even as they were victimized by the mob, Arabs during the revolution were also protected by African friends, neighbors, and even their employees. Their testimonies show that the polluting rhetoric of the previous decade had not completely destroyed good neighborly relations. Detainees might have ASP-supporting friends to help them obtain release from detention at Raha Leo or Kiinua Miguu Central prison.[76] A Zanzibar of Makonde extraction hid his Omani Arab friend in a field in Tunguu.[77] These stories demonstrate that even supporters of the revolution had a sense that many of those targeted were undeserving of mob violence and could act out of prior loyalties to protect neighbors and friends.[78]

Comorians, who like Shirazis were deemed exogenous to Africa by the ASP, played key roles. In his self-published biography of his father, Ahmed Ali al-Riyami relates:

> The author's neighbors were Comorians in Kisiwandui. They saved our home from being attacked by armed mobs on Revolution Day. They spread rumors that Ali Ahmed gathered Manga Arabs hidden in the ceiling ready to face any attacking mobs. Ali Ahmed also defended the home [at Kazole] with a shotgun.[79]

The family lost several members, including Ahmed's sister and brother.[80] Despite his father's notoriety, Ahmed Riyami's and his father Ali Ahmed's lives were spared, although they were roughed up and detained at Raha Leo and later the Central Prison, before being released on May Day.[81]

Habiba al-Hinai relates that one of these criminal gangs went to Pemba to her aunt's house and demanded to be let in. She contrasts the behavior of her aunt's employee "John" and those she describes as "Karume's men." (As previously mentioned, it is not at all clear that these men were acting on direct orders from Karume; most revolutionary partisans were either under Okello's control or were Umma Party members.) Habiba describes John as "the African driver working for my aunt's husband. He was gentle in disposition and elevated in manners, and was sincere, loyal, and well-disposed ('muta'āṭif') to the wife of his boss."

John's ingenuity and quick thinking saved al-Hinai's aunt and her family; he met the revolutionaries at the door and told them his boss had a communicable disease, "for her protection and so that the revolutionaries would fear coming close to her and thus not injure her." This delayed the revolutionaries but did not dissuade them from ransacking the house, "and Karume's men entered the house to search it ('taftīshuh'), among them men who were kicking and flinging the contents of the house around." They contemptuously threw pictures of her relative on the ground and left. Al-Hinai further shows how John ended up saving the lives of her family by bundling them into the police vehicle parked at the house and driving them to safety as they huddled away from the windows, while John drove with one hand on the steering wheel, the other waving an ASP flag.[82]

In his memoir Hamoud Marhuby praised the role of the sheha (a governing authority at the village level) in the northern Zanzibar village of Nungwi for acting decisively to protect rural residents by offering them shelter in houses in the village rather than at the lighthouse, where they would stand out.[83] Marhuby and his family, like the al-Rawahi brothers, turned on the radio to try to get news of an event whose scope and motivations were still unknown to them. Then the attackers were in the village. The targeted killings were aimed at all supporters of the ZNP, evidenced in Nungwi by the flag of the independent 1963 state that flew over the village. The attackers pulled down the flag, hoisted their own, and then went around torching houses and shooting anyone who opposed them.[84]

Though many were detained without charges and released after several months, others were deemed a permanent threat to state security and eliminated directly. In an online memoir from 2006, a writer with the nom de guerre "al-Bahry" describes how prominent ZNP intellectual Muhammad Salim Jinja and several of his colleagues, including the father of Bi Ubwa Amour, Amour Zahor, were "disappeared" on January 13, 1964. They were rumored to have been shot outside of town. Bi Ubwa's biographer clarified that January 13 was only the date of the initial arrest, however; they were released and rearrested. The actual date of their killing was October 29, 1964.[85] Al-Bahry stated that they were told to dig a mass grave for themselves, and then

> the first to be called was Muhahmmad Salim Jinja. He was ordered to strip naked, and he did so. After that he was given a pen and paper that he may write down his will if he wanted to do so. Sheikh Muhammad refused to write. He was ordered to open his mouth. As he did so they put a pistol into his mouth and shot him dead. He was pushed into the pit.[86]

A major new narrative of the revolution was collected by Sauda Barwani from a Zanzibari of Comorian origin, Zainab Himid, a schoolteacher who lived with her family in Malindi. Starting on Saturday, January 11, 1964, at 4:00 p.m., she received various warnings that the government would be overthrown; at a wedding she attended that day attendees said, "Today the government is overthrown." Zainab Himid saw her pupils be killed; received news of the murder of her relatives in Kikwajuni; and witnessed the results of terrible violence in the rural, Manga-dominated areas of Zanzibar.[87]

Himid related that during the revolution they and most of those residing in Malindi, Shangani, Vuga, and Stone Town neighborhoods were not harmed by Okello, who came daily to check on residents but did not otherwise interfere.[88] However, those with multistory houses were able to look across and see the mob looting shops and homes in Darajani and Mlandege.[89] Himid's testimony supports the earlier argument of this chapter that the poorer, rural-dwelling Manga Arabs were far more affected by the violence than the urbanized Arabs of Stone Town.

THE RED CROSS, THE UNHCR, AND ARAB MIGRATION OUT OF ZANZIBAR

After the revolution, approximately 2,643 detainees were housed around the island. The detainees were initially spread between the Sayyida Matuka school, the Aga Khan school (both housing men), and women and children at Euan Smith Madrasa. Members of the overthrown government and known ZNP party members were housed in the Central Prison. Some 700 detainees were transferred to Prison Island on January 25, and most male detainees were later centralized at Sayyida Matuka.[90]

Even if they survived the ordeal of the pogrom, the violence they witnessed, along with the erosion of civil liberties and the expansion of the power of arbitrary detention, convinced many Arabs of the urgency of leaving Zanzibar, even while still detained. Migration out of Zanzibar continued well into the mid-1970s, but its most concentrated period was in the year after the revolution, during which several thousand people were shipped from Zanzibar to the Gulf with the assistance of the Red Cross and the UNHCR.[91] In total, at least 4,600 people left Zanzibar from February 1, 1964, to January 1965 with assistance from the Red Cross and UNHCR, not counting those who made private arrangements to leave.

The question of the national identity and territorial homeland of the "Manga Arabs" was at the core of the crisis: Were these stateless people/refugees? Much of the answer to that question came to rest on the refugees' own diverse and shifting claims on nationality and national belonging. Tensions between the Zanzibar government and the Red Cross spurred government officials to belatedly claim the refugees as Zanzibaris. The shifting rhetoric of their inclusion was prompted by the significance and future of the April 1964 union with Tanganyika. In practice, Zanzibar's 1964 "Manga Arab refugees" were of mixed birth and nationality and carried various passports.[92] The formalization of a naturalization process in the previous decade meant that thousands of Omani-born had become citizens of Zanzibar and remained so legally after formal independence in 1963.[93] Many refugees were not technically "Manga" at all but came from families that had resided in Zanzibar for several generations, as evidenced by their fluency in Swahili and lack of knowledge of Arabic.[94]

UNHCR correspondence and newspaper reports indicated that the Dutch ship (originally a cattle transport ship) *van Riebeeck* left Zanzibar with 140 Arabs on board, who "were expelled or deported from Zanzibar and may be refugees." The *van Riebeeck* stayed in Mombasa for five days. Though many of the displaced had family in the city, "*the Kenya authorities refused the group asylum.*"[95] UNHCR deputy commissioner Sadruddin Aga Khan added that at least a thousand more were awaiting deportation from Zanzibar, stressing that these actions were designed "to neutralize the minority population of Zanzibar."[96] The Foreign Office reported that the reasons for the deportations were "still obscure," but that stated that they were the "arbitrary action of the Zanzibar regime," "contrary to the international practice that Government of destination should give prior agreement to accept those departed."[97]

In February 1964, Mr. C. P. Scott, UK permanent representative to the European Office of the UN, argued that the Zanzibar government had expressed a desire to send fourteen hundred refugees to Muscat or Hadhramaut.[98] Of these, four hundred were screened and awaiting transport who had "close tribal connections with the Arabian Peninsula," six hundred wanted to go but had less close connection, and four hundred had "no present connection." Scott understood from BRC officials in Zanzibar that the majority of this last group were "almost certainly Zanzibar nationals either by birth of by naturalization."[99] In comments on their identity, one UN official emphasized that "very few of them possess passports or other tangible links with this country [Oman]; many do not even speak Arabic today although they are ethnically of Arab origin."[100] The government of Zanzibar initially was in favor of authorizing BRC officials there to facilitate the transport of the Manga Arabs out of the country.[101]

Janet Adams of the Red Cross, who served in the BRC in Zanzibar from November 1963 to June 27, 1964, stated something similar: "Very few of the remaining Arabs in Zanzibar have Omani documents, and since the great majority never possessed any documents of any kind or lost whatever papers they had during the revolution (probably in the fires)." Adams feared this would be "a handicap to the resettlement of the group."[102] Many identity documents had been destroyed in the revolution, and "many deportees," in lieu of documents, would "claim Omani status by invoking tribal relationships or other evidence."[103] Those who retained their Omani passports carried either green sultanate or red Imamate passports; the latter did not actually allow entry into Oman.[104] More than a few Manga destroyed their passports in fear; they were regarded as one of the symbols of the overthrown government.[105]

On February 22 the *van Riebeeck* arrived in Muscat. It turned out that there were 160 refugees aboard, to whom the sultan granted asylum.[106] The sultan's representative declared that they were "grateful for assistance rendered to *his subjects*" but that "owing to small means and absence of facilities, it will be appreciated if all possible particulars are given in advance." The letter requests that future asylum-seekers "be confined to bona fide nationals."[107] By early March, ICRC official Georges Hoffman estimated there were still nearly 1,000 people wanting to leave Zanzibar, most of them more or less "hostages" in five detention camps around the island (including Prison Island), over 90 percent of them Arab.[108] Hoffman obtained an estimate of £60,000 sterling from British Airways for an airlift of all of them.[109] Hoffman, in his late February visit to Zanzibar, managed to obtain unofficial agreement from the new government allowing this group to leave.[110] At the time, both the ICRC and British officials were reluctant to become directly involved in repatriation efforts and urged that the responsibility be the Zanzibar government's.[111] The Zanzibar government had asked Georges Hoffman of the ICRC for funding to support this during his visit to the islands in February and March.[112] This attitude and Hoffman's inability to find funds encouraged the new Zanzibar government to act on its own to resolve the crisis, which it did without communicating with the Omani government.[113]

In early April the Zanzibar government financed at least fifteen dhows to carry refugees to Oman. An article published in the *Times* and later reprinted in the *New York Times* reported that the Zanzibar government paid dhow captains £9 per head to transport refugees.[114] The government forbade the dhows to stop along the East African coast. The article stressed the overcrowded conditions on the dhows, claiming, "The Zanzibar port authority ruled that each dhow should carry no more than 32 passengers, but this was overruled by the government, apparently after the dhow masters complained that their journey would be uneconomic."[115]

The *Samhan* was the first recorded departure, on April 2, with 193 refugees aboard. The port officer in Zanzibar reported that *Samhan* was only authorized to carry 50 passengers, but he was "overruled by Karume personally." The officer direly warned: "Dhows carry insufficient food and water and lack safety equipment. No medical supplies. Red Cross here have done what they can. All passengers [are] more or less destitute."[116] Several days later, another ship, the *Salam*, sailed with 191 passengers.[117] The Red Cross supplied tinned milk, plastic sheets, soap, and a first aid kit.[118] By April 20, 1964, reports were coming from Zanzibar that eleven to sixteen hundred refugees had left on dhows and ships.[119] In letters to the district commissioner at the beginning of April, some of those scheduled to leave on dhows pleaded for their relatives to be released from detention so they might travel to Muscat together.[120]

Salim arrived in Muscat at the end of May on one of these dhows, with his family.[121] The ship departed from Nungwi on the northern tip of the island of

Unguja on April 20, 1964, with two hundred passengers. Salim and his family slept head to toe on the deck of the ship, along with the other refugees.[122] When they reached Muscat, they were taken in Bedford trucks by the sultan's armed forces to the interior.[123] According to UNHCR correspondence, "almost all of the former group who went to Oman in April and May this year, were allowed to stay, even though many of them were not acceptable."[124] Rumors circulated among the refugees that future transports to Oman would include large numbers of Zanzibar citizens and even Tanganyikans.[125]

The sailings generated negative international publicity for the revolutionary government and affected its attitude toward planning for later relief operations. In the *Times* articles the dhows were referred to as "grossly overcrowded," and the refugees were referred to as traveling the "slave route."[126] The negative publicity pushed the US Department of State to write to the British government asking what had been done to resolve an issue they perceived as the racially motivated deportation of Arab nationals from Zanzibar.[127] It also left a negative impression on Zanzibar's leadership, who felt that they were being chastised and criticized for acting when international organizations were reluctant to get involved at all.

REFUGEE RELIEF AND THE POLITICS OF THE UNION

In late April, Karume and Nyerere agreed to form a union between Zanzibar and Tanganyika. The Union was framed at the time as part of an overall progress toward East African federation.[128] Zanzibar possessed considerable autonomy within the Union structure, and most members of the Revolutionary Council retained their influence and leadership on the islands. The formation of the Union in April 1964 influenced the overall publicity around the regime in Zanzibar, including unresolved issues of internally displaced and detained persons there.[129] At least one British official in June suggested contacting Nyerere to move the displaced to mainland Tanzania.[130] In the immediate aftermath of the Union agreement and the dhow voyages, Zanzibar president Abeid Karume gained firmer control of Zanzibar's internal security situation, and this likely influenced his attitude to the remaining detainees.

To understand the attitude of the Zanzibar government and the way different elements within it exploited the Union, it is important to understand the jockeying for power caused by the sudden catapulting of ASP leaders into power without a broad and unified vision for governance aside from defeating their rivals. The Revolutionary Council was established by Karume and ASP leadership to consolidate control over left-wing elements in the new government.[131] There were five subgroups within the Revolutionary Council. First was the group led by Karume, which was older and more conservative in orientation and included ASP general secretary Thabit Kombo, ASP Youth League head Seif Bakari, and many former civil servants. Second were young Arab and Comorian radicals from Umma (led by Babu); third were leftist radical elements in the Youth League (a group around Hanga); and fourth were lumpen elements led by John Okello, Absolom Amoi (Injen), Abdulla Mfanyariki, and Jimmy Ringo. Fifth were moderates in favor of a rapprochement with elements of the defeated opposition (Othman Sharif, Aboud Jumbe).[132] Okello had the final say over many security decisions until he was expelled from Zanzibar in early March and declared a prohibited immigrant, a result of his increasingly unstable and capricious statements and actions.[133] Karume's disagreements with the "intellectuals" in the coalition dictated many of his subsequent actions, including the eventual elimination of Hanga and Saleh Saadalla.[134] For their part, Hanga and Saadalla apparently did not trust Umma members, and especially not Babu, leading to Babu's eventually receiving an appointment on the mainland.[135]

The struggle for power within different revolutionary factions was acted out in part through negotiations about refugee status and the ambit and mandate of the Red Cross in Zanzibar. The various elements within the Revolutionary Council differed in their approach: while the radicals desired a more hard-line stance toward international agencies that were viewed as agents of Western imperialism, Karume sought rapprochement in order to quietly wrap up the issue.[136] Karume needed the Red Cross as a temporary ally to resolve the crisis, even if it meant facing criticism from the younger leftist elements in the party.[137] Karume was managing his own distrust of Babu and Hanga in government, while Hanga and his ally Saadalla for their part sought to undermine Karume's influence, which they saw as reactionary.[138] Hanga's irritation with the operation likely stemmed in part from his frustrations with Karume in power.

At first the Red Cross refused to provide refugee transport to Oman, only agreeing to assist after Hoffman's visit. A letter from the Department of External Affairs of Zanzibar, sent to the International Red Cross, emphasized that permission for a planned summer 1964 Red Cross transport operation entailed the free will of the internally displaced in the camps to leave; there was no question of the government forcing them to leave.[139] The numerous bureaucratic obstacles encountered during this operation led Karume to become convinced that the Red Cross would act as an instrument of Western power in order to embarrass the new government.[140] By the end of July, some revolutionary leaders had grown irritated with the Red Cross's attitude to the remaining Manga Arabs. According to Nick Phillips, who replaced Janet Adams as the Red Cross representative in Zanzibar at the end of June, the Zanzibar government "regard the Red Cross as perpetuating a problem which they consider no longer exists."[141] Tanganyikan newspapers printed a report that the Red Cross was in Zanzibar as spies to transport the Arabs there out of Zanzibar, who were not in fact desirous of leaving the islands.[142] Red Cross official Nick Phillips was referred to Zanzibar's vice president Hanga and asked to explain why the Zanzibar Red Cross (ZRC) needed the revolutionary government's assurances to repatriate a large group of the island's residents.[143] While Karume was tentatively willing to cooperate with ongoing Red Cross operations, Hanga was in disagreement with continuing operations and skeptical of Red Cross motives. To Hanga, "the Red Cross was working for political ends and had manufactured the desire of the Arabs to leave just when President Nyerere had spoken in Cairo about amity between Arabs and Africans in Zanzibar."[144]

The other major factor in this power struggle was the international perception of the revolution, which was also tied to international perception of the newly minted Tanganyika-Zanzibar Union. The Union also made the exile issue into one with larger implications for the tenuous and fraught relationship between African countries and the Arab world. Nyerere and Babu convinced Egyptian president Gamal Abdel Nasser (the ZNP's former patron) to support the revolution on the grounds of its being a socialist uprising against a landed oligarchy.[145] An Egyptian delegation visited the islands in March 1964.[146] According to Muhammad Abdul-Muttalib Hashim, Ben Bella was himself questioned about his support for the revolution by the exiles when he visited the Emirates; he justified it by stating that he was removing "sultan al-jairu" (an oppressive ruler).[147]

Reports put the number of people officially transported out of Zanzibar from June 1964 to January 1965 at 1,100. UNHCR paid bills of £34,800 for their passage.[148] By May 1965, the sultanate government reiterated it would not accept anyone to land without a passport.[149] In June 1965 the revolutionary government in Zanzibar banned port calls by dhows that had called at Arabian ports in the previous year, effectively ending the possibility of dhow passage direct from Zanzibar.[150] Still, Manga Arabs kept being repatriated until 1966, with 175 still waiting in mid-October 1966, according to ICRC records.[151] Afro-Arabs by contrast often escaped covertly to Mombasa after 1967, where they had family connections and could register with the UNHCR office there to travel to the Arab Gulf.

CONCLUSION

Revolutionary violence affected different groups of Arabs differently. Manga Arabs were most of those killed and displaced in January 1964. The violence rendered them homeless and without documents and thus functionally stateless. Afro-Arabs were more likely to be protected by Karume at Raha Leo and thus to escape the worst mob violence. They largely went voluntarily into exile on the nearby mainland, especially Mombasa, after being released from detention. As Judith Marshall argued, it is a mistake to overemphasize the inevitability or universality of migration out of Zanzibar.[152] Many Afro-Arabs with murdered family members retained deep and abiding ties to living kin on the islands. These were an important factor in keeping a significant section of the Afro-Arab community in Zanzibar from 1964 to 1970, even after Manga refugees had obtained asylum in Oman.[153] From the late 1960s through the late 1970s, communication between the community remaining in Zanzibar and the exiles in the United Kingdom and United Arab Emirates (UAE) remained difficult. Letters smuggled out of Zanzibar by family members were turned into political journalism by exiles outside of Zanzibar, as a small but vocal minority emerged in diaspora to protest deteriorating political and economic conditions in Zanzibar. The revolution eventually led to the emigration of not only the Afro-Arabs and ZNP leadership, but nearly thirty-five thousand of the islands' most well-educated professionals.[154] E. B. Martin estimated that by 1970, only six thousand Arabs remained in Zanzibar. This mass emigration was a new phenomenon in the history of Zanzibar: thousands of exiles living semipermanently abroad, in the United Kingdom, the UAE, and later Oman.[155]

PART TWO

Belonging in Diaspora

THREE

"On Behalf of Zanzibaris Abroad"

THE ZANZIBAR ORGANIZATION AND
POSTCOLONIAL TANZANIAN POLITICS, 1964–1985

CHAPTER 3 DEALS WITH THE PERSPECTIVES of exiled Zanzibaris on the politics of citizenship in postcolonial Zanzibar and mainland Tanzania. Although they did not succeed in mounting a counterrevolution, the exiles used journalism to protest political conditions on the islands and to cultivate alternative historical interpretations of the revolution. Because of its taboo nature until the 1990s, the extant historiography of the Zanzibar Arab exile phenomenon remains quite sparse. This chapter draws on UNHCR archives; Zanzibar archives; and *Free Zanzibar Voice* (*FZV*), an exile journal founded in 1964 by the former editor of *Mwongozi*, Ahmed Seif Kharusi. It was typed up, originally cyclostyled, and later printed in Portsmouth and mailed by Kharusi to human rights advocates, journalists, and dignitaries in the United Kingdom, East Africa, and the Gulf.[1]

James Mayall noted that many groups who were losers in the battle for state power tried to challenge the fiction of self-determination within the transition to a globally homogenous community of nations.[2] Wolfgang Schivelbusch explored the myths and narratives of loss among social groups after periods of trauma and how they converted the feeling of humiliation into moral superiority over the winners.[3] The phrase "long-distance nationalism" was coined by Benedict Anderson to describe a conflictual orientation of exiles toward an imagined homeland while outside of it.[4] After the revolution, some exiled Afro-Arabs practiced a form of long-distance nationalism characterized by the gradual evolution of a "culture of defeat," in which they criticized the motives of the revolution in ways more radical than that of their compatriots in Zanzibar during the same period. Unlike many other Arab émigrés from Zanzibar, they did not disavow their Zanzibari national identity or their claim on African political belonging (a claim relevant to how they related to political blackness in the United Kingdom) and did not make such a pronounced turn to emphasizing either broader Arab ethnicity or Omani nationality until well into the 1970s.[5] An example is Ali Muhsin al-Barwani, imprisoned after the revolution and finally released from prison in May 1974. After his escape from Tanzania, he became a major figure in the Zanzibar Organization in Dubai, where he lived out the rest of his life. Though he visited Oman and eventually moved there to be close to where several of his offspring gained citizenship, he never became an Omani citizen.[6]

The socialist turn of the Zanzibar revolution put the Arab exiles in an odd position in the age of postcolonial nationalism, for much popular perception in Africa and Asia at the time placed them as the ideo-historical counterparts of the émigré European community of Kenya, Rhodesia, and South Africa, the "pied noirs" of Algeria, and the "retornados" of Portugal, as reactionary settlers opposed to progressive socialist transformation and thus rightfully expelled to their "real" homeland in Arabia.[7] Their advocacy for Zanzibar from exile generated conflict with the new government of Zanzibar, as well as the government of "Tanzania," formed out of the April 1964 Union between Zanzibar and Tanganyika.

The initial exile organization was facilitated through the banned ZNP and ZPPP and called the Committee of ZNP and ZPPP in Exile.[8] Its members saw themselves as diasporic liberation groups from Palestine or Eritrea saw themselves in the 1970s: as the true voice of a nation in exile.[9] They often claimed to speak as the rightful voice of the Zanzibar public whose voice on the islands had been repressed.[10] In doing so, they sought to spur Zanzibaris abroad and at home to adopt their analysis and to coordinate and organize to influence the direction of the country.[11] Though they did not succeed in unseating the new government, mobilized exiles successfully reinterpreted the revolution in ways that would prove influential in the long run.[12]

The exiles were involved in some minor and abortive efforts to militarily resist the regime in Zanzibar but could not surmount their disunity in exile.[13] Initially the major impetus seemed to come from elements of the former ZNP, especially Ahmed Hamoud al-Maamiry, who worked to bring together Ahmed Lamky in Cairo with Ahmed Seif Kharusi in Portsmouth, United Kingdom. The ZNP leadership in exile had to shift its idea of itself from a political party to being a "people's movement."[14] Dispersed across the Gulf, North Africa, and the United Kingdom, only small numbers of Zanzibar exiles continued to plan to overthrow the revolutionary regime and reinstall the sultan; that organizing impulse was mostly moribund by the mid-1970s. The exiles were ultimately unable to muster a counterinsurgency (although they made several inquiries into such a possibility with the governments of Eritrea and Somalia) and did not realize a viable path to reestablishing a social presence on the island until the advent of democratic elections in 1985.[15] Despite their failure to influence regime change, exiles from Zanzibar represent an important critique of postcolonial governance on the islands. Their emphasis became centered on pointing out the hypocrisy of the Tanzanian state, which was reluctant to intervene against human rights violations in nearby Zanzibar while condemning the human rights violations of the Portuguese in Mozambique.[16] This reluctance stemmed from Nyerere's belief that to intervene more aggressively would cause the breakup of the Union.

For much of the 1960s and 1970s, the emotional and intellectual center of exile life was in Portsmouth, around where the former Sultan Jamshid resided. In exile, a prominent Zanzibari elder kept a morning baraza from 7:00 to 11:00 a.m. in Portsmouth at 7 St. Edwards Road. Ahmed Seif Kharusi, the most ardent proponent of Zanzibar long-distance nationalism, lived nearby at 68 Hudson Road, which was the initial organizing center for the Zanzibar Organization (ZO), founded in 1965 and operating in several Gulf emirates and in Zanzibar.[17] By 1967, the ZO had nine to eleven overseas branches.[18] A branch of ZO called Zanzibar Elders Organisation operated out of Mombasa, Kenya.[19] Other major nodes of the network were in Baghdad, Cairo, Doha, Dubai, Kuwait, and Bahrain.[20] The Zanzibar Affairs Office in Baghdad was run by Rashid Hamadi; the Union of Zanzibari Students was also formed among exiles in Iraq.[21] Ahmed Lamky founded the organization Zanzibar Liberation Front in the Garden City neighborhood of Cairo. There were also more informal nodes of this network in Sharjah and Muscat.[22] The ZO relied on regular financial contributions from its members in diaspora, as well as discreet support from some British nationals.[23] Leadership in the United Kingdom also dispatched people to the Gulf to raise funds.[24] An official constitution of the organization was drawn up as early as March 1968, but the network of the organization existed informally in exile from the early months of 1964.[25]

The organization's official aim was to return democracy to Zanzibar through nonviolent means, though it engaged in a few failed covert negotiations to facilitate the overthrow of the ruling regime there through other means.[26] Members of the ZO were among the first to write to the

UNHCR to raise awareness of the severity of the refugee crisis after the revolution.[27] The exiles engaged in a campaign of letter writing with the rulers of Kuwait, Qatar, Dubai, Abu Dhabi, Saudi Arabia and Bahrain, and visited these places to raise awareness of their issues. The former Zanzibar district commissioner and radio announcer for Sauti ya Cairo, who was detained without trial for years after the revolution, Suleiman Malik stated that the ZO also took on a number of practical charitable ventures: "We were at the forefront of fighting for those people who were fired by Afro-Shirazi without being given a pension."[28]

As early as April 1964, British authorities were aware of the organization, then called the Zanzibar and Overseas Association, but knew little about it except that it was "a project of the ex-Sultan of Zanzibar's secretary, Kharusi, along with a couple others close to the Sultan and Zanzibari students in the UK." They issued a warning to Kharusi after he published "stenciled pamphlets denouncing the new government."[29] These pamphlets were the forerunner of the *FZV*; before the early 1970s, the newsletter was also called *Zanzibar Organization*. When the name was changed to *Free Zanzibar Voice* in August 1969, the masthead of the new publication contained the initials ZO, surrounded by seven cloves.[30] Kharusi's was the dominant editorial voice, but there were contributions from ex-ZNP members like Ali Muhsin and Aman Thani, as well as many anonymously published letters. Kharusi used the newspaper to keep the issue of human rights in Zanzibar in front of Amnesty International, other international organizations, and African and Arab heads of state. Kharusi hoped to put pressure on the Tanzanian state to compel Zanzibar leaders to reintroduce democratic reforms and free elections.[31]

This advocacy by Kharusi needs to be understood in contrast to an organization he was briefly associated with in the year after the revolution, the Seyyid Jamshid Group. This organization had a promonarchy focus and explicitly sought to oust the republic that had been formed after the revolution.[32] Over time, Kharusi strategically downplayed his closeness to the monarchy. Responding in 1975 to the idea that he and the ZO wanted to bring back the sultan, Kharusi corrected a local Portsmouth newspaper who had printed that the *FZV* "supports the return of the sultan." Kharusi disavowed that statement, stating that he privileged democratization, though he did not deem this as leaving out the possibility that this might lead to the return of the monarchy.[33] His and the ZO's advocated goal was a return to democracy on the islands.[34]

In Suleiman Malik's opinion, the significance of *FZV* was as a source of truth about Zanzibar. This its editor did through printing not only the newspaper but also small booklets explaining what was happening in Zanzibar.[35] The goal of the newsletter and the booklets was to spread news of "our global struggle and the atrocities committed ('ukatitli unofanywa') in Zanzibar by the Afro-Shirazi party, and later CCM [Chama Cha Mapinduzi, the 1977 fusion of ASP with the Tanganyika African National Union (TANU)]." Malik successfully petitioned the British government for political asylum in August 1971 and went to London, where he met Kharusi, who encouraged him to begin composing the story of his time in prison in Zanzibar.[36] While in Libya, Mr. Malik collected funds for the printing of *FZV*.[37] While the newspaper's impact cannot be denied, its reach cannot be quantified exactly.[38] Certainly copies circulated in the diaspora communities of Zanzibar in the United Kingdom, the Gulf, and beyond.

Both the ZO and *FZV* were associated with traitorous subversion by the Zanzibar government and had a negative reputation among mainland Tanzanian officials.[39] This was due to the extremely critical attitude the exiles maintained toward postcolonial Zanzibar and its Union with Tanganyika, a centerpiece of Nyerere's foreign policy advocacy with other African nations after independence. However, as more and more of Nyerere's political opponents and rivals went into exile, some of these disgruntled or alienated state elites, including Oscar Kambona, linked with the ZO in exile.[40]

The issue of the potential political subversion of refugees from Zanzibar was also reflected in the ambivalence toward them by elements of Omani leadership. Kharusi's pamphlets and newspapers also caused security concerns in Britain's client state of Oman because of the tendency to associate the political activity of exiled Afro-Arabs from Zanzibar in Dubai with "Omanis."[41] Though returnees in Oman remained sympathetic to the ZO, the government of Oman prohibited the formation of autonomous ethnic or ethnic diaspora associations of any kind. The ZO was technically separate from the Zanzibar communal associations accommodating community needs in the diaspora, but membership overlapped considerably. At one point Kharusi sent a copy of *FZV* to the new Sultan Qaboos, only to receive a sharp anonymous reply in English, most likely from someone well acquainted with Zanzibar, who accused him of "sucking the blood of your fellow Zanzibaris... using their sweat to utilize the building up and purchasing houses" and of being a liar and a stooge who received money from the Tanzania embassy. It goes on to accuse him of being against monarchy.[42]

In the November/December 1974 issue of *FZV*, Kharusi printed "An Open Letter to the Sultan of Oman", the only evidence of official correspondence between the ZO and the Gulf ruler. In it he describes how the last issue of *FZV* was returned "with an unprintable response." Writing to explain the aims of the newspaper, Kharusi alerted the sultan that "opening someone's mail is a crime" as a way of excusing the harshness of the response.[43]

Kharusi's contact in Oman, Salim M. Barwani, assured him that "Omani leaders do not oppose our plans nor Zanzibari nationalism" and that such opposition came from those (implied to be Zanzibaris) using Omani-ness to cover themselves ("kujipaka").[44] Perhaps the exiles who had reached Oman were attempting to distance themselves from their association with Zanzibar, as a result of the unpleasant association of migrating Zanzibaris with political subversion.An October 1977 letter written by Issa Salim Muhammad al-Rawahi to the Omani ambassador in Kenya, Sheikh Ahmed Mahmoud al-Harthi, tried to counter these stereotypes and explain the destitute and desperate situation of many Zanzibaris after the revolution. The letter explained that al-Rawahi had been writing to the ambassador since September 1975, urging him to put the issue of stateless refugees before Qaboos and the Omani government. Al-Harthi explained how difficult it was for people to leave Zanzibar, due to the risks involved and the lack of ability to be accepted elsewhere. He asked al-Harthi for assistance on three levels: to facilitate those with Omani passports being able to leave Zanzibar, entry visas for those with non-Omani passports, and financial assistance for those with no passport at all.[45]

Kharusi corresponded with a growing number of people besides the original supporters of the ex-sultan and former government ministers, including Umma and ZPPP dissidents (Muhammad Shamte and others), political exiles from Tanzania (Oscar Kambona), Rhodesian whites who wanted more information on communist rule in Zanzibar, the historian R. Pakenham, L.W. Hollingsworth (a former teacher in Zanzibar), the Sandhurst historian Anthony Clayton (who wanted to know about an Israeli businessman who allegedly carried Babu to Zanzibar during the revolution), the International Commission of Jurists, Kharusi's local Labour Party's Young Socialist chapter, Amnesty International officials, and the Conservative MP Harold Soref (chairman of the Africa Group at the Monday Club).[46] Kharusi also sent copies of the *FZV* to Tanzanian embassy officials like Haroub Othman (stationed in Cairo at the time).[47]

Kharusi helped to facilitate many other Zanzibaris' migration abroad to the United Kingdom, in order that they might turn in their Tanzanian passports and obtain an Omani passport in London.[48] He also helped many non-English-speaking Zanzibaris adjust to UK life and even wrote letters of recommendation for some.[49] Kharusi was in touch with many Zanzibaris in diaspora who sought information on employment prospects outside of Zanzibar or wanted to clarify their diverse legal situations. In the mid-1970s, the exile Salim M. Barwani sent Kharusi a poignant letter in Swahili, along with his CV, from Guyana, where he worked as an architect. Barwani related the difficulties of exile; he didn't feel comfortable in Guyana, where no one spoke Swahili or Arabic. Even the English they spoke sounded strange to his ears. His son, born in Guyana and now five years old, knew no other life.[50]

ZANZIBAR EXILES AND ISLAM AS SOCIAL CRITIQUE

As Jones and Ridout note, "from the 1950s to the 1980s, a significant part of the cold war was played out in the context of decolonization."[51] The philosophical basis of *FZV*'s political critique of postcolonial society was part of a larger debate among Africans and Asians about the different models of national independence and national development being proposed as solutions for inherited problems of colonial rule.[52] The economic failures of the Tanzanian state and its authoritarian character led significant numbers of the new citizens to turn to older forms of community to thematize a horizon of ethical appeal beyond the state in crisis. The turn toward "religion" as political critique in this period has its origins in resistance to the secular excesses of the postcolonial developmentalist state. While Muslims lined up on both sides of the Cold War, three factors were key to the disillusionment with the Left suffered by Zanzibar exiles after the Zanzibar revolution.[53] While the ZNP was accused of being communist by the ASP in the early 1960s, many exiles developed by the mid- 1970s a more antagonistic relationship to socialist ideas because of the belief that they contributed to the growth of state authoritarianism in postcolonial Tanzania.[54]

First was the general "Tanzaphilia" of the global Left in this period; it represented to many in the African diaspora not only the ideals of anticolonial unity but also an example of pan-Africanism in action, especially through the Union between Zanzibar and Tanganyika.[55] Tanzania's tensions as a secular state were (and continue to be) visible in the politics of this

Union.⁵⁶ To the exiles, the Union represented the ultimate betrayal of the national sovereignty they had fought for, and they saw Nyerere as a cynical political operator aiming at mainland domination of Zanzibar, not the "father of the nation" but the "enemy of the nation."⁵⁷ There was a distinct irony in exiles criticizing Nyerere for spreading socialism to Zanzibar—at least one prominent anticommunist writer saw the Union as the *containment* of communism emanating already from Zanzibar.⁵⁸

Second was a general lack of basic civil rights for citizens of the islands, caused by the monopolization of political power by a clique within the state. Zanzibar did not have a written constitution from 1964 until 1979. The new state was riven by internal suspicion and differing agendas. Internal surveillance of citizens became a more essential aspect of statecraft solidified by external aid from socialist countries and used to control and persecute political enemies.⁵⁹ Zanzibar's first postrevolution president, Abeid Karume, famously stated that he would not allow elections for sixty years.⁶⁰ This set of factors made the exiles into Muslim liberal democrats; they sought to puncture what they saw as the myth of civic equality in the revolutionary state by giving voice to internal currents of resistance to arbitrary and draconian rule in Zanzibar, which was characterized by the absence of rule of law and civil liberties.⁶¹ In his memoir, Ali Muhsin al-Barwani condemned Western liberal tendencies to excuse and rationalize the violations of the rule of law occurring under postcolonial African rulers, assuming that these were morally exceptional due to "African conditions."⁶² Meanwhile Nyerere, while he was reportedly outraged by human rights abuses on the islands, felt he could do little to influence the internal dynamics of governance in Zanzibar without breaking the fragile Union.

Third was the revolutionary state's crackdown on Islamic education and Muslim religious authorities, including the imprisonment and expulsion of some ulama and the shutting down of Quranic schools.⁶³ A similar marginalization was increasingly felt by numbers of Muslims in mainland Tanzania. Exile discourse portrayed postcolonial governance in Tanzania as an issue of civilizational and religious values, between an amoral and despotic secular state and a righteous oppressed resistance of true Muslims.⁶⁴ Exiles argued that secularism in Tanzania was authoritarian and anti-Muslim. Secular rule could not but fail to overreach itself and thus fail to transcend prenational ethnic and religious identities.⁶⁵ In this emphasis on the civilizational corruption of the secular socialist state, the discourse of Zanzibar nationalism in exile anticipated in certain respects a political trend among

Muslims in Tanzania that would fully emerge only in the 1990s, in which Muslims were portrayed as an oppressed "majority" nationality in the country (Ahmed Baalawy, an exile imprisoned by Nyerere, claimed they were 70% of Tanzania).[66]

DEVELOPMENT AND CITIZENSHIP IN ZANZIBAR, 1964–1972

The revolutionary government offered a vision of nation-building meant to be defined by values of equality and development.[67] In the euphoric climate of postwar decolonization, the masses of people expected dramatic change and general improvement in the overall standard of living; Karume promised such a bright future in his speeches after the revolution.[68] Zanzibar's new leadership faced the enormous challenge of reconstructing the economic basis for development in the wake of the destruction of the old order. Communist support from East Germans and Soviets aided development projects in Zanzibar until 1970, when the regime sought Chinese assistance.[69] The material developments they helped to fund were presented by state leadership as the fruits of the revolution.

Socialist reforms did promote developmental reforms in ways the colonial state had been reluctant to do, with mixed results. Karume's socialist vision was rooted in the idea of producing modern housing for the impoverished citizens of Zanzibar. Zanzibar spent 70 percent of its development budget in 1971 building houses for citizens.[70] The state's plans had some limited success. In the major housing initiative of the postcolonial state, East Germans provided funds to build over one hundred apartments in a major building project called New Berlin. Yet only one-third of 150 new homeowners accepted the flats; by mid-1966, 95 flats were still vacant.[71]

In addition to housing, land redistribution was also at the top of the new regime's priority list. In March 1964 the revolutionary government nationalized all land and introduced a land redistribution program.[72] The government expropriated about 745 farms, owned by seventy-two landlords, most of which were distributed to members of the Revolutionary Council. The "eka tatu" (three acres) redistribution began on November 11, 1965, at Dole in Unguja, and the government redistributed tens of thousands of plots over four years. Approximately twenty-two to twenty-three thousand families received land of at least three acres.[73]

The distributed land came with a catch: those who did not productively utilize it to the government's satisfaction would be fined.⁷⁴ However, many people who were issued land had no deed and could not obtain one because of a lack of communication between the Ministry of State, in charge of distributing land, and the Ministry of Agriculture, responsible for distributing deeds. The latter complained that some people distributed land of their own accord, without permission. Those given land were not actually given title to the land, which was still vested in the government.⁷⁵ Some squatters even refused to take government land and remained on their former landlords' farms, out of a basic conservatism in outlook.⁷⁶ After 1967, land redistribution was halted because of mismanagement and reserved for emergencies only.⁷⁷ By 1974 land distribution was stopped completely, after the Ministry of Agriculture took over the distribution process.⁷⁸

Karume also had a vision of autarky, or economic self-reliance.⁷⁹ To him, as to his mainland colleague Nyerere, this was symbolized by rural forms of self-sufficiency.⁸⁰ Karume stopped rice imports in 1968 and tried to foster local rice cultivation.⁸¹ The major obstacle to implementing autarky, however, was the poor price paid to agricultural producers; the state mandated the sale of cloves to itself, then resold them for export at a rate up to seven times more than their purchase price.⁸² This policy prompted the increased smuggling of cloves off the island for direct sale.⁸³ Famine, an unheard-of phenomenon on the agriculturally abundant islands, became a recurring feature of island life from the late 1960s through the mid-1980s.⁸⁴ Famine conditions also compelled more people to leave.⁸⁵ Queues for bread became a regular feature of life, rationing was instituted, and cassava (otherwise a famine food) became a daily staple.⁸⁶ An *FZV* editorial reported, "In the ... queues for food rationing at the State shops some participants shout loudly, 'these are the fruits of the revolution.'"⁸⁷ In desperation, the state ended up spending £1,840,000 from 1970 to 1973 on importing rice, sugar, and grains, after drastically reducing such imports two years earlier.⁸⁸

For Karume, autarky also had a practical meaning in producing equality between national citizens. His government stopped the seasonal labor migration from the mainland, to encourage clove cultivation by locals.⁸⁹ The state had originally imposed this labor corvée on all citizens in the name of nationalist and socialist values.⁹⁰ The state then required a period of two years' service of every high school leaver, during which they would help to farm, including hoeing, planting, and weeding, followed by a year's stint in National Service, before being allowed to attend university.⁹¹ As Burgess noted, Zanzibar's postcolonial nationalists appropriated the language of socialism to express communal, grievances.[92] To the Zanzibari Arabs interviewed for this study, these government decisions compelling school leavers to cultivate could take on strong ethnic and racial overtones, motivated by the new government's zeal to eliminate the remnants of social privilege left over from the old order. Exiles also began to voice support and approval for acts of protest they disapproved of in Zanzibar before the revolution. Articles in *FZV* commented approvingly on acts of sabotage and destruction of crops on the farms of top state officials.[93]

In Zanzibar, the rising price of cloves was the main reason that the post-revolution government was relatively successful initially. In 1967–1968 the price per ton of cloves doubled from $1,500 to almost $3,000, and in April 1971 Zanzibar had foreign reserves of £14 million. But the relations of production continued to depend on labor to pick cloves, the primary export. The revolutionary government's ban on mainlanders coming to pick cloves meant that "up to 40% of cloves went unpicked in the 1970s."[94] By the mid-1970s the compulsory labor requirement from every citizen was inadequately compensating for shortages in the labor market; primary and secondary schoolchildren were even forced to pick cloves in 1976 in order to bring in the crop.[95] By the end of the 1970s, clove production had declined precipitously because of these factors, as well as neglect, tree disease, and insufficient replanting. State intervention in the clove sector did not achieve the desired result: the average percentage of domestic price compared to export price declined from 33 percent in 1965 to 7 percent by 1978.[96] At the same time, Zanzibar's economic dependence on cloves continued to rise, from 74 percent of export revenue in 1963 to a high of 99.6 percent in 1986, while prices continued to fall.[97] By the late 1980s, farmers were worse off than they had been even in the late 1970s.[98]

CITIZENSHIP AND POLITICAL RIGHTS OF THE INDIVIDUAL IN ZANZIBAR, 1964–1972

Crawford Young notes that "the rapid displacement in most countries of the fragile democratic institutions of decolonization by autocratic structures of rule, emptied citizenship of its political content."[99] In her study of the Grenadian revolution, historian Laurie Lambert notes its dark side of internal security: the violation of individual rights in the name of revolutionary advancement.[100] The nearly decade-long rule of Abeid Karume in Zanzibar exemplifies a logic of "dictatorship in the name of democracy" in which a permanent state of emergency, wrought by fear of an exile counterrevolution, justified Karume's rule by decree.[101] In 1970 he attempted to declare himself president of Zanzibar for life.[102] A dynamic of sinister suspicion and terror pervaded Zanzibar in this period and hollowed out the idea of civic belonging.[103]

For state leaders in Zanzibar, national security often trumped national development.[104] Fear of a monarchical restoration movement provided the justification for the Revolutionary Council to impose the death penalty for anyone found to be engaged in counterrevolutionary actions, and twenty years in prison for anyone found to be entering Zanzibar without authorization.[105] Detention without trial was legalized by a January 31, 1964 decree.[106] The new government set up "secret police" with East German training, instituting new methods of surveillance and torture.[107] Karume made this force (whose members were derisively termed by locals "panya," rat) an instrument of his rule. Security services claimed to have uncovered nine coup plots since 1964, including the assassination of Karume. In 1971, a year before his death, Karume held a rally to parade in front of a large crowd "traitors" who he promised would be executed for treason for conspiring to overthrow the government. It was alleged that the accused had been given $20 million by Great Britain and the United States, were conspiring with the overthrown Sultan Jamshid in the United Kingdom, and had been undergoing military training in Dubai and Saudi Arabia in preparation.[108] Even after Karume's death, the regime continued to fear being overthrown or invaded and often sent its spies to Tanzania and Kenya to monitor Zanzibaris in Dar-es-Salaam, Nairobi, and Mombasa.[109]

This inability of the Revolutionary Council to share power could be seen early on after the revolution, in the response of the regime to different sets of political actors. Sheikh Abdullah Suleiman al-Harthi, the former head of the Arab Association, who had facilitated the emigration of hundreds of refugees, was served a deportation order to Oman.[110] In 1965 the regime sentenced ZNP stalwarts Suleiman Malik and Aman Thani, among ten people, to ten years' imprisonment and hard labor.[111] What happened to Aman Thani, a ZNP member and government minister first detained along with twenty-five others closely associated with the ZNP, is typical of the experiences of the banned party's central cadres.[112] Though released in 1965 and free for two years while living in Dar-es-Salaam, he was rearrested on October 21, 1968. He was taken to Unguja, where he was imprisoned without charge along with seventeen others. Later in November of that year, he and other detainees were transferred to the security jail and tortured regularly throughout the end of 1968 and into 1969.[113]

The regime enforced loyalty through intimidation among former ZNP supporters who remained in Zanzibar after having been released from detention. Before being released by the new government, detainees at Raha Leo were asked to sign loyalty oaths in Swahili, which reminded them of the threat of violence that would attend any perceived lack of allegiance to the new government. A detainee had to be vouched for by the ASP chairman in a particular district andwas then pardoned by the government ("asamehewe na serikali") and released. The detainee and the ASP district chairman signed together, agreeing that they would be dutiful citizens ("raiya watiifu") and that if either of the two were found to be in error against the republic ("anagunduliwa na makosa dhidi ya Jamhuri"), the government had the right to shoot them both ("serikali itakuwa na haki ya kutupiga risasi sote wawili").[114]

Karume's autocratic tendencies extended to his own rivals within the ASP and to the citizens of Zanzibar. The same paranoid and inhumane tactics used on the exiles naturally soon found application beyond specific members of the old political opposition, to whole ethnic categories and eventually to the Zanzibar masses as a whole.[115] Zanzibar postcolonial citizens with multiple or mixed nationalities were particularly affected, as Karume attempted to make African ancestry the condition of island citizenship, in violation of the governing structure of the 1964 Union.[116] Karume initiated a program to abolish Shirazi identity. In rhetoric, he continued to double down on anti-Asian animus; by 1971 he declared that all noncitizen Asians would be forced to leave Zanzibar, and 234 people were designated as prohibited immigrants.[117] In 1968 Karume warned Comorians of Zanzibari descent to renounce their status as French subjects and naturalize as Tanzanian citizens, and eventually he stripped them of citizenship.[118] He warned Zanzibar's remaining Asians that they must "integrate themselves into the nation, because people would not tolerate forever exclusive groups of foreigners living among them."[119]

The forced marriage crisis of the early 1970s, which brought about an international outcry against Zanzibar, was ostensibly conducted in the name of producing ethnic harmony in the state and overcoming the legacy of slavery.[120] In June 1970 Karume asserted that young Asian women from

Zanzibar were not to refuse marriage proposals from top party officials, justifying this dictate with reference to the old practice of Arabs taking African concubines.[121] In September 1970 the government released an official marriage decree mandating family acceptance of a valid proposal, prompting an international outcry.[122] One interviewee in Muscat reported that the paranoia at the time led to her family marrying her off at a very young age.[123] At the same time, the government served deportation orders to citizens, including families who objected to marriage proposals from leading members of the Revolutionary Council.[124]

That Karume distrusted the formally educated is well known.[125] In late 1969 he lured several of his political opponents within the ASP, including Kassim Hanga and Othman Sharif, back to Zanzibar with promises of forgiveness, then promptly had them executed.[126] ASP party members who approached Karume about his decision-making in July 1970 were thrown in prison.[127] At a rally in 1971 Karume announced that nineteen alleged plotters against his government would be executed.[128] Enemies of the state were even sought on the nearby mainland.

The combination of the autocratic and erratic policies of the new government accelerated the emigration of skilled professionals. The mass emigration from the late 1960s to the mid-1970s led to shortages in skilled labor; a schoolteacher working in Zanzibar at this time reported that many secondary school graduates worked as teachers to cover the loss of professional trained educators.[129] Though Karume was initially dismissive of the exodus, the regime tried to prevent citizens from leaving Zanzibar after 1965 and fully prohibited it by 1967 to prevent further population loss among white-collar classes it viewed as crucial to state development.[130] The regime penalized people for leaving without state consent, including confiscation of their passports; a "departure tax" of 56,000 shillings, representing a lifetime of school fees and medical expenses; and being pursued on the East African mainland by agents of the security state.[131] From 1965 to 1974, even those from Zanzibar wishing to visit nearby Prison Island had to get permission from six different ministries. Even a close friend of Karume, Bi Ubwa Amour, had to petition Karume to get permission to travel; their passports were delivered to her and her husband on the order of Karume.[132] After 1968 emigration from Zanzibar was restricted wholesale. From 1968 to 1972, only six Zanzibaris were sent to overseas universities.[133] Nor did privileges of the Union afford freedom of visitation; all mainland visitors were required to have their passport stamped.[134] The government went so far as to threaten countries that admitted escaping Zanzibaris without exit visas.[135] *FZV* condemned measures denying the right of a passport to the island's citizens, which it recognized as "*aimed at halting the island's exodus of females (thousands of young and old have fled the country for the past six years) while at the same time, robbing people of their money.*"[136] Family members of those who escaped without permission were also often punished arbitrarily, as happened to Habiba al-Hinai's family (described in the introduction). When former ZNP minister Rashid Hamadi was released from prison in 1967 and escaped from the islands in 1968, his mother was imprisoned, and residents of his home village were flogged.[137]

THE COUNTERHISTORY OF THE ZANZIBAR REVOLUTION IN THE *FREE ZANZIBAR VOICE*

As a moral and legal ethos whose authority predated that of any national state as an arbiter of public order, Islam was for exiles a prominent resource for "grounding" their ethical critique of state behavior in Zanzibar in a more durable and communicable symbolic form, a kind of nationalist bona fide in exile.[138] A July 11, 1973, editorial in *FZV*, entitled "Cowboys and Indians" and written by a ZO member, analogized Zanzibar's current regime as the cowboys and the indigenous people of Zanzibar as the oppressed Indians. The author wrote, "How do the oppressed 'Injuns' of Zanzibar, those whose heartfelt wish is to join all people in fellowship and overthrow the veritable 'army of occupation', acquire the strength to do that, when the cowboys outride and outgun them? The answer can be found in the history of Islam."[139] Aman Thani asserted that Nyerere's famous statement about a secular Tanzania, "serikali ya Tanzania haina dini" (the government of Tanzania has no religion), was really "a stick with which to control the Muslims of the country."[140] On the ninth anniversary of the revolution (1973), *FZV* released a long-form article including many of the major themes of the exile counterhistory, in which Zanzibar is portrayed as an oppressed Muslim nation.[141]

Though fears of mainlander infiltration of Zanzibar were present during the islands' early 1960s elections, the accusations that the ASP organized mainlanders to come over and vote illegally in elections appeared in *FZV* as a full-fledged invasion plan.[142] It took nearly a decade for these thoughts, rumors, and speculations about the revolution as invasion to reach full narrative form. By 1978 Kharusi had obtained stills from the film *Africa Addio*, a cynical portrayal of African decolonization by two Italian pioneers of "shock cinema." According to Kharusi, the still revealed that the victims shown fleeing the pogrom "were mostly Black Africans and not Arabs. . . . [T]hey were all Zanzibaris and supporters of the Zanzibar Nationalist Party.[143] By the mid-1980s, in proofs titled "The Tragic Story of Zanzibar" (later published as the *Political Plight of Zanzibar*), "Zanzibar—Isles of Horror," and in an issue of *FZV* commemorating the twenty-two-year anniversary of the revolution, Kharusi called the revolution a foreign organized coup implemented by armed mainlanders, in which thirteen thousand people were killed.

As the 1960s ended, a top lieutenant of Nyerere in the Tanzanian government, Oscar Kambona, defected to the United Kingdom. There he met with Kharusi and other exiles who had previously regarded him with suspicion. Kambona helped to shift the exile discourse to emphasize the need to challenge Nyerere's rule in addition to Karume's; Zanzibar was posed as a victim of Nyerere's tyranny and complacency.[144]

The interpretations of the revolution in *FZV* are filled with bitter and highly ideological invectives, understandable considering that many of its writers were imprisoned and tortured by Zanzibar's revolutionary leadership.[145] Having witnessed shocking violence and then gone into exile, they were stripped of regular contact with social dynamics internal to Zanzibar. As they strained to understand an event that they found fundamentally irrational, many embraced conspiracies of mainland invasion and British colonial subversion, motivated by anti-Islamic animus. The alienation of the diaspora from the geographical context of its homeland increased the risk of their transmitting a counternarrative history of the revolution as a form of historical dogma, robbed of its dynamic dialectic.[146]

This is particularly evident in how exiles began to negatively mythologize Nyerere (who was very deserving of careful critique) as an almost cartoon-like villain.[147] Issa Shivji, in his book on the politics of the Union, criticized Nyerere for his various misunderstandings of the political situation in Zanzibar and for acting from pragmatism rather than idealism.[148] But the exiles went further: Nyerere was portrayed as an evil, manipulative powermonger. He was damned as a "safe African leader" dependent on, and useful to, British interests, and accused of being unable to divest himself of deeply rooted anti-Muslim prejudice.[149] It was alleged that his ambitions toward the island were annexation all along and that he orchestrated the

1964 revolution to distract from his failed economic policies on the mainland.[150] He was accused of being a Zionist tool; of having fond relations with Golda Meir; of having a secretary who was a "Jewess"; and of offering cover to fishing ships, which "ferried men and arms from Tanganyika for the massacres [in Zanzibar]."[151] Kharusi held Nyerere responsible for "unleashing" in Zanzibar "in January 1964, terror and murder on a scale unequalled in recent history."[152] Though Kharusi grudgingly credited Nyerere with curbing the power of the Revolutionary Council and restricting the power of preventive detention, he indicted him for failing to take action to curb human rights violations in Zanzibar.[153] Ali Muhsin accused Nyerere of the "rape" of Zanzibar and blamed him not only for the death of Kassim Hanga and Othman Sharif but also for the assassination of Karume, "whom Nyerere had especially groomed to serve as his tool for conquest and subjugation of Zanzibar."[154]

By the late 1970s, Nyerere was being portrayed by articles in *FZV* and other exile publications as an African neo-imperialist and fledgling colonizer who wanted to take over and control not only Tanzania but also Uganda. In Ali Muhsin's virulent critique of Nyerere, published by *FZV* while the author was in a Tanzanian prison in Bukoba, Nyerere's hatred of monarchy is blamed for the overall insecure climate of the whole East African region.[155]

By the early 1980s, Nyerere was also being portrayed as an Islamophobe by the exiles. Baalawy singled out Nyerere as having a "pathological" hatred of Islam and Muslims and of being a racial and religious bigot.[156] While this is hyperbolic rhetoric (Nyerere had close working relationships with many Muslims, and a Muslim succeeded him as president of Tanzania), Baalawy does pick up an association implicit in much of Nyerere's thought and in Zanzibar's anticolonial and postcolonial politics, between the so-called Arab slave trade of the nineteenth century and the presence of Arab minorities in Tanzania. Baalawy reported an alleged public address by Mwalimu after the revolution in Zanzibar, in which he told a Zanzibari crowd: "The Arabs sold us as slaves, and if we wished we could auction them in the marketplace as they used to do (to us). Do you want me to do that? Just allow me a period of one week."[157] He also allegedly urged that African leaders should distrust the "white Arabs" to the north, more than the European colonialists, because of their history of enslaving Africans.[158] Baalawy noted that "the present generation of East Africans of Arab origin, nor their parents, had ever met a slave, let alone being guilty of slave trading."[159] By the

2000s this discourse critical of Nyerere was cropping up again among Zanzibari nationalists opposed to the Union. They portrayed the revolution as a crusade by Nyerere against an independent Islamic state.[160] Critiques from exile that in the 1960s had been acutely focused on the corruption of the Revolutionary Council and Karume became part of a broader criticism of the place of Muslims in Tanzania as a whole.[161]

THE ASSASSINATION OF KARUME AND THE ZANZIBAR TREASON TRIAL

On April 7, 1972, the modern history of Zanzibar was changed again through violence, with the assassination of Zanzibar president Abeid Karume by a former member of the disbanded Umma Party whose father had been killed in a criminal attack during the revolution.[162] The nature of the assassination tended to reignite old paranoia about an Arab-led counterrevolution. The assassin Humud was killed immediately.[163] His co-conspirator, a fellow Umma Party member, was coerced into implicating nineteen people in an alleged Umma plot to overthrow the government. The "plot" was likely individualistically motivated, to revenge Humud's father who had been murdered in prison after the revolution.[164] After the assassination, large numbers of people were detained by the state and tortured until they confessed. The Revolutionary Council, seeing the hand of the (now dissolved) Umma Party in the assassination, moved to arrest some members and remove others from power. Eighty-one Zanzibaris, mostly Umma Party members but including many others, were formally charged with plotting to overthrow the government. Almost all the eighty men and one woman who had been charged were Arabs or Comorians."[165] To his credit, Nyerere refused to hand over suspects detained on the mainland to Zanzibar.[166] April 10 was Karume's janaza (funeral prayer), and the Revolutionary Council regrouped and chose Aboud Jumbe as the new president of Zanzibar.[167]

On April 9, 1972, a group of exiles made a statement connecting the autocracy of Karume's rule to his untimely end and made several demands. First, they called for Nyerere to dissolve the Revolutionary Council. Additionally, they asked for the return of democratic elections, a referendum on the Union, and the release of political prisoners. More than forty exiles signed the letter, including Ibuni Saleh, A. S. Kharusi, Maulid Mshangama, and Ali Muhsin.

A more strongly worded statement by the "Central Committee of the Zanzibar Liberation Front," located in Cairo, was published on the same day, and it condemned Karume as a despot, "head of the ruling gang of pirates," whose fate was deserved after the abuses he had committed against the citizens of Zanzibar: "*The Central Committee* [of the ZLF] congratulates the clean hands which stand guard over the interests of the people, and hails at the heroism of its innocent sons who did their duty. May they be a living example to their brothers, the youths of our people, and let the end of Karume be the beginning of the end of the corrupt puppet regime."[168]

The trial of those charged with collusion in Karume's assassination began in early May 1973 and was closely covered by international correspondents.[169] The government's case was argued by Wolfgang Dourado. The accused would not be allowed defense lawyers and had no right of appeal. Nine people pleaded guilty, fifty-four not guilty, and the remaining eighteen were held on the mainland, with Nyerere refusing to hand them over to the Revolutionary Council until guarantees of appropriate legal representation were made. The cases of those who pled guilty were to be heard first, on May 15, while the remainder would begin their trial on May 21. The trial was expected to last two months.[170] Among the nine who pleaded guilty was Ahmed Badawi Quallatein (Qulatein), the island's junior minister of communications until two months before the assassination. Among those held on the mainland were Abdulrahman Babu and Ali Mahfoudh.[171] Their arrests had the effect of bringing the ZNP exiles closer to their erstwhile Umma compatriots, because many of the Umma radicals who opposed Karume's hold on power ended up sharing Tanzanian prison cells with former ministers from the overthrown government of 1963.[172] Moreover, the revolutionary government, reflecting its basic paranoia since 1964, used racial populism to frame former Umma members as foreigners seeking the return of the Arab sultanate.[173] Even on the mainland, Babu remained in prison for six years before being released by Nyerere and settling in London.[174]

In *FZV* Kharusi laid out the human rights abuses of the treason trial. He urged his readers to "intervene with the Tanzanian and Zanzibar authorities in order to make as wide representation as possible on behalf of the detainees" and to "conduct an independent judicial enquiry." In a handwritten note on the trial report he stated, "may strain relations with the mainland."[175] With Nyerere protecting former Umma members in the Union government and refusing to recognize the trial, the exiles found themselves caught between desiring Nyerere to do more to stymie the power of the Revolutionary Council and the desire to defend the isle's judicial sovereignty from Nyerere as a sign of the persistence of Zanzibar nationalism. Kharusi understood that the Union government was a more formidable obstacle to reclaiming Zanzibar's lost autonomy than the Revolutionary Council; Nyerere's interference in this case would strengthen the Union.[176]

Karume's death did not end the generally paranoid and authoritarian character of the regime but did help to resolve the confusing relationship between ASP and the Revolutionary Council.[177] After Karume's assassination, the party leadership worked to limit the council's powers and to establish a mythology for itself as the architect of the revolution, with the "martyr" Karume at the head of revolutionary planning. The Union government was also strengthened as a result of these developments. With the 1977 merger of the ASP into TANU to create the Chama Cha Mapinduzi (CCM), the "Party of the Revolution," there finally existed a mechanism through which Zanzibar and mainland policy could be fully coordinated within the Union structure.[178] Legislative elections in 1977 sent seventy-two Zanzibari representatives to a Union Parliament for the first time.[179]

The exiles saw in the death of Karume an opportunity to launch a counterrevolution.[180] They stepped up fundraising and organizing efforts greatly; Kharusi's correspondence with the exile network was particularly thick in 1973 and 1974, with talk of fundraising, plans, and meetings with the Libyan ambassador in Cairo. After the use of Tanzanian territory and military support by exiled former president Milton Obote to launch a September 1972 invasion of Uganda ended in a fiasco, Amin's main supporter, the Qaddafi regime in Libya, invited the Zanzibar exiles to Tripoli to air their grievances about the Tanzanian regime. This was facilitated through the World Islamic Call Society, also founded in 1972.[181] The exiles felt that Mu'ammar Qaddafi's generosity might fall on their cause and worked assiduously to cultivate his patronage. Zanzibari exile delegates attended the International Muslim Youth Conference on July 2–12, 1973, in Tripoli, Libya. In a prepared speech, the delegates from Zanzibar condemned "the rulers of Zanzibar who came to power through the diabolical massacre of . . . *15,000* Zanzibaris," and who "have done everything in their power to suppress Islam in all its manifestations." The delegates strongly criticized the Union and accused it of being a vehicle in the struggle, "to destroy Islam completely." They accused the rulers of Zanzibar of having betrayed Islam by the adoption of the "materialistic" doctrine of communism, "mixed with rabid racialism."[182] The speakers portrayed Ali Muhsin as a champion of Islam in East Africa, claiming he "had a well thought out blueprint for revival of Islam in Zanzibar."[183] They closed with praise for Qaddafi, especially highlighting the letter from World Islamic Call to Nyerere linking the political plight of Zanzibaris under the Union to the "terrorism" experienced by Muslim minorities in the new African and Asian nation-states.[184] In Tripoli, many exiles also met with Ahmed Lamky, who by 1973 was no longer an exile but an Omani citizen and prominent ambassador.[185]

EXILE CRITIQUE AND ECONOMIC CRISIS IN TANZANIA

By the late 1970s, many states in Africa and Asia were in severe fiscal crisis, especially after the oil price boom of 1973 meant that ever larger percentages of export earnings went to servicing the petroleum bills of the state.[186] In 1972 Tanzania spent $29 million on petroleum. In 1978 the figure was $278 million.[187] During that same period, it also was forced to import large amounts of grain to feed its population in response to a multiyear drought.[188] After the Uganda-Tanzania war of 1979 (Kiswahili: "Vita vya Kagera"), hard-pressed Tanzanian farmers turned to subsistence farming and barter economy to ward off famine.[189] By the end of the 1970s the Tanzanian government was servicing debt in the billions, spending more than half its foreign exchange earnings to pay down that debt. A global recession in 1981–1982 meant an increase in overall interest rates, as developed countries tried to squeeze more of a financial margin out of debtor countries.

Karume's successor Aboud Jumbe inherited substantial foreign reserves of £25 million in 1972. From 1972 to 1982 those reserves were dramatically drained by over £17 million.[190] Export numbers declined at the end of the 1970s, but prices momentarily tripled, stabilizing export earnings.[191] However, between 1976 and 1985 the performance of Zanzibar's economy declined by a full 27 percent under various pressures.[192] Destructive and ill-advised local policy choices by paranoid leadership undoubtedly worsened a difficult situation. By the mid-1980s the collapse of international clove prices had eroded the Zanzibar government's capacity to facilitate continued projects of human development. These straitened economic conditions were not unique to Zanzibar, but rather wrought political instability on the mainland and across Africa and the world.[193]

Fiscal shortfalls in Tanzania during this period spurred the creation of a large black market for basic goods, including soap, sugar, toothpaste, and razor blades, and high prices for goods from abroad. The one-party state lost prestige among the public as a result; Tanzanians sardonically reworked state messages: "wananchi" (citizens) became "wenyenchi" (owners of the nation), then "walanchi" (eaters of the nation). CCM was called "sisi mmmm" (no, not us) and "Chukua Chako Mapema" (grab your share early).[194] These mocking expressions were the public's cynical reaction to their political rulers' inability to control runaway economic inflation that ballooned the price of basic commodities and accelerated government corruption.[195]

In June 1984 the Tanzanian government devalued the shilling by 26 percent against the US dollar.[196] In early 1986 negotiations with the International Monetary Fund, Tanzania tried to get credit of $200 million toward economic recovery, but the IMF first asked that it further devalue the shilling versus the dollar, as the official rate of 38 shillings/dollar was being supplanted through illicit channels by exchanges as high as 170 shillings/dollar.[197] By late 1986 the first post-Nyerere Tanzanian government, under Ali Hassan Mwinyi, had begun to privatize some debt-ridden parastatals and offer aid for the private farming sector. New government incentives also allowed exporters to retain foreign exchange earnings to import raw materials, spare parts, and other in-demand commodities.[198]

Nyerere's perceived mismanagement of these crises led to sharp criticism from the exiles. Much of it was from an explicitly "religious' viewpoint, portraying Nyerere as a Catholic biased against Islam.[199] A poem in the February 1984 pages of *FZV* exemplified this form of critique. It was published under the pseudonym "Binti Zinjibariya" and was a satirical response to a speech Mwalimu Nyerere had given on February 5, 1984, at a public meeting in Dar-es-Salaam. Poetry in Swahili culture has a long pedigree as an instrument of social critique.[200] In its repeated interweaving of specific political critiques with broad-based religious condemnation, the poem amply demonstrated the use of Islam as an alternative location from which to hold accountable the self-serving declarations of permanent sovereignty made by postcolonial governing classes. The author of the poem compared Nyerere to pharoah. The poet accused Nyerere of intending to break Islam and to subordinate all religions to the state and promised that God would enable his destruction out of displeasure. Increasingly religious themes are then turned to: Nyerere is accused of having no shame, of being overly fond of his own opinions, of building "kufr" (unbelief) with the "clothes of iman (belief)," of having no "deen" (religion), of not knowing the difference between good and evil. The poem promises punishment for his "dhambi" (sins) and that "ndio" (yes), Nyerere's ultimate destination will be the flames of hell.

A sense of the anti-Union character of Zanzibari nationalism among the exiles can also be gleaned from the poem. Events in the previous year (1983), particularly the debate over whether to create a three-government federal system that granted autonomy to Unguja and Pemba, made the Union issue once again a live and important one.[201] Kharusi told his readers that those who observed the meetings in Dodoma to debate the Tanzanian constitution and the Zanzibar question within it would understand the meaning of "ndio" (which simply means yes, in Swahili).[202] The poem condemned the Union: "Zanzibaris in truth / they don't want muungano" (Union) and claimed that even Tanganyikans were tired of Nyerere. Nyerere's "oppression" had led to a situation in which the people were cowed into silence, where "no one remains to tell you, ndio" ("Hunaye aliye baki atayekwambia ndio"). In these circumstances, "ndio" had become the cry of those without concern for justice and morality. The author condemned the fact that people had been thrown into prison and deprived of their guaranteed legal rights, called traitors ("makhaini") and dividers of the nation. The author claimed in the next stanza that the postcolonial rulers were worse than the colonialists ("They 'judge' with bullets / better than the colonialist) because they unjustly imprisoned and killed people they had earlier claimed were citizens. The "party of revolution" (CCM) was called sardonically "a party of black marketeers." "Ujamaa" socialism was equated to theft, and postcolonial citizens were satirically portrayed as being in the eyes of their corrupt rulers like mere flesh, not humans with rights. Nyerere was accused of having no vision for solving the nation's intractable economic crisis, of being an "accursed python" swallowing up the people's economic livelihoods. This was followed by a poetic declaration that the postcolonial state in Tanzania, far from advancing the interests of the public it claimed to represent, had retarded the educational and material development of its citizens. The poet pointed to the emigration of doctors and the lack of medicine (even aspirin) in hospitals.

This poem exemplifies a mode of poetic critique that has deep roots in Swahili culture and society.[203] Its critiques are not an apology for colonialism and do not evince nostalgia for it; a critique of colonialism—its denial of rights and the failure to develop—was logically extended to the apparatus of power in the postcolonial state. In this respect, the "religious" overtones of the critique may misleadingly give the reader an impression of a purist and extremist vision of social reality, when in fact the significance of the religious angle is to remind the state of its core duty to uphold the rights of the individual as the basis for just development. At the same time, the religiously themed critique of the poet and of the exiles often exaggerated a conspiratorial attitude of victimhood common to many exile diasporas. The poem shows that the exile critiques informed a broader critique of the politics of the Tanzanian Union that would increasingly be shared between elements inside and outside Zanzibar.

From 1983, a new diaspora organization, Maendeleo Zanzibar, was formed, with branches in London and Dubai. Its membership had its roots in the exiled Afro-Arab radicals who had once been part of the Umma Party. Its platform was substantially like the liberal democratic platform of the former ZNP exiles and shared with it a demand for Zanzibar to be an independent state.[204] From the end of the 1980s and the beginning of the 1990s, many other new organizations representing Zanzibaris in diaspora rose up, supplanting the dominant two-decade importance of the Zanzibar Association and the ZO in the politics of Zanzibaris in diaspora. In August 1989, a new diaspora association formed in Sweden convened a gathering in London called Hamaki (Harakati za Mabadaliko ya Kidemokrasia Zanzibar, or the Movement for Democratic Transformation in Zanzibar) to bring together the different branches of the political opposition abroad.[205] Its statement also expressed opposition to the Union in Zanzibar, a position influenced by the important position of the ZO within the coalition. Even after the death of Kharusi, *FZV* also continued to voice opposition to the Union. As the 1990s dawned and authoritarian states appeared to be at their last gasp, it seemed it would be impossible any longer to keep the exiles out of the scope of legitimate politics in Zanzibar, especially as Tanzania increasingly sought loans and investment from Gulf states.

CONCLUSION

Chapter 3 historicized the two-decade period after the Zanzibar revolution from the perspective of a marginalized narrative in postcolonial African history: the Afro-Arab exiles and their diasporic advocacy for political rights in Zanzibar. The exiles initially worked within a horizon of the first decade of the revolution, when it still seemed possible to mount a counterrevolution. This influenced their strident insistence that they were the real Zanzibar nationalists and the revolution was an illegitimate foreign coup.

As the 1990s dawned, continued exile transformed their desire for regime change and return of the duly elected ZNP to power into a general call for democracy in Zanzibar, combined with a call for the Union to end. In a February 1990 special issue "Uhuru" (Freedom), the author of an article titled "Unguja ni Njema" (Zanzibar is good) maintains that "what Zanzibar needs is not reform but a complete break with the bogus and illegitimate union. We cannot have reforms or democracy when we do not have a state. We had a state, and we had a democracy. We want both."[206] These same demands had been made from within Zanzibar since 1983–1984 from elements actively opposed to interference by ex-ZNP exiles, and despite a government ban on *FZV*, penalizing those found in possession of it with up to five years in prison.[207] The internal critique expressed dismay that Karume was not remembered in Zanzibar, while photographs of Nyerere's were in every government office, and asserted that Zanzibar was an independent state held in an exploitative relationship with the mainland by the Tanzanian constitution.[208]

The exiles were participants in new Muslim-themed currents and languages of dissent emerging from fraught interactions between secular and religious authorities in the developmental state, and they used this language to comment on governance in Zanzibar. A pamphlet circulating in Zanzibar at the end of 1988 and the beginning of 1989 called for an "intifada" against the government and provocatively portrayed the Union as a Christian plot overseen by Nyerere, portrayed as a pope, with Ali Hassan Mwinyi as his "cardinal."[209] But some of the original exiles had already dropped this inflammatory rhetoric and their separatist demands before they were embraced by the political opposition in Zanzibar. By the time of Ali Muhsin's release from prison in Tanzania in 1974 and his emigration to Cairo, the ex-prime minister of Zanzibar was himself ready to forgo both the covert military action dreamed of by the covert wing of the ZO and the public-facing "pamphleteering" approach, to the distress of his colleagues in the organization. Instead, Ali Muhsin believed a turn inward toward piety and self-reflection was needed, to build a solid new foundation for change inside Zanzibar.[210]

The critiques by the exiles would inform a broad historiography on Zanzibar in Swahili, Arabic, and English that emerged beginning in the late

1990s and was largely written by authors in Oman. This development was parallel to a heightened interest by the Omani state in the history of the nineteenth-century sultanate of Zanzibar. Chapter 6 will reveal the tensions and contradictions of this historiography for belonging in, and affiliation to, Zanzibar. The democratic transition of the 1990s in Zanzibar successfully reset relations with exiles as they and their offspring were invited back to the former homeland as guests, tourists, and investment partners. But renewed relations were haunted by the ghosts of old discourses about slavery, colonialism, and revolution.

FOUR

Zanzibari Diaspora Communities in the Arabian Gulf, 1964–1977

BECAUSE OF THE DIFFICULTIES associated with life under the new regime, many Zanzibaris escaped from Zanzibar from the last half of the 1960s into the early 1970s and settled in various Gulf emirates. From the end of the 1960s to the middle of the 1970s, the center of Zanzibari diaspora life came to reside briefly in the Trucial States and UAE during a period when the UAE was forming and the British were beginning a phased withdrawal as military protectors of their rulers.[1] Some fifteen hundred Zanzibaris resided in the UAE by 1975. The bulk of them were found in Dubai and Abu Dhabi. Dubai, as the most open of the emirates, was the center of Zanzibari community life in the Gulf until Oman's opening in the latter part of 1970. Outside the UAE, smaller numbers resided in Dammam, Doha, and Kuwait. This chapter relays the activities and dilemmas of Zanzibar's diaspora communities in the Gulf, through interviews with migrants as well as official UNHCR reports about the community.

Because of the difficulties associated with life under the new regime in Zanzibar, a common trend for Zanzibaris in this period was to escape from Zanzibar, from the last half of the 1960s into the early 1970s. Their ad hoc journeys to the Gulf also reveal changes in state practices around border regulation as well as the impact of new modes of travel. Air travel was gradually making sea travel between East Africa and the Gulf uneconomical. As UNHCR official Leslie Goodyear observed, "Shipping lines have cancelled their regular passenger service from Mombasa to the Arabian Gulf, so that the only reliable means of transportation is by air."[2] Zanzibaris were part of the story of ramped up immigration enforcement in the Trucial States because they arrived by boat and often stayed past the expiration of their residence permits, as they did not have anywhere else to go.[3] They could claim refugee status and then convert that into asylum, leading to permanent residence. But this could take a decade or more of residence in the Gulf.

If a refugee is defined as someone involuntarily displaced from their country of nationality, then the Zanzibaris in the Gulf ought to be seen as refugees when they arrived in the Gulf because by leaving Zanzibar without authorization they effectively became stateless. Moreover, the kind of nationality they could obtain in Dubai and Abu Dhabi was not a federal status but a form of local recognition, different than the national citizenship Zanzibaris would obtain in nearby Oman after 1970.[4] Though most of these escapees became Omani citizens by the mid- to late 1970s, they spent between five and ten years of uneasy shifting nationality status in various Gulf emirates.

The emirates differed in their approach to integrating foreigners into the national state as long-term residents, largely driven by the structural differences in approaches to revenue accumulation. For instance, while Abu Dhabi's oil rich economy meant a greater emphasis on restrictive incorporation, Dubai's economy was based on "mobile assets and trade" and the free issue of passports to diverse ethnicities.[5] Abu Dhabi had begun a rapid growth period under the new ruler Sheikh Zayed bin Sultan al-Nehayan. He encouraged the return migration of thousands of families who had left Abu Dhabi in the 1950s, a policy that was to be repeated by his counterpart Sultan Qaboos in Oman after 1970.[6] Dubai as a municipality was formally registered by Sheikh Rashid bin Said al-Maktoum in 1957.[7] In this period when neighbor Abu Dhabi had begun to exploit vast oil reserves, Dubai sought to attract commercial activity by introducing favorable tax structures and relatively liberal residence laws.[8] Between 1960 and 1966, port income and the taxes from the transit trade in gold allowed for the ruler to embark on a rapid campaign of modern development.[9] To do so, the government needed to import skilled labor that could not be obtained locally. Minor petroleum discoveries prompted further rapid in-migration to Dubai from India, Pakistan, and Iran, as well as further afield."[10]

CLAIMING NATIONAL STATUS AFTER EMPIRE

For Zanzibaris to obtain a UK visa from the colonies also became increasingly difficult during the 1960s. Great Britain took steps to limit citizenship, deliberately making it difficult or even impossible for most colonial subjects to obtain British nationality.[11] The Commonwealth Immigration Act of 1962 imposed specific immigration quotas limiting emigration from former colonies to the United Kingdom.[12] This was done largely in order to avoid having to give residence, asylum, or nationality to refugees and other persons displaced by decolonization.[13] Migration to the United Kingdom for Zanzibaris was further complicated by the need for a Ministry of Labour voucher (meaning a definite job was required as a condition of immigration), an entry certificate for the United Kingdom, and a recognized national passport.

The Tanzanian government was unwilling to recognize the exiled Zanzibaris as nationals eligible for a passport, as they were considered political subversives by the Zanzibar authorities and had fallen through the cracks because of their covert migrations before and after Zanzibar's union with mainland Tanganyika. Kharusi had struggled to normalize his immigration status and residence in the United Kingdom and faced the paradoxical issue of being unable to become a British national because of his lack of a national status in Tanzania, a country only formed after he left Zanzibar the day of the revolution with the sultan.[14] Since it was impossible for most exiled Zanzibaris to obtain a Tanzanian passport, they could not obtain other state documents contingent on an acknowledged national status.

Those who could prove their origin in Zanzibar could obtain from the British political agent in Dubai "a limited British passport identifying them as Citizens of the British Commonwealth," valid only for six months. This did not allow them to settle in the United Kingdom, as many desired to do, but only to possibly regularize their status as Tanzanian nationals and obtain a Tanzanian passport. But at the time in 1967 when these issues were being debated, Tanzania and the United Kingdom had broken off diplomatic relations, and British consular issues were being handled through the Canadian embassy in Dar-es-Salaam. To break through this "vicious circle," Goodyear asked the British political agent in Dubai, David Roberts, to accept applications for Dubai entry without the completion of the travel document particulars and to agree to the issuing of a visa "subject to a travel document being obtained."[15]

Roberts's objections were remembered by some Zanzibaris, even though the British withdrew from the region in 1971. According to Saud Ahmed, "There was a British immigration officer in Dubai who tried to prevent the [Zanzibari] immigrants from landing. I was told by someone who was there that whenever the Zanzibaris had trouble coming down off the boats (many of whom were de facto stateless) they sent a delegation to this officer for help, and he consistently refused."[16] The presence of undocumented Zanzibaris caused Roberts consternation. The recurring issue was that those already in Dubai wishing to sponsor visas for people in Zanzibar could not do so, because their applications were not being accepted by Roberts due to their lack of a travel document. Roberts was skeptical of the de facto policy for Zanzibari refugees because it involved treating a No Objection Certificate (NOC) as a valid visa. The position was urged on him by UNHCR officials, who stated that it would allow family members outside East Africa to apply to sponsor the departure of their relatives from Zanzibar and Mombasa.

In a May 12, 1967, letter written in the wake of Goodyear's February visit to Dubai, the UNHCR branch office representative in London advocated, despite the general foot-dragging attitude of Roberts, encouraging Zanzibaris to naturalize in Dubai.[17] Goodyear wrote in late January 1968 to Roberts, urging him to get agreement from the Dubai government for transit visas for Zanzibaris turned away at Muscat, reasoning that since the applicants were clearly Oman-born Arabs settled in Zanzibar, "they have good prospects of being able to enter Muscat and Oman if they can prove their nationality."[18] Roberts was skeptical; he thought that it would not be easier to enter Muscat through Dubai unless the travelers could first reside in Dubai long enough to obtain a Dubai passport. Roberts suggested involving the Zanzibar Association in Dubai to sponsor the persons concerned.

The struggles of Zanzibari refugees in the Gulf are evident in a story related in the UNHCR archives. "Muhammad", who owned a fleet of taxis before the revolution, lost most of them to revolutionary expropriation. He decided to leave and go to Dubai, and he left his four children with his brother until he was settled enough to send for them. On the three-week voyage by dhow to the Gulf, his wife bonded with another refugee family with four children, and the two families became closely intertwined. Shortly after arrival in Dubai, his wife's friend, the other mother, died. Her husband then returned to Zanzibar to marry his wife's sister, to have someone to look after the four children. He (temporarily) entrusted the children to Muhammad and his wife. However, after arriving back on the islands, he was prevented from leaving again. Muhammad got a job as a taxi driver in Dubai but faced difficulties as he spoke neither English nor Arabic. In the end, he and his wife were supporting another couple's four children in Dubai on a meager income, while their own four children could not leave Zanzibar.[19] The UNHCR worked with the ruler of Dubai to make available emergency funds for him to buy a taxi and obtain a taxi license (normally reserved only for Dubai citizens).[20]

ESCAPING ZANZIBAR, 1966–1977

Many Afro-Arabs rode out the initial events of the revolution without leaving Zanzibar. By the end of 1965, it began to dawn on many of them that the scope for a future in Zanzibar was rapidly diminishing because of the autocratic turn in governance after the revolution. Their first and most important preoccupation thus became escaping Zanzibar, a difficult prospect when few dhows called at Zanzibar's port and there were severe legal penalties for leaving without obtaining government permission. To leave Zanzibar, one needed a specific document, called colloquially "mkeka" (Swahili: mat), a special piece of paper that served as a passport.[21] Because postcolonial Zanzibar prohibited movement out of the country, and because obtaining this document was difficult and expensive, Zanzibaris planned covert escapes to the mainland in this period, with their goal usually to reach Mombasa, where they could obtain access to the UN office.[22]

According to Goodyear, who visited the Zanzibar diaspora communities in the Gulf several times in the late 1960s and early 1970s, by early March 1970, large numbers of Zanzibaris were sitting in Mombasa (at least a thousand) awaiting the start of the monsoons when they could catch dhows up to the Arabian Gulf.[23] Most had entered Kenya illegally.[24] Many Zanzibari refugees were afraid of registering in Mombasa for fear of being sent back to the islands.[25] British officials noted that in Mombasa, "the group causing most concern is the wives and children of persons already in the Trucial States, and I would ask whether anything could be done through the office of the Legal Advisor for Africa to legalize the status, and hopefully, provide travel documents for members of separated families to facilitate their move to Dubai. Arrangements could then be made in Dubai for the issue of N.O.C.s so that airlines would be ready to accept the persons."[26]

By late 1971 many in Dar-es-Salaam or Mombasa remained without documents enabling them to go to the Gulf.[27] Those who went from Zanzibar to Dar-es-Salaam were "pressed by the authorities to move on after a month or two."[28] Muscat passports were harder and harder to get, and the direct shipping line from Mombasa to Dubai had by then ceased. Thus, to escape people were forced to rely on dhows that departed from September to January during the 1971 monsoon season. Due to the difficulty of the journey, this cohort was mostly men. At the end of 1971 the Zanzibar Association members in Dubai believed that approximately 150 to 200 people were still stuck in Mombasa, and hundreds of people continued to attempt escape from the islands in the first three months of 1972.[29] The political crackdown in the wake of Karume's death provoked a new exodus. Thousands of undocumented immigrants from Zanzibar flooded the Mombasa port, seeking shelter in the city and eventual passage to the Gulf. Their ability to obtain an NOC, normally issued by the British high commissioner in many Commonwealth countries, was complicated by their having no legal immigration status within Kenya.[30] Three years later, in 1975, the city was still filled with Zanzibari refugees. A letter from Mombasa published in *FZV* in July 1975 related, "You can't walk two steps in Mombasa without meeting Zanzibaris."[31]

The influx of refugees from Zanzibar into coastal cities presented delicate security problems for Kenya and Tanzania.[32] This migration provoked new levels of surveillance of Zanzibaris by the Zanzibar government in Dar-es-Salaam and Mombasa. In the 1970s Aboud Jumbe and Hassan Nassor Moyo approached Tanzanian president Nyerere to allow Zanzibari interrogators to carry out investigations into Zanzibari dissidents on the mainland.[33] In 1973 and 1974, Zanzibar government security forces surveilled and detained Zanzibari refugees in Kenya. Revolutionary Council member Yusuf Himidi and others made visits to Mombasa to confirm whether there was an underground movement there to overthrow Zanzibar with support from exiled Zanzibaris in the Gulf.[34] Some refugees were even kidnapped in Mombasa by Zanzibar security police and taken back to Zanzibar.

Many from the nationalist generation, especially those who were political prisoners of the Tanzanian state, made similar journeys after their release or escape from Tanzanian prisons in the late 1960s and early to mid-1970s, going to Dubai, including Rashid Hamadi and Aman Thani. Muhammad Abdul-Muttalib Hashim left directly from Zanzibar on July 19, 1966, in a group that included Said Seif al-Riyami (who later became chief of Oman police). The ship stopped in Mombasa before arriving at Dubai.[35] The ex-ZNP minister Aman Thani went to Mombasa after his release from a Tanzanian prison. He went immediately to Salim Muhashami, the representative of the UNHCR in the city, to declare himself a refugee. He was helped to settle in Dubai, where he was first welcomed by Hashim, then president of the Zanzibar Association of Dubai, and given by the ruler a "shaksiya," permitting him to access the right to residence on a temporary renewable basis.[36] The Shirazi leader and exiled Zanzibar prime minister Rashid Hamadi made his way to Dubai from Kuwait in the early 1970s, after his 1967 release from prison. Ali Muhsin al-Barwani was released from a Tanzanian prison in 1974.[37] He then left Tanzania without authorization, fearing further imprisonment. He crossed the border into Kenya and to Mombasa, from where he attempted to join his family in Cairo, and later settled in Dubai.[38]

A younger generation was also escaping on fishing boats to Dar-es-Salaam, before traveling overland to Mombasa. Muhammad was in kindergarten when his older brother left Zanzibar. Muhammad left the island covertly at age nineteen. On an April evening in 1972, he boarded a small local fishing craft called a *ngalawa* (like a canoe) and took it to Bagamoyo on the Tanzanian mainland. In Bagamoyo he took a bus to Dar-es-Salaam, and then to Tanga. He did not have a passport, so in Tanga family members told him, "You look like an Msambaa. If you take a train and get stopped at the border in Kenya, tell them you are Msambaa."[39] The ruse failed. Muhammad was stopped at the border, asked to present his nonexistent passport, and identified as someone who was running away from Zanzibar. Although items in the *FZV* report that the Zanzibar government was rounding up escaped Zanzibaris in Dar-es-Salaam at this time, Muhammad was fortunate. Either Nyerere had determined to turn a blind eye to those escaping Zanzibar, or the Tanzanian border officials were sympathetic to those fleeing. Muhammad made his way to Mombasa, where he obtained a UN refugee passport, which he then used to fly to Dubai, before settling in Ras al-Khaymah, where he obtained citizenship.[40] He later became an Omani citizen.

A man from Pemba, "Rashid." escaped the islands in 1971 to go to Mombasa. He declared, "No one in those days was allowed to have a passport. It was not something you would just go and apply for and get. You had to find other means of leaving. If caught, you would go five years in prison. So, it was quite risky to leave the country." He was a teacher and used one of his students' outings to Mombasa to escape there. Like Habiba, he did not feel safe telling his family about his plans: "I did not tell my family. It is a risky thing to do. What will happen is the police will go to them and ask, 'where is he now?' My elder brother had left at that time, he found his own way as well." In Mombasa, he was dropped offshore without a passport. He was potentially at the mercy of the authorities if discovered. He slept in the mosque in Kibokoni for several months and did occasional work while waiting for papers that would enable him to travel. Said's family members in the Gulf assisted him in his efforts. Leaving Mombasa was a delicate operation, but there were more legal options for departure than for leaving Zanzibar. In 1971, after declaring himself with the UN representative Sheikh Salim Muhashim, he hired a lawyer and received legal permission to leave Kenya. The UN helped him purchase a one-way ticket to Abu Dhabi, while his brother, who was already there, sent him a one-way pass allowing him to enter the country. After a month in Abu Dhabi, Rashid's father, who was already in Oman, procured an Omani passport for him.[41]

"Seif" told the story of a man he knew who escaped Zanzibar by airplane. He managed to sneak his wife and daughter out with his wife's father, who went to Kuwait to get medical treatment. Noticing security state agents at the door of his home, he hid in a local bar, parked his car there, and then slipped into the house via the back door. As a member of the middle class who worked at a local bank, he was able to use his connections to purchase an air ticket and get through airport security. He moved through the airport paranoid that he would be seen by a member of the Revolutionary Council. All the flights were booked to Dar-es-Salaam, so he approached the captain of a TWA plane that had been waved down the previous day by revolutionaries and detained in the airport. The captain asked him where he was going; he said "Dar," and the captain, an American, said, "We are going to Mombasa."

"Oh," he answered, "that is just a few miles from Dar."

The captain gave him a look and let him get on the plane. The plane took off; Seif was sitting in his seat hunched up, still scared he would be discovered and turned over to the authorities. Suddenly the captain came out of the cockpit as the plane turned toward Pemba. He came up to Seif's seat. "You lied to me! Dar is not a few miles from Mombasa. Where are you really going? Are you running away?"

Shivering in his seat, Seif protested, "No, I'm not running away."

"You are a runaway!" the captain continued. "And I want to help you! I hate those bastards down there."[42]

BORDERS AND NATIONALITY: MUSCAT, DUBAI, AND THE ZANZIBARIS, 1966–1972

Dubai was also a destination for hundreds of Zanzibaris who had unsuccessfully attempted to find asylum in Oman. Well into the late 1960s,

Zanzibaris were routinely denied the possibility of entry into Muscat.[43] Saud Ahmed al-Busaidi from Zanzibar was denied entry to Oman in the 1960s and went to Libya. Ahmed Lamky, in Cairo, tried to establish the possibility of the resettlement of Zanzibaris resident in Egypt in Oman. British officials debating the case threw up their hands, reasoning there was no special intervention they could make, and urged Lamky to apply for an Omani passport.[44]

The Omani immigration authorities had even worked out a system to send migrants seeking asylum in Oman across to Dubai. On January 23, 1965, Hassan Abdalla, the de facto coordinator of the Red Cross relief operation in Zanzibar after the expulsion of British Red Cross official Nick Phillips, wrote directly to the British Red Cross Society. He was traveling on the sailing vessel *van Riebeeck* to Muscat with three sick refugees.[45] He observed the process of disembarkation and reported that "69 of our passengers were not allowed to land in Muscat even though some have Muscat passports, some had visas or NOCs. . . . They claim they sent us a telegram on or about the 10th of Jan that no refugees should be sent to Muscat [during] this month of Ramadan. I have not seen that telegram until I left Zanzibar on the 13th, I think they sent it to London and London was late to act." Hassan Abdalla reported that the refugees refused landing would go to Dubai and "make their own way to Oman by buses." He commented, "In Muscat even if a passenger is Muscat born and has a visa, a sheikh from his hometown must come on board to guarantee him, otherwise he will not be allowed to land."[46] Eventually the remaining passengers from the *van Riebeeck* were granted entry into Dubai on January 30, 1965.[47] At the end of 1965 approximately one hundred individuals from Zanzibar lived in Dubai, which was becoming the "Mecca" of Zanzibaris without papers.[48]

In October 1966 the UNHCR representative in Geneva wrote to his counterpart in London, relating a letter about the experience of one hundred "Manga Arabs" denied entry into Oman, who went to Dubai. Many of the refugees, especially the very old and the very young, were in extremely poor health and psychologically traumatized by the violence they had experienced. As "farmers and shopkeepers" in Zanzibar, they found it challenging to adapt those skills to the new urban context of Dubai. According to the UNHCR, "almost none of the Manga Arabs speak Arabic," and this created problems for placing younger children in the Arabic-language primary schools of the Emirates.[49] The secondary school graduates among them lacked money for university tuition, and there were insufficient scholarships available for their numbers.[50]

Not only Arab Zanzibaris left Zanzibar for Oman; in the 1970s many Shirazis also made landings in the Trucial States to escape Zanzibar, a result of the regime's shifting attitude toward them. As part of a program intending to do away with Shirazi identity, Karume required every self-identified Shirazi to sign a short declaration that they no longer wished to identify as Shirazis. There are seven volumes of these in the Zanzibar Archives.[51] In June 1970, an individual named Janu Hassan wrote to Kharusi about his travails with the Zanzibar regime and the difficulties he had obtaining a passport to leave.[52] Many Shirazi settled in the Deira neighborhood of Dubai.

In 1972 a group of escaping Zanzibaris wrote to Kharusi in Swahili, relating their rare and fascinating account of postcolonial travel, which highlights the role of ships, not as heterotopias, but as risky and dangerous vessels delivering stateless and displaced peoples to foreign shores. The escapees boarded various fishing boats and canoes to reach Mombasa. From Mombasa they were able to find passage on a dhow to the Gulf. However, their ship sprang a leak ("jahazi yetu ilitoboka") between Somalia and the southern Yemen coastal town of Shihr, obliging them to go to Shihr harbor for repairs. They continued to southern Oman, where their dhow ran aground on a rock in the harbor. "Luckily, we were very near shore, and were able to swim and arrive safely to this dry, desert country ('nchi kavu'), although several of us had a little of the skin stripped from our feet ('athari za kuchunika chunika'), but it was not too bad."

The Zanzibaris were met onshore by Omani soldiers, who took them to a nearby village and questioned them. "We stayed in the village for 8 days. We were asked various questions about the objective of our journey, and where we had intended to go." They were then sent to various detainment encampments in Salalah, and then in Ruwi:

> After answering as long as we were able, we were taken and placed in an army truck and taken to a camp called "Mid-Way Garrison." After a short time remaining there, we were removed again and placed into a detention center ("kizuwizi") in Salalah. We remained there six days, then placed in another detention center in Ruwi. Here we remained 33 days.

The letter writers stressed they were without any documents at all ("nyaraka zo zote za safari"), or anything that would enable them to enter the country in the customary manner ("njia kawaida"), or any sponsor. However, they claimed to have been well treated in detainment in Oman: "We thank God, that although we were placed in these, we suffered neither misery ('tabu') nor oppression ('dhiki') of any kind."

The writers then detail how four of their number had relational ties to Zanzibaris in Oman and were able to call on these to obtain release. However, the rest did not have the sponsors necessary to obtain their release. The Omani authorities thus gave them a little money and placed them in transport overland to Dubai, where they were received by the authorities. The writers related that in Dubai, "We were able to busy ourselves with our affairs ('Na hapo tuliweza kuhangaika hangaika'), and after a short time we met some Zanzibaris." The journey and experiences of these displaced Zanzibaris, related the writers, was not strange to the Zanzibaris in Dubai, *"for almost everyone who has come here has come in the same ways as we have come."* They received assistance from the community and began to settle in.[53]

Ali Muhsin al-Barwani praised the liberal attitudes of Emirati rulers: "A Zanzibari really felt at home on his landing anywhere in the UAE. This was home away from home."[54] At a 1973 conference in Libya attended by Zanzibari exiles, the Zanzibari delegate drew attention to "thousands of Zanzibari Muslim youths of all sexes [who] have fled from their motherland and are exiled in many parts of the world." The delegate praised Sheikh Rashid of Dubai as the refugees' main benefactor and the principal person responsible for their gaining asylum in the Gulf.[55]

ZANZIBARI MIGRATION AND RESIDENCE POLICY IN DUBAI AND ABU DHABI

Zanzibaris and other East African migrants were arriving in the Emirates in the mid-1960s, at a time before the UAE existed officially as a federation; only in 1971 did Dubai and Abu Dhabi become founding members of the UAE, with the Dubai Immigration Office given authority over all immigration in the UAE. Goodyear estimated the population of Dubai as 55,000 in 1966, with Indians, Pakistanis and Iranians outnumbering the Arabs.[56] Peter Liendhardt's research from 1967 showed that "the number of people living in Dubai who came originally from elsewhere probably outnumbered the indigenous inhabitants."[57] This was likely because there were approximately fifteen thousand illegal residents out of the fifty-five thousand estimated residents.[58] A 1968 population census of Dubai in the Gulf similarly found that the foreign born were more than half of the population of fifty-eight thousand.[59] The previously mentioned NOCs "provided a record of every foreigner employed in the territories" and linked them to a national sponsor, who would be responsible if they defected.[60] While obtaining NOCs for those from Zanzibar was relatively easy in Dubai, it was almost impossible in Abu Dhabi.[61] Entering the federation did not affect either ruler's willingness to admit Zanzibaris. However, it did appear to mean that NOCs issued to enable entry of refugees to Dubai would now need to be approved at the federal level by all the federation's rulers. Moreover, in the Emirates acquiring a passport did not mean acquiring federal status as an Emirati national, which still rested on being registered in a book of official ancestries accepted as authentic nationals. As Noora Lori showed, this effectively created a distinction between those with full nationality, those with passports but no nationality, and those who were long-term residents with neither.[62]

Initially, the somewhat irregular governance of many areas of life in both Dubai and Abu Dhabi worked to the advantage of the Zanzibaris, as they were able to find patrons and exploit a general openness then pervading the region. For instance, according to Liendhardt, the system of land title registration was still partially based in an old system of personal recognition by a patron, rather than bureaucratic guarantee and administrative title.[63] Muhammad Abdul-Muttalib Hashim's arrival demonstrated the ad hoc character of immigration at the time; he arrived in 1966 before there was an official port. An immigration official came aboard their ship, asked the Zanzibaris to stand to one side, and were told they were allowed, by direct order of Sheikh Rashid, to enter the country without hindrance.[64] Not all those who sought asylum in the Emirates were of Arab ancestry; moreover, even many Arabs from Zanzibar were not viewed as Arab or "people of the Gulf" by immigration authorities, despite the attenuated family connections of many refugees to prominent Omani tribes.[65] Dubai and Abu Dhabi differed on whether they saw Zanzibaris as Arab (Dubai) or non-Arab (Abu Dhabi). Their approach to integrating foreigners into the national state as long-term residents differed according to the structural differences in approaches to revenue accumulation. Abu Dhabi had only begun a rapid growth period under the new ruler, Sheikh Zayed. He encouraged the return migration of thousands of families who had left Abu Dhabi in the 1950s, a policy that was to be repeated by his counterpart, Sultan Qaboos, in Oman after 1970.[66] Abu Dhabi's oil-rich economy meant a greater emphasis on restrictive incorporation; few Zanzibaris were granted citizenship there. Dubai's economy was thus based on "mobile assets and trade" and Sheikh Rashid freely issued passports to diverse ethnicities, including many Zanzibaris.[67]

In Dubai there had been a large migration of nearly a hundred Zanzibaris in 1965, but most migrants came in smaller bursts, averaging about ten per month during 1965. A letter dated December 29, 1965, described the community as "small, well-organized, and comparatively well-educated" and "lower-middle class in outlook."[68] These arrivals continued well into the late 1960s: between April and June 1967, 37 new people arrived in Dubai from Zanzibar.[69] A 1966 breakdown found that 134 refugees from Zanzibar were residing in Dubai, and that most of them had large numbers of family members still in Zanzibar. Of the persons in Dubai, most (88) had incomes of over 250 rupees/month, with the most of this subset (60) making 250–500 rupees/month. The largest number of refugees had no documents at all (20), while smaller numbers (9) had Zanzibar emergency certificates. Two wealthier refugee families were in possession of Dubai passports, four carried Muscat passports (old sultanate passport), and five had British commonwealth passports.[70] By the end of 1967 there were some two hundred Zanzibaris (approximately eighty families) living in Dubai. Some Zanzibaris were given a provisional form of nationality, outside of full recognition, while others had one-year renewable work permits, enabling them to open a shop and engage in trade.[71] But while refugees in Dubai did receive passports and a path to permanent settlement, they faced obstacles to buying land, owning businesses, and educating their children, and many of them were functionally stateless.

Mr. William Duff, adviser to Sheikh Rashid al-Maktoum, was put in charge of the Zanzibari and Ugandan Asian refugees who arrived in Dubai from the late 1960s through the mid-1970s.[72] The British immigration official David Roberts also had tremendous power to shape migration policy, or at least to block certain actions he felt were undesirable. UNHCR official Leslie Goodyear's papers are the largest source in the UNHCR files. In March 1966 he was allocated funds for a fact-finding mission on the state of refugees in Dubai and Muscat, and he would return for visits to various Zanzibari communities in the Gulf over the late 1960s through the late 1970s.[73] The UNHCR assisted Zanzibaris in the Gulf often through the leadership of the Zanzibar Association by smoothing relations between the British government representatives and the local rulers and by soliciting donations from the Dubai and Abu Dhabi rulers for assistance to needy Zanzibaris.[74]

By Goodyear's visit to Dubai on February 2–10, 1967, he noted thousands of Zanzibari refugees had migrated to Dubai since 1964, with various forms of documentation, including Imamate passports, NOCs, and laissez-passers.[75] The UNHCR representative noted that emigration without documentation had effectively ended their status as Zanzibar nationals and affected their overall living standard. Some had no travel documents at all; very few had Tanzanian passports. The overwhelming desire of most who arrived in Dubai was to find money and resources to get their relatives out of Zanzibar.[76] Goodyear noted, "They are unable to maintain the same standard of living as they had in Zanzibar and most of their money is either sent to their unfortunate relatives at home or else put towards the cost of bringing them from Zanzibar to the Gulf."[77] UNHCR authorities in London recommended arriving émigrés from Zanzibar wait five years and pursue local nationality.[78] Having concluded operations in Zanzibar, the UNHCR deemed it still had responsibility to those refugees who had not gained entry into their "sheikhdoms of origin" (in Oman) and thus continued to come under UNHCR purview.[79]

In the middle of 1968, Mr. Goodyear reported on his trip to Dubai, where, he said, "Mr. Mohamed Said al-Mulla, the UNHCR honorary counsellor, has been preparing the ground for a general decision to give Dubai nationality to all Zanzibari refugees." While some of the Zanzibaris in Dubai were able to obtain citizenship after a period of years, most others lingered without national citizenship for five or six years. UNHCR officials visited the community in 1967 and 1968 and tried to arrange a more secure solution to the problem of nationality and citizenship. Goodyear noted that it was the opinion of community leadership that it was better to take up individual cases than to "press for a legal approach."[80] Goodyear spoke about the need for discretion, since the granting of a general nationality status on a group basis had the potential to inflame ethnic tensions with other communities.[81]

THE ZANZIBAR ASSOCIATION IN DUBAI AND ABU DHABI

Most Zanzibar exile communities in the Gulf lacked a public sphere to pursue protest and advocacy politics. Unlike the Zanzibari diaspora in the United Kingdom any political work done on behalf of Zanzibar by

Zanzibaris in the Gulf had to be, for the most part, clandestine. Many communities formed "Zanzibar Associations" (ZA) in the Gulf. These were generally relief and support organizations premised on a paid subscription model, in which monies were pooled for needy members of the community. The community associations provided for the social welfare of new arrivals and facilitated solutions to the unique problems faced by the community. They helped to take in and feed new arrivals, among other social welfare functions, including classes and assistance with education. Leadership also regularly met with the minister of foreign affairs and other UAE government officials to discuss the issues facing the community.[82] Association members also played a role in dramatizing the human rights abuses in Zanzibar as part of their efforts to gain the right of asylum in the Gulf.[83] As such it had non-Zanzibari members in both Tanzania and Kenya.[84] According to Muhammad Abdul-Muttalib Hashim, without the association, "the Zanzibari people would have disintegrated."[85]

According to Hashim, by the time he arrived in Dubai in 1966 the Zanzibar Association had already been formed. He quoted a letter from July 13, 1964, to Sheikh Rashid from Ali Masoud Thani, explaining the plight of the Zanzibaris in diaspora and asking for the ruler's permission to establish the association as a charitable organization under the ruler's supervision. Sheikh Rashid wrote directly on the letter that he had no objection.[86] Jamshid even came from the United Kingdom to Dubai to thank Sheikh Rashid for his strong support of the Zanzibaris in exile. The ZA had a constitution and was originally formed with dues of five rupees per month per family.[87] The ZA petitioned the UNHCR to fund it directly, though the organization balked at the future commitments that would entail, to begin providing funding for vocational training.[88] The ZA underwent leadership turnover after 1970 as leaders of Omani descent migrated to Oman after 1970.[89] The networks of the association also overlapped with that of the ZO, which caused no little consternation in certain circles and led to controversy over the "Omani" clan affiliation of Zanzibari exiles in Dubai.[90]

The entrance of Zanzibari refugees into Dubai and their access to permanent residence in Dubai had much to do not only with the intervention of the Zanzibar Association but also with their good personal relations with Sheikh Rashid (who ruled Dubai until October 1990). The Dubai ruler consistently overlooked the refugees' lack of documentation and did much to aid Zanzibari resettlement in the Gulf. It helped that one of Dubai's top immigration officials was Seyyid Ahmed Thabit, a member of the Zanzibar royal family in charge of disembarkation from sea vessels.[91] Thabit was also president of the Zanzibar Association. Through his personal intervention with Rashid, Thabit helped to bring thousands of Zanzibaris to settle in Dubai.

Sheikh Rashid gave small grants to the refugees to cover food expenses for one month after arrival. In some cases the Zanzibar Association was granted permission to submit NOC requests directly, meaning they could take petitions from East Africa to the immigration office. The government allocated $10,000, partially subsidized by the UNHCR, for 1968 for new arrivals, including job training, language instruction, and "special help to particularly difficult cases."[92] This fund was managed by Mohamed al-Mulla, Dubai minister of state and vice president of the Chamber of Commerce, as well as the UNHCR counselor for refugee affairs in the Gulf.[93] Noted Goodyear, "At a time when increasing restrictions are being placed on all other groups, Zanzibaris are allowed in even without papers or entry visas. This facility has now been extended to persons arriving by air, a concession previously denied."[94] Housing was a significant obstacle in the way of the Dubai community normalizing themselves as citizens. High rent rates caused by rapid urbanization meant many residents were spending half their yearly income on housing.[95] The UNHCR proposed a project whereby the Dubai ruler would provide land, the refugees a further 25 percent of the cost through a loan, and the UNHCR the remainder. The goal was to build fifty houses, at a total cost of $135,000. The ruler built seventy-five homes for Zanzibaris in the Rashidiya neighborhood of Dubai, for 36,000 dirhams. The occupants paid a mortgage of 500 dirhams/month.[96]

In Abu Dhabi in the early 1970s there were some fifty Zanzibari families, a total of four hundred persons. Mr. Said Mohamed Lamky was president of the Zanzibar Association.[97] Direct communication between the Zanzibar Association and the rulers is less evident, perhaps due to the UNHCR's more restricted role there. The cost of living was higher, and the community standard of living lower, than in Dubai; the Zanzibar Association was aiding eight needy families. Abu Dhabi's government also sent money to the UNHCR to support the community's needs. There was virtually no route to local nationality; only a few Zanzibaris had obtained Abu Dhabi passports after five years' residence and naturalization. Fifty refugee families in Abu Dhabi were also trying to obtain national passports for similar reasons; many possessed only an entry visa or NOC from Dubai, but not a full passport.[98]

ZANZIBARIS IN DAMMAN, DOHA, AND KUWAIT

The community in Damman, Saudi Arabia, was organized around the exiled Imam of Oman and made up of two to three hundred people, with another twenty-seven families (approximately one hundred people) in Jeddah, all of whom held Imamate passports, including the former qadi of Zanzibar. As elsewhere, the community faced difficulty normalizing their residence and obtaining access to higher education.[99] The exiled Omani Imam in exile had issued Imamate passports to Zanzibaris with the knowledge of the government of Saudi Arabia.[100] Zanzibari refugees in Saudi Arabia strategically used them to position themselves as refugees of Omani origin. In a letter to Saudi representatives, they claimed that "it was not correct to claim there has been expulsion of Zanzibaris. The issue is one of expulsion of Omani Arabs of Zanzibar origin." Refugees in Saudi Arabia, although not legally Omani citizens, protested that "they ha[d] been granted the privilege to settle ... as Omanis and not as Zanzibaris or refugees from Zanzibar."[101]

Zanzibaris also went to Kuwait and to the smaller Emirates; Muhammad Abdul-Muttalib Hashim went there from Dubai in 1966 on a scholarship facilitated by Ahmed Lamky. Some of them had moved there from Zanzibar or Oman in the early to mid-1950s to seek employment.[102] Ali Ahmed al-Riyami's sons and daughters spent the last part of the 1960s moving between Kuwait, Ras al-Khaymah, and Dubai.[103] Ahmed al-Riyami left Zanzibar in 1965, went to Mombasa, and from there boarded the ship SS *Camphuys* to Mukallah, Hadhramaut. He had been sent an Imamate passport to be able to travel freely. From Mukallah he attempted to enter Oman but was refused, and went to Dubai instead. On his arrival in Dubai, he was hosted by Zanzibaris and obtained temporary employment, before joining his brothers in Kuwait, via Dammam.[104]

In Kuwait in 1965–1967, Ahmed, his brother, and a schoolmate from Zanzibar all shared an apartment in the Mirqaab neighborhood of Kuwait City. While his roommates had white-collar jobs (at an insurance company and a bank, respectively), there were ten other bachelors from Zanzibar staying in the flat who were looking for work, including, for a time, Ahmed Hamoud al-Maamiry.[105] The men relied on support from Zanzibaris already in Kuwait, as well as members of the Imamate office there. Ahmed's younger brothers, Muhammad and Said, completed their secondary education in Dubai.[106] Ali's daughters enrolled in nursing school in Dubai.[107] Of their associations with other Zanzibaris in Ras al-Khaymah,

Ahmed observed, "We lived a very communal life amongst ourselves, Zanzibari refugees."[108] The Zanzibaris were employed in various industries, at the oil company, in the hospitals, in the ruler's office, and at the banks. Ahmed narrated that he was able to purchase a home in Ras al-Khaymah through financing available from Sheikh Saqr Muhammad Salim al-Qasimi.[109]

The situation of the Zanzibaris in Doha, Qatar, was also very different than that of Dubai, and this affected the viability of a separate organization for community interests. In the late 1960s, the emirate of Qatar was not yet formally independent of the British.[110] Approximately forty Zanzibari families (ninety persons) were living in Doha in late 1967. Most of them had arrived at another Gulf destination first. Qatar was also an educational destination for Zanzibaris.[111] In other cases, Zanzibaris had migrated there because wages were significantly higher than in the other Emirates.[112] Many unemployed Zanzibaris from Dubai, and even from Muscat, were migrating temporarily to Doha (and Bahrain and Dammam). Goodyear noted the diversity of passports of the Zanzibari Association members living in Doha, most of whom had Muscati (twenty) or Omani (seventeen) passports, issued by the Omani Imam in exile in Saudia Arabia. A few (three) had certificates of identity, having come direct from Zanzibar. Two others carried Dubai travel documents.[113]

In Doha, the refugees were prohibited from having an officially recognized Zanzibar Association, as were most all expatriate, non-Qatari groups.[114] The Zanzibari refugees (mostly immigrants from other Emirates) believed being allowed to form an association would assist them in obtaining residence permits, by enabling the association itself to act as a sponsor. Their reason for thinking this was Qatari recognition of the Palestinian Liberation Organization (PLO). Zanzibaris asserted to Goodyear that job seekers were prioritized by national origin, with Arabs from the Gulf allegedly just below Qataris in priority, and Palestinians after that. Nevertheless, they complained, they were not treated as Arabs from the Gulf, and Palestinians often received priority in employment (according to them). As a result, the refugees had difficulty obtaining sponsorship required for a residence permit and thus faced discrimination in the labor market.[115] Qatari authorities countered that this priority in employment applied only to the petroleum industry, and that at any rate, Zanzibaris' lack of fluency in Arabic barred them access to some jobs. The Qatari director of immigration stressed that Qatar faced problems finding its own citizens' employment after their return from higher education abroad, much less immigrants.[116]

In an unusual case, three Zanzibaris who were cousins of the exiled Sultan Jamshid were issued "certificates of identity" by the British political agent in Doha, after being refused renewal of their Tanzanian passport and being denied an Imamate passport (on account of their association with the Busaidi ruling family). One of the three used this certificate to visit family from Zanzibar living in Mombasa, Kenya. Mr. Ward, the political agent, pressed Goodyear to ask the Qatari immigration director, Ali Ansari, to issue red booklets granting the three permanent residence in Qatar without nationality.

In another case, a Zanzibari refugee had struck and killed a pedestrian, leading to his imprisonment and the imposition of a sizable fine of QDR 16,000, or approximately $3,368. The community, through appeals to the network of Zanzibaris in the Gulf, had raised QDR 10,000. UNHCR paid half of the remaining 6,000, with the remainder guaranteed by two Zanzibari employees of the British Bank of the Middle East. Goodyear held out hope that the Zanzibaris could obtain more success in the Emirate with a powerful Qatari patron, and as such he entreated Sheikh Faleh bin Nasser al-Thani, a member of the Qatari ruling family, to intercede on the community's behalf.[117]

By the early 1970s, Goodyear reported that the community in Qatar had almost all converted their Imamate passports into a claim on Omani sultanate nationality. "Since my last visit in late 1970, a number of families have moved to Muscat, following the opening up of development there, leaving only a total of 8 families (27 persons) living in Qatar on a permanent basis."[118] Goodyear stressed that "those remaining had permanent employment, but remained concerned about reuniting with other family members.... They also wished to obtain higher education for themselves or offspring, and to access a passport that would enable them of free movement." In 1971, four families still held soon-to-be-useless Imamate passports, now rendered invalid by the Arab League's recognition of the sultanate. Goodyear was working with a Zanzibari personal adviser to the sultan of Oman to arrange the conversion of these documents into a claim on Omani citizenship.[119]

THE OMANI COUP AND NEGOTIATING OMANI NATIONALITY IN DUBAI

In 1970 the first wave of Zanzibari refugees were eligible for Dubai naturalization.[120] They nevertheless faced a dilemma brought on by political change in nearby Oman. A July 1970 palace coup, engineered and encouraged by British officials within the state, installed Said bin Taimur's son Qaboos as the new sultan. To jump-start development, the state began to liberally issue passports to Omani nationals outside the country, including in East Africa.

Reaching Dubai as a Zanzibari exile in the late 1960s already potentially promised an easier route to Omani nationality for those escaping Zanzibar on the increasingly rare Imamate passport. As one official wrote to Goodyear, "It may be easier in practice for an Omani to establish his claim to Sultanate nationality if he is in Dubai then if he in Tanzania simply because of the greater speed with which mails between Dubai and Muscat."[121] Imamate passports were issued abroad for a short time, while the Imamate itself was underground or co-opted within Oman. Neither the Trucial States (later to become the UAE) nor Muscat recognized the Imamate passport, although Bahrain and Qatar did.[122] Of these, Goodyear clarified in a later memo that "the Omani passports cannot be considered as providing nationality as the Iman(sic) of Oman is presently living in exile and the country forms part of Muscat and Oman. Those on Muscati passports are presumably not refugees."[123]

Goodyear noted that the general procedure was for families in the Emirates to obtain an Imamate passport from the exiled Imam in Saudi Arabia and send this to family members in Zanzibar privately; the passport could also be obtained from the Imamate's offices in Cairo and Kuwait. The family would then send the Imamate passport with its stamps privately to family in Zanzibar, prestamped for entry to the UAE. In Dar-es-Salaam, the passport could also enable the issuing of an NOC from Dubai or Abu Dhabi, which would serve as a de facto entry visa and allow the British official in Dar-es-Salaam to authorize travel.[124] This passport allowed some Zanzibar refugees to reach Dubai, even though Imamate passports were not recognized by the Sultanate of Muscat and Oman, and although UNHCR officials opined that the Imamate passport could not be considered as providing nationality.

By the end of 1970, watching events unfold in Oman, Zanzibaris in Dubai increasingly wondered if they should wait for Dubai naturalization or risk a "return" to Oman. Many ended up converting their contingent national status in the Emirates to full Omani citizenship in the 1970s.[125] This proved to be an advantageous move; Zanzibaris in the Emirates finally received a passport in 1974, but it was not a full federal passport.[126] To this day there are Zanzibaris residing permanently in Dubai and other places in the UAE, many with family in Oman. Many are effectively stateless as a result of the failure of the UAE federal government to approve their citizenship claims.

WORKING AND STUDYING IN THE GULF: LABOR, EMPLOYMENT, AND EDUCATION PATTERNS

Higher education was a paramount goal for Zanzibaris coming of age in diaspora. A major problem was that Zanzibaris were generally better educated and required a higher level of primary and secondary education than was available almost anywhere in the Gulf during this period. As Goodyear observed, "Academic standards in Zanzibar seem to have been very high; here they are abysmally low."[127] Another major issue was transitioning to a new language environment and learning Arabic. The language transition most directly affected adolescents arriving from Zanzibar who had to transition from an English system in primary or secondary school to an Arabic system. To continue with their education locally they needed to demonstrate Arabic fluency.[128]

In Dubai and in Doha, the Zanzibaris' lack of fluency in Arabic was mentioned as a distinct liability. Some Zanzibaris drove taxis, and though they were part of a select group able to get taxi licenses, their lack of fluency in Arabic limited their employment.[129] The association in Dubai worked to hire teachers and rent a facility to teach Arabic and start classes in English typing, shorthand, and bookkeeping. Arabic classes, which initially had a Zanzibari enrollment of fifty to sixty people. The teacher also spoke Swahili and could assist in translating between the two languages.[130] Goodyear committed UNHCR to pay 50 percent of the fees for refugee children attending the English-language school in Dubai who were cut off from completing secondary education in Zanzibar.[131] The Zanzibar Association also ran Arabic classes for young children to enable them to enter the Kuwait School in Dubai. In Goodyear's 1971 report, he noted, "There are presently plans for the commencement of a six-month crash course in Arabic to be given to all candidates for technical training before the entrance examination next July."[132]

Literacy in English drastically increased one's employment chances in some sectors of the Gulf in the 1960s and 1970s. Some Zanzibaris found jobs in various white-collar professions in the Gulf as a result. For instance, in Fujairah, a small number of Zanzibaris were employed at the British Bank of the Middle East.[133] Ahmed Ali al-Riyami and some of his Zanzibari colleagues also found jobs in banks. Others opened private tutoring businesses. A number worked for the oil companies, both state and private.[134]

Gulf rulers made scholarships available to some. In the late 1960s, Sheikh Zayed in Abu Dhabi offered ten scholarships for Zanzibaris in the Trucial States to attend the new Gulf Technical College in Bahrain or alternately the trade schools in Dubai, Sharjah, and Ras al-Khaymah. By 1971 several Zanzibaris from Oman were attending the former institution. In the late 1960s and early 1970s some Zanzibaris worked as nurses in Dubai or another emirate, then used their resident status to apply to the United Kingdom for higher studies.[135] The Qatari government offered six scholarships to Zanzibaris for study abroad. The exiled Imam of Oman in Saudi Arabia sponsored two scholarships for community members to study in Iraq.

The keenness of the displaced Zanzibaris in Dubai for educational opportunities led them to approach Ali Hassan Abdulla, secretary to the Sudanese Ministry of Local Government, who had traveled as a representative of the Sudan Ministry of Education to meet Sudanese schoolteachers employed in Dubai. The Zanzibaris asked for primary education for ages nine to fourteen, vocational training, and "higher education for gymnasium graduates."[136] Younger children adjusted to primary school in Arabic, while older children had to search for further opportunities in English. A visit from Dr. Jack Barakat of the UN Relief and Works Agency (UNRWA) staff in Beirut led him to select eight candidates for vocational training in Beirut. Barakat said the main difficulty would be in "obtaining passports for the Zanzibaris, who were stateless." Goodyear advised Barakat to approach the ruler of Dubai and to consider "offering scholarships for training in nursing to Zanzibaris next year. . . . [T]he training of Zanzibaris in medical work might help us to overcome here the shortage of local nurses. There is no lack of candidates."[137] Dr. Barakat said the main difficulty would be obtaining passports for the Zanzibaris, who were stateless. T. J. Clark of British Political Agency Trucial States, Dubai, declined to give assistance but recommended approaching the ruler of Dubai for Dubai passports for the students.[138]

ZANZIBARI WOMEN IN DIASPORA

As they would be later in Oman, women from Zanzibar were some of the earliest Arab women to enter the modern Gulf workforce. Some of this was by necessity, as jobs were scarce, and whichever family member had the most secure residence status often worked to support the rest, as well as any new arrivals. Still, Zanzibari women especially faced lack of suitable educational and employment opportunities. Dubai law at the time, according to the UNHCR, officially prevented women from working outside the home. In 1971 "Khadija," the vice president of the Zanzibar Women's Welfare Association in Dubai, wrote to Goodyear requesting attention to the needs of Zanzibar refugee women. The organization was founded in mid-1970 and now had more than ninety women as members. The organization met once a month at the Zanzibar Association premises.[139] Khadija requested more English schools; postsecondary education assistance, especially scholarships; and secure housing. Not insensitive to the ongoing plight of those in Zanzibar, the organization requested the UN to help those escaping forced marriages in Zanzibar.[140] Finally, they requested national passports.[141]

In June 1970, "Faiza" wrote to the UN office in Riyadh requesting consideration of her case. Faiza requested a scholarship to study abroad, preferably in an English system, and to work as a stenographer. She had found it difficult to obtain employment in Saudi Arabia. She had only completed secondary school in Zanzibar just before independence. Her father had passed away during the revolution, and the family often depended on her irregular income.[142]

Other female refugees faced painful dilemmas in their search for gainful employment. One case was "Firdaws" and her two sons, aged three and five. Her husband had been an education officer and owner of a large clove plantation in Zanzibar. He was imprisoned for three months after the revolution before being released on Karume's intervention. A few months later he was again apprehended and taken outside of town, where he was executed without trial. Firdaws's brother shared in this ordeal but survived and thereafter escaped Zanzibar and went to Dubai, along with Firdaws and their families. Though she was the widow of a wealthy member of the elite, Firdaws faced straitened employment prospects as a forty-year-old woman without formal education. Her brother was already supporting six children, as well as his mother-in-law back in Zanzibar. Her brother's salary was unstable; he had been a merchant in Zanzibar but had few goods to sell as a refugee in Dubai. Firdaws's sister-in-law supported the entire family on the meager salary she earned giving tutoring lessons in her home.[143] Displacement made the value of education acutely evident to the generation raised and educated in exile.

SOCIAL AND IDEOLOGICAL DIMENSIONS OF ZANZIBARI DIASPORA COMMUNITIES

The struggles of Zanzibari refugee in the Gulf are evident in a story related in the UNHCR archives. "Muhammad," who owned a fleet of taxis before the revolution, lost most of them to revolutionary expropriation. He decided to leave and go to Dubai, and he left his four children with his brother until he was settled enough to send for them. On the three-week voyage by dhow to the Gulf, his wife bonded with another refugee family with four children, and the two families became closely intertwined. Shortly after arrival in Dubai, his wife's friend, the other mother, died. Her husband then returned to Zanzibar to marry his wife's sister, to have someone to look after the four children. He (temporarily) entrusted the children to Muhammad and his wife. However, after arriving back on the islands, he was prevented from leaving again. Muhammad worked as a taxi driver in Dubai but faced difficulties, as he spoke neither English nor Arabic. In the end, he and his wife were supporting another couple's four children in Dubai, on a meager income, while their own four children could not leave Zanzibar.[144] The UNHCR worked with the ruler of Dubai to make available emergency funds for him to buy a taxi and obtain a taxi license (normally reserved only for Dubai citizens).[145]

Displacement from the islands and living in diaspora caused a generational shift. To some imprisoned exiles individual conversion and cultivation of believers in prison became a task as important as the tasks of national development had been. Among older members in diaspora, this involved an inward turn and heightened levels of social conservatism. In short, they became more pragmatic, more private, and more pious. Many also actively resisted efforts by more politically mobilized exiles to participate in what they deemed quixotic schemes for counterrevolution.[146] Their pragmatism was generally shared by Zanzibaris in the Gulf, who were striving in the burgeoning economy while attempting to reconstitute families and secure a future outside Zanzibar. As a dispersed and then reconstituted community in the Gulf, they confirm Yuval-Davis's description of diaspora communities as more ideologically flexible than political exiles, as shown in their actions to obtain local national or resident status, obtain employment, get married, and buy property. They were interested primarily in higher education and employment and were necessarily attuned to the matter of nationality and right of residence, since employment and education were privileges rendered by nationality or other official state recognitions of legal resident status.[147] The forms of piety they cultivated in diaspora justified a healthy distance from secular political engagement.

An example of these trends can be found in the work of the Zanzibari exile Ahmed Hamoud al-Maamiry. After the revolution he emigrated to Dubai, where he served as secretary of the Zanzibar Association.[148] In his 1983 book, *Islamism and Economic Prosperity in Third World Countries*, written after his ethnic return migration to Oman, al-Maamiry's thirst for an alternative to his frustration with the great Western world blocs and their philosophies (basically capitalism and socialism) found an outlet in an older ideologies, which he deemed to have more harmoniously combined elements of both.[149] Al-Maamiry unambiguously declared his faith in Islam as the solution for many of the world's ills. He argued for Islam as the golden mean between capitalism and socialism, "but unlike any of them ... not man-made."[150] While living in an absolutist state, he praised Islam as a universal, nonracial, nondoctrinal solution, the only alternative to the hero worship of state dictatorship.[151]

TENSIONS BETWEEN ZANZIBARI EXILE DISCOURSE AND DIASPORA COMMUNITIES

As Zanzibaris outside of Zanzibar began to naturalize locally and even take up citizenship in the UAE and Oman, Kharusi and the more politically minded exiles voiced concern about what they saw as a disconnect by exiles from the suffering in Zanzibar. The criticism reflected a generational divide generated by two basic sets of fissures generated in diaspora. First was the distinction between politically active exiles and more locally embedded diaspora communities, the latter generally eschewing controversial political involvement. Second was the distinction between a Zanzibar nationalist generation who continued to think of Zanzibar as their national homeland

and a generation who, because of increasingly difficult circumstances in Zanzibar, decided to "cut their losses" and focus on more immediate and careerist goals of making a living and ensuring a future for their offspring.

At the end of December 1970, a Zanzibari exile wrote to Kharusi asking how the opening of Oman would influence a return to Zanzibar. There is suggestive evidence from Kharusi's later editorial writing that he thought that migration to Oman was influencing that desire. In a criticism written in 1973 Kharusi described a "type of exile who lives in prosperity and forgets the oppression that drove into foreign climes," arguing that such individuals were a liability to their adopted countries because he (Kharusi used the masculine singular) was "only concerned in saving his own skin, and on first signs of trouble in his new surroundings he packs his bags and leaves." He criticized those who took "greater pride that they have started from scratch and are now heads of this department or that firm." They could be found everywhere, he wrote, from Britain, Kenya, Tanganyika, Kuwait, Oman, and the Comoros. "Their acquisition of local nationality has made them feel safe and secure, and thus complacent about the ongoing atrocities in their homeland." An exile who "forgets and rejects his country of origin," opined Kharusi, "is not fit to live in any other country."[152] Kharusi urged the exiles, regardless of what new passport or citizenship they secured, to maintain a feeling of duty and obligation to the Zanzibar homeland.[153]

Kharusi's characterization reflected broader generational change in the diaspora. Kharusi's generation largely saw little contradiction between Islam and their articulations of nationalism and nationality. Other Afro-Arabs in diaspora developed a contrasting vision of Islam as a form of purposeful withdrawal into personal spiritual development and fell back on what transnational networks they still possessed for access to higher education. They rejected strong-arm tactics by some exiles to demand funds and commitment from the diaspora.[154] As this chapter has shown, Zanzibari exiles in the Gulf during the late 1960s and early 1970s, despite the links of some to the ruler in Dubai, were hardly generally prosperous. Instead, most struggled with securing residence, education, and employment, to say nothing of the trauma they processed privately. The gap between them and Kharusi was ideological and generational, a reflection of naturally divergent preoccupations caused by the contingent circumstances of a muwalladūn Zanzibari community split by the revolution and their displacement from Zanzibar during a crucial period of their education and development. A resistance to this vulnerability manifested itself as a conscious decision in diaspora to identify outside Zanzibar as "Arab" first and then Zanzibari.[155]

CONCLUSION

This chapter showed the development of Zanzibari diaspora communities in the Gulf Emirates during a period of intense economic and political development in the history of Dubai and other Gulf Emirates. Escaping political repression and economic privation on the islands, Zanzibaris entered the Emirates when processes of urbanization and formalization of national citizenship were rapidly accelerating. They proved useful to several Emirati rulers, especially Sheikh Rashid in Dubai. With Dubai as a base, Zanzibaris spread throughout the Gulf, seeking employment and educational opportunities, with small communities in Abu Dhabi, Damman, Kuwait City, and Doha. As the 1960s turned into the 1970s, it seemed increasingly unlikely to many of the exiled children that it would be possible to ever return to Zanzibar. Some of them subsequently converted a Dubai form of conditional nationality into Omani citizenship, after the 1970 palace coup that brought Sultan Qaboos to power. The dynamic of the ethnic return migration to Oman is examined in chapter 5.

PART THREE

Belonging in Oman

FIVE

Return Migration from East Africa and the Politics of Citizenship in Oman, 1970–2020

REVERSING THE INTERWAR TREND of impoverished members of families from interior Oman coming to Zanzibar, after 1970 Oman became a receiving country for migration.[1] The phrase "ethnic return migration"' refers to later generations of a diaspora returning to an ancestral homeland, usually to assume permanent national status, often due to political upheaval in their state of residence or in response to a particular economic incentive.[2] Return migration from East Africa to Oman was shaped by the push factor of deteriorating quality of life in East Africa after 1973 and the pull factor of the dearth of an indigenous technically educated labor force in Oman.[3] Eventually Omani state policy facilitated the admission and settlement of a substantial number of Swahili-speaking professionals from East Africa with attenuated Omani roots, including many from Zanzibar.[4]

Today perhaps as much of a tenth of the population of three million Omani citizens has family ties to East Africa.[5] Because of the lack of desire to advertise their exogenous birthplaces, and because the state does not officially keep records on the subject, there are really no reliable estimates. Out of all returnees from East Africa, those from Zanzibar, because of their statelessness, were uniquely invested in the ideology of Qaboos's accession to rule, and they eagerly cultivated his patronage, offering the state their service as professionals and managers of the new "modern" state bureaucracy.[6] In the process of return and assumption of leadership in the new state institutions, most accommodated themselves very smoothly to their professional roles. While the returnee experience was not unitary, and some were disgruntled by the experience, the stateless returnees from Zanzibar were overwhelmingly promonarchy, and many of them provided a bulwark against more republican sympathies among Omanis by serving in the Omani police forces, armed forces, and security services.[7]

Studies of European empire in East Africa have focused our attention on moments when imperial citizens made claims on metropolitan citizenship and the tragic and often callous way metropolitan governments retreated from earlier promises of civic, imperial citizenship for all colonial subjects. Although Omani imperial rule was dissolved in 1861, not 1964, the legacy of Busaidi rule in Zanzibar and Omani migration throughout East Africa meant that the 1970 call for an Omani diaspora to return was broadly similar to other postimperial situations in which former colonial metropoles defined the content of their new national citizenship in relation to former colonial subjects with mixed or exogenous origins.[8] The history of the returnees thus gives insight into the sociohistorical evolution of Omani citizenship after 1970 and its connections to various sources of legitimation, including the passport, paternal ancestry, linguistic fluency, and cultural behavior. It also shows how contestation over the "ordinary habits" of returnees from East Africa helped define the legal and socio-cultural contents of Omani national citizenship.[9]

Liisa Malkki has observed that "the range of different meanings attaching to citizenship and to the documentary construction of identity shows how inadequate is the common assumption that when a person 'assimilates', he or she simply gains elements of a new cultural identity while losing something definite from the old identity in the bargain."[10] Returnees from East Africa are a unique case study of the fractures and sutures between the legal possession of an Omani passport and the broader social criteria for national belonging in Oman.[11] Afro-Arabs from Zanzibar pluralized the legal and social dimensions of Omani citizenship, which was being reimagined in the 1970s as a newly hegemonic national territorial identity. Their political quiescence allowed them space to make skilled internal contestations of others' assumptions about the presumed cultural homogeneity of the new Omani nationalist imagination.

RETURN MIGRATION FROM EAST AFRICA AND OBTAINING OMANI CITIZENSHIP

Uniquely in modern times, becoming an Omani national citizen was a process involving application and acquisition of the Omani passport, with paternal ancestry as the basic criteria for its legal acquisition. Citizenship was thus based on the selection of a limited set of patrilineal kin relationships that could be bureaucratically secured by the modern state, proving one's membership in a set of larger clan groups deemed to be indigenous to the territory.[12] All ethnic communities in Oman were legally "tribalized" in their relations with the state by taking an approved tribal identity, and some people served the Ministry of Interior as representatives of the tribe.[13]

Early on in his reign, Sultan Qaboos expressed that the stateless condition of the Zanzibaris was not merely an Omani issue but concerned the whole world and all the Arab countries.[14] He was also well aware of the boon returnees were to the state; he told a Zanzibar government minister that "they came when Omanis were not educated and took most of the senior government positions. . . . Oman didn't spend a single cent on their education."[15] The common practice, to which the state gave its imprimatur, was for tribal authorities to write "recommendation letters" containing a sworn declaration establishing a claimant as a member of that tribe, which were approved by the local *wali* of the district where the returnee claimed a kinship connection, and then by a committee of local authorities. Returnees would be issued passports based on being "vouched for" by local authorities. After 1970, this role was often filled by the "sheikh rashid," a state intermediary between individuals and the public administration who would certify a person's lineage in order to deliver a passport.[16] Increasingly the passport was understood as an instrument of national identity, and a single exclusive passport was the proof of one's true intentions and loyalties vis-à-vis the imagined community of the nation.

A returnee recounted the process of getting Omani visas for East African family members after the sultan first extended the invitation to return. The official invitation was propagated through word of mouth among Omani family networks. He said that usually a family member in Oman, such as a sheikh or *wali* of a tribe, would go to the ministry with the paperwork and the passports. He would then send letters to applicants asking for their biodata and photos. With these in hand, he would proceed with the photos, fill out the passports himself at the ministry, and have them stamped before they were sent to applicants in East Africa. During the first half of the 1970s, Omani communities in Africa had begun to receive information trickled back from relatives and friends that it was possible for the first time to come to Oman and apply for Omani citizenship based on a descent claim.[17] Omani passports also began to be sent to the many family members escaping Zanzibar to Mombasa, Dubai, and the United Kingdom.[18] The Ministry of Foreign Affairs processed thousands of visa applications in the early 1970s, many of them for return migrants from East Africa.[19] Five of Ali Muhsin's children were granted Omani citizenship in the early 1970s, while he was still imprisoned in Tanzania.[20]

Instead of going back to the interior villages their ancestors had left in the nineteenth and early twentieth centuries, the Zanzibaris settled in new urban neighborhoods: initially Medinat Qaboos (a planned development completed in 1973), Ruwi, Wattayah, Qurum, and later Mina al-Fahal and Medinat al-Nahda. Ibtisam al-Habsi captured the ad hoc character of the rapid changes in Muscat because of rapid in-migration, urbanization, and various development plans: "Things didn't go smoothly. Muscat, or rather the Mutrah area where we came ashore, was still underdeveloped in 1972. The number of people slowly returning, arriving, responding to the change in regime, had caused a kind of euphoria but also chaos in the districts beyond the main mercantile area. Most people had no real idea what was going on."[21] Many returnees commented on the low state of development in Oman at the time. A member of the Omani State Council (Majlis al-Dawla), born in Tanzania, recalled that although his father was "very patriotic about Oman," when his relatives invited him back to Ibra in the interior, he found there was no basic sanitation in the town.[22]

The last half of the decade of the 1970s saw Oman's development plans in full swing.[23] Oman's first major growth era occurred from 1973 to 1986. By 1973 a new harbor was completed at Mina al-Qaboos; in 1974, a new national telephone company, Omantel, was founded; and in 1976 an international airport and a dual carriageway constructed in Muscat.[24] The country was for the first time connected independently via a satellite station in the Hajar Bowl, to a larger network of satellites in the Middle East, Europe, and the United States.[25] Construction was booming everywhere, as returnees built houses on lands given to them by the state.[26]

LABOR, DEVELOPMENT, AND THE RETURNEES

During the first five years of the Qaboos regime, ministries in Oman were heavily dependent on expatriate expertise and labor. The process of nation-building in Oman depended on training a new national bourgeoisie in European and American metropolitan universities to return and indigenize the various ministries and other state institutions. Zanzibari return migration helped speed up this process by providing a class of skilled laborers and administrators to fill positions that otherwise would have been filled by European expatriates. As one returnee put it, "In early days of Omani renaissance, someone with a diploma could have an advanced position."[27]

Ahmed al-Riyami shows the rapidity with which many of the returnees from East Africa became managers and supervisors because of their prior experience in Zanzibar. In 1958–1959 he had been a station clerk for East African Airways, and in 1959–1960 he worked as a cashier with the Zanzibar Electricity Board.[28] Reaching Oman in 1973, Ahmed worked first for an international fishery and then for the American embassy. He was subsequently selected for a management trainee program at the Qaboos Port Authority, and his family moved into villas provided by the government.[29]

The national oil corporation is another case in point. Many returnees worked for Petroleum Development Oman (PDO), the national oil and gas company (now Oman Oil). In 1970, all but 3 of 210 senior staff positions at the company were filled by European (mostly British) expatriates.[30] Returnees from East Africa educated in technical fields were among the first trained as their replacements.[31] Some received scholarships to study petroleum engineering in the United Kingdom or United States. The company also provided employees with loans to buy land and houses. Salim Muhammad al-Mawaly was a public health inspector in Zanzibar before joining PDO.[32] Saif Hamed al-Hinai came from Tanzania thinking of a career in journalism but joined PDO under the influence of his relatives and became oil director of PDO's northern directorate in 2002. Abdullah Lamky, another returnee, was formerly the number two executive at PDO. The Omani billionaire Muhammad al-Barwani, chair of MB Holdings and current CEO of Oman Air, also began his career at PDO. He is the son of a returnee from Zanzibar, Ali Muhammad al-Barwani.[33] Similarly, Warith al-Kharusi, born in Zanzibar and raised in the United Kingdom, came to Oman in 1979 and joined PDO, before starting al-Kharusi motors with his brothers and then in 1986 setting up al-Safwa Group, managing businesses in logistics, property, information, communication, and tourism.[34] Hamed al-Harassy, who grew up in Zanzibar, worked from 1975 to 2005 for PDO and later continued running the business he had founded while still a PDO employee, the Teejan Group. His father, an Omani emigrant to Zanzibar, had run a small shop in Zanzibar.[35] The former minister of gas and oil, Muhammad al-Rumhi, was born in Zanzibar and is fluent in

Swahili. He, along with Salem ben Nasser al-Ismaily, led a high-level Omani state visit to Tanzania in 2017.

A main characteristic of the growth of the developmental state is the growth of the civil service as employer, which by the 1990s composed nearly a quarter of Oman's total work force.[36] Zanzibaris were very active in the civil service and other managerial-level government positions. For instance, a returnee educated in engineering at Brighton Technical College and originally posted as a civil engineering assistant in Zanzibar's Public Works Department, Obed Saif al-Hatmi, became the technical director of Greater Mutrah, with planning authority for Muscat.[37] His vision of the new urban space of the city was eventually sidelined, leading to his resignation.[38] A returnee, Ahmed Muhammad Ali al-Hinawy, was president of the Chamber of Commerce.[39] Seif Hamoud al-Bahlani was a general manager at Oman's national airline, Oman Air.[40] The first deputy minister of health in Qaboos Oman was Said Shaksy, who had previously served in the Zanzibari civil service. By 1996 the health network included 48 hospitals, 5 polyclinics, 114 health centers, and 28 mobile health units.[41] In an interview in Muscat, Shaksy reflected:

> In 1970, Seyyid Tariq appointed me in the Ministry of Finance, and then as the first Undersecretary in the Health Department. Dr. Asim Jamali was head of the Health Department in Dubai, and was later appointed Minister of Health in Oman, but he had no idea how to set up a ministry.... *I had good experience setting up ministry during the transition from the British protectorate to independence in Zanzibar.* We inherited about 35 employees all together, including 11 doctors. I spent five years in the Ministry of Health and during that time we built the ministry from almost zero to a staff of 4,000.... There were no housing facilities in Oman, there were no roads. We had to do many things simultaneously.[42]

Another prominent returnee in the Ministry of Health was Dr. Wahid al-Kharusi, who was born in Zanzibar and educated in England. He arrived in Oman in 1971 and helped to contribute to the organization and expansion of the Ministry.[43]

Because of their fluency in English and wider experience of the world, returnees were often tapped for the Omani diplomatic corps in the Ministry of Foreign Relations. A returnee from mainland Tanzania, Nasser al-Bualy served in the first post-1970 Omani diplomatic corps; he also assisted the Omani diaspora in East Africa with their resettlement in the sultanate. Fareed al-Hinai, who served in the Kenya diplomatic corps before returning to Oman, was at one time the Omani ambassador to the United States and to China.⁴⁴ Saud Ahmed al-Busaidi, a former Zanzibar civil servant who witnessed the Libyan revolution and the ascension of Qaddafi while living for seven years in Tripoli, returned in the early 1970s and worked for the Ministry of Foreign Affairs in Iran and Qatar and then in the Ministry of the Interior.⁴⁵ The Cairo-educated Ahmed al-Lamky, who helped pioneer militant anticolonial nationalism in Zanzibar and helped connect Zanzibar's communities in diaspora, later became a member of the diplomatic corps and for a time was chief of African affairs in the Ministry of Foreign Affairs.⁴⁶ Ahmed Hamoud al-Maamiry, former president of the Zanzibar Association in Dubai, became Omani ambassador to India.⁴⁷ The Cairo- and UK-educated Omani diplomat Lyutha Sultan al-Mugheiry (appointed ambassador to Germany in 2016) is a returnee from Dar-es-Salaam, Tanzania, but her family has Zanzibari roots; her father, Sultan Ahmed, was famously assassinated for refusing to join with Arab nationalists in boycotting the Legislative Council.⁴⁸ Her younger sister, Hunaina Sultan al-Mugheiry, is also an influential Omani diplomat. Perhaps the most prominent returnee of all at the ministry is Dr. Salem ben Nasser al-Ismaily, who has been involved with Oman-Tanzania relations and was responsible for opening a back channel with US officials to broker the 2009 Iran deal.⁴⁹

Returnees were also very involved in the higher education sector; almost all of the Afro-Arabs trained as teachers by the Zanzibar protectorate ended up in Oman. Amour Ali Ameir al-Marhuby was a graduate of Oxford and a former director of education in the government of Zanzibar. He worked at the Jeanes School in Zomba Nyasaland between 1926 and 1930.⁵⁰ He rose through the ranks of Zanzibar's educational administration, eventually attaining the role of assistant director of education in September 1963, just a few months before the revolution. He was briefly imprisoned after the revolution and then went to Dar-es-Salaam. He eventually arrived in Oman in 1971 and was appointed as an adviser to the sultan for the establishment of scholastic and academic institutions. Al-Marhuby made recommendations in early 1980 for the creation of Sultan Qaboos University (SQU) and was its first vice chancellor.⁵¹ Plans for SQU began in 1980, announced on National Day. In September 1986 the university began instruction with 580 students.⁵² The first Omani faculty member in that university's chemistry department and first Omani full professor in the College of Sciences was a female returnee from Zanzibar, Dr. Salma al-Kindy.⁵³ Dr. Samir al-Adawi, professor of behavioral sciences at SQU, came from Zanzibar to Oman at the age of twelve; his family was one of those who escaped from the islands to the Tanzanian mainland and later came to Oman. Maulid Mshangama Haj, originally a district officer in Pemba, and who had as a young man in Zanzibar married into the Zanzibari royal family, moved to Oman in 1978 and in 1988 joined the College of Engineering at SQU, retiring in 1996.[54]

Many returning Zanzibaris had careers in the Ministry of Defense, the police force, and the security services.[55] One of the most remarkable was Fatma Salem al-Maamiry, aunt of the former minister of higher education. Dr. al-Maamiry obtained her PhD in Latin at University College London in 1955 and trained a generation of Arab Zanzibaris who went to Cairo for schooling. She migrated to Oman in the 1980s to teach English language to officers at the Defense Ministry.[56] Samira Salim Seif al-Maamiry, who began her teaching career in Zanzibar in 1948 at the Government Secondary School and became senior women's education officer before the revolution, later taught police cadets at the academy in Oman.

In spite of the stereotype of returnees not speaking Arabic fluently, among the returnees were prominent members of the ulama class in Zanzibar; they played a role in shaping religious education in the country. The most prominent modern Ibadi religious authority, the mufti of Oman, is Ahmed al-Khalili, a returnee from Zanzibar who came to Oman in January 1965, after his father's release from a Zanzibar prison, as part of the "Manga refugee" emigration described in chapter 2. When Khalili reached the family's ancestral home Baḥla in the interior, the local qadi praised God, "who brought him [al-Khalili] from Zanzibar so that we and our children may benefit."[57]

Because of their fluency in English, the returnees found themselves in demand as teachers. Shaaban Saleh al-Farsy (also spelled al-Farsi) migrated from Zanzibar to Mombasa in June 1975, where he was helped by Salim Muhashami to register as a refugee in order to immigrate to Oman.[58] Al-Farsy's son Muntasir, now an Omani author and lecturer, also migrated to Oman at this time. Al-Farsy's wife was given Omani citizenship and an Omani passport in 1987.[59] Al-Farsy, who was also a teacher in Zanzibar, continued his teaching career in Oman. Many returnees also entered the Ministry of Higher Education as lecturers. Said Abdulla Seif al-Hatimy had been a writer for a popular magazine for teachers published in Zanzibar, and had written various books on religion in English and Swahili before the 1964 revolution. He completed secondary school in the UAE and later became an English teacher there, before going to Oman in the early 1970s, where he taught English and Arabic at PDO and later at Oman's Religious Institute (the Ma'ahad al-Dīn).[60]

As they had been elsewhere in the Gulf, returnees were active in the growing Omani banking sector, as founders, managers, and midlevel employees. Said Shaksy was a founding member of Bank Muscat. The most highly trained returnees from Zanzibar frequently also became administrators; Issa Nasser al-Ismaily arrived in Oman in April 1976 and quickly moved through the ranks of the Central Bank of Oman, retiring in 1987.[61] Being fluent in English and often multilingual, returnees were often bank tellers and filled other public-facing customer service roles interfacing with expatriates from India, the United Kingdom, and the United States.

Some returnees were recruited into the new regime by the network of powerful British advisers within the state. Muhammad Ali al-Riyami was born in Zanzibar on October 17, 1953, and left the islands in 1972, after the assassination of Karume. He lived in Ras al-Khaymah before moving to Oman, where he was proceeded by brothers. After getting his higher education in Cairo, Muhammad took a job in the Ministry of Information, where he mainly worked in the Department of Public Relations. One day he was asked to accompany Anthony Ashworth to the airport. As Muhammad describes him, Ashworth was "His Majesty's Advisor, one of the very rare powerful British citizens. . . . [T]here were two or three of them. Number one was Tim Landon, number two was Tony Ashworth, and the only living one, General Bennett."[62] When he went with the driver to collect Mr. Ashworth, Ashworth got in and asked Muhammad to move from the front to sit in the back and talk with him. Muhammad was asked what he thought about Qaboos's policies, and Muhammad gave his opinions. He was, as he recalls, "a typical fresh graduate, full of ideas." The following day, at Ashworth's request, he was transferred to the Ministers Office within the Ministry of Information, at the time Ashworth's portfolio.

Returnees were thus well-represented in the civil service and other integral parts of the workforce that modernized the Omani state; they enjoyed proximity to British elites influential within the new Omani regime and were active in representing Oman internationally.[63] Several returnees were employed at the US embassy in Muscat.[64] The social capital they possessed due to their modern education more than counterbalanced their extraterritorial birth, lack of fluency in Arabic, and liberal social mores.

STATE APPROACHES TO RETURNEE CITIZENSHIP

Internally, Omani nationalism portrays the national citizen as a religiously and culturally homogenous ideal, substantially based on a reinvented Arabism. But there is also awareness and embrace by some Omanis of the historically multiethnic, multilingual, and multireligious dimensions of the national citizenry.⁶⁵ This diversity is not only something acquired through Indian Ocean travel but is a deeper legacy of the particular status of Ibadis as a "minority" madhab within the ummah. Along with Ibadism, the country's long history in the Indian Ocean has served as a motif for an Omani monarchy-centered cultural heritage of harmonious ethnic and religious pluralism among diverse ethnic and religious groups. The Omani national museum emphasizes the exceptionality of this Omani national-cultural heritage, positing the anchorage of the national character in histories of maritime exchange and the tolerant spread of Islam. The al-Busaidi dynasty in Zanzibar's cultural heritage exemplifies a past instantiation of this ideal, even as the living presence of Swahili speakers within the body of the Omani nation is viewed more ambivalently with respect to the nationalist emphasis on Arabism.

In official Omani state discourse, the Zanzibaris interviewed were referred to in Arabic as *'ā'idūn* (returnees). The Zanzibaris were portrayed as *mahjar* (temporary migrants) in East Africa and as merely on a sojourn from the Omani motherland. While this designation as temporary migrants was partly applicable to those who went from Oman to Zanzibar as children and later returned directly to Oman after the revolution, it did not apply to those third- and fourth-generation Afro-Arab families who had localized as Zanzibaris during the nationalist struggle there and later returned to Oman.⁶⁶ For them, the assumption of the social dimension of Omani citizenship was an act of imagination and invention.

Authorities sometimes interrogated the paternal genealogy of these returnees upon arrival and demanded they give up their Tanzanian or Kenyan passports. Once the returnees were in country, the state also made efforts to nativize them. The state incentivized endogamous marriage to fellow nationals.⁶⁷ The returnees were retribalized, taking on an official *nisba* (a clan or tribe name indicating paternal ancestry or corporate identity) as a surname if they didn't already have one. Many began wearing the newly proclaimed Omani "national" dress. They were also discouraged by other

Omanis from speaking Swahili in public, and their relatively "freer" attitudes to gender mixing were condemned as alien to traditional Omani society.[68]

Many Omanis also conceived of the returnees as a distinct ethnoracial category, the Zanjiyya. Though the Zanzibaris themselves are not a tribe, in common parlance, they were often thought of as a unified cultural group associated with certain cultural traits, sociolinguistic practices, and occupations.[69] The parallel but distinct trajectories of East African returnees and former slaves of African descent within Omani citizenship illuminate the old and new meanings of these contrasting expressions of exogenous origins as they confront each other in everyday social understandings and also show the fluidity of the term Zanj as both ethnonym and toponym.[70] Returnees to Oman from Zanzibar and mainland East Africa had mixed nationalities and long histories of cross-ethnic intermarriage with Swahili-speaking coastal East Africans. Third- and fourth-generation Arabs in East Africa had attenuated roots in the Omani homeland. They used the term *return* as a metaphor for becoming an Omani citizen, even when it was not expressive of a living connection to Omani kin. Former slaves, on the other hand, had formed historic relations of clientship with prominent Omani tribes and often adopted their patron's nisba.[71] Speaking Swahili and sometimes appearing darker skinned than other Omanis meant that muwalladūn Zanzibaris were sometimes assumed by some Omanis to be African and thus non-Arab, and thus possibly of khādim (slave) descent.[72]

The nickname for the Muscat neighborhood Medinat al-Naḥda—Chicago—reflects these tensions of race and ethnicity.[73] Some Omanis joked that the nickname came about because the area was overrun with drugs and gangs at one time. However, according to one returnee, the nickname really came about because "the government gave all the Africans [meaning in this case returnees] houses there." These overlapping dynamics between being from Africa and being of slave descent are also evident around families with deceased Omani fathers and in the discourse of the preservation of patrilineal and matrilineal purity among certain Arab groups.[74] It is also evident in the culturally rehearsed performances of loyalty and affiliation of the families of former slaves to the families of former masters, which I witnessed at an Omani wedding of a member of the royal family. However, it is important to emphasize that in the Omani context, language and culture are much more significant markers of difference in Oman than skin color; nonfluency in Arabic marks one out to others as non-Arab more than does one's complexion. In this respect, the returnees were sometimes regarded as more alien than the descendants of slaves, especially because of their "modern' lifestyles acquired through long residence in East Africa.

RETURNEE CONCEPTIONS OF OMANI CITIZENSHIP

The lived experiences of Omani nationalism among the returnees were considerably more complex than its representation in the official script. National formation of the returnees occurred in a dialectic between returnees' complex affiliation to Arabism or Africanity and the state's idealized image of an Omani citizen.[75] While many returnees also explicitly embraced the official vision of Omani nationalism, their oral histories reflect the complexity of their lived experience of Omani citizenship. Some embraced their "Omani-ness" as a natural extension of their primordial ancestry.[76] Many reaffirmed to me vernacular understandings of Omani citizenship in terms of purity of, if not ancestry alone, then ancestry and culture together, imagining their time in East Africa as a mere sojourn, in which their Omani culture was preserved from external influence and other effects of long-term residence abroad.[77] More than a few returnees glorified rural Tanzania as a place where Omani culture had been preserved in diaspora, which allowed them to assert that East African Arabs in the interior of Tanzania were more authentically Omani than the more modern urbanized Arabs of Muscat.

Others celebrated their culturally cosmopolitan attitude obtained through long East African residence, alongside the preservation of their ancestry and culture.[78] The Swahili novelist and Omani returnee Naila Barwani wrote a poetic commentary in Swahili on the entanglement of Omani identity with East Africa. Known in East African literary circles for such works as *Imepita Jana*, *Usinisahau* (Forget Me Not), and *Tamasha*, Naila's cosmopolitan family roots encompass Shirazi, Omani, Egyptian, Syrian, Yemeni, and Somali ancestry. In the early 1980s she came to Oman with her husband and family. In 1983 she authored a poem entitled "Zinjibari," emphasizing her pride in being from Zanzibar, knowing the Swahili language, and having Omani roots. Her poem translated shows returnees confirming the logic of ethnic descent, rather than refuting it. She gave greater weight to affective registers of belonging than to legal ones, but ultimately confirmed the possibility of a knowable nationality that is inextricable from the self as race:

> Waarabu wa Omani / Tumekuja Duniyani
> Jinsi Yetu Yakini / Mzizi Uliyo Ndani
> Ni Damu Yetu Mwilini / Hadi Kesho Kaburini
> Mu Omani Passpoti / Hiyo Siyo Hoja Yangu
> Kuwa Nayo si Shariti / Nithibiti Ulimwengu
> Sihitaji Makoriti / Kumjua Baba Yangu
>
> *Arabs of Oman, We Came into this World*
> *Indeed, this our nationality,*
> *that which is the blood in our bodies, until tomorrow we face death.*
> *Not an Omani passport, this is not my need*
> *To possess one is not necessary to prove to the world*
> *I don't need the courts in order to know who my father is*

In the next stanza, Barwani writes about Arab identity:

> Mwafrika Hawi China / Muhindi Hawi Mzungu
> Mwarabu Aso Shina / Hadanganyi ulimwengu
> Na Omani shaka sina / ninayo nasabu yangu
>
> *An African is not a Chinaman, an Indian is not a European.*
> *An Arab without roots cannot deceive the world*
> *And in Oman is my lineage, without a doubt.*

Still others attached themselves to the late Sultan Qaboos as emblematic of their acceptance as an Omani citizen.[79] The returnees interviewed were devoted to and reverential about Sultan Qaboos. In the words of Saud Ahmed al-Busaidi, "With wisdom and experience, His Majesty Sultan Qaboos bin Said welcomed all overseas Omanis to return to their ancestral homes."[80] In their recollections and genuine effusive admiration, he became for returnees a body that by revering they symbolized their loyalty to the nation and the promise of progress.[81] Ahmed al-Riyami described Qaboos as "the young, educated Ruler of Oman, under whose reign ... we have experienced ... development in all walks of life."[82] For the returnees from Zanzibar in particular, the sultan existed at the juncture of the affective and legal regimes of recognition, as many had fled the islands after the overthrow of Zanzibar's sultan. The ideological symbolism of Omani monarchy was significant to returnees because there had not been a severing of vertical sovereignty in Oman as had occurred in Zanzibar.[83] Qaboos's descent from the house of al-Said linked him to a historical legacy of Omani maritime empire in the Indian Ocean.[84]

A letter to the editor in the October 29, 1984, issue of the *Oman Observer* reflects the ideological tensions among returnees between "soil" and "blood" visions of national citizenship, in this case birth in Zanzibar and descent from Omani parents. Writing from Sharjah, the author, Mohammed Nasser al-Kharusi, wrote to defend a writer (Ali Ahmed Jahdhmy) of an earlier *Oman Observer* article about political changes in Zanzibar against a letter criticizing the article by Mrs. Raya al-Kharusi. Though this letter is not in the file, the author believed the letter not only misrepresented facts about the Omani presence but was overly suspicious of the Zanzibar links of some of the returnees. He argued, "that there are Zanzibar refugees in Oman is a statement which neither Mrs. Kharusi nor anyone else who has not checked the motives of the immigrants from 1964 to date, can deny." He further insisted, "Mrs. Kharusi and many like her were accepted and given Omani citizenship not because they were Arabs, but because they were of Omani descent."[85]

Many other returnees emphasized the significance of the Omani passport itself as the foundation of their citizenship.[86] While most returnees obtained the passport legally, there were many liminal and extralegal situations that demonstrated how eligibility for the passport was formalized in the recognition and registration of ancestry as a sign of membership. In a system built on recognition through the sheikhs, the potential for slippage between bureaucratic and social recognition was large. As one returnee from East Africa put it, "As long as someone from the interior claimed you as his relative, you were Omani."[87] One of my interviewees told me his father saw an elderly man at the docks in Muscat who had disembarked with the refugees but who had no documentation of any sort. As my interviewee described it, his father recognized that this man was "a pure Omani"—he was dressed in the Omani traditional white robe, wore an Omani-style turban, spoke Arabic, and had a very long beard. My interlocutor's father began putting pressure on officials to let the man in, even without documentation. In the context of the interview, my interlocutor meant to demonstrate the generosity of his father, but it also shows that there was an inextricable element of visual and auditory confirmation of cultural belonging that buttressed the formal legal procedures of obtaining citizenship documents.

Finally, many linked their citizenship to an unquestioned loyalty to the state. They were loath to challenge the state, and most interviewees expressed their disdain for popular protests, including those that occurred in Oman in 2011 and 2012. Their preponderance in the military and security services also meant they were more active in the suppression of, than participation in, these and earlier Omani workers' protests of 1971 and 1989.[88]

WORKING WOMEN, MARRIAGE, AND CITIZENSHIP IN THE OMANI DEVELOPMENTAL STATE

Whatever the cultural tensions engendered by their presence, the economic imperatives of state-building meant that many returnees and especially returnee women were full participants in the 1970s Omani workforce. While men tended to be the bearers of citizenship legally because of the importance of paternal descent, women tended to be the bearers of citizenship culturally.[89] There were additional pressures for them to downplay their "non-Omani" cultural expressions in public places.[90] Returnee women were among the first to enter the modern Omani workforce, bearing the burden of the state's need to portray working women as pious paragons publicly active in national development in order to counter deeply entrenched conservative attitudes that would normally forbid women from working in this manner.[91] Zanzibari women are still perceived today by some Omanis as having less formal shyness about their public presence. The presence of Zanzibaris who didn't cover "properly" could offend more religiously conservative returnees. A March 12, 1970, circular reflected the cultural tensions introduced by the newcomers: "It has been observed that increasing numbers of women are frequently entering the souqs (markets) and stores wearing foreign dress and not national dress. This is a denounced innovation, and it is desired that you forbid it."[92] For their part, Zanzibari women saw themselves as able to maintain their piety even while mixing with men, since the more extreme practices of gender segregation and isolation of women common in traditional Omani culture were not common among the more modern returnee families, and many had long experience in international higher education contexts.[93]

According to Dawn Chatty, the presence of women in a diverse set of occupations continued until the early 1980s, when the number of job seekers outpaced the available positions.[94] By the late 1980s, according to Chatty, women were being actively discouraged out of certain labor markets and prevented from organizing in groups.[95] These new cultural attitudes of the late 1980s emerged out of transnational purist currents of Islamic revival sweeping the region. One interviewee noted the newly ostentatious conservative cultural attitudes: "Abeya did not come in until the late 1990s. In the beginning it was open like a smock and with no hijab. People have become more religious now."[96] That shift was evident for a returnee from Mombasa who came to Abu Dhabi in 1980 and to Oman in 1986. As she put it, "The culture in Mombasa was completely different. . . . [I]n Kenya it is a Western area and here in Oman it is an Arabic culture. . . . *I had to 'change myself to be an Arab because it is my country.'*"[97] She began to wear abeya and cover her hair.[98]

By the early 1980s, marriage had become a site of state surveillance as it pertained to the politics of citizenship for spouses. Cleavages around citizenship developed in relation to exogenous marriages of both Omani men and Omani women to non-Omanis (especially East Africans).[99] Marriage to someone of Omani descent was itself not enough to guarantee a nontribally descended woman citizenship. Sometimes non-Omani family members (such as a spouse) were prevented from legally entering the country. Omani men who had non-Omani wives often skirted immigration regulations to enable their families to join them immediately in Oman. Several returnees related illicit border crossings between the Emirates and Oman, bringing their wives in and out of Oman in the trunk of a car for lack of legal status.[100] Another interviewee left his wife and six children in Tanzania in 1975 to go to Oman, traveling on a Tanzanian passport up to the airport, where he received an unstamped Omani passport after surrendering his Tanzanian document. He managed to arrange for his family to travel to Abu Dhabi in 1977, from which point the family was forced to cross illicitly into Oman to be reunited with him, because his spouse did not have legal standing at the time.[101]

MULTIPLE PASSPORTS AND FLEXIBLE USES

Omani ethnic return migration fragmented households of extended kin in Zanzibar and East Africa. Many non-Arab family and household members were left behind by the exclusions of ethnic citizenship. Omanis occasionally passed off household help from Africa as cousins or close kin to gain them admittance as permanent residents and even citizens in Oman. This strategy was sometimes encouraged by the desire of tribal leadership to expand membership to increase their own domestic power base.

One Omani-born interviewee contrasted these surreptitious strategies with his East African–born wife's legal path to citizenship by showing a picture of his old Sultanate of Oman and Muscat passport from 1979. He described how in the 1970s "there was a lot of funny business with passports, people coming back and forth under the same five names. . . . [T]he government knew many Zanzibaris were in Oman illegally."[102] Letters from the UK mission in Geneva in August 1966 show that a few Zanzibaris were using the repurposed passports of others to go to Oman. In one case, a man traveling with his two wives and four children was stopped because he presented two Omani passports, each with various combinations of spouses and children on them. He claimed he had lost his first passport, applied for a second, and then found the first again. Another two families were turned away after it was discovered that both fathers (each traveling with his wife and two children) were presenting another person's passport, in which they had altered the photograph.[103] As Will Hanley notes, "Fraudulent use is a mark of the value of papers."[104] Most illicit uses of the Omani passport were not done out of an attempt to "conceal" one's "true" national identity, but out of the search for security and opportunity.

In another case, a father wrote the names of his family members on the passport application (in the early 1970s, a single family could travel on one passport), but the *wali* made the family a part of one tribe when they considered themselves as being from another. In another example, a female relative, a grandmother, was listed under the passport of her son, but after the original passport holder died, the grandmother had to apply for an individual passport. Moments like these could allow other family members in East Africa to use the passport of deceased individuals or those who had already entered, coming back under an assumed name. In certain situations, a younger brother might use the name of an elder brother listed on the passport.[105] One Omani returnee even applied to the court to change his official name because he was legally listed under the name of his brother who was already resident there, the result of the use of this older style of passport.

According to one interviewee, there was one sheikh of the al-Harthi tribal confederation who had a close friend in Zanzibar of non-Omani background. In the early 1970s, this sheikh signed off on a passport for his friend and adopted him into the tribe even though he was neither Omani nor al-Harthi. This adopted tribal person lived in the interior for many years. When the sheikh's son took over after his father's death, he found out his father's friend was charging people money to bring them to Oman, where they would pose as his family members. He had begun paperwork to bring two children, who would pose as his sons, and then he planned to bring the mother as a maid, and the father later. He promised them a route to the passport through his facilitation.[106] This anecdote was also related to me by another returnee. While it was impossible for me to confirm or corroborate it without indiscretion, the story indicated to me that there were ongoing anxieties about the "integrity" of Omani nationality, anxieties that Omanis of visibly mixed African ancestry and Swahili-speaking returnees could find themselves subject to.

It is also evident from the oral history interviews that many Omanis continued to attempt to maintain multiple citizenships and to live the translocal pattern of life they had been leading in earlier decades, using the 30/90 schedule maintained by some PDO employees (one month leave, three months continuous work) and taking advantage of the favorable exchange rate of the Omani riyal compared to the shilling to support a family in Tanzania.[107]

The possession of multiple passports was subject to increasing levels of state surveillance as the modern Omani state consolidated itself. One interviewee related how her father was able to maintain multiple passports well into the 1970s, until he arrived with her mother in 1981. At the airport, authorities asked her father to surrender his Tanzanian passport and asked the interviewee if that really was her mother.[108]

OMANI NATIONALITY LAW REFORMS AND EXTRATERRITORIAL BIRTH

Scholar Mayuko Okawa described three documents defining Oman's nationality law over this period from the early 1970s to the early 1980s: the Nationality Law of 1972 and Amendments A & B of 1983. The November 30, 1972, Omani citizenship law sets forth the conditions governing the acquisition and loss of citizenship in Oman. The law states that the following conditions need to be met for an individual to be eligible for Omani citizenship: (1) born inside or outside Oman to an Omani father, (2) born in Oman to unknown parents, and (3) born in or outside Oman to an

Omani mother and an unknown father or a father without a legal nisba.[109] The most significant clause of the 1972 law was clause 6, which granted nationality to all those who were "originally Omani" and had not acquired another nationality. This was important for returnees from East Africa with attenuated roots (meaning those whose grandfathers' generation or older had migrated to Africa).[110] The law also stated that an Omani woman marrying a foreigner remained an Omani unless she sought a waiver of her citizenship to gain her spouse's citizenship. Legally, such women could even regain their lost Omani citizenship if they divorced their spouses. However, a woman's ability to pass this status on to her children was conditional on marrying a man of Omani ancestry.

David Cook-Martin noted a conflict between state goals of gaining children of settled immigrants and maintaining nationality links to émigrés. He observed that this conflict occurs especially in cases of marriage between a "national' woman and a "nonnational" man.[111] The Omani citizenship laws provided an illuminating case of this. In 1983 the nationality law was revised for the first time in over a decade. The new law stated that a child born of an Omani mother and a non-Omani father outside Oman was now considered non-Omani.[112] It also decisively tightened citizenship requirements, requiring two additional characteristics other than origin: long residence in Oman (up to two decades) and Arabic proficiency.[113] According to Okawa, the most significant change with an impact on the returnees was the deletion of clause "y" in the Amendment to the Nationality Law of 1983. Okawa argued that this effectively meant that if one parent was not already an Omani citizen, it was prohibitively difficult to acquire nationality. As noted by Okawa, the basic difficulty this created for the returnees was that it was impossible to make a claim on ancestry unless, as a returnee, your father or mother was born in Oman and immigrated to Africa, and then you were the one trying to return. Most African returnees came from families that had been in Africa for several generations. All of Okawa's ninety-one interviewees were in this latter category. Okawa noted the case of a 1988 female "returnee" to Oman born in Tanganyika to an Omani-born father and a Tanganyikan-born mother of Omani descent. Upon their giving up their Tanzanian passports on arrival, the returnee's husband obtained Omani nationality after three years, while the woman waited thirteen for hers (officially, non-Omani wives of Omani nationals are entitled to naturalization as citizens after five years' residence in the country).

There are two likely reasons for the state's policy making some applicants wait longer than others. First, as we have been discussing, was the combination of being a woman and being born in East Africa. The second influential factor was economic. The delay and even closure of the possibility of return migration for citizenship was motivated by declining oil prices during 1981–1986, culminating in state spending outstripping state income in 1985–1986.[114] State fiscal concerns dictated a temporizing approach to return migrants after the mid-1980s. By 1990 it had become difficult to impossible to easily obtain Omani citizenship based on a descent claim alone; one also needed a prolonged residence in the country.[115] Thousands of East African–born returnees with Omani ancestry waited a decade or more to receive their citizenship.

ARABISM, SWAHILI LANGUAGE, AND THE RETURNEES

An Omani writer for the Ministry of National Heritage emphasized that "Omani society shares with the Arab nation in firm belief in the existence of an Arab destiny."[116] Oman has always had significant numbers of non-Arab or culturally Arabized linguistic minorities among its citizens, including some rare and near extinct non-Arabic languages, like "Jabali" in the south, as well as Baluchi, Lawati, and Zadjali.[117] While they are linked closely to the Omani tribal structure, the returnees from Zanzibar are also connected to a larger community of returnees from East Africa by their shared vernacular, Swahili.[118] In the social life of the returnees and their descendants, Arabic is the national language, Swahili is the language of the Omani-Zanzibari "in group," and English is the language of business and higher education.[119] There is a substantial amount of code-switching between these three languages among younger generations of Omanis descended from Swahili-speaking returnees.

Languages, like other forms of symbolic capital, change prestige levels when transplanted by migrants to a new context. As historian Jan Vansina notes, "Usually the speakers of the losing eroding linguistic community become bilingual in a second language of higher prestige, and eventually their descendants may abandon their original language. This process is called language shift."[120] Linguist Nafla Kharusi observed processes of convergence, divergence, and maintenance in language shift among Zanzibari returnees, who typically were fluent in Swahili and English but spoke broken Arabic.[121] The Swahili-speaking returnees, though advantaged by speaking English fluently, often decided to downplay their fluency in Swahili. Sometimes this was a purely pragmatic decision, shaped by Swahili fluency not being economically valuable or socially prestigious in Oman.[122] At other times this was related to cultural pressures stemming from the Arabism dominant as a value within Omani national identity. The competing linguistic hierarchies of Arabic and English in Oman's employment sector often drove this shift, as did one's early educational context. It could be driven by one parent attempting to ban the speaking of Swahili among their children, both in Zanzibar and in the Gulf, or by those who preferred to keep it as a parental language while not teaching it to their kids.[123] Some East African returnees even insisted to other Omanis that they didn't know SwahiliOne returnee cautioned that it was not necessarily true that Swahili-speaking Omanis were not fluent in Arabic; from her perspective, one's linguistic practices depended on "who you mix with." Even within returnee families, linguistic practices and fluency in Swahili could vary widely. While the grandmother of one female returnee spoke Swahili fluently, the returnee's mother spoke English better than Arabic. The returnee's sister was fluent in Arabic. This same returnee observed that Zanzibaris often spoke Arabic with a distinctive East African accent, elongating cognate words from Swahili.[124] A returnee from mainland Tanzania related that although her grandfather spoke Arabic and her father spoke to his children in simple Arabic sentences, she was more comfortable speaking Swahili to her own children. She grew up learning how to read Arabic in the Quran but not how to speak it conversationally.[125]

Many interviewees reported not knowing Arabic when they returned in the 1970s and 1980s. Some younger returnees who had first lived elsewhere in the Arab world quickly gained fluency before they arrived in Oman; one returnee learned Arabic in Cairo, from watching Egyptian soap operas.[126] One interviewee and his brother remember being teased mercilessly in school: "Zanzibari ma ya'arif Arabi" (a Zanzibari doesn't know Arabic). They learned Arabic in three years, from Egyptian teachers. Another learned Arabic in one year while living in Sinaw, in the Omani interior, also from Egyptian teachers.[127] Another returnee from Tanzania related, "When I came to Oman . . . it was tough to go to school, because you had to speak Arabic all the time, and you only learned English in class 4. People would laugh at you if you spoke Swahili."[128]

Older returnees by and large did not learn to converse in Arabic. In the mid-1970s, the Ministry of Education began a program of adult education teaching Arabic to this older generation of returnees. The program ran until the late 1980s and was deemed a success.[129] But it did not extinguish the speaking of Swahili from public places in Oman, nor the unease many Omanis still felt about the language. In a 2011 editorial, Omani academic Saida al-Farsiyya linked Omani citizenship to speaking Arabic by denigrating the public speaking of Swahili and Baluchi: "We have in Oman have some Omanis who insist on speaking languages other than Arabic. Those coming from Africa speak Swahili and those coming from Asia speak Urdu or Baluchi, although they have lived in Oman for many years, an issue which detracts from the citizenship of both groups."[130] Speaking Swahili, the author felt, was evidence of insufficient patriotism and disrespect for Omani citizenship.[131] Dr. Asya al-Bualy, the daughter of the returnee Nasser Seif al-Bualy, vigorously rejected this idea in an editorial published in Arabic and English. Her response glorified the Omani role in East Africa and the risks the ancestors of modern returnees took to go there.[132] In defending Swahili-speaking Omanis, Dr. Bualy suggested their sojourn in East Africa was the experience preparing them to serve the Omani nation at the highest levels.

A situation of "triglossia" has developed over the last five decades among descendants of the returnees born in Oman. As mentioned, the first generation of adult returnees from Zanzibar were fluent in Swahili and English. The generation who left Zanzibar as children were usually also conversant in Swahili but later became more fluent in Arabic, especially if they arrived in Oman before the end of primary school.[133] A generation born to the returnees in Oman and educated there in Arabic can understand Swahili, but they often respond in English to Swahili conversation initiated by their parents. The grandchildren of returnees also grew up with Swahili primarily as an oral language; unlike their parents and grandparents, they do not relate to it written in Roman or Arabic script.[134] To some in the new generation, there is nothing sentimental about this loss; it simply marks their cultural integration as Omani national citizens.[135] To others, Swahili is an index of their unique cultural heritage and, even if they are fluent in Arabic, they wish to preserve Swahili as an aspect of their identity and are interested in it as an Ajami language written in the Arabic script.[136]

In a book he first published in the early 2000s and that has gone through multiple editions, the returnee Abu Jadham Nasser al-Jahadhamy aimed to teach Arabic to Swahili speakers and Swahili to Arabic speakers. Al-Jahadhamy noted that multilingualism was an asset of the shrewd and intelligent: "[W]e are safe from the conniving of peoples, if we learn their languages." A native Arabic speaker, al-Jahadhamy learned Swahili from his extended family, who had deep roots in Mombasa and on the Swahili coast. The book, according to him, was "for two types of readers, for that type that reads Arabic without Swahili (if it is written in non-Arabic letters), and the second type is that which reads Swahili without Arabic (if it is written in its letters)." Al-Jahadhamy presented Swahili knowledge as the garland of the educated person, who "is never satisfied with knowledge."[137]

Many returnees and their children wanted to be understood as both Omani citizens and of East African heritage. Some linked their facility with Swahili to a cosmopolitan and multicultural identity rooted in a Swahili Coast idea of urban Muslim refinement, *ustaraabu*. This ideological link of Swahili to Arabism is a part of the pride returnees take in the language. In her poem "Zinjibari," writer Naila Barwani argued that the Zanzibaris' bringing of Arabic vocabulary helped to perfect Swahili, and that the two languages are interlinked. She urged her fellow Zanzibaris to "be proud of our language, to teach it to our children" ("Tukisema kufakhari / wenetu watalaamu"). *"Many languages are cleverness, understand this fruit To scorn Swahili is a sign of ignorance"* ("Lugha nyingi uhodari / hili tunda tufahamu/ Kudharau tuhadhari / ni uchache wa elimu").[138] Scholar Harith Ghassany similarly urged returnees "to not be afraid (kutoogopa) to use Swahili nor to assert their Africanness."[139]

In 2013 the popular Omani serial *Youm wara Youm* released a short clip of an office conversation between a Zanzibari lady and one of the serial's main characters, a Dhofari man. The Dhofari man is shown waiting, looking piqued, as the ministry lady talks in Swahili about what she will cook for dinner for her guest that evening. The Dhofari man expresses indignation that she is speaking Swahili in the office: "There are two languages spoken in this country: English and the language we inherited from our ancestors (Arabic)." The Swahili lady simply laughs at his naivete, stating that she knows people speaking many languages, and that it is "hamna neno" (no problem). The clip plays as comedy, but even as a comedic representation, it is an unprecedented and welcome portrayal of the realities of linguistic and cultural diversity in modern Oman, a heartening parody of monolingualism and of those who are unable to adapt to Oman's polyglossic society.[140] But it also underscores Swahili as an ambiguous sign of foreignness, misinterpreted by other Omanis who have internalized some of the dominant and ethnocentric scripts of Omani nationalism's link to Arabism. With the opening up of a Swahili language classes at Knowledge Oasis Muscat and the enthusiastic reception of Tanzanian artists like Mbosso in Muscat in recent years, Swahili in Oman is not going anywhere; Oman will likely continue to have the largest community of Swahili speakers outside East Africa. The Omani state has also begun to recognize and exploit the advantage of a Swahiliphone citizenry to its relations with East African countries.

CONCLUSION

The existence of "back-from-Africa" return migrants today living in Muscat shows the role of extraterritorial dynamics in renewing the Omani territorial state as modern. Through attention to the process of return migration and the assumption of Omani citizenship, as well as "returnee" negotiation of the politics of language and citizenship, this chapter has shown the material impact of returnees from East Africa on the making of Oman's developmental state and their ideological impact on the "crafting" of Omani citizenship. Their unique structural position made them in many ways arch-Omani nationalists, and the state's material wealth and (relatively) late modernization pulled them decisively within its ambit, outweighing whatever ambivalence others felt about their presence.

From 1970 to 1990, the issuing of Omani citizenship evolved into a modern rationalized bureaucratic procedure. This increasingly rationalized character of state bureaucracy meant that citizenship policy post-1970 was linked more than ever to state economic development goals. However, national citizenship did not always surmount, but in many cases entrenched, older notions of social value. If anything, the increasing economic value of Omani nationality in this era accelerated conflicts and anxieties over the precise ethnic demarcation of national identity even when citizenship did not depend on any explicit physiognomic criteria. Rather, the undecidability of "liminal" cases of East African returnees shows the complexities of state attempts to define national belonging through paternal ancestry and the cultural expectations of Arabism.[141]

Becoming an Omani citizen had a significant ideological impact on the returnees. A secure citizenship status was the precondition allowing them to gain distance from the events in Zanzibar, sufficient to analyze and relate their personal experience to the larger history of modern Zanzibar. By the time Tanzania and Zanzibari leadership opened a dialogue with the Zanzibari diaspora community in the early 1980s, the Afro-Arabs from Zanzibar were ensconced as Omani. This was a positive development for Tanzanian state elites, as it largely removed the existence of a large and vocal Zanzibari exile force critical of Tanzanian governance in Great Britain. It was also a positive development for the Omani state, which gained a cadre of loyal citizens with world-class white-collar educations obtained in colonial Africa. The returnees today exemplify the persistence of a distinct form of transnational belonging and express this through writing connected histories of Arabia and East Africa. Their creations are taken up in chapter 6 as part of a more general Omani state turn after 1990 toward the instrumentalization of the material and documentary heritage of Zanzibar.

SIX

Transregional Relations, Omani Heritage, and a Vernacular Historiography of Zanzibar, 1990–2020

IN OMANI SOCIETY, returnees' interactions with the dominant paradigm of nationalism eventually raised a more historical question relevant to the meaning of both Zanzibar and Oman's national heritage. What was the nature of, character of, and motivation for Omani imperial rule on the East African coast during the nineteenth century? More acutely, what was the meaning of the post-1861 "rump" state inherited from the division of that empire to the 1963 Sultanate of Zanzibar and Pemba? This chapter explores what the idea of Zanzibar as a country has meant for the "invented tradition" of Omani cultural heritage in the Indian Ocean and how it persists in history writing about Zanzibar by the returnees.[1]

Here I refer to writing emerging from within a community interested in its own history as "vernacular historiography." A vernacular historiography is a corpus of historical work originating out of the writings of nonhistorians about history. In these works audiences internalize imaginations of belonging by relating it to the past.[2] A spate of new works over the last decade has attempted to address remembrance of the past as political and social work by nonacademic historians.[3] There has also been interest in developing a critical approach to heritage in the Gulf.[4] Approaches to history among Muslim intellectuals from Africa remain understudied and undertheorized.

This chapter draws on scores of works written by returnees from Zanzibar and a corpus of works about East Africa published by the Omani Ministry of Heritage and Culture. Taken together, and addressed comparatively in this chapter, these interrelated works articulate "multidirectional memory" and show negotiating, borrowing, and cross-referencing between the Omani national heritage project and the vernacular historiography of the returnees.[5] The overlap between the two discourses has been stimulated by the renewal of transregional links between the Gulf and East Africa after 1990.[6] The communicative memory of Afro-Arabs from Zanzibar is key to the vernacular historiography.[7] We can discern the fears, expectations, desires, and repressed elements of a larger community of Afro-Arabs from Zanzibar by considering how they gave form to the islands' history while negotiating their Omani national citizenship.[8]

National heritage is the imagined link between cultural heritage and contemporary national identity; as one scholar from the UAE put it in a December 1992 Literary Forum lecture in Muscat sponsored by the Ministry of Heritage and Culture, "The search for heritage ... is a search for the 'spirit' (rūḥ) of a people and its history. The spirit of a people is that hidden movement which directs the behavior (sulūk) of an individual towards the group."[9] Gulf states have placed national heritage at the ideological cornerstone of narrating the nation, where the ruptures of modern development are portrayed as a seamless historical and cultural transition from a virtuous past.[10] As Rosie Bsheer noted about Oman's neighbor, Saudi Arabia, "Heritage reflects the power to subjugate the past to the politics of the present."[11] Even when acknowledging continuity with the past, modern heritage projects in the Gulf are forms of invented tradition, mobilized to antedate the existence of the nation within the historical culture of a given territory.[12]

How does the twentieth century history of Omani muwalladūn as political actors in Zanzibar fit into Omani national heritage? The vernacular historiography of the Zanzibar returnees has a unique twentieth-century focus that the historiography of Oman emerging from the National Ministry of Heritage and Culture eschews. Zanzibar's history under al-Yaʿaraba and al-Busaidi rule can plausibly be articulated as part of Omani national heritage.[13] The history of nationalist political participation by the Afro-Arabs in Zanzibar, on the other hand, goes unmentioned in state-sanctioned publications. Insofar as Omani state officials do evince interest in Zanzibar, they are mainly interested in the material culture of the nineteenth-century sultanate rather than the intellectual musings of former nationalists. While the eighteenth and nineteenth centuries stand outside the bounds of shared memory retained by a living generation, the twentieth involves events experienced by still-living individuals, including many returnees.[14] While the Omani heritage historiography allows the returnees to connect their transnational past in East Africa to durable concepts of Islam, "ḥāḍara" (civilization) and "tijāra" (trade) within a cosmopolitan vision of Omani global influence, Zanzibar's twentieth-century history under British colonial rule has little value to the Oman state in terms of an invented tradition or a "usable" past, and anticolonial movements there still have a "whiff" of antimonarchical subversion about them.

The emphasis on politics and revolution in the vernacular historiography of the Zanzibari returnees is largely driven by their desire to educate their offspring about their unique history of involvement in Zanzibar's sovereignty of pre-1890, as well as 1963. Distinct from the exile discourse, that written from the space of Omani citizenship was preoccupied with the lost homeland of Zanzibar as a memory space rather than an object of irredentist concern.[15] This is not to deny that the historiography possessed the potential to influence how Zanzibaris think of themselves in relation to the Union and Zanzibar's history as an independent state. But rather than a political war fought over territory and sovereignty, the vernacular historians waged an ideological war over narrative, concerning sensitive topics such as the nature of Arab slavery in Zanzibar, the meaning of territorial nationalism in Zanzibar, and the origins of the Zanzibar revolution. This discourse has only marginally affected the evolution of multiparty politics in Zanzibar from 1995; most voters in Zanzibar's hotly contested elections in the 2000s were born after the revolution.[16]

RELATIONS BETWEEN TANZANIA, THE GULF COUNTRIES, AND THE ZANZIBAR EXILES, 1973–1985

Structural transformations in Zanzibar's economy eventually led to a reopening that brought many exiles back to Zanzibar for the first time since the revolution, the by-product of a set of diplomatic initiatives of Tanzanian and Zanzibari leadership with Gulf countries, seeking in-country investment and loans to meet state fiscal challenges. In the mid- to late 1970s, the Zanzibar government was almost bankrupt and was compelled to look outside for assistance.[17] The Union government was in similarly bad shape, hit hard by the rising oil prices that undermined the import-substitution industrializing strategy of developing countries.[18]

At the time there was a growing global trend of state outreach to wealthy overseas investors, including diasporas living outside the country. A growing number of states had sought to recruit former émigrés back to the former homeland as investors and nonresident citizens, expressed through voluntaristic ties to their country of origin.[19] Similarly, Tanzania turned to court Zanzibari exiles.[20] In 1975 and 1978 Zanzibar president Aboud Jumbe took a Zanzibar delegation to the Middle East; they met with some exiles in the Gulf during the latter visit.[21] The former president of the Zanzibar Association in Dubai (at the time an Omani diplomat), Ahmed Hamoud al-Maamiry, commented on the interest of the Zanzibar government in the diaspora: "The Government has now left the doors open for the interested emigrants to come back. . . .Whether this come 'come back' sign is genuine or not remains to be seen when the conditions put forward by those emigrants to facilitate their return are discussed by the authorities in Zanzibar."[22]

Other ex-ZNP politicos were highly skeptical about Tanzania's new overtures to the Gulf. Ahmed Baalawy, for instance, called Nyerere a "tyrant" and condemned the visits by Tanzanian officials as self-serving and materialistic. "To [President Nyerere]" alleged Baalawy, "the Arabs are to be befriended only for what they can give."[23] He cynically anticipated the appeals of the East African delegation: "With their mind's eye on the Arab riyals, the Tanzanian envoys would try to invoke, by way of setting the scene, the ancient cultural and commercial ties between the Gulf and East Africa, and the need to renew and strengthen those ties."[24] In the mid-1970s, A. S. Kharusi had taken a skeptical attitude to East African overtures to wealthy Arab Gulf countries. in "Statement on Tanzanian Goodwill Mission to the Gulf," *FZV* described the 1975 Zanzibar delegation in cynical terms: "What is to be done? Since all economic roads now lead to Arabia, so to Arabia they must go, and exploit the traditional Arab hospitality and generosity."[25] Kharusi nevertheless sounded an optimistic note: "Exiles are now freer to visit their relatives in Zanzibar than had previously been the practice."[26] In an editorial in a mid-1980 issue of *FZV*, "he urged Nyerere to invite the exiles back to Zanzibar, as their skills and education would drive economic reform as long as a secure environment for those investments was created."[27]

In Zanzibar, some were skeptical of these overtures, though for different reasons. The specter of Arab domination and Arab slavery still played a role in the political culture of revolutionary elites. Many regarded multipartyism in Zanzibar as little more than a pretext for the return of elements of the ZNP and Arab hegemony.[28] The faction within the Revolutionary Council known as the liberators felt that a rapprochement with exiles would lead to the return of undesirable elements in politics.[29] This older clique was increasingly isolated and attempting to protect their autonomy against the assertion of power by Tanzania's ruling party, CCM. In 1982 Jumbe and Tanzanian diplomat Salim Ahmed Salim again made a tour of Gulf states, especially the Emirates, Oman, and Bahrain, seeking investment and capital.[30] In 1984 Zanzibari diplomats visited exiles in the Middle East, Europe, and the Americas to encourage them to come back to Zanzibar.[31] Mohamed Bakari notes that "due to a high degree of suspicion and mistrust between the two governments, [these] earlier efforts did not yield substantial fruits."[32] Even after 1985, when a Zanzibari became president of the Union, the former newspaper editor Jamal Ramadhan Nasibu warned that the exiles had attempted to take advantage of crises in Zanzibar and would try to break the Union and reconquer Zanzibar.[33] The specter of their interference was still used as a justification for violent actions by security services and police against citizens of Zanzibar.[34] As late as the 1990s, at celebrations commemorating the revolution, the government staged ritual reenactments of Arabs in 1964 having their beards shaved off and being publicly humiliated.[35]

Two developments from the mid-1980s heralded a new opening. First, Ali Hassan Mwinyi was elected as Zanzibar's president in the wake of Jumbe's fall from grace in 1983; he had liberalized the islands by facilitating freedom of movement and opening it up to private investment.[36] In 1985, in the most significant political transition in Zanzibar's modern history, he became president of Tanzania. The symbolism of a Zanzibari presiding over the Union and the smooth handover of the office from Nyerere to Mwinyi in October 1985 gave Nyerere the political security he needed to join in the economic and diplomatic overtures to Gulf states. Second was an initiative within the exile community. Muhammad Abdul-Muttalib Hashim was president of the Zanzibar Association from the mid-1970s to the mid-1980s and wrote a letter to President Ali Hassan Mwinyi (then president of Zanzibar) in 1984, advising him to hold discussions between the government of Zanzibar and Zanzibaris in exile.[37] Eventually Nyerere joined Mwinyi on a historic state visit to Oman and other Gulf states.[38] The Tanzanian ambassador to Oman, Ali Ahmed Saleh, presented the rapprochement of Tanzania and Oman as the convergence of projects of national development and attributed the reset to a rethinking between Sultan Qaboos and Ali Hassan Mwinyi.[39] After Mwinyi became president of Tanzania in 1985, the Zanzibar government under new president Idris Wakil began to lay down regulatory guidelines governing outside investment.[40] Zanzibar chief minister Seif Sharif Hamad visited the Gulf in 1987 with other Zanzibar government ministers, and Hamad visited for two hours with Sultan Qaboos.[41] Both Mwinyi and Hamad also took the unprecedented step of visiting with the ex-ZNP leader Ali Muhsin al-Barwani, then living in Dubai.[42] These visits yielded fruit in Oman in spite of political tensions in Zanzibar. In 1988, in a historic move, Oman established a consulate in Zanzibar.[43] Omani aid helped in the construction of a new hospital and a new airport in Zanzibar.

With the collapse of the Soviet bloc, transnational Islam became a new focal point for many African and Asian Muslims.[44] Nongovernmental organizations (NGOs), especially Muslim ones, grew rapidly between 1980 and 2000.[45] There were also many new private educational and religious initiatives launched in Zanzibar from Oman, most notable among them by Al-Jam'iyya al-Istiqāma al-Khayriyya al-Islāmiyya al-'ālamiyya (the Istiqāma International Muslim Charitable Society).[46] The new intellectual currents have driven a kind of Islamic resurgence in Zanzibar, characterized by both Islamist and nationalist tendencies.[47]

GLOBALIZATION, TRANSREGIONAL RELATIONS, AND SOCIAL MEMORIES OF ZANZIBAR IN THE 1990S AND 2000S

In the wake of the breakdown of the most robust political and economic alternatives to the capitalist system, the 1990s was a decade of global economic integration and optimism about what it might portend.[48] Increasingly, alternative development models seemed to converge on liberal democracy as the only remaining viable system of governance and economic development.[49] By the end of the Cold War, a new grassroots wave of democratic movements had crested, and many autocratic regimes became ungovernable as the Soviet economy collapsed.[50] Events in Eastern Europe and Romania put pressure on developmental states to democratize governance, with even the venerable Nyerere embracing multiparty competition as inevitable.[51] International donors in the dominant capitalist countries pushed African states "to adopt political and economic systems that resembled political and economic systems in donor countries."[52] It was alleged that the free movement of capital would generate an enduring global prosperity that the developmental state model and its social welfare programs had been unable to do.

Jeremy Prestholdt argued for these themes as significant developments in the Indian Ocean. First, the economic insularity of the region diminished because of the lowering of trade barriers in the unification of a global trading sphere in the wake of Soviet collapse. Second, the restriction of movement and migration by states grew, as nation-states continued to dominate political life. Third, the Indian Ocean was "revivified as a unit of social exchange and analysis," becoming increasingly germane to how nations around its rim conceived of their own national heritage.[53] The "Indian Ocean" as theme was highly relevant to the renewal of relationships between Zanzibaris and Omanis forged after 1990. The idea of the Indian Ocean as a unit of analysis was consonant with the generally optimistic attitude among exiles and new state leadership about the economic possibility of diasporas. Transregional pasts of connection were mobilized as evidence supporting the new trade relations.

The growth and acceleration of information's availability helped expand a growing disaggregation between territory, national culture, and state management of the economy. Digital technologies linked "dominant groups and territories across the globe" into "a new technological system."[54] According to Arjun Appadurai, electronic mediations and mass migrations made "experiential engagement with vernacular globalization" part of daily life for much broader sectors of global population."[55] It became more possible than ever to narrate one's story, spread it rapidly to audiences in far-flung corners of the globe, and achieve a level of audience penetration many earlier state leaders could only dream of.[56] As a result, small groups had more potential than ever to drive sentiment, affect, and action, even at a distance.[57] The digital revolution provided an opportunity for Zanzibaris in and out of the country to meet in new online forums.[58] Virtual places like Zanzinet provided a new kind of platform for Swahili-phone Muslim discourse, a new "Swahili Muslim public sphere," or what Irene Brunotti calls the "cyber-baraza," where Zanzibar's history could be debated.[59] The spread of digital information aided the proliferation of "Indian Ocean" as a symbol of transregional and transnational affiliation, reinforcing its centrality to national cultural heritage in the countries of the basin.[60]

At the same time that these digital forms of linkage emerged, there was a renewal of visits to the islands by the former exiles, as well as visits by Zanzibaris to Oman. Gulf Air initiated a direct flight from Muscat to Zanzibar beginning in 1992, and a major international conference on the history of Zanzibar was held in December that year, attended by Omani dignitaries.[61] Many Omani-Zanzibaris took advantage of the ability to travel to their former homeland; between 1991 and 1994 more than six thousand people from Oman visited the islands.[62] There they renewed deep translocal ties of family and friendship that had been partially severed (or confined to outside Zanzibar) because of the revolution. While some Omanis obtained residence permits and were living at least part of the year on the islands, Zanzibari relatives of Omanis often spent several months a year with family in Oman on a "relative visa."[63] They accessed medical care and higher education in the sultanate, and others obtained a work visa in order to send remittances back to family members.[64] Students of religious knowledge in East Africa also sought out Oman as a destination for religious education.[65]

These dynamics allowed the former exiles to "sustain multi-stranded social relations" linking "their societies of origin and settlement."[66] What this meant in terms of exile consciousness was the "respatialization" of Zanzibar within their memories. In making visits back home, in walking old paths or visiting schools or other landmarks, the exiles recalled the richness of their past on the island and its cosmopolitan milieu. The nationalist generation—Issa Nasser al-Ismaily, Aman Thani, Maulid Haj, Saud Ahmed al-Busaidi, and Ali Muhsin al-Barwani—all revisited Zanzibar during this period. They also began to publish memoirs to reflect on the turbulent moments of their lives as they settled into retirement, whether in Oman or the UAE. Their books of history and memoir began to be published in the mid- to late 1990s (Juma Aley published *Enduring Links* in 1994, the same year as a new commitment by the Omani government to "Omani heritage"), and at the same time that a Zanzibar government conservation plan was created for Zanzibar's urban "Stone Town" (1993–1994).[67]

In Oman, beginning in the 1990s there was increasing interest in East Africa, expressed through radio programs, news articles, and eventually television documentaries.[68] Omanis with an interest in East African history began visiting Zanzibar at this time. The Omani scholar Dr. Muhammad al-Mahrooqi, whose mother grew up in East Africa and was fluent in Swahili, translated literary works from Swahili culture and edited a travelogue of a prominent nineteenth-century Zanzibar intellectual.[69] Al-Mahrooqi learned Swahili in five weeks in Tanzania, a visit he wrote about in a short account of that visit published in 2013, called *Min Forodhani*.[70] Another Omani writer, Nasir Ghalib al-Busaidi, used Zanzibar as a launch pad to travel around the rest of East Africa.[71] The Omani writer Salḥa Bint Seif

Sulaiman al-Miskery first visited in August 1995 and was attracted by the palaces, ruins, and other material remains of nineteenth-century Omani heritage there.⁷²

The renewal of travel helped to redevelop linkages between the Omani-Zanzibaris and a larger community of scholars and writers from the coast, foremost among them one of Africa's most well-known public intellectuals, Dr. Ali Mazrui. Mazrui made his first trip to Oman in 1992. In his newsletter, he wrote about adopting his "clan" name Mazrui, instead of Al-Amin, upon the invitation and urging of an Omani of Kenyan origin, Khamis Hashar, to visit and lecture on the concept of "Afrabia."⁷³ Mazrui also had an audience with Sheikh Sultan bin Muhammad al-Qasimi of Sharjah, whose works on Zanzibar are a notable part of the new Arabic-language historiography of the islands.⁷⁴ He also met Ahmed Hamoud al-Maamiry, who like many exiles planned to spend more time in Zanzibar and Pemba after his retirement from Oman's foreign service in the early 1990s.⁷⁵

Some exiles remained skeptical after 1990 and refused to go back to the islands. Habiba al-Hinai's mother was among those who refused to visit Zanzibar, even when it was open to do so. When asked why, she referred (half-jokingly) to a sentence of eighty lashes passed against her when she had escaped in 1970. Muhammad Ali Muhsin, the son of Ali Muhsin, who was nineteen at the time of the revolution, categorically refused to visit Zanzibar. Others similarly refused to return to Zanzibar because of the trauma they had witnessed in 1964.⁷⁶ And critical Zanzibari writers continued to fall afoul of the regime in Zanzibar, as in the case of Ahmed Diria in 2002–2003.⁷⁷

The younger generation of Zanzibari exiles also visited Zanzibar in the 1990s, and they began publishing works on Zanzibar as their parents aged. Most notable among these works are Nasser al-Riyami's landmark Omani bestseller, *Zanjibar: Shaksiyat wa Aḥdath* (first edition published 2009, with an English version released in 2012, and subsequent Arabic editions) and Habiba al-Hinai's memoir, discussed in the introduction.⁷⁸ The deaths of elders and the desire to communicate with a new generation of their offspring motivated their writing and research.⁷⁹ In turn their work has inspired others. Al-Riyami inspired al-Ghonaimi's novel about the revolution and was available in a popular Stone Town bookshop in the summer of 2014.⁸⁰ Other Omani fiction writers have also turned to East Africa as a subject. A speculative novel published in 2011 by Omani author Muhammad Seif al-Rahbi has its protagonist meet a madman with a black bag full of papers in Mutrah souq, a large and popular market in

Muscat. After copying and beginning to read the papers, the narrator was transported through various episodes in the life of Seyyid Said bin Sultan, whom he follows to Zanzibar, where he learned about Arab and Islamic culture there and the great historical personalities of the era.[81] The novel ended with the death of Seyyid Said on a ship, surrounded by his sons Bargash and Majid. A more critical treatment of Zanzibar, which also brings in the dimension of the Zanzibar revolution, is Huda Hamed's *I Saw Her in My Dreams*, which explores the desire of Omanis from Zanzibar to find lost relatives against the backdrop of tensions of class and status within the Omani household.[82]

OMANI CULTURAL HERITAGE AND THE "OMANI EMPIRE" OF SEYYID SAID IN EAST AFRICA

The Omani economic crises of the late 1980s, the liberalization of the 1990s, and the new consciousness of the importance of East Africa to Oman's history helped make cultural heritage increasingly important to Omani statecraft. The idea of an Omani empire is a modern anachronism and thus an invented tradition; there is no language from Seyyid Said's time in which he refers to his domains as such. The language of Omani empire dates back to colonial-era texts about the Busaidi state, but the term was used in Oman by the returnees and their offspring to legitimate their cultural claims to citizenship, as well as by the Zanzibar-born mufti of Oman, Sheikh Ahmed al-Khalili, to place Oman's cultural heritage within a global Islamic context.[83] In this imagination of the past meant to resound among the imagined community of the nation, Omanis rule overseas was conducted by civilized, tolerant, and elevated ancestors, whose offspring now inform the national populace's refined and hospitable attitude toward other religions and ethnicities.

The concept of the Omani empire allowed the exiles to imagine the diverse strands of the Omani diaspora in East Africa as a shared community. Ali Muhsin al-Barwani argued that the earliest political attempt at East African unity was the empire of Seyyid Said.[84] At the beginning of a two-and-one-half-hour interview given before his death in March 2006, he defined Zanzibar in a remarkable way. Eschewing the idea that Zanzibar was merely the islands of Unguja and Pemba, al-Barwani instead defined a much vaster area "under Omani rule" as being "Dawlat Zanjibār," divided after the founder's death by the "kinyanganyiro" (scramble) for Africa by European powers.[85] It follows that all Omanis in Africa were (and are) its subjects and that Zanzibari identity is an expansive one, connecting the Zanzibar-island dwellers to the "Zanzibara"—that is, the Omani diaspora in Tanganyika, Kenya, Burundi, Rwanda, Uganda, and The Congo.[86]

Representations of Oman's East African empire appear in works of Omani history and in Omani school textbooks.[87] The Ministry of Heritage and Culture has from the early 1980s republished several classic and out-of-print Arabic works on East Africa, for instance *Fatḥ al-Mubīn fī Sīrat-l-Sādat-l-Busaʿidīn*, a history of Busaidi state formation, an Arabic translation of Abdullah Saleh al-Farsy's history of the Busaidi sultans in Zanzibar, multiple travel narratives of Zanzibar's sultans, and a history of the Mazrui clan in Mombasa.[88] One of the most famous works the ministry republished was Said al-Mugheiry's *Juhaynat al-Akhbār fī Tārīkh Zanjibār*, a history of Zanzibar originally written in the 1950s.[89] Al-Mugheiry, writing in the 1930s in Zanzibar, was keen to differentiate between the colonialism ("istiʿamār") of the Portuguese and the Islamic governance ("dawla") of the Omanis in East Africa, stating that the Omanis came as brothers, at the invitation of local people. In al-Mugheiry's view Omani sovereignty on the coast was a benevolent protective move, the culmination of a longue durée cultural relationship. This view was attractive to those interested in globalizing the Omani heritage impulse to East Africa. Several collections of Omani history cite and rely heavily on al-Mugheiry.[90]

In a Ministry of Heritage publication published in 1991, Said al-Unsi described the founder of the Busaidi dynasty, Ahmed, in glowing terms as a national redeemer and noted the continuity of Busaidi rule to the present day.[91] Ahmed's successor, Seyyid Said, is described as the renewer ("mujaddid") of the Omani empire, who recaptured the empire's East African provinces after the Yaʿaraba wars of the eighteenth century. Al-Unsi makes clear that maritime power was key to the empire; Seyyid Said controlled the oceans "from Basra to the Cape of Good Hope with his navy."[92] All this culminates in the statement that "history bears witness ('wa yashhad al-tārīkh') to Oman's prestigious civilizational status since before 5000 years B.C." Al-Unsi asked citizens to consider 1856, the death date of the Busaidi sultan Seyyid Said, as a turning point ("nuqtat taḥawwul") in the life of the Omani empire that disintegrated ("tafkak") after being split into two parts.[93] Al-Unsi described this as an event impacting Oman's coastal provinces, because trade with East Africa deteriorated. Immediately after this, al-Unsi jumped rapidly forward to celebrate events since the accession of Qaboos on July 23, 1970.

Both Mandana Limbert and Mayuko Okawa have previously analyzed Omani social studies textbooks, noting their presentation of East African history.[94] A social studies textbook from Level 8 explored the life of Seyyid Said. The textbook praised his consultative governance, his skillful diplomacy, and his outstanding business mentality as key elements of his ability to raise the status of Zanzibar and form a vast empire ("īmbraturiyyāt wasiyyāt") that extended in Asia to include Oman, parts of the coasts of the Arabian Gulf, the eastern coast of Africa from Mogadishu in the north to Mozambique, and into the African interior.[95] The textbook described Zanzibar as the second capital of Seyyid Said's empire, which he developed "from a humble island to a metropolis, a political, economic and cultural center for the upliftment ("li-shurfi") of central Africa."[96] According to the text, the accompanying maps of the empire reflect not just the claimed domains of the Busaidis but also "the extent of Omani civilization in East Africa."[97]

A more advanced school textbook, *Hadhā waṭanī* (This is my nation), devoted a section to "the cultural role of the Omanis in East Africa."[98] The author describes Sayyid Said Bin Sultan and the Omanis as "active in spreading the values of a tolerant civilization from the coast to the interior until it reached, thanks to the Arabs of Oman, to the region of the tropical lakes and the upper Congo. It also reached distant places in Central Africa, such as Uganda, which was brought Islam thanks to the pioneering role played by Ahmed Ibrahim Al-Amiri around 1844." This text also has a map of the Indian Ocean with Oman, the Swahili coast, the Horn of Africa, and Gwadar, shaded red as part of "Oman in the age of al-Yaʿaraba and al-Busaidi."[99]

Ibrahim al-Shaʿarāwī's book *al-ʿUmāniyyun fī Sharq 'Afrīqiyā*, published by the Ministry of Education, illustrates the spatial contexts in which memory and history of Oman's East African history are transmitted from the East African–born returnees to a younger generation of Omanis. The story is based in scenarios that likely occurred before the 1990s, since the main narrator of the history is portrayed as being a small boy in Zanzibar in 1900. The book begins with the visit of Sheikh Nasser and Rahma to the family of Hamza and Sheikha, where the family engages them in conversations about East African history. Over the next few days, after Maghrib and Jummah prayers, Nasser comes to the house to discuss East African history with the children, sometimes over a delicious banquet of food cooked in the East African coastal way. Their dialogues were infused with Omani nationalist values, such as when Nasser described Omanis as "people of pride and dignity, who refused dishonor and subservience."[100] The Omani presence in East Africa was dated to antiquity, and Omani mastery of the art of maritime navigation treated as a proud civilizational heritage. The Omanis are described as East Africa's liberators from the Portuguese, and Zanzibar is praised as a center of social progress and religious tolerance.

In one memory session during Eid in Oman, Zanzibar-born Sheikh Nasser reminisced about his days celebrating Eid there, with the fluttering red flags, the rows of Sultan's soldiers, the cannon salute, the adornment of palaces, and ships in the harbor lit with hundreds of lamps.[101] The Eid sermon in Muscat revolved around the theme of Omani unity, and the seventeenth-century East African history of Omani resistance against the Portuguese was invoked as a lesson about the results of political infighting.[102] Seyyid Said's political acumen was praised, and his polity was explicitly referred to as "the Omani empire." This Arab entity ("al-Kiyān al-ʿArabī") in Zanzibar is portrayed as having been exterminated by a spirit of racism ("rūḥ al-ʿunṣurīyya") manufactured by European colonialism.[103]

These conceptions of Omani empire in Zanzibar were also celebrated by Zanzibaris for creating cultural connections that would facilitate a revival of prosperity in East Africa. Juma Aley was born in Zanzibar in 1915, was a student of L.W. Hollingsworth, majored in biology at Makerere University, was active with the ZNP, and was a close confidant of Ali Muhsin.[104] Imprisoned for a decade by Nyerere but later pardoned and rehabilitated by the Tanzanian government, his work on Zanzibar from 1994 strongly emphasized the importance of the post-1990 renewal of these overseas connections forged in the past, a force he termed, "enduring links."

A younger generation in Zanzibar has also demonstrated interest in the vernacular historiography of the Omani empire. In Hussein Abdallah's Swahili-language work, *Dola Kongwe ya Zanzibar: Kutoka Oman hadi Kongo*, he detailed the influence of Seyyid Said's state on the spread of Islam in East Africa, showing masjids established by traders in the interior, as well as the work of prominent Muslim scholars from the coastal towns. The geographical scope of the work encompasses everywhere Omani coastal traders established settlements in the nineteenth century, including Bujumbura, Burundi, Tabora, Kigoma, and Uganda.[105] This influence is meant to reflect the one-time greatness of Zanzibar that can be recovered through its residents' devotion to Islam. An earlier work of his, *Utukufu wa Zanzibar*, published in 2010, is a general compendium of historical facts about Zanzibar, including the origin of the name, the arrival of Islam there, the role of Comorians in spreading Islam in Zanzibar, major ulama and their students, Zanzibar's joining of the OIC, and the negative effects of tourism on the island's cultural and religious life.[106] In a section called "Biashara ya masafa marefu," Abdallah quoted from Issa Nasser al-Ismaily's *Kingang'anyiro na Utumwa*, showing that the latter book was available in Zanzibar and read by Zanzibaris. Abdallah showed Seyyid Said's actions of sending ambassadors to various countries and kingdoms on the African mainland. He noted this was a business mainly involving not slavery but ivory, gold, copper, and animal skins; he praised Zanzibar as the foremost international market of the nineteenth century.[107]

TENSIONS OF OMANI CULTURAL HERITAGE DISCOURSE IN ZANZIBAR AND EAST AFRICA

Is framing the Busaidi state in Zanzibar as an Omani cultural heritage conceptually irredentist? Because of the complexity of Oman's historical presence in Zanzibar, and because of the repudiation of that legacy in the revolution, the cultivation of new forms of transregional affiliation has not been without significant tensions. Three main tensions emerge at the intersection between the nineteenth-century transregional history of the Omani empire and the rapid late twentieth-century shift in national citizenship, raising questions about the conceptual and cultural irredentism of the heritage concept.

First, are the nineteenth-century Arabic documents in the Zanzibar Archives, especially the correspondence of the Omani sultans of Zanzibar, a lost Omani cultural heritage? This question occurs against the background of wealthy Gulf collectors acquiring Islamic manuscripts and other archival material from East Africa.[108] Educated Omanis who are aware of this dynamic feel that their wealthier Gulf neighbors are horning in on an East African Muslim heritage that although it belongs territorially to Zanzibar is also properly an Omani cultural heritage.[109] The papers presented at the September 2013 symposium History of Islamic Civilization in East Africa, hosted in Zanzibar by the State University of Zanzibar and attended by the Omani chair of National Records and Archives Authority (NRAA), and at the 2012 International Conference on the Omani Role in East Africa at Sultan Qaboos University, are evidence of keen continued interest in this heritage outside of Zanzibar, which has only intensified over the past decade. The opening of the Oman National Archives (ONA) to the public in 2017 showed that it drew part of its collection from photocopies and scans of Zanzibar archival documents.

Second, what is the heritage and preservation status of buildings of the former sultanate, including the former royal palace and other nineteenth-century buildings? They have been an object of concern by Zanzibari preservationists as well as the returnees because of their steady decay. One side of the former royal palace in Zanzibar collapsed in 2020, triggering outraged comments by many former Zanzibaris in Oman.[110] Many felt that the CCM government in Zanzibar was deliberately allowing the building to disintegrate, feeling that it was an alien cultural heritage.[111] The issue of the expropriated property of the former exiles also lies at this same intersection. Some of the largest and finest houses in urban Stone Town were built in the nineteenth century by the Afro-Arab elite and appropriated as government buildings after the revolution. The Omani attorney and author Nasser al-Riyami (along with other Omani-Zanzibaris) raised the issue of the return of these houses in a meeting with Tanzanian president Jakaya Kikwete during Kikwete's visit to Oman in October 2012. Kikwete advised that it was an issue best taken up with the Zanzibar government directly. In a bid to attract investment, some of these homes have also been turned into boutique hotels as Stone Town is rebranded as an Arabesque playground for foreign tourists.[112]

Third, the rediscovery of East Africa's "Omani heritage" has stirred interest in broader issues of citizenship for muwalladūn families of long-standing East African residence. The issue was illustrated to the Omani public through the work of the Omani broadcast journalist Muhammad al-Murjebi. His family migrated from Oman to mainland Tanganyika in the early 1950s and returned to Oman in 1963. Al-Murjebi's parents never learned Swahili, but al-Murjebi learned the language from his cousins. He produced two important multi-episode specials, *Influence of the Omani Presence in Zanzibar* (2002) and *From the Coast* (2013). The shows helped dramatize to Omanis the existence of people with Omani clan names living throughout East Africa and interviewed some of them with a frustrated desire to claim Omani nationality.[113] Al-Murjebi explained that after the airing of his first series, a ninety-six-year-old man he interviewed in Zanzibar was able to get back in touch with his relatives after seventy years of lost contact.[114]

In a 2013 editorial in the Omani daily *al-Watan*, Dr. Saleh Hashil al-Miskery issued a call for those languishing in this citizenship limbo to be given their human right to asylum and a national identity. Al-Miskery called for Oman to recognize and give citizenship to stateless Omanis in East Africa who are the remnants of Omani imperial rule and have the right to Omani citizenship based on descent.[115] Al-Miskery thus drew on the idea of "Omani empire" to argue for a contemporary human rights obligation to Omani nationals in diaspora.[116]

OMANI-ZANZIBARI AUTHORS ANALYZE THE SLAVE TRADE AND SLAVERY IN EAST AFRICA

Slavery is an important, albeit dreadful, modern heritage of Zanzibar. As Harith Ghassany has put it, "Every nation has its 'fitna', and the 'fitna' of the Zanzibar state is slavery" ("kila taifa lina fitina yake na fitina ya dola Zanzibar ni utumwa").[117] Zanzibar's symbolic significance to Western histories of slavery and abolition is enormous, and its material landscape of Zanzibar is marked with two large, prominent reminders of slavery as a "cultural heritage": a massive cathedral established by British abolitionists and a museum meant to explain slavery to western tourists.[118]

The history of slavery in Zanzibar is closely ideologically linked to justifications for the revolution and in many ways recapitulates debates from the Time of Politics.[119] Ghassany identified the ideological construct of "Arab slavery" as one of the justifications for the attribution of collective guilt as well as the killings carried out on the islands in 1964.[120] The writers of the vernacular historiography, responding to the association of the Sultanate of Zanzibar and Pemba with slavery, endeavor to show that slavery is largely an externally imposed colonial theme on Zanzibar's history, fundamentally stemming from European imperialism.[121] Al-Barwani writes about the myths and distortions of Islamic slavery that "it is the duty of writers and historians among the Swahili themselves to disabuse the minds of this generation and the generations to come."[122] The ideological connection between slavery and the Zanzibar revolution, not the defense of slavery qua slavery, is what is really at stake in this historiography.[123] The writers engage with the discourse of slavery not to defend the contemporary practice of slavery but to delink what they see as a selective, deterministic, and damaging association of slavery's history with Arabs and Islam by abolitionist rhetoric.[124] Ahmed Hamoud al-Maamiry accused European colonial writers of positing an ideological construct of "Arab slavery," with which they wanted to "undermine Arabs and Islam."[125] In *Kinyanganyiro na Utumwa*, Issa Nasser al-Ismaily called such associations slander ("usingiziaji"). According to al-Ismaily, Europeans had three goals in East Africa: "to destroy Islam, to build up Christianity, and to enrich their own nation."[126] In another work, *Uzanzibari na Usultani*, al-Ismaily emphasized Seyyid Said and other Omani rulers' contributions in ending slavery.[127]

The writers are keen to emphasize slavery as a "secular" issue, not particular to one religion or ethnicity in terms of either demand or supply; however, many treat it through a modernist lens, seeing it as having the potential both to indict the character of Muslim civilization in East Africa more generally. Al-Haddad, in a separate section on slavery in Islam, treated slavery as many of the aforementioned authors do: as having a "civilizational" character that differs from culture to culture, rather than a class character determined by the kinds of labor slaves did.[128] Babakerim described Arabs on the caravan routes to the coast as only building on the slavery practiced by African tribes, an argument also made by the Swahili poet Robert Shaaban.[129] However, nowhere is slavery engaged in terms of its specific historical character in Zanzibar, on the African mainland, or in terms of the evolution of relations between the servile and elite classes of society.

At times the historiography reanimates the trope of "Islamic slavery" as a form of positive rather than negative exceptionalism, emphasizing that it was a mode of slavery less cruel and more socially assimilationist than its Western counterpart.[130] The euphemism of slaves as family also recurs repeatedly in this historiography.[131] In al-Rahbi's novel, the narrator listened to slaveowners from Zanzibar insist that slaves are family members, manumitted and given land by their masters and limited to five days a week of work.[132] While many slaves in history may have patiently endured their lot and even come to be grateful for the benevolence of their masters, one wonders if this trope of "family" accords with the private thoughts of the enslaved on the nature of the relationship; nowhere is the testimony of slaves offered as evidence to bolster such assertions.

A recent work in this vein is Ibrahim Noor Sharrif's *Tanzania na Propaganda za Udini*. The book explores the world history of the slave trade, the participation of different ethnicities, the cruelty of European-led slavery in the Americas, colonial propaganda about Arab slavery, and beliefs by Africans about the slave trade.[133] Shariff also critiqued the portrayal of the East African slave trade in colonial and postcolonial Tanzanian education textbooks, noting the manner in which images derived from the Western historiography of slavery were transplanted to East Africa with an orientalist visual touch added.[134] In the introduction, "Professor Ibrahim," who taught Swahili literature at Rutgers University for years before immigrating to Oman in the 1980s, related an incident in 1960 when he was a young man in Zanzibar. He stopped to listen to a speech by Abeid Karume given near the Anglican Church. Karume incited the audience against Arabs, detailing all the horrors they had allegedly inflicted on hapless Africans, painting them as grotesque villains.[135] Shariff recalled his blood running cold listening. He argued that anti-Arab and anti-Swahili rhetoric are forms of anti-Muslim propaganda originating in the colonial moment and picked up by Tanzanian intellectuals and politicians. He detailed a number of the most common myths linking Arabs in Zanzibar to the dead and murdered bodies of African slaves.[136]

Since the renewal of relations with Oman and other Gulf countries in the 1980s, wild rumors have occasionally flown in Zanzibar and on the mainland about East Africans being sold into slavery to rich Arabs.[137] The fundamental structural asymmetry between the national economies of the two countries helps the persistence of the symbolic linkage between Arabs and slavery among East Africans; the negative experiences of some Tanzanian and Kenyan labor migrants in Oman and the broader Gulf have also tended to revive this discourse.[138] Given the prominent role of slavery talk in Zanzibar's contemporary cultural heritage discourse, Omani-Zanzibari intellectuals are keenly attuned to the issue of slavery's representation in East African literature and media, which globalization has helped to expand interest in. While one does not need to agree with the overall characterization of slavery in the vernacular historiography and can indeed criticize some of it as self-interested, an unmistakably important argument it makes is that the multifocal heritage of Zanzibar has been narrowed in the Western historical imagination to a story of Arab slavery and African liberation, which is patently unable to engage the politics of Zanzibar's present political crisis. The vernacular historians do not see slavery as a fatalistic or deterministic element in Zanzibar's history as many Western writers tend to.

The vernacular authors are proud of the Sultanate of Zanzibar as the fountain and center of Muslim life on the coast, the only Muslim majority "country" in the region, and as a global symbol of national pride for all those born and residing there.[139] Their writing is grounded in what Marie-Aude Fouéré describes as "the idea that the Isles' independence is the product of a century of slow maturation, throughout the nineteenth century, of a body politic rooted in a clearly delimited island territory."[140] Unlike many Omani authors, who often position the Zanzibar revolution as "the end of Omani rule (ḥukm al-ʿUmanī) in Zanzibar," the authors understand that this framing essentially accepts the arguments of their critics in the ASP, which denied muwalladūn claims on territorial belonging and denigrated the idea of a "Zanzibari" territorial identity.[141] The forms of progress toward a specifically Muslim modernity (symbolized in these works by the printing press, the railroad, electric lighting, and schools) made by its nineteenth- and twentieth-century rulers in Zanzibar are posited as either the ideological forerunner of the modern Omani developmental state or an ideological resource for renewing development in Zanzibar. Zanzibar's 1963 independence is remembered by the authors as the fulfillment of sovereignty denied to the Sultanate of Zanzibar after 1890. Issa Nasser al-Ismaily argued that Zanzibar at independence was "a shining star in the whole of East Africa."[142]

POLITICS AND REVOLUTION IN THE VERNACULAR HISTORIOGRAPHY

Arif Dirlik notes the challenge of reconciling memory with history for revolutionary legacies, when the problems of the revolution stem from its contemporary representations.[143] If the Zanzibar sultanate did not survive the contentious politics of decolonization, the memories of its onetime supporters did, outlasting their post-1964 exile and the assumption of Omani citizenship from 1970 to 1990 to return as a form of historical imagination in the next generation. The nationalist generation, several of whom had been members of the civil service administration in Zanzibar in the 1950s, took the most authoritative role as active transmitters of their memories of the revolution, while the generation who came of age in exile was also very influential in shaping these into a historical narrative. Radical muwalladūn who sided with the Zanzibar revolutionaries in 1964 have also joined the conversation. They are all interested in fundamentally challenging the hegemonic narrative of the revolution and rewriting its history.[144]

The narrative of the exiles was largely devoted to undermining a narrative created in Zanzibar after the revolution, which portrayed Zanzibar's 1963 independence as a false independence ("uhuru bandia"). Their time in Oman had changed the Omani-Zanzibaris by the time they sat down to write their memoirs and works of history. Many had grown more conservative because of living for decades in an absolute monarchy with a carefully managed public sphere for debate. The distance of those raised in exile from East Africa, their proximity to narratives of victimization and conspiracy, their elite social standing, and their promonarchy views influenced their interpretations of the revolution.

This was evident in how they began to portray mass politics and republican ideas themselves as the problem in Zanzibar.[145] Many of the authors were critical of what they saw as the excesses of anticolonial nationalism. Saud Ahmed al-Busaidi opined that populist politicians promised the world to their constituents, who lacked the education to take advantage of national independence.[146] The outlook of many in this generation on the revolution is captured in al-Maamiry's *Oman and East Africa*, first published in 1979. In chapter 14, "Why a Revolution in Zanzibar?," al-Maamiry explained that Zanzibar's ethnic tensions lay within the more immediate past of the protectorate after 1890 and the subsequent three-quarters of a century, especially with food rationing on the basis of race during World War II.[147] Al-Maamiry argued the British government was hostile to this party, the ZNP, and that the Zanzibar revolution was a conspiracy by the mainland government of Tanganyika.[148] Al-Maamiry portrayed Zanzibar politics in the 1960s as manipulating people's desires to be wealthy by dispossessing others: "The dream was that when the Arabs are turned out and their lands are confiscated and re-distributed to the Africans, everybody would be rich in the country."[149]

Vernacular authors tended to portray Africans in Zanzibar as victims of a colonial propaganda campaign to undermine Arabs and Islam. Al-Haddad portrayed the revolution as a repudiation of the spread and influence of Arabs and Islam throughout all East Africa, rather than just Zanzibar.[150] Al-Barwani saw the revolution as fundamentally continuous and connected to the nineteenth-century colonial effort to undermine

Islam in East Africa, motivated by jealousy about Zanzibar's level of development and payback for the anti-Zionist stance of the ZNP.[151] Al-Barwani and al-Ismaily both accused the British of not wanting to see an independent Arab Muslim country succeed, in order to punish ZNP leadership for supporting Egyptian anticolonialism.[152] Al-Maamiry accused the British of preventing "other races from joining with the Arabs."[153] Al-Ismaily opined that British officials had helped to create the ASP "on purpose to oppose a nationalist party."[154] In *Sowing the Wind*, a fictionalized account of the time of politics, Haj had one of his characters argue that the ASP was founded with the support of British colonial officials who wanted to offset the ZNP.[155] Haj had this character opine that the ASP was not even a genuine political party, "just a hastily organized mass movement for winning one election."[156] Shaaban al-Farsy accused the ASP of fomenting ethnic division among Muslims and importing mainland voters illegally to swing elections.[157]

Most if not all the vernacular historians, as well as many interviewees, believed the revolution was a mainland invasion, planned by members of the Tanganyikan government, including Nyerere and Kambona, in alliance with sympathetic British officials.[158] This idea had long circulated in exile journalism and in private testimony; after 1990 it found its way into biography, memoir, and historical narrative.[159] Issa Nasser al-Ismaily titled a section of his book "No Revolution without Tanganyika." Al-Ismaily argued that the existence of an independent Zanzibar posed a threat to Nyerere's vision of a greater Tanganyika.[160] Ibrahim Noor Shariff argued that the goal of the propaganda against Swahili and Arabs in Zanzibar was ultimately to make Zanzibar a province of the larger country.[161] This position was echoed in the 2019 account of the revolution by Egyptian author Dr. Saleh Mahrous Muhammad Muhammad, subtitled, "The Last Days Omani Rule in East Africa."[162]

These views of mainland interference in the politics of Zanzibar were given additional support by the publication of Harith Ghassany's *Kwa Heri Ukoloni, Kwa Heri Uhuru!* In his interview with Ghassany, Muhammad Abdul-Muttalib Hashim claimed that Daniel Moi chided Nyerere in the early 1990s, for his role in the invasion of Zanzibar and that Kambona openly admitted to the exiles his role in facilitation.[163] A supporting piece of evidence often presented and discussed is a shipment of Algerian weapons. Dr. Salem al-Ismaily, whose historical novel is really an explanation of the revolution, claimed Israelis helped to arm Babu's and Hanga's supporters with these Algerian arms.¹⁶⁴ Ghassany's interviewees added testimony about this shipment; Mzee Aboud declared that the guns were stolen from the Algerian ship by Oscar Kambona's men and then smuggled from Tanga to Pemba and then through Forodhani in Unguja. However, the actual use of these weapons in the revolution has never been demonstrated; Mzee Aboud claimed most of them were not used.¹⁶⁵ Al-Riyami argued that a large number of men arrived from the African mainland, "but only after the overthrow of the government, not before."¹⁶⁶

The young socialist Arabs of the Umma Party who enthusiastically joined the revolution come in for special criticism by the authors of the vernacular historiography; there is especially vituperative dislike of Abdulrahman Babu among the former ZNP ministers especially. In *Ukweli ni Huu*, ex-ZNP minister Aman Thani characterized him as a talented but selfish individual who destroyed the ZNP. Al-Ismaily likened the political party Babu founded, Umma, to a parasitic plant growing on the nationalist movement.¹⁶⁷ Al-Maamiry blamed the Umma Party for planning the revolution.¹⁶⁸ Al-Busaidi argued that "Babu was the one who planned the coup and brought Tanganyikan fighters to Zanzibar."¹⁶⁹ The dislike of Babu sometimes resulted in overestimating his influence; as when Shahbal claimed the formation of the Tanganyika-Zanzibar Union was a US-led conspiracy to isolate Babu.¹⁷⁰ Al-Farsy condemned "Makomred" (Umma) for a list of eighteen crimes, including killing civilians, expropriating land and property illegally, forced marriages, public beatings, violation of mosques, stealing of waqf properties, and imprisonment without trial.¹⁷¹

The vernacular historiography was often sharply critical of Karume. Shariff called him an "evil man" and asserted that he was a foreigner born in Congo.¹⁷² The muwalladūn author Hamad Ahmed al-Haddad had particularly bitter and racially tinged words for Karume. Remembering Karume's speeches, he recalled his imposing physical presence, including his "broad shoulders," "sharp eyelashes," "bulging red eyes," and "huge head." The author described him as a gloomy-faced human who you think will assault you.¹⁷³ A 2017 picture book of Omanis in Zanzibar claimed Karume was responsible for bringing armed mainlanders to attack islanders, despite the evidence that he was not involved in revolutionary planning at all and actually took steps to halt the violence.¹⁷⁴ Some of the vernacular historians partially rehabilitated the image of Karume as a Zanzibar nationalist. Despite his failings, Karume was portrayed as someone who put Zanzibar first.

Some went so far as to imply that he was assassinated on the eve of plans to break the Union.[175] Salem ben Nasser Al-Ismaily held Karume innocent of the violent actions of the revolution, claiming "he was horrified by the whole business."[176] In her 2021 memoir, Bi Ubwa, who was very close to Karume, denied that Karume had any knowledge of her father's extrajudicial killing, placed the blame on other, more impulsive and vengeful members of the Revolutionary Council, and said that she believed that Karume had tried to stop the killing.[177]

Regarding the violence, the arguments of the vernacular historiography refer to it as a genocide. The evidence they use to do so is an object lesson in the new intermingling of digital resources with traditional historical evidence. Most Zanzibaris, including those in exile, had not seen the film *Africa Addio* before the founding of YouTube in 2005. But sometime in the late 2000s the film was uploaded there. Notably the film contains extended footage of mass graves allegedly from Zanzibar. Subsequently the footage was repurposed into video narratives in Arabic.[178] Stills from the film were also used on a website commemorating the revolution and have proliferated in new digital platforms like Twitter and TikTok.[179] Shariff also used numerous stills from the film in *Tanzania na Propaganda za Udini*.[180] The credulous use of video stills as evidence is a product of the new digital information economy; despite the massive expansion in availability of information, video narratives are even more liable than written sources to become the source of uncritical and dogmatic conclusions.

There is an increasing openness to public criticism on both sides that was not present in earlier decades. The sensitive questions of human rights in postcolonial Tanzanian history have even begun to be discussed by intellectuals in Tanzania.[181] More recent works by Omani-Zanzibaris show signs of willingness to be critical of the mistakes of the ZNP. The coastal Kenyan politician Suleiman Shahbal wrote a landmark work analyzing the revolution in which he was critical of the ZNP leadership.[182] Dr. Salem al-Ismaily's novel has one of the characters express criticisms of Ali Muhsin's mistakes, including the ZNP attempt to deny Karume the right to stand for elections on citizenship grounds (discussed in chapter 1). Al-Ismaily also had his narrator criticize Ali Muhsin's closeness to Egyptian president Gamal Abdel Nasser and inability to see Babu's threat.[183] Al-Ismaily also demonstrated keen awareness of generational divisions within the ASP and the ZNP. In his 2018 memoir, former Umma cadre Hashil S. Hashil argued that the revolution could have been avoided if ZNP and

ZPPP leadership had listened to warnings about the security situation in Zanzibar. He criticized the ZNP for refusing to cooperate with the ASP after winning the 1963 elections; a national unity government might have staved off a revolutionary conspiracy.[184] In a short essay on "political problems in Zanzibar," the Zanzibari writer Ally Saleh criticized the revolutionaries, arguing that they could have avoided many problems by being more gracious to their defeated enemies.[185] A few of my interviewees were similarly critical of what they saw as an entrenched and reflexive need by some former Zanzibar exiles to put down anyone associated with the ASP or the Umma Party.

As we saw in the novels of Maulid Haj and Salem al-Ismaily, interpretations of the revolution were not confined to memoirs and history.[186] Increasingly the revolution has been dramatized in fiction. Exiled Zanzibari writer Abdulrazak Gurnah was one of the earliest to tackle the questions of what the revolution meant for Zanzibar's diaspora in works of fiction like *Memory of Departure* (1987) and *Pilgrims Way* (1988). The Zanzibari novelist Adam Shafi (b. 1940) had in the 1970s published an indictment of social relations in Zanzibar's agricultural sector (*Kasri ya Mwinyi Fuad*) and a fictional rendering of the 1948 dockworkers' strike (*Kuli*). But he turned in 2003 to fictionalizing the experiences of torture and indefinite detention suffered by Zanzibaris under the Karume regime (*Haini*).[187] The descriptions of life in Zanzibar before and during the revolution have also found expression in a remarkable bildungsroman-style Swahili novel of a young woman's coming of age, *Imepita Jana* (translated into English as *Gone Is Yesterday*) by Naila Kharusi.[188] Former Umma Party writers have recently contributed to the works of fiction narrativizing politics and revolution.[189] The authors have stated their purpose as "stimulating Zanzibaris to come forward and relate their experiences of what happened during the 1964 Revolution that took place on the islands of Zanzibar and Pemba" and as a "vent for my inner anguish and lament with respect to my country of birth, Zanzibar."[190]

In *Zanjibār: Wa Akfān min Raḥim Al-'Alam* (Zanzibar: Shrouds from the womb of pain), Zanzibar-born Omani author Sheikha al-Ghonaimi portrayed the gripping experience of an Omani-born boy who moves to Zanzibar at age eight with his father, where he lives through the 1964 revolution in Zanzibar. During the revolution, Mohammed and his younger brother are hidden in a well during the revolution by Mohammed's African friend, Yusuf, and Yusuf's family, while outside they hear the terrifying din and cry of an anti-Arab pogrom nearby. They witness other atrocities before dramatically escaping the islands.[191]

CONCLUSION

An aging generation in Oman still preserves the living memory of a turbulent era in East African history. These traumatic memories of the Zanzibar revolution shaped the contemporary political identity of Zanzibar-born Omani citizens and the Omani state's reconstruction and promotion of the cultural and national heritage of modern Oman.[192] The coming decades have tremendous potential for transcending the terms on which politics has been conducted in both countries for a generation. The generation of exiles turned Omani citizens born immediately after World War I are now mostly deceased. Even those born between 1930 and 1940 are in their eighties and nineties. Those born in 1964 are nearing sixty now. Fewer and fewer people in either Zanzibar or Oman have any connection to the conditions that brought about the revolution; most Zanzibaris and Omanis today have no direct memory of it.

Transmission of memory in the form of narrative is marked by the assimilation of memories from a smaller group into a much larger receiving group, thus becoming the imagined collective "property" of a larger group who did not experience them directly. In this way, memory transmitted in written narratives becomes a form of increasingly generic group inheritance, and each successive generation must go back to study the past to avoid its trivialization as heritage.[193] As the transmitting generation ages and dies, the opportunity to verify or rediscuss with speakers their own statements is lost. All that is left then are their recorded utterances and inscriptions. The Tanzanian ambassador to Oman Ahmed Saleh emphasized this transition as an opportunity to look to the future of a new generation in both Arabia and East Africa.[194] Elders who lived through the harrowing events of that time now affirm what Tony Judt has called "a future-oriented vocabulary of social harmony and material improvement" meant to "occupy a public space hitherto filled with older, divisive, and more provincial claims and resentments."[195] The multiplication of biographical narratives by Zanzibari exiles in Oman, the United Kingdom, and elsewhere shows the diversity of historical experiences *within* the community of muwalladūn returnees from Zanzibar and their relation to other branches of the "Omani" diaspora throughout East and Central Africa.[196]

Is it possible to integrate the history of the independence of 1963 into the history of the 1964 revolution? Is that narrative also compatible with the history of the Union? Or are the two narratives fundamentally irreconcilable? Paradoxically, memory transmission meant to explode the mythologies embedded in traditional narratives of history may help create and reinforce other mythologies of its own. Even though we now have more materials than ever to portray the events of mid-twentieth-century Zanzibar, the aging out of a generation in both Zanzibar and Oman can also mean the next generation is dependent more and more on versions of Zanzibar's history transmitted directly from their elders. Integrating narratives about Zanzibar produced on opposite sides of the Indian Ocean can compensate for the flattening that occurs in memory transmission in diaspora and the possible biases introduced by that context. Without this integration, there will continue to be histories in which the essentializations of race and ethnicity are reified into Manichean narratives, imprisoning future readers in stale and hackneyed narratives of either angelic ancestral heroism or collective historical guilt, complicity, and blame. The transmission of the memories of Afro-Arabs during the Zanzibar revolution has the potential to challenge mythical constructions of the revolution by exiles and revolutionaries, a process already being engaged in by Zanzibar intellectuals.[197]

Educated members of its political leadership, now that the risk of a diaspora-sponsored counterrevolution has passed, have engaged in a more critical and balanced process about the positives and negatives of the revolution, including its negative impact on the rights of the individual and the uneven results of the development process assembled ad hoc in the revolution's wake.[198] The revolution, regardless of whether it was "necessary" or "inevitable," actually impeded and stalled necessary processes of consultation and democratization, whereby a robust popular democracy might still be legitimized in both Unguja *and* Pemba.[199] Had there been some political prudence, more restraint, and more willing power sharing exhibited in the late 1950s and early 1960s, Zanzibar easily might have been able to transition its economy in the manner of Mauritius, Seychelles, Singapore, or Brunei and become a middle-income country. History is open ended, and the tragedy of human existence is that although we cannot exist socially without the transmission of our memories to each other, present action can never be perfectly informed by the past. Memory is ever imperfect, never an infallible guide to the changing conditions of the future, and liable to be shorn into projects that confine it within a more static realm of national heritage.

Conclusion

EVERY ELECTION from the early 2000s in Zanzibar have brought fresh tensions that reanimate the ghosts of race, religion, and national origin in the complex politics of Zanzibar.[1] CCM and the opposition party Civic United Front (CUF) have fought six hotly contested elections, in 1995, 2000, 2005, 2010, 2015, and 2020, characterized by intimidation, violent and xenophobic political rhetoric, and even outright fraud.[2] In the wake of the Electoral Commission's decision to abruptly "cancel" the October 2000 election results of sixteen constituencies, more than thirty protestors against the election results were killed by police, and nearly six hundred people were seriously injured.[3] More than two thousand displaced people fled to nearby Shimoni, on the Kenya Coast.[4] Although a "Government of National Unity" was formed in 2010 out of a historic agreement between the parties, it lasted only one term, and the 2015 election was controversially annulled, then rerun (with a lower turnout) in 2016.[5] The requirement to show a Zanzibar ID document proving one's citizenship in order to vote was a controversial issue in these elections.[6] These rivalries have inflamed an old division between mainlanders and islanders, as well as that between Pembans (the majority of whom support CUF) and Ungujans (who largely support CCM).[7]

Arab-African tensions appear mostly subdued in modern Zanzibar, as mixed lineages of the ruling class have ensured that the politics of Arabophobia have little purchase, although one sometimes hears disgruntled sentiments about Zanzibar from mainland politicians.[8] Zanzibar's first family, the Karumes, are a product of African and Arab lineages: Abeid Karume's wife was Arab. Their son Amani married the daughter of Fatima Jinja and Yusuf Hemedi, Shadia. Shadia and Amani had a daughter named Fatma

Karume, who today writes about politics in Zanzibar. This intermixture of lineages, even though it occurred during one of the most difficult periods in Zanzibar's history, has produced a new generation of Afro-Arab Zanzibari leadership who are interested in moving beyond the old antagonisms and debates. Zanzibar president Salmin Amour went so far as to invite the exiled Sultan Jamshid to return to Zanzibar as a private citizen. Ironically, Jamshid was permitted to visit Zanzibar in 2010, before he was allowed to retire in Oman, a move that only occurred under Sultan Qaboos's successor, Sultan Haitham bin Tariq, after Qaboos's death in 2020.

The wealth accumulation of certain Arab muwalladūn groups as a result of petroleum rents has enabled them to continue older strategies of mobility between states. Their wealth, the images of Gulf prosperity broadcast around the world, the harrowing stories of some African migrant laborers, and images of the African composition of Qatar's national football team animate old tensions and create new expectations in East Africa about the meaning of the Gulf in the East African imagination. Meanwhile the liberalization of Tanzania's economy has meant increased migration to Oman and especially the Gulf.

More pragmatic, material concerns appear paramount in the current relationship. Tanzanian president Jakaya Kikwete made a historic visit to Oman in October 2012, and the two countries exchanged delegations to discuss economic assistance and development. In January 2014 a joint agreement between Shell and the Zanzibar government gave Shell the right to develop the tremendous natural gas resources offshore of the islands.[9] As Tanzania embarked on a project to exploit these offshore hydrocarbon deposits, Oman saw an opportunity to diversify its economy by investing in Tanzanian development. State elites in each country stand to gain economically from the relationship, and Omani-Zanzibaris are particularly well placed to ideologically legitimate Oman's economic interests in the region.[10] In October 2017 the then minister of oil and gas, Muhammad al-Rumhi, a returnee, led a major delegation to Tanzania to discuss development cooperation.[11] In 2021 the Oman Investment Authority signed a memorandum of understanding to develop a new port in Zanzibar. There has been no shortage of philanthropic and educational cooperation over the last thirty years.

Muwalladūn ancestry, a liability in the revolutionary period, has today became a symbol of international cooperation; politicians on both sides referred to the ties of blood linking the two countries.[12] There has been a scholarship program for Zanzibari students to study in Oman, as well as festivals and academic conferences celebrating the shared culture between the two regions. The family trips by former Zanzibaris have been joined by a younger generation of Omanis interested in Oman's East African presence and influential in promoting Swahili coast folkways, foodways, and fashion in modern Muscat. The city is a node on an Afropolitan network of Swahili-speaking Indian Ocean Muslims. One wonders if, without a class analysis, this emphasis can really challenge the ethnoracial reification that pervades contemporary and commonsense understandings of who or what an Omani or a Zanzibari is.[13] Can the new generation transcend the paradigm of ethnonational citizenship?

National citizenship in both Oman and Zanzibar continues to be marked by contention and controversy over what Jon Soske calls the "internal frontier" of the nation.[14] The developmental state, even in its neoliberal phase, continues to generate expectations and dreams about citizenship among ordinary people, on both sides of the Indian Ocean. In 2012 there was a proposal by the Tanzanian government for dual citizenship for émigrés born in Tanzania, in order to spur the return of the diaspora populations who may have nationalized in their host countries. These efforts included outreach to Omanis born in Zanzibar and mainland Tanzania.[15] The news created a stir among Tanzanian-born Omanis in Muscat.

Debates about Zanzibar nationality have also tried to define who is a Zanzibari within the structure of the Union.[16] The government continues to use identity documents, specifically Zanzibar identification residency cards, to differentiate citizens from noncitizens.[17] The citizenship status of those who departed in 1964 has been important to the debate. In Tanzania, the failure to proactively address Zanzibar's place within the Union—by either seeking popular ratification by majorities in both countries or creating a federal structure whereby the mainland and the islands can both enter as equal partners—guarantees the issue will continue to remain a vulnerability for Tanzania and create frustration among Zanzibaris.[18]

The imagined community of Zanzibar has signal importance for the politics of citizenship in Zanzibar. Some Zanzibaris assert that "Zanzibar ni nchi kamili" (Zanzibar is a "complete" [sovereign] country) and question the legality and benefit of the union with the mainland, asserting that it is another form of neocolonialism; they find in Zanzibar's 1963 independence a precedent for their vision. This assertion of Zanzibari sovereignty by Zanzibar politicians does not imply their approval of the return of the ex-ZNP ministers or the Arab sultan.[19] By 1990, as we have seen, there was already a substantial portion of Zanzibar's new political elites who were determined to maintain Zanzibar's autonomy within the Union, without promoting open conflict with the Union government, and they did not need exile support. This element's influence has continued to grow. The imagined community of "Zanzibar" draws its power from the islands' longer history of nineteenth-century sovereignty. This imagination will remain important to the Afro-Arabs, their Omani descendants, and the larger community of muwalladūn historians writing about Zanzibar in the wake of the sixtieth anniversary of the revolution in January 2024.

In Oman, the "time of oil," while bringing tremendous progress, has also increasingly been characterized by an awareness among state elites of petroleum as a finite resource. Oman thus faces first and foremost a fiscal challenge of meeting the expectations of a new generation of school leavers that the state will find them gainful employment, in the face of declining petroleum reserves. It must meet these expectations at the same time that it diversifies its economy, and it must find a way to reduce its dependence on noncitizen expatriate labor, a difficult prospect when most Omani citizens have acquired a taste for the kinds of goods and services that low-wage labor can provide. This, in essence, is the dilemma of Omanization, an indigenization process.[20] Moreover, the sources of citizenship in the Gulf continue to be a point of contention; Habiba al-Hinai's son's citizenship was revoked as punishment for marrying a non-Omani, and al-Hinai went into voluntary exile in Berlin as a result. There have been recent rumors that the law preventing Omani women from passing on nationality directly to their offspring will be rescinded, a hopeful development.

A group of stateless people of Omani descent in Burundi briefly captured international attention in 2011 and 2012. All were remnants of older waves of Omani migration that had reached into central Africa during the late nineteenth and early twentieth centuries. One of those stateless people in Burundi, Sultan Salum, told Agence France Press, "'What is said in the family, is that our ancestors came from Oman via Zanzibar to Kigoma,'" referring to a town on the eastern Tanzanian shores of Lake Tanganyika. "'Finally they landed in Burundi.'"[21] Most of this community were living in Bujumbura and surrounding areas without papers of any kind, except for temporary residence permits provided by the government and the UNHCR. The community has been advocating that Omani government recognize them as conationals, give them the right of return, and give them

Omani passports. Salum said, "'I want a passport from my home in Oman, to live on the land of our ancestors.'"[22]

Examining the salience of their memories to belonging across national contexts, this book has explored the twentieth-century history of muwalladūn of Omani descent and East African birth and their pursuit of "alternative political goals and strategies" to secure a national citizenship in a period of delineation of national borders and national identities.[23] Ideologies of ethnonationalism in both the Gulf and East Africa have obscured the ethnic and cultural mixing that occurred over the long history of interaction between Arabian and East African coastal regions of the Indian Ocean world and marginalized the Swahili in the postcolonial states of Kenya and Tanzania.[24] Their postcolonial migrations have been contextualized here against the rise of the developmental state and the economic divergence between the Gulf and East Africa, including monumental political transformations in state regimes.[25] Although nativism has been since World War II at the base of postcolonial Arab and African nation-states on both sides of the Indian Ocean rim, this book has demonstrated a more historically contingent reality of muwalladūn in different contexts negotiating Arab and African national citizenships. It has also demonstrated the persistence of a transregional Swahili-speaking Muslim public sphere that includes muwalladūn as well as many other East Africans, in which other forms of belonging are negotiated with the national frame.

NOTES

INTRODUCTION

1. Habiba al-Hinai, 'Ā'idūn Ḥaythu al-Ḥulm:, Mashāhid wa-Dhikriyyāt 'auda min Zanjibār wa al-Jazīrat-l-Khaḍrā' 'ilā 'Uman (Beirut: Beirut Bookshop, 2013), 77.
2. Al-Hinai, 'Ā'idūn, 88–89.
3. Ronald Aminzade, *Race, Nation and Citizenship in Post-Colonial Africa: The Case of Tanzania* (Cambridge: Cambridge University Press, 2014), 358; and James R. Brennan, "Julius Rex: Nyerere through the Eyes of His Critics, 1953–2013," in *Remembering Nyerere in Tanzania: History, Memory and Legacy*, ed. Marie-Aude Fouéré (Dar-es-Salaam: Mkuti wa Nyota, 2015), 158. For context on the political imaginations of revolutionary Zanzibar in relationship to establishing the union, see Marie-Aude Fouéré, "Recasting Julius Nyerere in Zanzibar: The Revolution, the Union and the Enemy of the Nation," *Journal of Eastern African Studies* 8, no. 3 (April 2014): 478–496.
4. Nienke Boer, *The Briny South: Displacement and Sentiment in the Indian Ocean World* (Durham, NC: Duke University Press, 2023), 2–3. See also May Joseph, "Indian Ocean Ontology: Nyerere, Memory and Place," in *Reimagining Indian Ocean Worlds*, ed. Smriti Srinivas, Bettina Ng'weno, and Neelima Jeychandran (London: Routledge, 2020), 44. For additional insights into the links between sentiment, memory, and the construction of narratives in relation to identity, see Andrew Shryrock, *Nationalism and the Genealogical Imagination: Oral History and Textual Authority in Tribal Jordan* (Berkeley: University of California Press, 1997), 243; Julia Creet, introduction to *Memory and Migration: Multidisciplinary Approaches to Memory Studies*, ed. Andrea Klitzmann and Julia Creet (Toronto: Toronto University Press, 2011), 10; Pierre Nora, "Between Memory and History: Les Lieux de Memoire" *Representations* 26 (Spring 1989): 7; S. N. Ankersmit, "The Sublime Dissociation of the Past: Or How to Be(come) What One Is No Longer," *History and Theory* 40, no. 3 (2001): 301–302; M. Medved and J. Brockmeier, "When Memory Goes Awry," in *Routledge International Handbook of Memory*

Studies, ed. Anna Lisa Tota and Trever Hagen (London: Routledge, 2016), 450; and Duncan Bell, ed., *Memory, Trauma and World Politics: Reflections on the Relationship between Past and Present* (New York: Palgrave Macmillan, 2006).

5. Ariel Crozon, "Zanzibar en Tanzanie: Essai D'histoire Politique," Universite de Pau et des Pays de L'adour, 1992, 112, 130.

6. Ron Eyerman and Giuseppe Sciortino, introduction to *The Cultural Trauma of Decolonization: Colonial Returnees in the National Imagination*, ed. Ron Eyerman and Giuseppe Sciortino (New York: Palgrave Macmillan, 2020), 6; Ron Eyerman, "The Past in the Present: Culture and the Transmission of Memory," in *The Collective Memory Reader*, ed. Jeffrey Olick, Vered Vinitzky Seroussi, and Daniel Levy (Oxford: Oxford University Press, 2011), 304; and Alon Confino, *The Nation as a Local Metaphor: Wurtemberg, Imperial Germany, and National Memory, 1871–1918* (Chapel Hill: University of North Carolina Press, 1997), 7–9.

7. Crozon, "Zanzibar en Tanzanie," 35, 112–13. See also Harith Ghassany's observations about the "wounds and scars" of the events. Harith Ghassany, *Kwa Heri Ukoloni, Kwa Heri Uhuru! Zanzibar na Mapinduzi ya Afrabia* (n.p.: Self-published, 2010), 321.

8. Sauda Barwani, R. Feindt, L. Gerhardt, L. Harding, and L. Wimmelbücker, eds., *Unser Leben von der Revolution und danach—Maisha yetu kabla ya mapinduzi na baadaye* (Cologne: Rüdiger Köppe, 2003), 281–282.

9. Al-Hinai, *'Āidūn*, 37.

10. Samira Salim Seif, Saud Ahmed Busaidy, Suleiman Mohamed Lamki, Hashim Muhamed Kindy, and Suleiman Sultan Malik to Ahmed Seif Kharusi, 9 May 1970, Kharusi Papers (hereafter KP) no. 6.

11. Citizenship is used in the following two senses: formal belonging to a nation-state and affective belonging to that entity of the collective within the state, society.

12. Christopher Lee, "Between a Moment and an Era: The Origins and Afterlives of Bandung," in *Making a World after Empire: Bandung and Its Afterlives* (Athens: Ohio University Press, 2010); Gijsbert Oonk, "Gujarati Asians in East Africa, 1880–2000: Colonization, De-colonization, and Complex Citizenship Issues," *Diaspora Studies* 8, no. 1 (2015): 66–79; George Roberts, "MOLINACO, the Comorian Diaspora, and Decolonisation in East Africa's Indian Ocean," *The Journal of African History* 62, no. 3 (2021): 411–429; Afshin Marashi, *Exile and the Nation: The Parsi Community of India and the Making of Modern Iran* (Austin: University of Texas, 2020); Iain Walker and Marie-Aude Fouéré, eds., *Across the Waves: Strategies of Belonging in Indian Ocean Island Societies* (Leiden: Brill, 2022); Christoph Kalter, *Postcolonial People: The Return from Africa and the Remaking of Portugal* (Cambridge: Cambridge University Press, 2022), xii; and Christopher Lee, "The Indian Ocean during the Cold War: Thinking Through a Critical Geography," *History Compass* 11, no. 7 (2013): 524–530. For a response to that challenge see Ismay Milford et al., "Another World? East Africa, Decolonisation, and the

Global History of the Mid-Twentieth Century," *The Journal of African History* 62, no. 3 (2021): 394–410.

13. Charles Tilly, *Big Structures, Large Processes, Huge Comparisons* (New York: Russell-Sage Foundation, 1984), 23. See also similar sentiments by Jerry Bentley, "A New Forum for Global History" *Journal of World History* 1 no.1 (1990): iii-v.

14. Gabriel Sheffer, *Diaspora Politics: At Home Abroad* (Cambridge: Cambridge University Press, 2009), 148.

15. Kevin C. Dunn and Martin Boas, *Politics of Origin in Africa: Autochthony, Citizenship and Conflict* (London: Zed Books, 2013), 20–22; Nelida Fuccaro, *Histories of City and State in the Persian Gulf: Manama since 1800* (New York: Cambridge University Press, 2009), 190, 207, 228; and Olaf Zenker, "Autochthony, Ethnicity, Indigeneity and Nationalism: Time-Honouring and State-Oriented Modes of Rooting Individual–Territory–Group Triads in a Globalizing World," *Critical Anthropology* 31 no. 1 (2011): 63–81. For state practices of registration tied to this assertion, see Keith Breckenridge, introduction to in *Registration and Recognition: Documenting the Person in World History*, ed. Keith Breckenridge and Simon Szreter (London: British Academy, 2012), 1–36; and John Torpey and Jane Caplan, eds., *The Development of State Practices in the Modern World* (Princeton, NJ: Princeton University Press, 2001).

16. Ulrike Freitag, *Indian Ocean Migrations and State Formation in Hadhramaut* (Leiden: Brill, 2003), 6; and Greg Mann, *From Empires to NGOs in the West African Sahel: The Road to Nongovernmentality* (Cambridge: Cambridge University Press, 2015), 91. See also May Joseph, *Nomadic Identities: The Performance of Citizenship* (Minneapolis: University of Minnesota Press, 1999).

17. David Greenslade, *Ibtisam al-Habsi and Her Zanzibar Court* (Muscat: Ministry of Heritage and Culture, 2013), 24–27.

18. James R. Brennan, *Taifa: Making Nation and Race in Urban Tanzania* (Athens: Ohio University Press, 2012); and Ned Bertz, *Diaspora and Nation in the Indian Ocean: Transnational Histories of Race and Urban Space in Tanzania* (Honolulu: University of Hawai'i Press, 2015).

19. Aiyar, *Indians in Kenya: The Politics of Diaspora* (Boston: Harvard University Press, 2015), 5, 299.

20. Earl Lewis, "'To Turn as on a Pivot': Writing African Americans into a History of Overlapping Diasporas," *American Historical Review* 100, no. 3 (1995): 782. To paraphrase Michael Gomez, the use of the term *diaspora* (Gomez uses the term *community*) does not necessarily entail conscious affinities. Michael Gomez, *Exchanging Our Country Marks: The Transformation of African Identities in the Colonial and Antebellum South* (Chapel Hill: University of North Carolina Press, 1998), 6.

21. Freitag, *Indian Ocean Migrations*, 452; Ninna Nyberg-Sorensen, Nicholas Van Hear, and Poul Engberg-Pedersen, "The Migration-Development Nexus: Evidence and Policy Options State-of-the-Art Overview" *International Migration* 3, no. 4 (2002): 69–70; Jef Huysmans, "Discussing Sovereignty and Transnational

Politics," in *Sovereignty in Transition*, ed. Neil Walker (London: Bloomsbury, 2010), 210; Margaret Kohn and Keally McBride, *Political Theories of Decolonization: Postcolonialism and the Problem of Foundations* (Oxford: Oxford University Press, 2011), 9; Sugata Bose, *A Hundred Horizons: The Indian Ocean in the Age of Global Empire* (Cambridge, MA: Harvard University Press, 2006), 148–150; Sumit Mandal, *Becoming Arab: Creole Histories and Modern Identity in the Malay World* (Cambridge: Cambridge University Press, 2018), 8–9. Pamila Gupta, *Portuguese Decolonization in the Indian Ocean World: History and Ethnography* (London: Bloomsbury, 2018), 2; and Ruth Craggs and Claire Wintle, eds., *Cultures of Decolonization: Transnational Productions and Practices, 1945–1970* (Manchester: Manchester University Press, 2016).

22. Richard Werbner, "Introduction: Multiple Identities, Plural Arenas," in *Postcolonial Identities in Africa*, ed. Richard Werbner and Terence Ranger (London: Zed Books, 1996), 1; and Mohammad Shahabuddin, "Minorities and the 'Ideology' of the Postcolonial State," in *Minorities and the Making of Postcolonial States in International Laws* (Cambridge: Cambridge University Press, 2021). The term *imagined community* is from Benedict Anderson, *Imagined Communities* (London: Verso, 2006).

23. James Brennan, "Lowering the Sultan's Flag: Sovereignty and Decolonization in Coastal Kenya," *Comparative Studies in Society and History* 50, no. 4 (2008): 831–861; Jeremy Prestholdt, "Politics of the Soil: Separatism, Autochthony, and Decolonization at the Kenyan Coast," *The Journal of African History* 55, no. 2 (2014): 249–270; A. I. Salim, "The Movement for 'Mwambao' or Coastal Autonomy in Kenya, 1956–63," in *Hadith 2*, ed. B. A. Ogot (Nairobi: East African Publishing House, 1970), 212–228; and James W. Robertson, *The Kenya Coastal Strip: Report of the Commissioner* (London: H. M. Stationery Office, 1961), Zanzibar National Archives (hereafter ZNA). See also "Purchase of Kenya Coast," ZNA, DD 1/6.

24. Taushif Kara, "Provincializing Mecca? (1924–1969)," *Global Intellectual History* 7, no. 6 (2022): 1037–1057. Reflected in the fact that Indians in Zanzibar during the 1950s were divided between the Indian Association and the Muslim Association.

25. Aiyar, *Indians in Kenya*; and Arif Dirlik. "It Is Not Where You Are from, It is Where You Are At: Place-Based Alternatives to Diaspora Discourse," in *World on the Move: Globalization, Migration and Cultural Security*, ed. Jonathan Friedman and Shalini Randeria (London: I. B. Tauris, 2004), 141–165.

26. Friedhelm Hartwig, "The Segmentation of the Indian Ocean Region: Arabs and the Implementation of Immigration Regulations in Zanzibar and British East Africa," in *Space on the Move: Transformations of the Indian Ocean Seascape in the Nineteenth and Twentieth Century*, ed. Jan-Georg Deutsch and Brigitte Reinwald (Berlin: Klaus Schwarz Verlag, 2002), 21; and Engseng Ho, "Empire through Diasporic Eyes: A View from the Other Boat," *Comparative Studies in Society and History* 46, no. 2 (2004): 210–246; See also Takashi Oishi, "Indian Muslim Merchants in Mozambique and South Africa: Intra-Regional Networks in Strategic Association with State Institutions, 1870s–1930s," *Journal of the Economic and Social History of the Orient* 50, nos. 2/3 (2007): 287–324.

27. Donald Rothchild, *Racial Bargaining in Independent Kenya: A Study of Minorities and Decolonization* (New York: Oxford University Press, 1973), 189–192.

28. John D. Kelly and Martha Kaplan, "Nation and Decolonization: Toward a New Anthropology of Nationalism," *Anthropological Theory* 1, no. 4 (2001): 419–437.

29. Though many of the Afro-Arabs obtained national citizenship in Oman, they remained culturally affiliated to Zanzibar and have used history writing to reshape the narrative history of modern Zanzibar, as well as to educate Omanis on the historical Omani presence in East Africa.

30. William Safran, "Diasporas in Modern Societies: Myths of Homeland and Return," *Diaspora* (Spring 1991): 83–99. The Omani-Zanzibaris fit three to four of Safran's six criteria for constituting a diaspora. See also Robin Cohen, *Global Diasporas* (New York: Routledge, 2008), 26. Some of the most influential and theoretically sophisticated works to have influenced this book are Stephane Dufoix, *Diasporas*, trans. William Rodamor and Roger Waldinger (Berkeley: University of California Press, 2008); Paul Johnson, *Diaspora Conversions: Black Carib Religion and the Recovery of Africa* (Berkeley: University of California Press, 2007); and Bryan Cheyette, *Diasporas of the Mind Jewish and Postcolonial Writing and the Nightmare of History* (New Haven, CT: Yale University Press, 2013). For the Swahili diaspora and long-distance nationalism, see Mohamed Ahmed Saleh, "Swahili Elites and the Concept of Long-Distance Nationalism within the Diaspora," in *Translocal Connections across the Indian Ocean: Swahili Speaking Networks on the Move*, ed. Francesca Declich (Leiden: Brill, 2018), 301–304.

31. Following an agenda suggested in Lydia Walker, "Decolonization in the 1960s: On Legitimate and Illegitimate Nationalist Claims-Making," *Past & Present* 242, no. 1 (February 2019): 233; Omnia El Shakry, "History without Documents: The Vexed Archives of Decolonization in the Middle East," *American Historical Review* 120, no. 3 (2015): 920–934; and Anthony Smith, *Nationalism: Theory, Ideology, History* (London: Polity Press, 2010), 135.

32. Toyin Falola, *Nationalism and African Intellectuals* (Rochester, NY: Boydell and Brewer, 2004), 108; Françoise Perret and François Bugnion, *From Budapest to Saigon: History of the ICRC, 1956–1965* (Geneva: ICRC, 2018), 533; and Ainslee Embree, "Imperialism and Decolonization," in *The Columbia History of the Twentieth Century*, ed. Richard Bulliet (New York: Columbia University Press, 1998), 152.

33. Fuccaro, *Histories of City and State in the Persian Gulf*, 207. See also Will Hanley, *Identifying with Nationality: Europeans, Ottomans and Egyptians in Alexandria* (New York: Columbia University Press, 2017). Comparative histories of citizenship and state have most often been oriented around western Europe instead of Africa and Asia. Quentin Skinner and Bo Strath, eds., *States and Citizens: History, Theory, Prospects* (Cambridge: Cambridge University Press, 2003); and Geoffrey Hosking and George Schopflin, eds., *Myths and Nationhood* (New York: Routledge, 1997).

34. A. G. Hopkins, "Rethinking Decolonization," *Past and Present* 200, no. 1 (2008): 227–228.

35. Fuccaro, *Histories of City and State in the Persian Gulf*, 188; and F. Gregory Gause, "Gulf Regional Politics: Revolution, War and Rivalry," in *Dynamics of Regional Politics: Four Systems on the Indian Ocean Rim*, ed. W. Howard Wriggins (New York: Columbia University Press, 1992), 25.

36. John Meyer et al., "World Society and the Nation-State," *American Journal of Sociology* 103, no. 1 (1997): 144–1581.

37. Eyerman and Sciortino, introduction to *Cultural Trauma of Decolonization*, 3.

38. One Omani returnee from Zanzibar associated the past with social conflict, emphasizing that "happy is the country which has no history." Ahmed Hamoud al-Maamiry, *Whither Oman* (New Delhi: Lancers Publishers, 1981), 11–12.

39. Even the late 1970s transition to democracy in Zanzibar was justified in terms of the need for economic development. Crozon, "Zanzibar en Tanzanie," 357.

40. Fred Cooper, "Africa and the World Economy," *African Studies Review* 24, nos. 2/3 (June–September 1981): 1–86.

41. See Joseph M. Hodge and Gerard Hodl, introduction to *Developing Africa: Concepts and Practices in Twentieth-Century Colonialism*, ed. Joseph M. Hodge, Gerard Hodl, and Martina Kopf (Manchester: Manchester University Press, 2014); and Elizabeth McMahon and Corrie Decker, *The Idea of Development in Africa: A History* (Cambridge: Cambridge University Press, 2020).

42. Mahmood Mamdani, *Citizen and Subject: Contemporary Africa and the Legacy of Late Colonialism* (Princeton, NJ: Princeton University Press, 1997); Crawford Young, *The African Colonial State in Comparative Perspective* (New Haven, CT: Yale University Press, 1994); Manu Goswami, *Producing India: From Colonial Economy to National Space* (Chicago: University of Chicago Press, 2004), 183; and Barry Hindess, "Citizenship and Empire," in *Sovereign Bodies: Citizens, Migrants, and States in the Postcolonial World*, ed. Thomas Blom Hansen and Finn Stepputat (Princeton, NJ: Princeton University Press, 2005), 243. For a comparative study of regional political cultures of the Indian Ocean, see W. Howard Wriggins et al., eds., *Dynamics of Regional Politics: 4 Systems on the Indian Ocean Rim* (New York: Columbia University Press, 1992). See also Robert Kaplan, *Monsoon: The Indian Ocean and the Future of American Power* (New York: Random House, 2010).

43. James Mayall, "Nationalism," in *The Columbia History of the 20th Century*, ed. Richard Bulliet (New York: Columbia University Press, 1998), 180.

44. Subir Sinha, "Lineages of the Developmentalist State: Transnationality and Village India," *Comparative Studies in Society and History* 50, no. 1 (2008): 57–90; and Piotr Dutkiewicz and Gavin Williams, "'All the King's Horses and All the King's Men Couldn't Put Humpty Dumpty Together,'" *IDS Bulletin* 18, no. 3 (1987): 1–6.

45. Christopher Freeman, "Technology and Invention," in *The Columbia History of the 20th Century*, ed. Richard Bulliet (New York: Columbia University Press, 1998), 328.

46. Christopher R. W. Dietrich, *Oil Revolution: Anticolonial Elites, Sovereign Rights, and the Economic Culture of Decolonization* (Cambridge: Cambridge University Press, 2017).

47. Jeremy Prestholdt, "Locating the Indian Ocean: Notes on the Postcolonial Reconstitution of Space," *Journal of Eastern African Studies* 9, no. 3 (2015): 443; and Katrin Bromber, "Working with 'Translocality': Conceptual Implications and Analytical Consequences," in *Regionalizing Oman: Political, Economic, and Social Dynamics* (New York: Springer, 2013), 68.

48. Dietrich, *Oil Revolution*, 251.

49. Peter Liendhardt, *Shaikhdoms of Eastern Arabia* (New York: Palgrave, 2001), 137; Rosemarie Said Zahlan, *The Origins of the United Arab Emirates: A Political and Social History of the Trucial States* (London: Macmillan Press, 1978), 193; Mohammed al-Fahim, *From Rags to Riches: A Story of Abu Dhabi* (London: London Centre of Arab Studies, 1995), 93; Eric Davis and Nicolas Gavrielides, eds., *Statecraft in the Middle East: Oil, Historical Memory, and Popular Culture* (Gainesville: University of Florida Press, 1991); Farah al-Nakib, *Kuwait Transformed: A History of Oil and Urban Life* (Stanford, CA: Stanford University Press, 2016); and Ragaei El Mallakh, *Kuwait: Economic Development and Regional Cooperation* (Chicago: University of Chicago Press, 1968), 2.

50. Erik Gilbert, *Dhows and the Colonial Economy of Zanzibar, 1860–1970* (Athens: Ohio University Press, 2005), 158; and Omar alShehabi, "Histories of Migration in the Gulf," in *Transit States: Labour, Migration and Citizenship in the Gulf*, ed. Abdulhadi Khalaf et al. (London: Pluto Press, 2015), 7–8. For the politics of oil in the Gulf, see Gregory Gause, *Oil Monarchies: Domestic and Security Challenges in the Arab Gulf States*. (New York: Council on Foreign Relations, 1994). Oil was discovered in 1964 in Oman. Christine Eickelman, *Women and Community in Oman* (New York: New York University Press, 1984), 222; and Abdulkhaleq Abdulla, "The Impact of Globalization on Arab Gulf States," in *Globalization and the Gulf*, ed. John W. Fox, Nada Mourtada-Sabbah, and Mohammed Al Mutawa (New York: Routledge, 2006).

51. Anh Nga Longva, "Citizenship in the Gulf States: Conceptualization and Practice," in *Citizenship and State in the Middle East: Approaches and Applications*, ed. Nils Butenschon, Uri Davis, and Manuel Hassassian (Syracuse: Syracuse University Press, 2000), 180. The Zanzibar revolution of 1964 is indicative of a trend in popular social mobilization of antimonarchical and republican ideas during decolonization in Africa and Asia, beginning with the overthrow of King Farouk of Egypt (1952); the abolition of the Tunisian monarchy (1957); the overthrow of monarchies in Rwanda (1961), Yemen (1962), Burundi (1966), and Libya (1969); and the deposing of Emperor Haile Selassie of Ethiopia (1975). Oman was challenged by these antimonarchical trends in the region from the mid-1950s all the way through the mid-1970s.

52. Jill Crystal, "Coalitions in Oil Monarchies: Kuwait and Qatar," *Comparative Politics* 21, no. 4 (1989): 433.

53. Timothy Mitchell, *Carbon Democracy: Political Power in the Age of Oil* (New York: Verso Books, 2011).

54. The modern twentieth century in the Gulf was also characterized by a change in the proportion of the urban population. By the mid-1950s over 50 percent of the population in the Gulf resided in larger urban areas. Liendhardt, *Shaikhdoms*, 143; and Esmond Bradley Martin, "The Geography of Present-Day Smuggling in the western Indian Ocean: The Case of the Dhow," *Great Circle* 1, no. 2 (October 1979): 18–35. Martin cites figures of 500,000 landed on Gulf beaches in that period, compared to 310,000 enslaved Africans landed in the Gulf during the nineteenth century.

55. Ali Mazrui, "Christian Power and Muslim Challenge in Africa's Experience," undated typescript, 14–16, Papers of Ahmed Seif Kharusi, KP. See also Mandana Limbert, *In the Time of Oil: Piety, Memory and Social Life in an Omani Town* (Palo Alto, CA: Stanford University Press, 2010), 163. The oil economies do not fit easily into existing histories of Afro-Asian and Afro-Arab solidarities, which emphasize transnational actors resisting the mainstream of political statecraft. Fuccaro, *Histories of City and State in the Persian Gulf*, 4–13; El Mallakh, *Kuwait*, 1, 237; Ferenc A. Vali, *Politics of the Indian Ocean Region: The Balances of Power* (New York: Free Press, 1976), 214; Gilbert, *Dhows*, 160; and Orne Westad, *The Global Cold War: Third World Interventions and the Making of Our Times* (Cambridge: Cambridge University Press, 2006), 91–92.

56. Marc Valeri, *Oman: Politics and Society in the Qaboos State* (London: Hurst 2009), 93. Valeri noted the dependency of the Interim Planning Council of March 1972 on emigrants from outside Oman: of ten, "six had been educated in Eastern Europe" and "two were born in Zanzibar and had never been in Oman before 1970."

57. Jon Soske, *Internal Frontiers: African Nationalism and the Indian Diaspora in Twentieth-Century South Africa* (Athens: Ohio University Press, 2017), 7.

58. Randall Pouwels, "Eastern Africa and the Indian Ocean to 1800: Reviewing Relations in Historical Perspective," *International Journal of African Historical Studies* 35 (2002): 385–425.

59. David Schoenbrun, personal communication with author, July 2016; and Lionel Casson, ed., *The Periplus Maris Erythraei: Text with Introduction, Translation, and Commentary* (Princeton, NJ: Princeton University Press, 1989).

60. E. S. Brielle et al., "Entwined African and Asian Genetic Roots of Medieval Peoples of the Swahili Coast," *Nature* 615 (2023): 866–873.

61. James McRitchie, and Sigvard von Sicard, *An Azanian Trio: Three East African Arabic Historical Documents* (Leiden: Brill, 2020), 32–33.

62. François Constantin, "Sur les modes populaires d'action diplomatique: Affaires de famille et affaires d'État en Afrique orientale," *Revue française de science politique* 36, no. 5 (1986): 676. For some examples of this intermarriage see Ghassany, *Kwa Heri*, 350. For Arab intermarriage with Manyema women, see Sheryl McCurdy, "Fashioning Sexuality: Desire, Manyema Ethnicity, and the Creation of the Kanga, 1880–1900," *International Journal of African Historical Studies* 39,

no. 3 (2006): 441–469. The phenomenon of intermarriage is widely discussed in the historical literature of the Swahili and bears centrally on the question of how one conceives of who the "Swahili" are. Chapurukha Kusimba, *The Rise and Fall of Swahili States* (Lanham, MD: AltaMira Press, 1999); Randall L. Pouwels, "The Medieval Foundations of East African Islam," *International Journal of African Historical Studies* 11, no. 3 (1978): 213; B. G. Martin, "Arab Migrations to East Africa in Medieval Times," *International Journal of African Historical Studies* 7, no. 3 (1974): 378–379; Neville Chittick, "A New Look at the History of Pate," *The Journal of African History* 10, no. 3 (1969): 383, 389; and Nafla Kharusi, "The Ethnic Label Zinjibari: Politics and Language Choice Implications among Swahili Speakers in Oman," *Ethnicities* 12, no. 3 (2012): 351.

63. Said Salim al-Naamāni, *Al-Hijrāt al-'Umaniyya ilā Sharq 'Ifriqiyyā: ma bain al-Qarnain al-Awal wa al-Sāb'a al-Hijrain, Dirāsa Siyāsa wa Ḥaḍāriyya* (Damascus: Dār al-Farqad, 2012), 313–333; and John Wilkinson, "Oman and East Africa: New Light on Early Kilwan History from the Omani Sources," *International Journal of African Historical Studies* 14, no. 2 (1981): 272–305.

64. Graham Connah, "Indian Ocean Networks: The East African Coast and Islands," in *African Civilizations: An Archaeological Perspective* (New York: Cambridge University Press, 2001), 181–222. As Marc Valeri notes, the category "Arab" "overlooks the varied stages through which Omanis in East Africa have been integrated within Swahili society." Marc Valeri, "Nation-Building and Communities in Oman since 1970: The Swahili-Speaking Omanis in Search of Identity," *African Affairs* 106, no. 424 (2007): 484.

65. Constantin, "Sur les modes populaires", 675; Darren Ray, "Defining the Swahili," in *The Swahili World*, ed. S. Wynne-Jones and A. LaViolette (New York: Routledge, 2017), 66–80. See also Abdullah Najib Muhammad, *Dirāsāt fī-l-adab al-Sawāḥilī: al-Qiṣaṣ al-Sha'bī* (Cairo: Maktaba al-Nahda al-Misriyya, 1987), 64–65. During the colonial period, many assimilated Swahili Arabs were classified as Bajuni, Shirazi, or Swahili, rather than Arab, leading to their petitioning of the Sultan. See letters in ZNA, AB 26/63. See Reda Bhacker, *Trade and Empire in Muscat and Zanzibar: Roots of British Domination* (New York: Routledge, 1992), 5. Bhacker argues that many of these nineteenth-century "Swahili" "may be regarded as more Omani than ... the Zanzibaris returning to Oman in the 1970s." A. I. Salim, "'Native or Non-native?' The Problem of Identity and the Social Stratification of the Arab-Swahili of Kenya," in *Hadith 6: History and Social Change in East Africa* (Nairobi: East African Literature Bureau, 1976), 70–71. Knowledge of Arabic script was widespread even among ordinary islanders well into the mid-twentieth century. See F. B. Wilson, *A Note on Adult Literacy amongst the Rural Population of the Zanzibar Protectorate* (Zanzibar: Government Printer, 1939).

66. Enseng Ho, "Hadhramis Abroad in Hadhramaut: The Muwalladīn," in *Hadhrami Traders, Scholars and Statesmen in the Indian Ocean, 1750s–1960s*, ed. Ulrike Freitag and W. G. Clarence-Smith (Leiden: Brill, 1997); and Leif O. Manger, *The Hadrami Diaspora: Community-Building on the Indian Ocean Rim* (New York: Berghahn Books, 2010).

67. Colette Le Cour Grandmaison, "Rich Cousins, Poor Cousins: Hidden Stratification among the Omani Arabs in Eastern Africa," *Africa: Journal of the International African Institute* 59, no. 2 (1989): 181; and R. E. S. Tanner, "Cousin Marriage in the Afro-Arab Community of Mombasa, Kenya," *Africa: Journal of the International African Institute* 34, no. 2 (April 1964): 127–138. For a suggestive argument for Arabness as "caste," see Mandana Limbert, "Caste, Ethnicity, and the Politics of Arabness in Southern Arabia," *Comparative Studies of South Asia, Africa, and the Middle East* 34, no. 3 (2014): 590–598. In an East African cultural context, an Omani in diaspora might be called "Mshashi," a synonym for an Arab in East Africa who has preserved their traditional homeland ways.

68. Dale F. Eickelman, "From Theocracy to Monarchy: Authority and Legitimacy in Inner Oman, 1935–1957," *International Journal of Middle East Studies* 17, no. 1 (1985): 4–6. Though as Eickelman also notes, in practice the leadership was "the nearly exclusive province of an oligarchic tribal elite." Uzi Rabi, "The Ibadhi Imamate of Muhammad Bin ʿAbdallah al-Khalili (1920–54): The Last Chapter of a Lost and Forgotten Legacy," *Middle Eastern Studies* 44, no. 2 (2008): 174.

69. Saada Wahab, *The History of Indians in Zanzibar from the 1870s to 1963* (Gottingen: Gottingen University Press, 2022), 25.

70. The controversy is discussed in C. F. Beckingham, "The Reign of Aḥmad Ibn Saʿīd, Imam of Oman," *Journal of the Royal Asiatic Society of Great Britain and Ireland* 3 (1941): 257–260. My thanks to Fahad Bishara for bringing my attention to this source. See also Said Ali al-Mugheiry, *Juhaynat-l-Akhbār fī Tārīkh Zanjibār*, ed. Muḥammad Ali al-Sulaibi (Muscat: Ministry of Heritage and Culture Oman, 2001), 206; Jummʿa Khalifa al-Busaidi, *Dirāsāt fī Maʿālim al-Dawlat-l-Busaʿidiyya: al-Haditha min al-Imāma ilā al-Sultana* (Seeb: Maktabat-l-Ḍāmri li-l-Nashr wa al-Tawzīʿ, 2015), 18; and John Wilkinson, *The Imamate Tradition of Oman*. (Cambridge: Cambridge University Press, 1987), 226.

71. Rabi, "Ibadhi Imamate", 175.

72. Bhacker, *Trade and Empire in Muscat and Zanzibar*, 52–53; Patricia Romero, "Seyyid Said bin Sultan BuSaid of Oman and Zanzibar: Women in the Life of this Arab Patriarch," *British Journal of Middle East Studies* 39, no. 3 (December 2012): 373. See also Muzah to Governor of Bombay, 8 April 1832, *Affairs of the Persian Gulf*, Vol. I [235v] (286/556), British Library: India Office Records and Private Papers, IOR/F/4/1435/56726, Qatar Digital Library, https://www.qdl.qa/archive/81055/vdc_100100333663.0x000057.

73. Al-Busaidi, *Dirasāt*, 92; Romero, "Seyyid Said bin Sultan BuSaid of Oman and Zanzibar," 379–380; and Abdullah Muhammad al-Ṭāʾi, *Tārīkh ʿUmān al-Siyāsī* (Maktabat-l-Rubiʿān lil-Nashara wa al-Tawzīʿ, 2008), 189–193.

74. Peter J. Martin, "The Zanzibar Clove Industry," *Economic Botany* 45, no.— (October–December 1991): 450–459.

75. Fahad Bishara, *Sea of Debt: Law and Economic Life in the Western Indian Ocean, 1780–1950* (Cambridge: Cambridge University Press, 2017).

76. Jonathon Glassman, *War of Words, War of Stones: Racial Thought and Violence in Colonial Zanzibar* (Bloomington, Indiana University Press, 2011),

29–30. See also Abdul Sheriff, *Slaves, Spices, & Ivory in Zanzibar: Integration of an East African Commercial Empire into the World Economy, 1770–1873* (London: J. Currey, 1987); Stephen Rockel, *Carriers of Culture: Labor on the Road in Nineteenth Century East Africa* (Portsmouth, NH: Heinemann, 2006); and John Wilkinson, *The Arabs and the Scramble for Africa* (Bristol, CT: Equinox Publishing Ltd., 2015).

77. While trading the first generation of Omanis relied on locally born coastal Muslims, who had experience and connections in the interior. Thomas F. McDow, *Buying Time: Debt and Mobility in the Western Indian Ocean* (Athens: Ohio University Press, 2018), 100–103.

78. Grandmaison, "Rich Cousins, Poor Cousins," 176–184.

79. Grandmaison, "Rich Cousins, Poor Cousins," 177, 179; Collete Grandmaison, *Turāthna: Hijrāt al-Ḥarth ilā 'Awāsiṭ al-Qāratl-l-Afriqiyya* (Muscat: Ministry of Heritage and Culture Oman, 1984); John R. L. Carter, *Tribes in Oman* (London: Peninsular Publishing, 1982), 127; and J. E. Peterson, *Oman: Political Foundations of an Emerging State* (London: Croom Helm, 1978), 119.

80. Grandmaison, "Rich Cousins," 180; and Grandmaison, *Turāthna*, 8.

81. Grandmaison, *Turāthna*, 22; and Ibrahim Zein Soghayrun, "Al-Ishām al-'Umānī fī al-Majālāt al-Thaqāfiyya wa al-Fikriyya wa al-Kashf 'An Majāhil al-Qārat-l-Ifrīqīyya fi Al-'Ahd al-Busa'īdī," in *Fa'āliyyāt wa Nāshiṭ: Ḥiṣād 'Anshiṭat al-Muntadā al-Adabī, 1991–1992*, edited by Salim Muhammad al-Ghailānī and Muhammad Ali al-Sulaibi (Muscat: Ministry of Heritage and Culture, 1993), 193–228.

82. Hamed bin Muhammed el-Murjebi, *Maisha Ya Hamed Bin Muhammed El Murjebi Yaani Tippu Tip Kwa Maneno Yake Mwenyewe* (Nairobi: East African Literature Bureau, 1958).

83. Steven Fabian, *Making Identity on the Swahili Coast: Urban Life, Community, and Belonging in Bagamoyo* (Cambridge: Cambridge University Press, 2019).

84. Chhaya Goswami, *The Call of the Sea: Kachhhi Traders in Muscat and Zanzibar* (New Delhi: Orient Blackswan, 2011); and Pedro Machado, *Ocean of Trade: South Asian Merchants, Africa and the Indian Ocean, c. 1750–1850* (Cambridge: Cambridge University Press, 2014).

85. The argument originates with Randall Pouwels, *Horn and Crescent: Cultural Change and Traditional Islam on the East African Coast, 800–1900* (Cambridge: Cambridge University Press, 1987, 2002). Elizabeth McMahon notes the fundamentally equivalent meaning of the two concepts. Elizabeth McMahon, "'A Solitary Tree Builds Not': Heshima, Community, and Shifting Identity in Postemancipation Pemba Island," *International Journal of African Historical Studies* 39, no. 2 (2006): 200.

86. Amal Ghazal, "Omani Fatwas and Zanzibari Cosmopolitanism: Modernity and Religious Authority in the Indian Ocean," *Muslim World* 105, no. 2 (April 2015): 236–250.

87. Ghazal, "Omani Fatwas," 239; and Valerie J. Hoffman, "Ibāḍīs in Zanzibar and the Nahḍa," in *Oman, Ibadism and Modernity*, ed. A. Al-Salimi &

R. Eisener, Studies on Ibadism and Oman, vol. 12 (Baden: Georg Olms Verlag, 2018), 129–144.

88. Sultan bin Muhammad Al-Qāsimī, *Taqsīm al-Imbrāṭūriyya al-'Umāniyya: 1856–1862* (Sharjah: Al-Qasimi Publications, 2012); Abdel Razzaq Takriti, *Monsoon Revolution: Republicans, Sultans and Empire in Oman, 1965–1976* (Oxford: Oxford University Press, 2013), 15; and Sebastian Żbik, "The Omani Prince in the Search for Protectors: Abdulaziz bin Said's Struggle for Power and Money in the Time of Growing British Dominance in the Indian Ocean Region," *Journal of Colonialism and Colonial History* 23, no. 1 (2022), https://doi.org/10.1353/cch.2022.0010.

89. Bhacker, *Trade and Empire in Muscat and Zanzibar*, 191; and Reda M. Bhacker, "Family Strife and Foreign Intervention: Causes in the Separation of Zanzibar from Oman: A Reappraisal," *Bulletin of the School of Oriental and African Studies* 54, no. 2 (1991): 269–280.

90. The award continued to be paid (albeit very sporadically) until the late 1960s. See P. Gent to Foreign Office, "The Zanzibar Subsidy," 8 December 1967, The National Archives (hereafter TNA), FCO 8/587.

91. James Onley, *The Arabian Frontier of the British Raj: Merchants, Rulers, and the British in the Nineteenth Century Gulf* (Oxford, Oxford University PresIoo7).

92. The agricultural productivity of Unguja's sister island Pemba saved the state from decline after the 1872 hurricane wiped out the clove trees of Unguja. Mohamed Bakari, *The Democratisation Process in Zanzibar: A Retarded Transition* (Hamburg: Institute of African Affairs, 2001), 49.

93. Amal Ghazal, *Islamic Reform and Arab Nationalism: Expanding the Crescent from the Mediterranean to the Indian Ocean, 1880s–1930s* (New York: Routledge, 2010), ch. 2; and Philip Sadgrove, "The Press: Engine of a Mini-renaissance in Zanzibar (1860–1920)," in *History of Printing and Publishing in the Languages and Countries of the Middle East*, ed. Philip Sadgrove (Oxford: Oxford University Press, 2009), 151–178.

94. Wahab, *Indians in Zanzibar*, 130.

95. Wahab, *Indians in Zanzibar*, 131–135.

96. Frederick Cooper, *From Slaves to Squatters: Plantation Labor and Agriculture in Zanzibar and Coastal Kenya* (Portsmouth, NH: Heinemann, 1997).

97. Glassman, *War of Words*, 49.

98. John Middleton and Jane Campbell, *Zanzibar: Its Society and Its Politics* (London: Oxford University Press, 1965), 11.

99. Leo Kuper, *Race, Class, and Power: Ideology and Revolutionary Change in Plural Societies* (London: Duckworth, 1974), 119; Middleton and Campbell, *Zanzibar*, 2; and Helen Louise Hunter, *The Hundred Days Revolution* (Santa Barbara, CA: ABC-CLIO, 2010), xxii.

100. Kuper, *Race, Class, and Power*, 120–121.

101. Michael Lofchie, *Zanzibar: Background to Revolution* (Princeton, NJ: Princeton University Press, 1965), 78–79.

102. Ironically, the other group were the Africans rescued from slave vessels and sent to missions around the British Empire to be educated. For their trajectory in colonial and postcolonial Kenya, see Joseph Harris, *Repatriates and Refugees in Colonial Society: The Case of Zanzibar* (Washington, DC: Howard University Press, 1987). For colonial education and the idea of social development, see Jurgen Osterhammel, "Epilogue: From Civilizing Missions to the Defence of Civility," in *Civilizing Missions in the Twentieth Century*, ed. Boris Barth and Rolf Hobson (Leiden: Brill, 2020), 209. See also Aram Ziai, *Development Discourse and Global History: From Colonialism to the Sustainable Development Goals* (New York: Routledge, 2016).

103. Anthony Marx defines nationalism as "a collective sentiment tied to the object of an existing or emergent state . . . that "potentially ties masses to elites within states."Anthony Marx, *Faith in Nation: Exclusionary Origins of Nationalism* (Oxford: Oxford University Press, 2003), xi; and Jonathon Glassman, "Racial Violence, Universal History, and Echoes of Abolition in Twentieth-Century Zanzibar," in *Abolition and Imperialism in Britain, Africa and the Atlantic*, ed. Derek Peterson (Athens: Ohio University/Swallow Press, 2010), 182–183. For territoriality, see John Gerard Ruggie, "Territoriality and Beyond: Problematizing Modernity in International Relations" *International Organization* 47, no. 1 (Winter 1993): 150; Margaret Moore argued that territory has to be understood as an important part of any project of collective self-determination. Margaret Moore, *A Political Theory of Territory* (Oxford: Oxford University Press, 2015).

104. Amal Ghazal, *Islamic Reform and Arab Nationalism: Expanding the Crescent from the Mediterranean to the Indian Ocean, 1880s–1930s* (New York: Routledge, 2010), 76.

105. Michael Lofchie, *Zanzibar: Background to Revolution* (Princeton, NJ: Princeton University Press, 1965), 131–132; Amal Ghazal, "The Other Frontiers of Arab Nationalism: Ibadis, Berbers, and the Arabist-Salafi Press in the Interward Period," *International Journal of Middle East Studies* 42, no. 1 (2010): 105–122.

106. Soghayrun, "Al-Ishām," 202; and Ghazal, *Islamic Reform*, 86. Many were inspired by the Omani-born poet Abu Muslim al-Bahlani, who lived in Zanzibar most of his life and died in 1920. Mohammad al-Mahrouqi, "Religious Discourse in the Poetry of Abū Muslim al-Bahlānī," *Journal of African Cultural Studies* 14, no. 1 (June 2001): 89–106. The work of Sheikh Al-Amin Mazrui in nearby Mombasa was tremendously influential. See Kai Kresse and Hassan Mwakimako, eds., *Guidance (Uwongozi) by Sheikh al-Amin Mazrui: Selections from the First Swahili Islamic Newspaper* (Leiden: Brill, 2016).

107. Wahab, *Indians in Zanzibar*, 160. The Indian Association was established in the 1910s, while the African Association was formed in 1934 and the Shirazi Association (by Thabit Kombo) in 1939. Roman Loimeier, *Between Social Skills and Marketable Skills: The Politics of Islamic Education in 20th Century Zanzibar* (Leiden: Brill Press, 2009), 28–29.

108. For instance as late as August 1963, al-Miskery mourned the death of Zanzibar monarch Seyyid Abdullah, celebrated the persistence of the monarchy in

Zanzibar, and decried the secularization of society there. Muhsin Ḥamud al-Kindi, *al-Ṣaḥāfat-l-ʿUmāniyyat-l-Muhājira wa Shakhṣiyyāthā: Shaikh Hāshil bin Rāshid al-Miskirī Numūdhajā* (Beirut: Riad al-Rayyes Books, 2009), 440.

109. Soghayrun, "Al-Ishām," 208; Ahmed Hamed al-Khalili, "al-ʿUmāniyyūn wa Atharahum fi al-Jawānab al-ʿIlmiyya wa al-Maʿarfiyya bi-Sharq Ifrīqīyya." In *Faʿāliyyāt wa Nāshiṭ: Ḥiṣād: Anshiṭat al-Muntadā al-Adabī, 1991–1992*, edited by Salim Muhammad al-Ghailānī and Muhammad Ali al-Sulaibi (Muscat: Ministry of Heritage and Culture, 1994); *Qirāʾāt wa Dirāsāt wa Buḥūth fi al-Fikr wa al-Adab wa al-Turāth al-ʿUmanī* (Muscat: Ministry of Heritage and Culture, 1994), 189; and al-Kindi, *al-Ṣaḥāfa al-ʿUmāniyya al-Muhājira wa Shakhṣiyyāthā*, 486.

110. Scott Reese, "'The Ink of Excellence': Print and Islamic Written Tradition of East Africa," in *Manuscript and Print in the Islamic Tradition*, ed. Scott Reese (Berlin: De Gruyter, 2022), 217–242; Anne Bang, "Authority, Piety, Writing and Print: A Preliminary Study of the Circulation of Islamic Texts in Late Nineteenth and Early Twentieth-Century Zanzibar," *Africa: Journal of the International African Institute* 81, no. 1 (2011): 89–107. See also essays in James Gelvin and Nile Green, eds., *Global Muslims in the Age of Steam and Print* (Berkeley: University of California Press, 2014).

111. Muhammad Ali Khamis al-Barwani, *Riḥla Abī al-Ḥārith* (Muscat: Ministry of Heritage and Culture Oman, 2010). This work was originally published in Cairo in 1914.

112. Kuper, *Race, Class, and Power*, 119; and Suleiman Shahbal, *Zanzibar: The Rise and Fall of an Independent State* (Dubai: Self-published, 2002), 184. Two excellent introductions to space and social class in Zanzibar are W. C. Bissell, *Urban Design, Chaos, and Colonial Power in Zanzibar* (Bloomington: Indiana University Press, 2011); and Garth Myers, *Verandahs of Power: Colonialism and Space in Urban Africa* (Syracuse: Syracuse University Press, 2003).

113. Fred Cooper, *Colonialism in Question: Theory, Knowledge, History* (Berkeley: University of California Press, 2005), 143; Justin Willis and George Gona, "Tradition, Tribe and State in Kenya: The Mijikenda Union, 1945–1980," *Comparative Studies in Society and History* 55, no. 2 (2013): 451; Tania Murray Li, *The Will to Improve: Governmentality, Development and the Practice of Politics* (Durham, NC: Duke University Press, 2007); Michael O. West, *The Rise of an African Middle Class: Colonial Zimbabwe, 1898–1965* (Bloomington: Indiana University Press, 2002); and Olufemi Taiwo, *How Colonialism Preempted Modernity in Africa* (Bloomington: Indiana University Press, 2010).

114. Middleton and Campbell, *Zanzibar*, 44; Lofchie, *Zanzibar*, 77; Glassman, *War of Words*, 81; Loimeier, *Between Social Skills*, 272–273; Norman Bennett, *A History of the Arab State of Zanzibar* (London: Methuen, 1978), 240, 249; and Jonathon Glassman, "Sorting I the Tribes: The Creation of Racial Identities in Colonial Zanzibar's Newspaper Wars," *The Journal of African History* 41, no. 3 (2000): 395–428. For colonial education's impact in other contexts of British Africa, see Jonathon Earle, *Colonial Buganda and the End of Empire: Political*

Thought and Historical Imagination in Africa (New York: Cambridge University Press, 2017); Heather Sharkey, *Living with Colonialism: Nationalism and Culture in the Anglo-Egyptian Sudan* (Berkeley: University of California Press, 2003), 83–85; H. Marhuby, *My Zanzibar: From Idyllic to Upheaval* (n.p.: self-published, 2017), 309; and Ahmed al-Riyami, *My Pride and Joy* (Muscat: self-published, 2007), 59, 104.

115. A glimpse into some of the politically influential members of Zanzibari society is offered by scanning the list of attendees at the 1963 Eid celebration. "Idd El Fitr Baraza—1963," ZNA, AK 9/17.

116. Seth Markle, "'Brother Malcom, Comrade Babu': Black Internationalism and the Politics of Friendship," *Biography* 36, no. 3 (Summer 2013): 540–567. See also Maha Yassine Ziad al-Hassen, "To Tell What the Eye Beholds: A Post 1945 Transnational History of Afro-Arab 'Solidarity Politics'" (PhD diss., University of Southern California, 2017).

117. Anthony Clayton, *The Zanzibar Revolution and Its Aftermath: The Zanzibar Revolution and Its Aftermath* (London: C. Hurst, 1981), 38; Minutes of the Scholarship Selection Committee, 29 May 1961, ZNA, AK 15/1; and Passport and Visa Fees, "Passports to Makerere Students," 19 January 1943, ZNA, AB 26/43. Prominent among them was the education officer and principal of Seyyid Khalifa School, Muhammad Salim al-Barwani; see Loimeier, *Between Social Skills*, 566. Shaaban Saleh al-Farsy, Juma Aley, Ahmed Hamoud al-Maamiry, and Aboud Jumbe were also all trained teachers. Former president of Zanzibar Idris Wakil was also educated at Makerere.

118. Ghazal, *Islamic Reform*, 112; and Lofchie, *Zanzibar*, 128. Ahmed Lamky and Ahmed Hamoud al-Maamiry were among those who went to Cairo for higher education.

119. Loiemeier, *Between Social Skills*, 286; *Zanzibar Monthly Newsletter*, no. 14, October 1948, ZNA, AB 5/20. The most comprehensive account of women's education in Zanzibar is Corrie Decker, *Mobilizing Zanzibari Women: The Struggle for Respectability and Self-Reliance in Colonial East Africa* (New York: Palgrave Macmillan, 2014).

120. See, for instance, "Zanzibarisation: Returns and Training Programmes—Government Press," ZNA AO 1/183, and "Establishment of Zanzibar Foreign Service/Training of Diplomats," ZNA, AO 1/105.

121. "Training of Zanzibar Students Overseas out of Protectorate Funds," March 1947–September 1952, ZNA, AB 1/147.

122. For public health initiatives in post–World War II Zanzibar, see Amina Ameir Issa, "'From Stinkibar to Zanzibar': Disease, Medicine, and Public Health in Colonial Urban Zanzibar, 1870–1963" (PhD diss., University of Kwa-Zulu Natal, 2009).

123. Many Zanzibaris who studied in the United Kingdom at this time were members of the Communist Party of Great Britain. Saleh, "Swahili Elites," 296–314; Loimeier, *Between Social Skills*, 286; G. Thomas Burgess, "An Imagined Generation," in *In Search of a Nation: Histories of Authority and Dissidence in Tanzania*, ed.

Gregory Maddox and James Giblin (Dar-es-Salaam: Mkuti wa Nkota, 2005), 216–249; and Andrew Burton and Helene Charton-Bigot, eds., *Generations Past: Youth in East African History* (Athens: Ohio University Press, 2010).

124. Glassman, "Racial Violence," 180; Emma Hunter, *Political Thought and the Public Sphere in Tanzania: Freedom, Democracy, and Citizenship in the Age of Decolonization* (Cambridge: Cambridge University Press, 2015), 44; and Geoffrey Barraclough, *An Introduction to Contemporary History* (New York: Penguin, 1967), 175–176.

125. Prasenjit Duara, "Transnationalism and the Predicament of Sovereignty: China, 1900–1945," *American Historical Review* 102, no. 4 (October 1997): 1030–1051. Naim Kattan captures some of this sentiment in his memoir of growing up Jewish in 1940s Baghdad. Naim Kattan, *Farewell Babylon: Coming of Age in Jewish Baghdad*, trans. Sheila Fischman (Vancouver, BC: Raincoat Books, 2005).

126. This generation began to join the civil service as a response to the general crisis of profitability in the plantation sector in the 1930s. Abdul Sheriff, "Race and Class in the Politics of Zanzibar," *Afrika Spectrum* 36, no. 3 (2001): 302. For instance, Issa Nasser al-Ismaily entered the administration department in January 1947. Issa Nasser al-Ismaily, *Will Zanzibar Regain Her Past Prosperity* (Muscat: self-published, 2015), xii.

127. "Appointment of Immigration Officer," The Immigration (Control) Decree 1947 Appointment of an Immigration Officer, 29 May 1952 and 28 December 1953, ZNA, AB 26/57.

128. al-Riyami, *Pride and Joy*, 56–57; and Jonathon Glassman, "Slower Than a Massacre: The Multiple Sources of Racial Thought in Colonial Africa," *American Historical Review* 109, no. 3 (June 2004), 736–739.

129. Naturalization 1959 December–1963 May, ZNA, AK 24/7.

130. Crozon, "Zanzibar en Tanzanie," 76–77.

131. Wahab, *Indians in Zanzibar*, 166.

132. Bennett, *History of the Arab State of Zanzibar*, 252–253; and Maulid M. Haj, *Zanzibar: The Last Years of the Protectorate A Constitutional and Political Account* (Muscat: Al Roya Publishing, 2006), 28–29. Alison Smith, "The End of the Arab Sultanate: Zanzibar, 1945–1964," in *History of East Africa*, ed. D. A. Low and Alison Smith (Oxford: Clarendon Press, 1976), 3:196–211. For the shifting emphasis on African nationalism in the Afro-Arab newspapers of the time, see, for instance, the following items in the Michael Lofchie Collection (hereafter MLC) at the Charles Young Research Library, UCLA: Sheikh Juma Aley, "Zanzibar Nationalists Celebrate Independence of Ghana," *The Adal Insaf* 10, no. 34, 8 March 1958; "Uhuru Hivi Sasa, Tumechoka Kutawaliwa," *The Adal Insaf*, 12 July 1958); and Said Humoud Nasser, "Bw. Smithyman na Bw. Woodland—Musituleze yasiyotukhusu," *Mwongozi*, 27 December 1958.

133. Hashil S. Hashil, *Mimi, Umma Party na Mapinduzi ya Zanzibar* (Paris: DL₂A Buluu Publishing, 2018), 60. Lamky, according to Hashil S. Hashil, was a student in Egypt and was thrown in prison by King Farouk based on accusations of being a communist. At age twenty-five he was in Zanzibar as a coeditor of

al-Falaq. His father was Mohamed Nassor Lamky. Later the younger Lamky became head of the Africa department in Oman's Ministry of Foreign Affairs.

134. Wahab, *Indians in Zanzibar*, 174. Wahab identifies this as the Bandung Conference, which actually occurred two years earlier in 1955. The Cairo Conference of 1957, while related, was meant to build on the principles laid down at Bandung.

135. Glassman, "Sorting Out the Tribes", 406–407n48; and Jonathon Glassman, "Creole Nationalists and the Search for Nativist Authenticity in Twentieth Century Zanzibar: The Limits of Cosmopolitanism," *The Journal of African History* 55, no. 2 (July 2014): 229–247.

136. Barraclough, *Introduction to Contemporary History*, 178; and Marhuby, *My Zanzibar*, 351. In 1948 the protectorate government commissioned a social survey by E. Batston meant "to facilitate development planning." Anthony Clayton, "The General Strike in Zanzibar, 1948," *The Journal of African History* 17, no. 3 (1976): 417–434.

137. Al-Riyami, *Pride and Joy*, 116. See also Said Humoud Nasser, "Baada ya Vita Vya Pili," *Adal Insaf*, 13 December 1958, ZNA.

138. Ahmed al-Riyami, *Quite Another* (Muscat: self-published, 2010), 172–173. He later became secretary general of the Comoros Liberation Movement headquartered in Nairobi.

139. Ghassany, *Kwa Heri*, 193.

140. Timothy Oberst, "Transport Workers, Strikes and the 'Imperial Response': Africa and the Post World War II Conjuncture," *African Studies Review* 31, no. 1 (1988): 117–133; and Clayton, "General Strike in Zanzibar, 1948."

141. Bakari, *Democratisation*, 55; and Ghassany, *Kwa Heri*, 191.

142. Crozon, "Zanzibar en Tanzanie," 79.

143. Lofchie, *Zanzibar*, 160.

144. Don Petterson, *Revolution in Zanzibar: An American's Cold War Tale* (Boulder: Westview Press, 2002), 41.

145. Crozon, "Zanzibar en Tanzanie," 99.

146. "Manga Arabs—Evacuation out from Zanzibar," Felix Schnyder to U Thant, 12 August 1964, United Nations High Commission on Refugees (hereafter UNHCR) Archives, Fonds 11, Series 1, Box 280; F. Homann-Herimberg, "Refugees in Zanzibar," 24 June 1964, TNA, FO 371:178271; and "Proces-Verbal D'Entretien: M. Borsinger," 24–30 June 1964, International Committee of the Red Cross (hereafter ICRC) Archives, Geneva, B AG 233 203-002, 14/02/1964–05/08/1964.

147. A constitutional amendment in 1992 ended this practice.

148. For the Union's lack of legal ratification, see Issa Shivji, *Pan-Africanism or Pragmatism: Lessons of the Tanganyika-Zanzibar Union* (Dar-es-Salaam: Mkuti wa Nyota Publishers, 2008), 92. For those privy to discussions about the Union, prior to its ratification, see Haroub Othman, "The Union with Zanzibar," in *Mwalimu: The Influence of Nyerere*, ed. Colin Legum and Geoffrey Mmari (Oxford: James Currey, 1995), 174; and Haroub Othman, "Nyerere's Political Legacy," in *Tanzania*

After Nyerere, ed. Michael Dood (New York: Pinter Publishers, 1988), 158–164. For an evaluation of the different historiographical perspectives on the Union, see Paul K. Bjerk, "Sovereignty and Socialism in Tanzania: The Historiography of an African State," *History in Africa* 37 (2010): 275–319.

149. Crozon, "Zanzibar en Tanzanie," 160, 192; and Amrit Wilson, *The Threat of Liberation: Imperialism and Revolution in Zanzibar* (London: Pluto Press, 2013).

150. Crozon, "Zanzibar en Tanzanie," 157; and C. M. Vaughan, "The Politics of Regionalism and Federation in East Africa, 1958–1964," *Historical Journal* 62, no. 2 (2018): 519–540. A related project, the East African Community (EAC), advocated the lowering of trade barriers between the countries and the formation of a common market. Sena Eken, "Breakup of the East African Community," *Finance and Development* (December 1979): 36–40. This was also a project discussed by late-colonial British officials.

151. Godfrey Baldacchino, "Displaced Passengers: States, Movements, and Disappearances in the Indian Ocean," in *Connectivity in Motion: Island Hubs in the Indian Ocean World*, ed. Burkhard Schnepel and Ed Alpers (New York: Palgrave-Macmillan, 2018), 94.

152. Crozon, "Zanzibar en Tanzanie," 216–217. See, for instance, the debate over the nationality of Ahmed Seif Kharusi, "Modifications of British Nationality Acts," HC Debate 785, 17 June 1969, 406–412, http://hansard.millbanksystems.com/commons/1969/jun/17/modifications-of-british-nationality-acts: "[P]roviso (i) to paragraph 2(1) of the 4th Schedule of the Tanzanian Citizenship Decree of 3rd November, 1964, specifically excludes from citizenship of Tanzania 'any person who, prior to Union Day, had been deprived of his status as a Zanzibar subject, or deported or exiled from Zanzibar. . . . In view of your close association with the former Sultan of Zanzibar, we need to see confirmation from the Tanzanian authorities that you are currently regarded by them as a citizen of Tanzania before we can proceed with your application.'" B. P. Dave to Area Commissioner Zanzibar, 11 September 1967; Ali Said Akbary to B. P. Dave, 31 October 1967; S. A. Maswanya to Aboud Jumbe, N.D., ZNA, AK 14/5A. Aminzade, *Race, Nation, and Citizenship*, 99–103.

153. "Naturalisation–Uraia," Mwenyekiti ASP Shangani Branch to Mkuu wa Wilaya Mjini, 12 September 1966, ZNA, AK 14/5A.

154. Judith Marshall, "(Im)mobility in a Sea of Migration: Race, Mobilities, and Transnational Families in Zanzibar and Oman, 1856–2019" (PhD diss., Michigan State University, 2021).

155. Crozon, "Zanzibar en Tanzanie," 217.

156. Al-Hinai, *Ā'idūn*, 68.

157. Marhuby, *My Zanzibar*, 512–520; and al-Hinai, *Ā'idūn*, 87.

158. Interview subject (I.S.) 52, 6/23/2013. All interview subjects except those whom I have explicit permission from to use their names have been anonymized in accordance with institutional review board (IRB) regulations. All interviews were conducted in Oman unless otherwise noted in the bibliography.

159. I.S. 15, 8/26/2011. Within six months of arrival, he traveled back to Zanzibar to visit.

160. "Let Us Be Consistent" by "Zanzibaris Abroad", undated typescript, KP no. 8. This statement repeats the phrase "we Africans," and condemns apartheid alongside the revolution of 1964.

161. Susan Crane, "Writing the Individual Back into Collective Memory," *American Historical Review* 102, no. 5 (December 1997): 1372–1385.

162. L. Wimmelbücker, "Aspekte eines gesellschaftlichen Umbruchs: Die sansibarische Revolution von 1964," in *Unser Leben von der Revolution und danach— Maisha yetu kabla ya mapinduzi na baadaye*, ed. S. Barwani et al. (Cologne: Rüdiger Köppe, 2003), 482.

163. "Cowboys and Indians," *Free Zanzibar Voice (FZV)*, 11 July 1973, KP no. 6 (emphasis added). Issues of *FZV* are found in a digitized set of photographs taken by James Brennan of Ahmed Seif Kharusi's files and papers and used by the kind permission of Sauda Barwani.

164. "L. Goodyear to J. Reddaway," 3 June 1966, UNHCR, Fonds 11, Series 1, Box 256, 15/DUB/ZAN; and "Goodyear to High Commissioner," 30 May 1966, UNHCR 15/DUB/ZAN.

165. Domenyk Eades, ed., and Zayana al-Badaei, trans., *The Pioneer Professor Fatma Salem Seif Al-Maamary (1911-2002): A Historical, Documentary and Academic Study* (Muscat: The Ministry of Education, 2013). See "Report by M.L. Tait, Assistant Political Agent to Mr. M.R. Harris," "Refugees from Zanzibar in Dubai," UNHCR, Fonds 11, Series 1, Box 256, 15/DUB/ZAN.

166. I.S. 15, 8/26/2011.

167. Young, *African Colonial State*, 287–288; and Embree, "Imperialism and Decolonization", 169.

168. Young, *African Colonial* State, 266; Aminzade, *Race, Nation and Citizenship*, 9; Mayall, "Nationalism," 191; G. Thomas Burgess, "Mao in Zanzibar: Nationalism, Discipline, and the (De)Construction of Afro-Asian Solidarities," in *Making a World after Empire: The Bandung Movement and Its Political Afterlives*, ed. Christopher Lee (Athens: Ohio University Press, 2010), 199; Falola, *Nationalism and the Intellectuals*, 117, 128; Thomas Blom Hansen and Finn Stepputat, introduction to *Sovereign Bodies: Citizens, Migrants and States in the Postcolonial World*, ed. Hansen and Stepputat (Princeton, NJ: Princeton University Press, 2005), 4; Robert H. Bates, *Markets and States in Tropical Africa* (Berkeley: University of California Press, 1981), 14–18; Roland Burke, *Decolonization and the Evolution of International Human Rights* (Philadelphia: University of Pennsylvania Press, 2010), ch. 2; Dennis L. Cohen, "Class and the Analysis of African Politics," in *The Political Economy of Africa*, ed. D. Cohen and J. Daniel (London: Longman, 1981), 92; Achille Mbembe, *On the Postcolony* (Berkeley: University of California Press, 2001), 116–117, 120; and Paul Bjerk, *Building a Peaceful Nation: Julius Nyerere and the Establishment of Sovereignty in Tanzania* (Rochester, NY: University of Rochester, 2015), 5.

169. Aiyar, *Indians in Kenya*, 262; Westad, *Global Cold War*, 95; Lisa Wedeen, *Peripheral Visions: Publics, Power and Performance in Yemen* (Chicago: University of Chicago Press, 2008), 63; Mahmood Mamdani, *Define and Rule: Native as Political Identity* (Boston: Harvard University Press, 2012); and Manu Goswami, "Rethinking the Modular Nation Form" *Comparative Studies of Society and History* 44, no. 4 (2002): 770–799.

170. Fred Cooper, *Africa since 1940* (Cambridge: Cambridge University Press, 2002); and William McNeill, "Money and Economic Change," in *The Columbia History of the 20th Century*, ed. Richard Bulliet (Columbia University Press, 1998), 308.

171. Dietrich, *Oil Revolution*, 268, 283.

172. Mayall, "Nationalism," 192.

173. Clayton, *Zanzibar Revolution and Its Aftermath*, 153; and Keren Weitzberg, *We Do Not Have Borders: Greater Somalia and the Predicaments of Belonging in Kenya* (Athens: Ohio University Press, 2017), 120–121. In 1967 in Zanzibar, the state tried to centralize approval for all public cultural activities within the Zanzibar Information Office. Eric Burton, "Diverging Visions in Revolutionary Spaces: East German Advisers and Revolution from Above in Zanzibar, 1964–1970," in *Between East and South: Spaces of Interaction in the Globalizing Economy of the Cold War*, ed. Anna Calori et al. (Berlin: De Gruyter, 2019), f108.

174. In 1937 the first fruitful oil concession was signed by Said b. Taimur, and his allowing oil officials into the interior reactivated the political conflict with the Imamate. It took until March 1967 to conclude talks guaranteeing the government 50 percent of all petroleum profits and the rights to 12.5 percent of all petroleum exported; the first exports were in August 1967. J. E. Peterson, *Oman's Insurgencies: The Sultanate's Struggle for Supremacy* (London: Saqi Books, 2008), 61; and Mohamed Musa al-Yousef, *Oil and the Transformation of Oman* (London: Stacey International, 1995), 30. In the early 1970s this was converted to a 60 percent overall stake in PDO. For similar developments elsewhere, see Dietrich, *Oil Revolution*, 31.

175. *Development in Oman, 1970–1974* (Muscat: Ministry of Development, National Statistical Department, 1975).

176. J. E. Peterson, "L'Odyssee de l'Oman: De l'Imamat au Sultanat," in *L'Oman Contemporain: État, territoire, identité*, ed. Marc Lavergne and Brigitte Dumortier (Paris: Karthala, 2003), 37–39. In the late 1950s, Great Britain was providing Sultan Said bin Taimur with funding for the state's first development plan. Fehmi Alem, "The Question of Oman in the United Nations" (MA thesis, The American University, 1967), 55.

177. Eickelman, "From Theocracy to Monarchy", 10; and J. E. Peterson, *Historical Muscat: An Illustrated Guide and Gazetteer* (Leiden: Brill, 2007), 97–98.

178. Peterson, *Oman's Insurgencies*, 100–200; Wilkinson, *Imamate Tradition*, 312–328; and Uzi Rabi, *The Emergence of States in a Tribal Society: Oman Under Sa'id bin Taymur, 1932–1970* (Liverpool: Liverpool University Press, 2011), 61–90.

179. "The Words of Sultan Said bin Taimur," in Majid al-Khalili, "Oman's Foreign Policy: foundations and practice" (PhD diss., Florida International University, 2005), app. III, 303.

180. Talal al-Rashoud, "From Muscat to the Maghreb: Pan-Arab Networks, Anti-colonial Groups, and Kuwait's Arab Scholarships (1953–1961)," *Arabian Humanities* 12 (2019), https://doi.org/10.4000/cy.5004.

181. Nabeel A. Khoury, "The Politics of Intra-Regional Migration," in *International Migration in the Arab World: Proceedings of an ECWA Population Conference, Nicosia, Cyprus, 11–16 May 1981* (Beirut: UNECWA, 1982), 754.

182. Michael Herb, *All in the Family: Absolutism, Revolution and Democracy in Middle East Monarchies* (Albany: State University of New York Press, 1999), 14. In 1968 Said promised petroleum revenues would inaugurate development plans including offices, hospitals, schools, roads, and communications, "until modern projects spread over the whole of the Sultanate, to each area according to its needs." Al-Khalili, "Words of Sultan Said bin Taimur," app. III, 303.

183. *Development in Oman*, 69; Valeri, *Oman*, 73; and Donald Hawley, *Oman and Its Renaissance* (London: Stacey International, 1977), 204. This number has come down, and after 2006 it was steady at around 65 percent. Petroleum Development Oman Ltd. is the largest concession in Oman, with the Omani government as the major shareholder. Hawley, *Oman and Its Renaissance*, 211.

184. Dietrich, *Oil Revolution*, 263–264.

185. al-Yousef, *Oil and the Transformation of Oman*, 28, 30; and Takriti, *Monsoon Revolution*, 220. Takriti argued that petroleum revenue helped make up for the fact of profligate spending by Qaboos in the early years of his reign.

186. al-Yousef, *Oil and the Transformation of Oman*, 43; and S. G. Phillips and Jennifer Hunt, "'Without Sultan Qaboos, We Would Be Yemen': The Renaissance Narrative and the Political Settlement in Oman" *Journal of International Development* 29, no. 5 (July 2017): 649.

187. Dermot Gately, "Lessons from the 1986 Oil Price Collapse," Brookings Papers on Economic Activity, 1986, https://www.brookings.edu/wp-content/uploads/1986/06/1986b_bpea_gately_adelman_griffin.pdf, 246. Oman's import price index increase had offset these price gains by the early 1990s.

188. Limbert, *In the Time of Oil*; and Shiblak Abblas, "Arabia's Bidoon," in *Statelessness and Citizenship: A Comparative Study on the Benefits of Nationality*, ed. Brad Blitz and Maureen Lynch (Cheltenham: Edward Elgar, 2011), 174–186.

189. Peterson, *Oman's Insurgencies*, 78; Valeri, *Oman*, 56–57; Calvin Allen and W. Lynn Rigsbee II, *Oman under Qaboos: From Coup to Constitution, 1970–1996* (London: Routledge, 2000), 13; and Protection-General-Saudi Arabia, "Amour Barwani and Hashil Riyami and Abdullah Lemki to Hassan M. Hassan," 22 June 1970, "La questions des refugies originairee de Zanzibar et detenteurs de passports deliveres par l'Imam d'Oman," UNHCR, Fonds 11, Series 1, Box 165, 6/1/SAU.

190. "Amour Barwani to Hassan Mohammed al-Hassan," 22 June 1970.

191. For instance, Dr. Suad Lamky was a graduate of St. Joseph's Convent School in Zanzibar, the American Ghamra school in Cairo, and Trinity College

School of Law. She later worked in public prosecution, for PDO, and for the Omani Ministry of Legal Affairs. She was honored as the first female lawyer in the sultanate. Her sister Sharifa graduated from the American University in Cairo. Dr. Asya al Bualy, senior adviser for cultural sciences at the Council for Scientific Research, is Sharifa's daughter and Suad's niece. Her son Nasser al-Riyami is also a lawyer, serving in the public prosecution, and has authored a well-known Arabic-English history of Zanzibar, explored in chapter 6.

192. Liisa Malkki, *Purity and Exile: Violence, Memory and National Cosmology among Hutu Refugees in Tanzania* (Chicago: University of Chicago Press, 1995), 168–170.

193. Arguably tens of thousands more in East Africa could make at least some claim to Omani nationality through lineage. See Sheikh Saleh Hashil al-Miskery, "Ālāf min Ahlna Yantadhirūn I'tirāfna bihim," *Al-Watan*, May 9, 2013.

194. Harmut Lehmann and James J. Sheehan, *An Interrupted Past: German-Speaking Refugee Historians in the United States after 1933* (Cambridge: Cambridge University Press, 2002), 157.

195. François Constantin and François Le Guennec-Coppens, "Dubai Street: Zanzibar," *African Politics* 30 (1988): 13; Julia Verne, *Living Translocality: Space, Culture, and Economy in Contemporary Swahili Trade* (Stuttgart: Franz Steiner Verlag, 2012); Erik Gilbert, "Oman and Zanzibar: The Historical Roots of a Global Community," in *Cross Currents and Community Networks: The History of the Indian Ocean World*, ed. Himanshu Prabha Ray and Edward A. Alpers (Oxford: Oxford University Press, 2007), 163–178; and Zulfikar Hirji, "Relating Muscat to Mombasa: Spatial Tropes in the Kinship Narratives of an Extended Family Network in Oman," *Anthropology of the Middle East* 2, no. 1 (Spring 2007): 55–69.

196. Mann, *From Empires to NGOs*, 92, 143. See the call for exploring these issues as part of reconfiguring Middle East studies in an Indian Ocean frame. Fahad Bishara, "The Many Voyages of Fateh Al-Khayr: Unfurling the Gulf in the Age of Oceanic History," *International Journal of Middle East Studies* 52, no. 3 (2020): 397–412.

197. Pierre Nora quoted in Laurenn Guyot, "Locked in a Memory Ghetto: A Case Study of a Kurdish Community in France," in *Memory and Migration: Multidisciplinary Approaches to Memory Studies*, ed. Andrea Klitzmann and Julia Creet (Toronto: University of Toronto Press, 2014), 135–155.

198. Ali Muhsin al-Barwani, *Kujenga na Kubomolewa Zanzibar (Kumbukumbu)* (n.p.: self-published, 2004); and Ali Muhsin al-Barwani, *Al-Ṣirāʿāt wa Al-Wiʾām fī Zanjibār: Dhikriyyāt Ali Muhsin al-Barwani*, trans. Said Amir (Beirut: Dar al-Gharīr, 2010).

199. Kimberly Wortmann, "Ibadi Muslim Schools in Post-Revolutionary Zanzibar," *Africa* 92, no. 2 (March 2022): 249–264; and Nasser al-Riyami, *Zanzibar: Personalities and Events*, trans. Ali Rashid al-Abri (Beirut: Beirut Bookshop, 2012), 354.

200. Franziska Fay, "'Kuishi Ughaibuni': Emplaced Absence, the Zanzibar Diaspora Policy, and Young Men's Experiences of Belonging in Zanzibar and Oman,"

Journal of Indian Ocean World Studies 6, no. 1 (2022): 10–37. For an incisive look at the role of diasporas in shaping national belonging, see Robtel Pailey, *Development, Dual Citizenship and Its Discontents in Africa: The Political Economy of Belonging to Liberia* (Cambridge: Cambridge University Press, 2021).

201. For Zanzibaris accessing health care through temporary residence in Oman facilitated by Omani family members, see Sandra Staudacher, "Shifting Urban Margins: Accessing Unequal Spaces of Ageing and Care in Zanzibar and Muscat," *Anthropological Forum* 29, no. 1 (2019): 77–94. For a personal account of this process in the life of an Omani born in Rwanda, see Habiba al-Tawqi, *Diamond Life: Autobiography of Habiba al-Tawqi* (Dubai: Index Media, 2008). For status of noncitizens, see Linda Bosniak, *The Citizen and the Alien: Dilemmas of Contemporary Membership* (Princeton, NJ: Princeton University Press, 2008), 2–3.

1. IMMIGRATION, EXOGENOUS ORIGINS, AND THE POLITICS OF CITIZENSHIP IN ZANZIBAR, 1957–1963

1. John Middleton and Jane Campbell, *Zanzibar: Its Society and Its Politics* (London: Oxford University Press, 1965), 56.

2. A total of 165,000 were registered to vote by June 1963. Even the first election of 1957 had a nearly 90 percent participation rate. Middleton and Campbell, *Zanzibar*, 50. The question of women voting raised the issue of the documents they needed to obtain naturalization. "Supervisor of Elections to Senior Commissioner," 8 September 1959, ZNA, AK 14/8. For women's enfranchisement in Zanzibar, see Corrie Decker, *Mobilizing Zanzibari Women: The Struggle for Respectability and Self-Reliance in Colonial East Africa* (New York: Palgrave Macmillan, 2014), 136–142.

3. Zanzibar Census, March 1958 (Government of Zanzibar), 32, ZNA.

4. Jonathon Glassman, *War of Words, War of Stones: Racial Thought and Violence in Colonial Zanzibar* (Bloomington: Indiana University Press, 2011), 150–151; and Michael Lofchie, *Zanzibar: Background to Revolution* (Princeton, NJ: Princeton University Press, 1965), 210.

5. As they did in Malaysia; see James P. Ongkili, "The British and Malayan Nationalism, 1946–1957," *Journal of Southeast Asian Studies* 5, no. 2 (1974): 255–277.

6. Anthony Clayton, "The General Strike in Zanzibar, 1948," *The Journal of African History* 17, no. 3 (1976): 417–434.

7. Jonathon Glassman, "Sorting Out the Tribes: The Creation of Racial Identities in Colonial Zanzibar's Newspaper Wars," *The Journal of African History* 41, no. 3 (2000): 395–428.

8. *Report of a Commission of Inquiry into Disturbances in Zanzibar during June 1961* (London: Her Majesty's Stationery Office, 1961), MLC, 13–14.

9. Sidney Tarrow, "Social Movements in Contentious Politics: A Review Article," *American Political Science Review* 90, no. 4 (December 1996): 874–883.

10. Lofchie, *Zanzibar*, 204.

11. Leo Kuper, *Race, Class, and Power: Ideology and Revolutionary Change in Plural Societies* (London: Duckworth, 1974), 142; Charles Taylor, "Nationalism and Modernity," in *Theorizing Nationalism*, ed. Ronald Beiner (Albany: State University of New York Press, 1999), 225; and Robert Jackson, *Sovereignty: The Evolution of the Idea* (London: Polity, 2007), 7.

12. Norman Bennett, *A History of the Arab State of Zanzibar* (London: Methuen, 1978), 241.

13. Mohamed Bakari, *The Democratisation Process in Zanzibar: A Retarded Transition* (Hamburg: Institute of African Affairs, 2001), 125.

14. Valentin Mudimbe, *The Invention of Africa: Gnosis, Philosophy, and the Order of Knowledge* (Bloomington: Indiana University Press, 1988), 98–135; John Breuilly, *Nationalism and the State* (Manchester: Manchester University Press, 1993), 281–287; and P. Olisanwuche Esedebe, *Pan-Africanism: The Idea and the Movement* (Washington, DC: Howard University Press, 1982).

15. Jurgen Osterhammel, "Epilogue: From Civilizing Missions to the Defence of Civility," in *Civilizing Missions in the Twentieth Century*, ed. Boris Barth and Rolf Hobson (Leiden: Brill, 2020), 221; and J. Paul Martin, "Ethnicity and Racism," in *The Columbia History of the 20th Century* ed. Richard Bulliet (New York: Columbia University Press, 1998), 131. See also Michael Mann, *The Dark Side of Democracy: Explaining Ethnic Cleansing* (New York: Cambridge University Press, 2005).

16. Mahmood Mamdani, *Define and Rule: Native as Political Identity* (Boston: Harvard University Press, 2012), 104. Before 1925, in African colonial governance the word *native* included people whose place of origin was the protectorate of Aden or the dominions of the sultan of Muscat, because of the high number of what British officials referred to as "half-castes," those of mixed Arab and Bantu ancestry. See "Debate over Native Half-Castes," ZNA, AB 26/65.

17. S. N. Eisenstadt, *Paradoxes of Democracy: Fragility, Continuity, and Change* (Baltimore: Johns Hopkins University Press, 1999), 14–24; and Barrington Moore, *Social Origins of Dictatorship and Democracy: Lord and Peasant in the Making of the Modern World* (Boston: Beacon Press, 1966).

18. Sana Aiyar, *Indians in Kenya: The Politics of Diaspora* (Boston: Harvard University Press, 2015), 230, 233–234; Will Hanley, *Identifying with Nationality: Europeans, Ottomans and Egyptians in Alexandria* (New York: Columbia University Press, 2017), 282; Ronald Aminzade, *Race, Nation and Citizenship in Post-Colonial Africa: The Case of Tanzania* (Cambridge: Cambridge University Press, 2014), 205; and Elie Kedourie, *Nationalism in Asia and Africa* (New York: World Publishing, 1970), 92–105. For comments critical of anticolonial protest and opposed to common roll elections, see Mbarak al-Hinawy in Zulfikar Hirji, *Between Empires, Sheikh-Sir Mbarak al-Hinawy 1896–1959* (London: Azmuth Editions, 2012), 143. See also the advice of Sheikh Hashil Rashid al-Miskery to the Arab Association in the early 1960s in Nasser al-Riyami, *Zanzibar: Personalities and Events*, trans. Ali Rashid al-Abri (Beirut: Beirut Bookshop, 2012), 346. H. Marhuby's father warned his nationalist-sympathizing colleagues that the populace was not

"politically mature" and thus not ready for independence. H. Marhuby, *My Zanzibar: From Idyllic to Upheaval* (n.p.: self-published, 2017), 412.

19. Abdin Chande, *Islam, Ujamaa, and Community Development: A Case Study of Religious Currents in East Africa* (San Francisco: Austin and Winfield, 1998), 234.

20. Lofchie, *Zanzibar*, 136–143; Suleiman Shahbal, *Zanzibar: The Rise and Fall of an Independent State* (Dubai: self-published, 2002), 127, 158; Salem Ben Nasser Al Ismaily, *The Sultanate of Zanzibar* (Indianapolis: Dog Ear Publishing, 2014), 129.

21. Muḥsin Ḥamūd al-Kindi, *al-Saḥafa al-ʿUmāniyya al-Muhājira wa Shakhṣiyyāthā: Shaikh Hāshil bin Rāshid al-Maskarī numūdhajā* (Beirut: Riad al-Rayyes Books, 2009), 73; see also Ibrahim Zein Soghayrun, "Al-Ishām al-ʿUmāni fī al-Majālāt al-Thaqāfiyya wa al-Fikriyya wa Al-Kashf ʿAn Majāhil al-Qārat-ul-Ifrīqīyya fī Al-ʿAhd al-Busaʿīdī," in *Faʿāliyyāt wa Nāshiṭ: Ḥiṣād Anshiṭat al-Muntadā al-Adabī, 1991–1992*, ed Salim Muhammad al-Ghailānī and Muhammad Ali al-Sulaibi (Muscat: Ministry of Heritage and Culture, 1993), 203.

22. Arthur H. Hardinge, "Legislative Methods in the Zanzibar and East Africa Protectorates," *Journal of the Society of Comparative Legislation* 1, no. 1 (March 1899): 1–10, describes early governance of the protectorate.

23. Middleton and Campbell, *Zanzibar*, 43.

24. W. H. Ingrams, *Zanzibar: Its History and Its* People (London: Stacey International, 2007).

25. Al-Kindi, *al-Saḥafa al-ʿUmāniyya*, 378; Bennett, *History of the Arab State of Zanzibar*, 237–238. Ethnic associations in Zanzibar date from the interwar years, originating in the reaction to onerous distinctions of communal wartime rationing. There was also intra-elite competition between Arabs and Indians caused by the indebtedness of the landed sector to the islands' merchant classes.

26. Bennett, *History of the Arab State of Zanzibar*, 245.

27. Timothy Parsons, *The 1964 Army Mutinies and the Making of Modern East* Africa (Westport, CT: Praeger, 2003), 41. See also Mark Baynham, "The East African mutinies of 1964," *Journal of Contemporary African Studies* 8, no. 1 (1989): 153–180.

28. Lofchie, *Zanzibar*, 132–133.

29. Maulid M. Haj, *Zanzibar: The Last Years of the Protectorate A Constitutional and Political Account* (Muscat: Al Roya Publishing, 2006), 18.

30. Bennett, *History of the Arab State of Zanzibar*, 246. For the construction of Shirazi identity in Zanzibar, see Glassman, *War of Words*, 49–58.

31. Middleton and Campbell, *Zanzibar*, 36.

32. Ingrams, *Zanzibar*, 147–150.

33. A. H. J. Prins, *The Swahili-Speaking Peoples of Zanzibar and the East African Coast, Arabs, Shirazi, and Swahili*(London: International African Institute, 1967), 11.

34. Lofchie, *Zanzibar*, 44–47; and Kuper, *Race, Class, and Power*, 118.

35. Glassman, "Sorting Out the Tribes," 403n36.

36. Anne Bang, "Cosmopolitanism Colonised?: Three Cases from Zanzibar, 1890–1920," in *Struggling with History: Islam and Cosmopolitanism in the Western Indian Ocean*, ed. Kai Kresse and Ed Simpson (New York: Columbia University Press, 2008. See also Anthony Anghie, *Imperialism, Sovereignty and the Making of International Law* (Cambridge: Cambridge University Press, 2004).

37. Engseng Ho, *Graves of Tarim: Geneaology and Mobility Across the Indian Ocean* (Berkeley: University of California Press), 2006, 324. For similar efforts to control movement and migration of Lebanese and Syrians in French West Africa, see Andrew Arsan, *Interlopers of Empire: The Lebanese Diaspora in Colonial French West Africa* (Oxford: Oxford University Press, 2014), ch. 4.

38. Abdul Sheriff, "Race and Class in the Politics of Zanzibar," *Afrika Spectrum* 36, no. 3 (2001): 303–304.

39. "Immigration Officer to Chief Secretary," 5 January 1950, ZNA, AB 26/11.

40. "Acting Senior Commissioner to Chief Secretary," 24 April 1956, ZNA, AK 9/17.

41. Passport Office, "The Zanzibar Ports Decree, 1911," and "The Zanzibar (Provisional) Administration Decree, 1914," ZNA, AB 26/40. See also Graham McPhee and Prem Poddar, introduction to *Empire and After: Englishness in Post-Colonial Perspective*, ed. Graham McPhee and Prem Poddar (New York: Berghahn Books, 2007), 8. After World War I, in 1923, this decree was revised, outlining the requirements of a passport. Mandana Limbert, "Escape from Zanzibar: Refugees, Documents, and the Indian Ocean Shipping Regime," *International Journal of Middle East Studies* 54 (2022): 753–757.

42. Passport Regulations for India, "Rules Governing the Issue of Passports and Visas," ZNA, AB 26/24.

43. A deposit was expected to guarantee return passage in case the passenger was refused entry to East African ports. The AB series in the Zanzibar National Archives is filled with exchanges regarding Manga migrants requesting the refund of the deposit they had given to immigration authorities in Muscat; the Zanzibar authorities typically had to then request this money from the government in Muscat. See, for instance, "Deportation of Undesirable Persons," ZNA, AB 28/82. See also "Passports for Aliens," AB 26/47. In Kenya, the authorities could refuse admission to a passenger unless they could pay the required deposit. The deposit could be paid in Zanzibar or at Mombasa. In Tanganyika, the authorities had the right to order the shipping company to carry the passenger back to their port of embarkation for up to two months after arrival. This caused the shipping companies to collect deposits to hedge themselves against the cost of returning the passenger to their destination. See "Security Bonds for Immigrants under the Immigration Regulation and Restriction Decree," 1923, and H. H. Robinson to Provisional Commissioner, 16 October 1941, AB 26/16. Immigration regulations were further revised in 1923, 1924, 1934, 1935, and 1939. The Immigration Regulation and Restriction Decree, no. 8 of 1923, ZNA, AB 26/15.

44. The Immigration Regulation and Restriction Decree, no. 8 of 1923, ZNA, AB 26/15. See also "Sailing of Dhows to Muscat from Pemba without obtaining a

clearance at Zanzibar," ZNA, AB 45/44; and "Police Reports: Arrival of Dhows," ZNA, AB 45/45. Throughout the 1930s and 1940s vessels from southern Arabia continued to dock in unauthorized ports in Pemba, evading colonial authority. See "Control of Manga Arab Immigrants," ZNA, DO 40/52.

45. Commissioner of Police to Honorable Chief Secretary, 18 August 1939, ZNA, AB 26/13.

46. Glassman, *War of Words*, 194–198; Mahmoud Abel Rahman El Sheikh, "State, Cloves, and Planters: A Reappraisal of British Colonialism in Zanzibar, 1890–1934" (PhD diss., UCLA, 1986), 254–256; and "Disturbances Created by Manga Arabs at Wete, Pemba," July 1941, ZNA, AB 70/3.

47. See, for instance, "Sinhalese Buddhist association Renewal of Passports," ZNA, AB 26/50.

48. Eventually the 1954 Immigration Control Decree supplanted the 1948 guidelines. "The Immigration Control Decree 1954," ZNA, AB 26/13.

49. Sultan Khalifa bin Harub, "A Decree to Make Provisions for Zanzibar Nationality and for Purposes Connected Therewith," 24 December 1952, ZNA, BA 14/43.

50. "The Status of Native Half-Castes in East Africa" 13 October 1949, and "General Notice: Zanzibar Nationality," ZNA, AB 26/65: "Every person born within the Dominions of His Highness the Sultan, whether before or after the date of commencement of the Nationality Decree, 1952, is a Zanzibar subject by birth. on production of proof of his birth to the Passport Officers such a person can apply for a passport."

51. Middleton and Campbell, *Zanzibar*, 12.

52. "The Status of Native Half-Castes in East Africa," ZNA, AB 26/65; and "Identity Documents for African Residents of Zanzibar Visiting the Mainland," 13 October 1949, M.O. Wray to Chief Secretaries, ZNA, AB 26/69. An objection to this proposal in the file states that the document would legally entail bringing Africans within the ambit of the 1947 Immigration Decree.

53. "Imposing of Immigration Restrictions Africans coming from mainland and Portuguese Africa," and "Immigration of Africans in Zanzibar," 29 December 1954, ZNA, AB 26/79. This identification requirement for Africans was further formalized in 1954, with a system of registration that required documentation and surveillance of Africans, while not requiring them to carry a passport.

54. Abdulla Delo Baluchi, "Birth Certificates," *Adal Insaf*, 7 March 1959, 5, MLC.

55. "Immigration, Emigration, and Naturalisation 1958 Feb–1963 Jun," P. A. P. Robertson, "Minute 69 A," 17 October 1958; and AG Senior District Commissioner, Memo "Birth Certificates," 18 December 1962, ZNA, AKP 24/4; and "Naturalization 1959 Dec–1963 May," Mudir Wete to DC Pemba, "Application for Naturalisation," 12 September 1962, ZNA, AKP 24/7.

56. Khamis Ameir, District Officer Chake Chake/Mkoani Pemba, to District Commissioner Pemba, "Immigration Control," 20 November 1962, ZNA, AK 9/20. For birth affidavits in Pemba, see "Affidavits of Births," ZNA, AKP 32/7.

57. Yahya Alawi to Senior Commissioner, 14 May 1958, ZNA, AK 9/20.

58. "Immigration General" Secretary, Ithadi El Umma Party to Chief Secretary, 12 December 1956; J. D. Doherty to Khamis Ameir, 28 July 1959; Permanent Secretary to Senior District Commissioner, 18 January 1962; Civil Secretary to Permanent Secretary, 13 February 1962; and Permanent Secretary to Senior District Commissioner, 5 March 1962, ZNA, AK 9/20.

59. Secretary Ithadi El Umma Party to Chief Secretary, December 12, 1956, ZNA, AK 9/20. Muhammad Shamte and Ali Sharif Mussa formed the Ittihad al-Umma (The People's Union). Lofchie, *Zanzibar*, 172–173; Glassman, *War of Words*, 154–155. The party never contested any elections. Its leaders would later bring supporters into the ZPPP in 1958.

60. M. T. Guthey, "For Zanzibaris Only," *The Adal Insaf* 10, no. 46, 31 May 1958, MLC.

61. "Immigration," Abdulla Rashid, DC, Pemba to District Officer, Chake; and "Immigration Control," 5 December 1962, ZNA, AK 9/17.

62. "Unguja na Utawala: Kurithiwa Hatujafa," *Agozi*, 2 November 1959, MLC.

63. "Naturalization," *Sauti ya Afro Shirazi*, 9 February 1960, MLC.

64. "The Nationality: Amri ya Tajnisi, Lipi Linalo Kizuwizi Kwa Watu Juu ya Tajnisi," *Afrika Kwetu*, 19 November 1962, MLC.

65. *Report of a Commission of Inquiry into Disturbances in Zanzibar*, 2.

66. Al Ismaily, *Sultanate of Zanzibar*, 178; Bennett, *History of the Arab State of Zanzibar*, 255; Helen Louise Hunter, *The Hundred Days Revolution* (Santa Barbara, CA: ABC-CLIO, 2010), 19; and Harith Ghassany, *Kwa Heri Ukoloni, Kwa Heri Uhuru! Zanzibar na Mapinduzi ya Afrabia* (n.p.: Lulu Press, 2010), 22.

67. Lofchie, *Zanzibar*, 217.

68. Saada Wahab, *The History of Indians in Zanzibar from the 1870s to 1963* (Gottingen: Gottingen University Press, 2022), 169–170.

69. Glassman, *War of Words*, 170. See characterization of ASP's opposition to ZNP in B.F. Mrina and W.T. Mattoke. *Mapambano ya Ukombozi Zanzibar* (Dar-es-Salaam, 1980), 100.

70. Ghassany, *Kwa Heri Ukoloni*, 100.

71. For red baiting in the ASP, see Glassman, *War of Words*, 272–273. For ASU conservatism, see Lofchie, *Zanzibar*, 166–168.

72. Ariel Crozon, "Zanzibar en Tanzanie: Essai D'histoire Politique" (Universite de Pau et des Pays de L'adour, 1992), 250.

73. Glassman, *War of Words*, 61, 159.

74. Glassman, "Sorting Out the Tribes," 417; Lofchie, *Zanzibar*, 209–210. See also Haroub Othman, "Tanzania: The Withering Away of the Union," in *Yes, in My Lifetime: Selected Works of Haroub Othman*, ed. Saida Yahya-Othman (Dar-es-Salaam: Mkuti wa Nyota, 2013), 192.

75. Lofchie, *Zanzibar*, 186.

76. Glassman, *War of Words*, 106–107.

77. Jonathon Glassman, "Creole Nationalists and the Search for Nativist Authenticity in Twentieth-Century Zanzibar: The Limits of Cosmopolitanism," *The Journal of African History* 55, no. 2 (July 2014): 239. In their own self-understanding,

"mixing of the blood" is important to their identity, and in some sense they believe it makes them "superior" to those who eschew such associations. For similar dynamics in Latin America, see Marisol de la Cadena, *Indigenous Mestizos: The Politics of Race and Culture in Cuzco, Peru, 1910–1991* (Durham, NC: Duke University Press, 2000).

78. See Ibrahim Shao, *The Political Economy of Land Reforms in Zanzibar: Before and after the Revolution* (Dar-es-Salaam: UDSM Press, 1992), 37; and Frederick Cooper, *From Slaves to Squatters: Plantation Labor and Agriculture in Zanzibar and Coastal Kenya* (Portsmouth, NH: Heinemann, 1997), 280n13.

79. Zanzibar Census, March 1958, 9.

80. Glassman, *War of Words*, 156–157.

81. Lofchie, *Zanzibar*, 207–208. In the discourse of the exiles, it was often claimed that ASP was a party founded and supported by mainlanders with the goal of undermining Islam, but this rhetoric dates back to the time of politics and the way in which nativism was utilized by the class interests in both parties to maintain or improve their economic position and control over labor.

82. Shahbal, *Zanzibar*, 159–160; and Al Ismaily, *Sultanate of Zanzibar*, 174–175.

83. For Ibrahim Noor's recollection of the rhetoric at one of Karume's 1960 rallies, see Ibrahim Noor Shariff, *Tanzania na Propaganda za Udini* (Muscat: self published, 2014), 23–27. In a December 2009 informal conversation in Muscat with a friend of Ali Muhsin, this individual, who was from Mombasa, related a story of being chastised by some Zanzibar Arabs for greeting Karume at a gathering. He retorted, "Why?! I can't greet them?! Just because I disagree with them, I can't greet them!?"

84. Claims (without citations) in Al Ismaily, *Sultanate of Zanzibar*, 174–175. The author claims the issue began two years earlier when Karume stood up at the first meeting of the abortive Zanzibar National Union and asked, "Can a man like myself, born in the Congo and a Belgian subject, be accepted for membership?" Glassman calls the case a form of "slave-baiting" to discredit Karume by exposing his origins, but does not investigate the veracity of Karume's claims. Glassman, *War of Words*, 157.

85. Laura Fair, *Pastimes and Politics: Culture, Community, and Identity in Post-Abolition Urban Zanzibar, 1890–1945* (Athens: Ohio University Press, 2001).

86. Other sources claim he was born in Nyasaland that year. Crozon, "Zanzibar en Tanzanie," 146.

87. Issa Nasser al-Ismaily was unable to find any record of Karume's enrollment in the school registers of 1938–1961. Issa Nasser al-Ismaily, *Will Zanzibar Regain Her Past Prosperity* (Muscat: self-published, 2015), 251.

88. Minael-Hosanna O. Mdundo, *Masimulizi ya Sheikh Thabit Kombo Jecha* (Dar-es-Salaam: DUP, 1995), 74–75. In Ali Shaaban Juma's biography of Karume, his birth neighborhood is listed as Pongwe, in Mudiria Mwera. Juma also states that his father Amani and his mother Amina binti Kadir were married in Mwera. See Ali Shaaban Juma, *Abeid Karume, 1905–1972* (Zanzibar: Rafiki Publishers, 2013). In Karume's obituary reprinted in Crozon's dissertation, Lt. Colonel Mussa

Maisara states that he was born in Kiongoni, Mwera. Glassman, *War of Words*, has a summary of this issue (344n35).

89. These views were also shared by Julius Nyerere, who spoke up about the need to end the "imperialism" of the ZNP-British-sultan triad. Ann Grimstad, "Zanzibar: The Nine-Hour Revolution" (PhD thesis, University of Florida, 2018), 58.

90. Shahbal, *Zanzibar*, 98–100, 256, 364.

91. Bennett, *History of the Arab State of Zanzibar*, 254; and Dieter Nohlen, Michael Krennerich, and Bernard Thibaut, eds., *Elections in Africa: A Data Handbook* (Oxford: Oxford University Press, 1999), 876, 879, 882. A sense of the social constitution of a portion of the electorate can be obtained by studying Zanzibar Protectorate, *List of Electors, Constituency: Ngambo* (Zanzibar: The Legislative Council (Elections) Decree, 1957), ZNA.

92. Lofchie, *Zanzibar*, 177.

93. For naturalization applications and certificates of Omani-born as Zanzibar nationals, see ZNA, Secretariat Files DC 8/4-15, 18, 21.

94. Chief Secretary to Hon. Senior Commissioner 2 January 1960, ZNA, AK 14/8 AG.

95. Middleton and Campbell, *Zanzibar*, 64.

96. ZNA AK 14/8, AG. Chief Secretary to Hon. Senior Commissioner 2 January 1960.

97. Ghassany, *Kwa Heri Ukoloni*, 25.

98. Lofchie, *Zanzibar*, 189.

99. Bennett, *History of the Arab State of Zanzibar*, 258.

100. Hunter, *Hundred Days*, 15; and Al Ismaily, *Sultanate of Zanzibar*, 237.

101. Hunter, *Hundred Days*, 16.

102. Lofchie, *Zanzibar*, 197, 213.

103. *Report of a Commission of Inquiry into Disturbances in Zanzibar*, 4.

104. Ironically Sultan Khalifa was not born in Zanzibar, but in Muscat, and only came to Zanzibar at age thirteen. See "The Sultanate of Zanzibar," *al-Falaq*, 5 September 1956, ZNA.

105. For an ASP communiqué that affirms this, see Haj, *Zanzibar*, 9.

106. Lofchie, *Zanzibar*, 216. For the puzzle of the late emergence of antimonarchical politics, see Glassman, *War of Words*, 319n75. For ASP's use of antisocialist rhetoric in relation to pledges of loyalty to the monarchy, see Glassman, *War of Words*, 338n87. For the antimonarchy of *Agozi* editor J. R. Nasibu, see Glassman, *War of Words*, 372n58. Hanga was also strongly opposed to the monarchy. Glassman, "Sorting Out the Tribes", 423. Also see Nasibu's apology for "an attack on the Person and Throne" of the new sultan Abdulla: J.R. Nasibu, "Apology," *Afrika Kwetu*, 1 November 1962, 4, MLC. For Mapuri's assertion that Jamshid campaigned for the ZNP, see Omar Mapuri, *The 1964 Revolution: Achievements and Prospects* (Dar-es-Salaam: TEMA Publishers, 1996), 47.

107. Abdul Kassim Hanga was among the latter.

108. Bennett, *History of the Arab State of Zanzibar*, 259.

109. Hunter, *Hundred Days*, 15.

110. Dieter Nohlen, Michael Krennerich, and Bernard Thibaut, eds., *Elections in Africa: A Data Handbook* (Oxford: Oxford University Press, 1999), 876, 879, 882.

111. *Report of a Commission of Inquiry into Disturbances in Zanzibar*, 5.

112. *Report of a Commission of Inquiry into Disturbances in Zanzibar*, 8–13.

113. The Zanzibar Refugee Relief Fund Committee, "Refugee Relief Coordinating Committee," 28 August 1961, ZNA, AB 26/72.

114. Glassman, *War of Words*, 234.

115. Ahmed Ida Salim, *The Swahili-Speaking Peoples of Kenya's Coast, 1895–1965* (Nairobi: East African Publishing House, 1973).

116. Shahbal, *Zanzibar*, 300.

117. Ghassany, *War of Words*, 21, 32.

118. Hunter, *Hundred Days*, 35; and Bennett, *History of the Arab State of Zanzibar*, 264.

119. Lofchie, *Zanzibar*, 258–259; and Zuhura Yunus, *Biubwa Amour Zahor: Mwanamke Mapinduzi* (Dar-es-Salaam: Vision Publishing Ltd., 2021), 92–93, 101–104. In Bi Ubwa's account, Babu's falling out with the ZNP stemmed from Ali Muhsin's insisting that the Malindi seat must be held by an Arab. Thank you to Kimberly Wortmann for bringing my attention to this source.

120. Yunus, *Bi Ubwa*, 103–104.

121. Shahbal, *Zanzibar*, 355–361.

122. Glassman, *War of Words*, 173.

123. Ghassany, *Kwa Heri Ukoloni*, xxiii

124. P. A. Robertson, "Zanzibar—Crossroads of East Africa," *Journal of the royal Society for the Encouragement of Arts, Manufactures and Commerce* 112, no. 5096 (July 1964): 610.

125. Lofchie, *Zanzibar*, 220; and Crozon, "Zanzibar en Tanzanie," 92.

126. Middleton and Campbell, *Zanzibar*, 61.

127. Crozon, "Zanzibar en Tanzanie," 97.

128. Crozon, "Zanzibar en Tanzanie," 98.

129. Lofchie, *Zanzibar*, 265–267; Anthony Clayton, *The Zanzibar Revolution and Its Aftermath* (London: C. Hurst, 1981), 63; and Crozon, "Zanzibar en Tanzanie," 96.

130. Bennett, *History of the Arab State of Zanzibar*, 263.

131. Martin Shipway, *Decolonization and Its Impact: A Comparative Approach to the End of Colonial Empires* (New York: Wiley-Blackwell, 2008),174.

132. Cooper, *From Slaves to Squatters*, 286.

133. Lofchie, *Zanzibar*, 269.

134. Lofchie, *Zanzibar*, 265, 267.

135. Ghassany, *Kwa Heri Ukoloni*, 292. Juma Aley infamously stated at the time that the government was not a "cup of tea to be overturned so easily."

136. Cooper, *From Slaves to Squatters*, 286–287; Hunter, *Hundred Days*, 35; Shahbal, *Zanzibar*, 372–375; and Samuel G. Ayany, *A History of Zanzibar: A Study in Constitutional Development* (Nairobi: East African Literature Bureau, 1970, 129.

137. Lofchie, *Zanzibar*, 272.
138. Lofchie, *Zanzibar*, 270.
139. Lofchie, *Zanzibar*, 257.
140. Ghassany, *Kwa Heri Ukoloni*, 34.

2. VIOLENCE AND EMIGRATION IN THE ZANZIBAR REVOLUTION, 1964–1965

1. Jonathon Glassman, *War of Words, War of Stones: Racial Thought and Violence in Colonial Zanzibar* (Bloomington: Indiana University Press, 2011), 212, 214; *Report of a Commission of Inquiry into Disturbances in Zanzibar during June 1961* (London: Her Majesty's Stationery Office, 1961), 10, 13, MLC; Saud Busaidi to Mudir Maghrib, DC Urban Suleiman b. Muhammad al-Kindy, ZNA, AK 16/48. The letter mentions an overheard chant: "'Bring a panga to kill Wamanga."

2. Glassman, *War of Words*, 221. For a flavor of the ominous and conspiratorial character of these rumors, see "Coffee-Ship Gossips," October, November 1962, ZNA, AK 17/20.

3. Glassman, *War of Words*, 227.

4. Chambi Chachage, "Dispensing Survivor's Justice in Zanzibar," *Pambazuka News*, April 15, 2010, www.pambazuka.org/governance/dispensing-survivors-justice-zanzibar. For social histories of partition, see Mushirul Hasan, "Partition Narratives," *Social Scientist* 30 (2002): 24–53. Glassman's discussion of the literature on violence is illuminating. Jonathon Glassman, *War of Words, War of Stones: Racial Thought and Violence in Colonial Zanzibar* (Bloomington: Indiana University Press, 2011); Caroline Elkins, "Looking beyond Mau Mau: Archiving Violence in the Era of Decolonization," *American Historical Review* 120, no. 3 (June 2015): 852–868.

5. Jeffrey C. Alexander, Ron Eyerman, Bernhard Giesen, Neil J. Smelser, and Piotr Sztompka, *Cultural Trauma and Collective Identity* (Berkeley: University of California Press, 2004),12; Liisa Malkki, *Purity and Exile: Violence, Memory and National Cosmology among Hutu Refugees in Tanzania* (Chicago: University of Chicago Press, 1995), 135; and Stef Jansen, "The Violence of Memories: Local Narratives of the Past after Ethnic Cleansing in Croatia," *Rethinking History: The Journal of Theory and Practice* 6, no. 1 (2002): 78.

6. Most of the video footage of the Zanzibar revolution is from the makers of the film *Africa Addio*, available at www.youtube.com/watch?v=UQoSOrHcExY. Sandra Lockwood, "Nightmare in Paradise: The 1964 Zanzibar Revolution and Genocide," in *Hushed Voices: Unacknowledged Atrocities of the 20th Century*, ed. Heribert Adam (Berkshire: Berkshire Academic Press, 2011), 23, offers the film as "concrete proof of the genocide." This is further discussed in chapter 6. Ibrahim Noor's book, *Tanzania na Propaganda za Udini*, (Muscat: Self published, 2014) reprints stills of the film with discussion of what they reveal about the victims' ethnicities.

7. Mira Seigelberg, *Statelessness: A Modern History* (Cambridge, MA: Harvard University Press, 2020).

8. Abdullahi Ali Ibrahim, "The 1964 Zanzibar Genocide: The Politics of Denial," in *Africa and the Gulf Region: Blurred Boundaries and Shifting Ties*, ed. Dale Eickelman and Rogaia Abu-Sharaf (Berlin: Gerlach Press, 2015).

9. Elisa von Joeden-Forgey, "Life Force Atrocities Are Early Indicators of Genocide," in *At Issue: Genocide*, ed. Barbara Krasner (New York: Greenhaven Publishing, 2021); and Arthur Kleinman et al., eds., *Violence and Subjectivity* (Berkeley: University of California Press, 1997).

10. Sascha O. Becker, Sharun Mukand, and Ivan Yotzov, "Persecution, Pogroms and Genocide: A Conceptual Framework and New Evidence," *Explorations in Economic History* 86 (2022): 1–18.

11. G. Thomas Burgess, *Race, Revolution and the Struggle for Human Rights in Zanzibar: The Memoirs of Ali Sultan Issa and Seif Sharif Hamad* (Ohio: Ohio University Press, 2009), 86. Ali Sultan's own reported actions contradict his story. His family alleged that he traveled to Pemba to confront Issa Nasser al-Ismaily's wife with a pistol and threatened to kill her unless she confessed to her husband's whereabouts. Shahira al-Ismailiya, *The Story of Our Father* (Muscat: self-published, 2014), 49. For Prison Island detainees, see Sauda Barwani and Regina Feindt, "Aman Thani," in *Unser Leben von der Revolution und danach—Maisha yetu kabla ya mapinduzi na baadaye*, ed. Sauda Barwani et al. (Cologne: Rüdiger Köppe, 2003), 190–191.

12. Paul Brass, "On the Study of Riots, Pogroms, and Genocide" (prepared for the Sawyer Seminar session "Processes of Mass Killing" at the Center for Advanced Study in the Behavioral Sciences, Stanford University, December 6–7, 2002), www.anveshi.org.in/wp-content/uploads/2017/04/Ripogen.pdf.

13. Paul Brass, *Theft of an Idol: Text and Context in the Representation of Collective Violence* (Princeton, NJ: Princeton University Press, 1997). Writing on the revolution in 1995, Omar Mapuri argued that "Arab intentions" toward Africans in the 1960s justified the 1964 mass killings. Omar Mapuri, *The 1964 Revolution: Achievements and Prospects* (Dar-es-Salaam: TEMA Publishers, 1996), 56–57. Some of the errors of Mapuri's interpretation are addressed in Abdul Sheriff, "Race and Class in the Politics of Zanzibar," *Afrika Spectrum* 36, no. 3 (2001): 306–307.

14. Suleiman Shahbal, *Zanzibar: The Rise and Fall of an Independent State* (Dubai: self-published, 2002), 400–407.

15. Hashil S. Hashil claims Umma members were planning a revolution after their party was banned by the government on January 6, 1964, and were the ones who encouraged the storming of the military barracks and police station. Hashil S. Hashil, *Mimi, Umma Party na Mapinduziya Zanzibar* (Paris: DL₂A Buluu Publishing, 2018), 73–75.

16. Nasser al-Riyami, *Zanzibar: Personalities and Events*, trans. Ali Rashid al-Abri (Beirut: Beirut Bookshop, 2012), 179. Others have argued that the radical elements within the ASP essentially used Okello's army to take power. Ann Grimstad tries to restore Okello to his preeminence in the successful and strategic execution of the revolution; see Ann Lee Grimstad, "The Voice of the Revolution: Remembering and Re-Envisioning Field Marshal John Okello," in *Social Memory, Silenced*

Voices, and Political Struggle: Remembering the Revolution in Zanzibar, ed. W. C. Bissell and Marie-Aude Fouéré (Dar-es-Salaam: Mkuti wa Nyota, 2018), 79–107. See also Michael Lofchie, "Was Okello's Revolution a Conspiracy?," *Transition* 33 (1967): 36–42.

17. Harith Ghassany, *Kwa Heri Ukoloni, Kwa Heri Uhuru! Zanzibar na Mapinduzi ya Afrabia* (n.p.: Lulu Press, 2010), 120.

18. Ariel Crozon, "Zanzibar en Tanzanie: Essai D'histoire Politique" (Science politique, Universite de Pau et des Pays de L'adour, 1992), 117.

19. Crozon, "Zanzibar en Tanzanie," 117–118n4.

20. Helen Louise Hunter, *The Hundred Days Revolution* (Santa Barbara, CA: ABC-CLIO, 2010), 40–41.

21. Ghassany, *Kwa Heri Ukoloni*, 38, 71, 122; and Michael Lofchie, *Zanzibar: Background to Revolution* (Princeton, NJ: Princeton University Press, 1965), 276.

22. Ghassany, *Kwa Heri Ukoloni*, 23, 150, 167, 177; and Crozon, "Zanzibar en Tanzanie," 117.

23. Ghassany, *Kwa Heri Ukoloni*, 54, 59–61, 65–72, 73–86. According to this narrative, Mkello and Mohamed Omari Mkwawa recruited mainland laborers to take an oath to be initiated into a covert organization. They then learned Zanzibari Swahili, were slipped covertly into Zanzibar, and illegally participated in the 1963 election. Later these same mainlanders were alleged to have assisted in overthrowing the government with the help of Jumanne Abdullah Ali and Ali Mwinyi Tambwe in Tanga. They received financial and logistical assistance from Oscar Kambona and tacit approval from Nyerere. In her microhistory of the revolution, Ann Grimstad criticized Ghassany's methods and approaches and disagreed with him about the key role of armed Makonde mainlanders. Ann Grimstad, "Zanzibar: The Nine-Hour Revolution" (PhD diss., University of Florida, 2018), 27, 94–95. Marie-Aude Fouéré has a largely dismissive discussion of the book in "Recasting Julius Nyerere in Zanzibar: The Revolution, the Union and the Enemy of the Nation," in *Remembering Nyerere in Tanzania: History, Memory, Legacy* (Nairobi: Africae, 2015), 180.

24. Ghassany, *Kwa Heri Ukoloni*, 91.

25. Ghassany, *Kwa Heri Ukoloni*, 253.

26. Ghassany, *Kwa Heri Ukoloni*, 106–107, 253–254.

27. "Siyo kweli hata kidogo kama Mapinduzi ya Zanzibar yalifanywa na Watanganyika, yalipangwa na kufanywa na Wazanzibari." Tanzanian president Jakaya Kikwete, quoted in *Mwananchi*, 23 February 2014.

28. Glassman, *War of Words*, 237–240; Grimstad, "Zanzibar," 204; Don Petterson, *Revolution in Zanzibar: An American's Cold War Tale* (Boulder: Westview Press, 2002), 191; Ludger Wimmelbücker, "Aspekte eines gesellschaftlichen Umbruchs: die sansibarische Revolution von 1964," in *Unser Leben von der Revolution und danach—Maisha yetu kabla ya mapinduzi na baadaye*, ed. Sauda Barwani et al. (Cologne: Rüdiger Köppe, 2003), 480–481. Ali Muhsin's estimate is 13,000. A. M. al-Barwani, *Conflict and Harmony in Zanzibar* (Dubai: self-published, 1997), 35, 150. A. Ledger, Zanzibar general manager of the shipping firm Smith

Mackenzie, estimated eight thousand dead. Anthony Clayton, *The Zanzibar Revolution and Its Aftermath: The Zanzibar Revolution and Its Aftermath* (London: C. Hurst, 1981), 81n63. The British Red Cross files on the subject cite various numbers, including two hundred hospitalized and three thousand killed. "Zanzibari, Disturbances In, Vol. 1," British Red Cross, London, RCC/1/2/4/190. Harith Ghassany has a range of five to eighteen thousand, Ghassany, *Kwa Heri Ukoloni*, 320. Ghassany also quotes a letter putting the numbers issue in comparative national perspective: Ghassany, *Kwa Heri Ukoloni*, 320–321, 403n82. For a discussion of minimization, see Issa Shivji, *Pan-Africanism or Pragmatism: Lessons of the Tanganyika-Zanzibar Union* (Dar-es-Salaam: Mkuti wa Nyota Publishers, 2008), 3. For a helpful contextualization see Riikka Suhonen, "Mapinduzi Daima—Revolution Forever: Using the 1964 Revolution in Nationalistic Political Discourses in Zanzibar" (MA thesis, University of Helsinki, 2009), 47. "Letter from Area Commissioner, Rural," 13 April 1964, ZNA, AK 17/10.

29. Burgess, *Race, Revolution*, 87.

30. "Press Communique," ZNA, AK 17/12 has Babu's estimate of "less than 150." Shivji argued that the Umma Party helped halt further violence. Shivji, *Pan-Africanism or Pragmatism*, 3. See also Hashil, *Mimi, Umma Party, na Mapinduzi*, 102; Umma's role in the revolution is contested. Some Omani-Zanzibaris emphasized Umma's role as the revolution's "brain box," while others derided them as opportunists. I.S. 32, 2/20/2013; and I.S. 35, 3/27/13.

31. R. Gallopin to E. Bark, ICRC, B AG 233 203-002, 14/02/1964–05/08/1964.

32. "Zanzibar, Disturbances In, Vol. 1," British Red Cross, RCC/1/2/4/190.

33. Ibrahim, "1964 Zanzibar Genocide" has a good discussion of the controversy.

34. According to Nasser al-Riyami, *Zanzibar: Personalities and Events*, trans. Ali Rashid al-Abri (Beirut: Beirut Bookshop, 2012), 187, this characterization was first made by Ahmed Lamky. See also al-Riyami, *Zanzibar*, 17–19. In conversation with Ibrahim Noor Shariff, he called the revolution 'the first genocide in that part of the world. See also Ibrahim, "1964 Zanzibar Genocide," 68–69; Abdul Sheriff calls the violence, "genocidal in proportion." See G. Thomas Burgess, "Memories, Myths, and Meanings of the Zanzibar Revolution," in *War and Peace in Africa*, ed. Toyin Falola and Raphael Chijioke Njoku (Durham, NC: Carolina Academic Press, 2010), 442–443.

35. Lemkin's original definition of *genocide*, as the intended annihilation of a particular group, was expanded considerably by subsequent theorists, who argued that any act of mass murder constitutes a genocide. Strauss largely concurs with Lemkin's original definition and advocates against the conceptual inflation the term has undoubtedly undergone. See Scott Strauss, "Contested Meanings and Conflicting Imperatives: A Conceptual Analysis of Genocide," *Journal of Genocide Research* 3, no. 3 (2001): 363–364.

36. This is highly significant because considering the tendency of latter-day accounts to "deceive posterity," we might expect more self-conscious references to

genocidal action to emerge from these accounts. That they do not ought to increase our faith in the accuracy of their personal testimony. But for a discussion of these issues see Glassman, *War of Words*, 285–286.

37. Glassman, *War of Words*, 247. But even that term falls short, since it implies a level of conscious preplanning likely absent from the violence. Glassman's explanation emphasizes the spontaneity of the moment and the semidirected actions of the mob. See also Crozon, "Zanzibar en Tanzanie," 35.

38. Ghassany, *Kwa Heri Ukoloni*, 90–91.

39. Glassman, *War of Words*, 246–247.

40. Glassman, *War of Words*, 247–248, 261. See also Ghassany, *Kwa Heri Ukoloni*, 111.

41. Ghassany, *Kwa Heri Ukoloni*, 41–43, 46–51. Among its alleged members were Ibrahim Makungu, Yusuf Himidi, and Sefu Bakari.

42. Ghassany, *Kwa Heri Ukoloni*, 90–91. Both groups claim they deliberately avoided recruiting Shirazis and the indigenous Tumbatu to their cause, because of their extensive kinship ties to Zanzibar's Arabs.

43. Ghassany, *Kwa Heri Ukoloni*, 45.

44. See Jonathon Glassman, "Racial Violence, Universal History, and Echoes of Abolition in Twentieth-Century Zanzibar," in *Abolition and Imperialism in Britain, Africa and the Atlantic*, ed. Derek Peterson (Athens: Ohio University/Swallow Press, 2010), 200n22.

45. I.S. 24, 12/8/2012.

46. Michael Lofchie, *Zanzibar: Background to Revolution* (Princeton, NJ: Princeton University Press, 1965), 206; and Garth Myers, "Narrative Representations of Revolutionary Zanzibar" *Journal of Historical Geography* 26.3 (July 2000): 429–448.

47. Lofchie, *Zanzibar*, 171–172, 254–255; and Ahmed Rajab, "Healing the Past, Reinventing the Present: From the Revolution to Maridhiano," in *Social Memory, Silenced Voices, and Political Struggle: Remembering the Revolution in Zanzibar*, ed. Bill Bissell and Marie-Aude Fouéré (Dar-es-Salaam: Mkuti wa Nyota, 2018), 337n3.

48. Ghassany, *Kwa Heri Ukoloni*, 93, 97, 139.

49. Ghassany, *Kwa Heri Ukoloni*, 84.

50. Ghassany, *Kwa Heri Ukoloni*, 173–174.

51. Ghassany, *Kwa Heri Ukoloni*, 256. For Okello in Pemba, see Burgess, "Memories, Myths, and Meanings", 441.

52. Ghassany, *Kwa Heri Ukoloni*, 255.

53. Ghassany, *Kwa Heri Ukoloni*, 257.

54. Timothy Parsons, *The 1964 Army Mutinies and the Making of Modern East Africa* (Westport, CT: Praeger, 2003), 109. As Parsons notes, there is a direct connection between the revolution and the army mutinies later that January.

55. Glassman, *War of Words*, 248–281.

56. John Okello, *Revolution in Zanzibar* (Nairobi: East African Publishing House, 1973), 61–64.

57. Ghassany, *Kwa Heri Ukoloni*, 110–111.

58. Ghassany, *Kwa Heri Ukoloni*, 256–257. See also Ali Sultan Issa's reflections in Burgess, *Race, Revolution*.

59. Kjersti Larsen, "Silenced Voices, Recaptured Memories: Historical Imprints within a Zanzibari Life-World," in *Social Memory, Silenced Voices, Political Struggle*, ed. Bill Bissell and Marie-Aude Fouéré (Dar-es-Salaam: Mkuti wa Nyota, 2018), 254–255; and Burgess, *Race, Revolution*, 7.

60. Such as where his father bought land, in Manga Pwani, northwest Unguja, a distance he described as fourteen miles from the city center. I.S. 49, 6/10/2013.

61. I.S. 49. I was not able to substantiate this account with other eyewitnesses, but it resonates substantially with Glassman's accounts of mob behaviors and political violence in 1961. See Glassman, *War of Words*, ch. 7. More robust substantiation of such narratives would require additional ethnographic work in rural Zanzibar and Oman. See Mandana Limbert, *In the Time of Oil: Piety, Memory and Social Life in an Omani Town* (Palo Alto, CA: Stanford University Press, 2010), 152–153, for an important oral account of violence against a rural Arab family.

62. I.S. 11, 8/24/2011.

63. I.S. 31, 2/19/2013.

64. al-Ismailiya, *Story of Our Father*, 19.

65. al-Ismailiya, *Story of Our Father*, 41.

66. These testimonies, mostly originating in an Arabophone oral register and then transcribed by others into written Arabic, are here analyzed for what they can tell us of the chaotic social dynamics of the seventy-two hours after the moment the revolution began in the early morning hours of January 12, 1964. Muhammad Abdullah Said Nasir al-Saifi, *Ḥikāyāt wa Riwāyāt al-Ibāḍiyya fī Zanjibār wa ma Jāwaruhā minDduwwal Sharq 'Ifriqiyā*. (Muscat: al-Numair, 2013).

67. Elke Stockreiter, *Islamic Law, Gender, and Social Change in Post-Abolition Zanzibar* (Cambridge: Cambridge University Press, 2015), 92; and Seyyid Hamad Ahmed Mashur al-Ḥaddad, *Dirāsat al-'Arab wa al-Islam fī Sharq 'Afrīqiyā* (Beirut: Dar al-Minhaj, 2007), 287.

68. See Certificate of Naturalization Applications, ZNA, DC 8/10.

69. See Ahmed Ali al-Riyami, *Saluting My Hero* (Muscat: self-published, 2006), 95. Some 217 political prisoners, most associated with the overthrown government, remained in the central prison. "Hoffman Note No. 14 visite a Zanzibar du 11 au 14 Juin 1964," 16 June 1964, ICRC, B AG 233 203-002, 14/02/1964–05/08/1964.

70. Zanzibar to CRO, 5 May 1964, Muscat to FO, 4 May 1964, "Muscat Annual Report, 1964," TNA, FO 371; and "M. Borsinger to Wiltshire," 17 June 1964, ICRC, B AG 233 203-002, 14/02/1964–05/08/1964.

71. Al-Saifi, *Ḥikāyāt*, 323–326.

72. Al-Saifi. *Ḥikāyāt*, 323–326.

73. Al-Haddad, *Dirāsāt*, 286.

74. Al-Saifi, *Ḥikāyāt*, 325.

75. Al-Saifi, *Ḥikāyāt*, 325.

76. Ahmed al-Riyami, *My Pride and Joy* (Muscat: self-published, 2007), 119–120. Sheikh Thabit Kombo later helps Issa Nasser al-Ismaily to escape Zanzibar, al-Ismailiya, 46–51.

77. Ghassany, *Kwa Heri Ukoloni*, 351–353.

78. A theme also present in the Rwandan genocide; see Malkki, *Purity and Exile*, 94.

79. Ahmed al-Riyami, *Quite Another* (Muscat: self-published, 2010), 50. "The family house, originally constructed to accommodate Ahmed Ali Zaher, bore a special significance. It represented family values, being a refuge to the entire members of the family, during celebrations or commemorations."

80. Al-Riyami. *Saluting My Hero*, 73

81. Al-Riyami, *My Pride and Joy*, 119–120.

82. Habiba al-Hinai, *'Ā'idūn Ḥaythu al-Ḥulm, Mashāhid wa-Dhikriyyāt 'awda min Zanjibār wa al-Jazīrah al-Khaḍrā' ila 'Uman* (Beirut: Beirut Bookshop, 2013), 56.

83. H. Marhuby, *My Zanzibar: From Idyllic to Upheaval* (n.p.: self-published, 2017), 421. Glassman demonstrates the dilemmas of participation for some sheha. Glassman, *War of Words*, 261–263.

84. Marhuby, *My Zanzibar*, 421.

85. Zuhura Yunus, *Biubwa Amour Zahor: Mwanamke Mapinduzi* (Dar-es-Salaam: Vision Publishing Ltd., 2021), 142.

86. Al-Bahry, "Death in Zanzibar 1964," August 18, 2009, http://zanzibarwebsite.com/m/discussion?id=2712669%3ATopic%3A59773. See also al-Riyami, *Zanzibar*, 201; Mohamed Bakari, *The Democratisation Process in Zanzibar: A Retarded Transition* (Hamburg: Institute of African Affairs, 2001), 111; al-Barwani, *Conflict and Harmony in Zanzibar*, 237; and Yunus, *Bi Ubwa*, 142. Shaaban S. al-Farsy alludes to this event in his memoirs, *Mzanzibari Asimilia Hadithi Yake* (Muscat: self-published, 1994), 72, as does Aman Thani Fairooz, *Ukweli ni Huu (Kuusuta Uwongo)* (Dubai: self-published, 1994), 53. A letter by Nasor Mansur Mohamed, "A Statement by a Tortured Zanzibari," provides the fullest account of the incident by an eyewitness. It is reprinted in Yunus, *Bi Ubwa*, 203.

87. Sauda Barwani and Ludwig Gerhart, eds., *Life and Poems of Bi Zainab Himid, 1920–2002* (Berlin: Rudiger Koppe, 2012), 121.

88. Barwani and Gerhart *Life and Poems*, 113.

89. Barwani and Gerhart, *Life and Poems*, 119. According to Himid, the revolutionaries "didn't go in the direction of the Sultan and Stone Town at all." This is broadly corroborated by a similar account by Anthony Clayton. Clayton, *Zanzibar Revolution and Its Aftermath*, 74. For reports of stolen property, see "Revolution," ZNA, AK 17/72.

90. "8.2.64 Report on Zanzibar–Sunday 12 January to Friday 7th February 1964," 17 February 1964, ICRC, B AG 233 203-002, 14/02/1964–05/08/1964.

91. A madhhab is a loose collection of Muslim scholars centered on the works of certain great legal and scholarly minds in Muslim history. Ibadism is something like the fifth or sixth major "madhhab" in Islam.

92. DHC E. R. Marlin, 'Note for the File: visit of Mr. Borsinger of the ICRC', 19 Feb. 1964, UNHCR, Box 280. The presence of British passport holders among the refugees indicates some were former civil servants in the colonial protectorate.

93. For naturalization applications and certificates of Omani-born as Zanzibar nationals, see ZNA, Secretariat Files, DC 8/4-15, 18, 21.

94. A. Burdett, ed., *Records of Oman, 1961–1965* (Cambridge: Cambridge University Press, 1997), Vol. IV (1964), 541, FO to R. Hickman, Esq., CRO, 8 February 1964, Oman National Archives, Muscat, Oman (hereafter ONA).

95. Burdett, ed., *Records of Oman*, FO to Hickman, 8 February 1964, ONA (emphasis added).

96. E.R. Marlin, "Note for the File," 19 February 1964, UNHCR, Box 280. The Aga Khan would contribute five thousand to the repatriation operations.

97. Burdett, *Records of Oman*, FO to Muscat, 17 February 1964, ONA.

98. Mr. C. P. Scott to UNHCR, 21 February 1964, UNHCR, Box 280.

99. Scott to UNHCR, 21 February 1964, UNHCR, Box 280.

100. Felix Schnyder to U Thant, 12 August 1964, UNHCR Box 280.

101. "Proces-Verbal D Telephone, M. Borsinger with E. Bark," 19 February 1964, ICRC, B AG 233 203-002, 14/02/1964–05/08/1964.

102. Prince Sadruddin Aga Khan, "Note for the File: Manga Arabs from Zanzibar," 6 July 1964, UNHCR, Box 280. For Mrs. Adams, see "Proces-Verbal D'Entretien: M. Borsinger," 1 July 1964, ICRC.

103. Prince Sadruddin Aga Khan, "Note for the File." See also John Torpey, *The Invention of the Passport: Surveillance, Citizenship, and the State* (Cambridge: Cambridge University Press, 1999).55.

104. The Imamate was a theocratic political community in the Omani interior that tried to become an independent state in the 1950s before being defeated by sultanate forces with the help of the British military advisers. The passport was issued by the Imam's offices in exile, which provided some with a means to leave Zanzibar but did not guarantee the ability to settle in Oman. Saud Ahmed al-Busaidi, *Memoirs of an Omani Gentleman from Zanzibar* (Muscat: al-Roya Press, 2012), 151–153; and Rabi, *Emergence*, 177.

105. Al-Riyami, *Zanzibar*, 198.

106. Otto Gobius, Note for the File: "Re: Group from Zanzibar," 21 February 1964, UNHCR, Box 280.

107. Muscat to Boissier, president intercrouxrouge, 24 February 1964, UNHCR, Box 280.

108. "Rapport Presente Par Georg Hoffman," 5 March 1964, 3, ICRC, B AG 233 203-002, 14/02/1964–05/08/1964. Hoffman was discouraged by Karume from going to Pemba.

109. Scott to Powell-Jones, 4 March 1964, TNA, UK FO 371: 178270.

110. R. Gallopin to P. Scott, 19 March 1964, ICRC, B AG 233 203-002 14/02/1964–05/08/1964.

111. C. D. Powell to Bark, 6 April 1964, TNA, UK FO 371.

112. "Hoffman Note No. 14 visite a Zanzibar du 11 au 14 Juin 1964," 16 June 1964, ICRC, B AG 233 203-002 14/02/1964–05/08/1964.

113. Geneva to FO, 11 March 1964, Zanzibar to CRO, 13 March 1964, and Muscat to FO, 15 March 1964, TNA, FO 371, 178270.

114. With many passages going for as much as £25/person.

115. "Arabs Shipped from Zanzibar to Oman by new Government," *New York Times*, 21 April 1964, extracted from *The Times*, 9 April 1964, and Ann S. Petluck to UN High Commissioner, 22 April 1964, UNHCR, Box 280.

116. "Manga Arabs," 7 April 1964, "Notes on Mrs. Brittain's Verbal Report on Conditions in Zanzibar," 20 April 1964, and "Port Officer information," 6 May 1964, UNHCR, Box 280. See also *Records of Oman*, 1964, de Burlet (N. Aspin) (CRO) to Crosthwait (BHC Zanzibar), 26 Mar. 1964, ONA; and Zanzibar to CRO, 3 April 1964, TNA FO 371.

117. "Manga Arabs," 7 April 1964, UNHCR, Box 280.

118. "Notes on Mrs. Brittain's Verbal Report," 20 April 1964, UNHCR, Box 280.

119. "Manga Arabs Sailings," 18 Apr. 1964, UNHCR, Box 280; and Zanzibar to CRO, 10 April 1964, TNA, UK FO 371.

120. "Revolution—Detainees," A.M.S. Lemki to Commissioner of Prisons, 11 August 1964, ZNA, AK 17/20.

121. I.S. 49.

122. I.S. 49; and UNHCR Geneva to UNHCR London, 4 May 1964, UNHCR, Box 280.

123. "Muscat Annual Report for the Year 1964," TNA, FO 371, 179813.

124. Marlin, "Note for the File: Manga Arabs in Zanzibar," 4 August 1964, UNHCR, Box 280.

125. Muscat to FO, 23 April 1964, Zanzibar to CRO, 25 April 1964, TNA FO 371.

126. *The Times*, 8 April 1964, TNA FO 371.

127. Washington to FO, 16 April 1964, Washington to FO, 18 April 1964, UK Mission, NY to FO, 21 April 1964, TNA FO 371; "Proces-Verbal de Telephone with Miss Wiesender, US permanent delegation," 20 April 1964, ICRC, B AG 233 203-002, 14/02/1964–05/08/1964.

128. Shivji, *Pan-Africanism or Pragmatism*, 98; and Petterson, *Revolution in Zanzibar*, 207.

129. Glassman, *War of Words*, 292–923; and Ronald Aminzade, *Race, Nation and Citizenship in Post-Colonial Africa: The Case of Tanzania* (Cambridge: Cambridge University Press, 2014), 101–102.

130. C. P. Scott to J. E. Powell-Jones, UN Department FO, 26 June 1964, TNA, FO 371, 178271.

131. Crozon, "Zanzibar en Tanzanie," 123–124.

132. Okello, *Revolution in Zanzibar*, 198; John Middleton and Jane Campbell, *Zanzibar: Its Society and Its Politics* (London: Oxford University Press, 1965), 68; Yunus, *Bi Ubwa*, 119; and Crozon, "Zanzibar en Tanzanie," 154.

133. Clayton, *Zanzibar Revolution and Its Aftermath*, 93–94.
134. Ghassany, *Kwa Heri Ukoloni*, 149, 169, 182.
135. Ghassany, *Kwa Heri Ukoloni*, 178.
136. Petterson, *Revolution in Zanzibar*, 158; and R. Gallopin to E. Bark, 10 March 1964, ICRC, B AG 233 203-002 14/02/1964–05/08/1964.
137. J. Bourn to W. G. Dawson, Esq, 4 September 1964, Fowler to Walsh Atkins, 7 September 1964, BHC Dar to CRO London, 10 September 1964, TNA, DO 185/61. The British High Commissioner in Dar-es-Salaam stated: "Karume's fear that Red Cross action might suggest that Arabs were unsafe here and thus be politically unwelcome to him." N. Aspin, East African Political Department CRO, 6 July 1964, TNA, UK FO 371.
138. Ghassany, *Kwa Heri Ukoloni*, 290.
139. "Principle Admin. Sec Dept of Ext Affairs to ICRC Geneva, 3 August 1964, ICRC, B AG 233 203-002, 14/02/1964–05/08/1964; E. R. Marlin, "Note for the File: Manga Arabs in Zanzibar," 5 August 1964, UNHCR, Box 280; "Message de Phillips A La Croix-Rouge Brittanique Expedie Le 11 Aout de Zanzibar," 10 August 1964, UNCHR, Box 280; and Hodgson, Red Cross, "Note for the File: Zanzibar—Manga Arabs," 21 September 1964, UNHCR Box 280, .
140. Nick Phillips c/o Tanganyikan Red Cross Society, 3 September 1964, ICRC, B AG 233 203-003.
141. Phillips, "Report Covering Period from Saturday 27th June to Friday 10 July 1964," UNHCR, Box 280; and "Joan Whittington British Red Cross to M. Borsinger ICRC," 26 June 1964, ICRC, B AG 233 203-002, 14/02/1964–05/08/1964.
142. E. R. Marlin, Note for the File, "Manga Arabs in Zanzibar," 4 August 1964, UNHCR, Box 280.
143. CRO to Dar-es-Salaam, 21 August 1964, 1 September 1964, DO 185/60, "Memo from Nick Phillips," 29 July 1964, TNA, DO 185/61. The same memo is in Annex to J.D. Kelley, London to E. R. Marlin, Geneva, 4 August 1964, UNHCR, Box 280. Clayton, *Zanzibar Revolution*, 104–5, also has additional detail.
144. D.F.B. Le Breton to R. De Burlet, 21 August 1964, DO 185/60, "Memo from Nick Phillips," 29 July 1964, FO 371 Dar-es-Salaam to CRO, 4 September 1964, TNA, DO 185/61. Nyerere was concerned about inciting Egyptian sympathy for the refugees, as many Zanzibari exiles had made a home in Cairo. The Egyptian president supported the revolution and even visited Zanzibar, where Nyerere explained to him that the revolution was not anti-Arab but had been led by revolutionary Arabs from the Umma Party. Fowler to Walsh Atkins, 7 September 1964, TNA, DO 185/61. "Rapport de M.G. Hoffman, sur Ses Missions a Zanzibar," ICRC, B AG 233 203-002, 14/02/1964–05/08/1964; Confidential Telegram Zanzibar to CRO, 23 July 1964, "Precis for Miss Joan Whittington," 26 June 1964, TNA, FO 371; Confidential Telegram Zanzibar to CRO, 23 July 1964, Zanzibar (Acting DHC) to CRO, From Phillips to Miss Whittington at Red Cross, 28 July 1964, Zanzibar to CRO, 4 August 1964, R. W. D. Fowler, British High Commish, Dar to L. B. Walsh Atkins, CRO, 7 September 1964, TNA, FO 371.

145. al-Barwani, *Conflict and Harmony*, 267

146. Crozon, "Zanzibar en Tanzanie," 139.

147. Ghassany, *Kwa Heri Ukoloni*, 198. Ben Bella also refused to meet with any of the Zanzibar exiles residing there.

148. A. Burdett, ed., *Records of Oman, 1966–1971*, Vol. III (1968) (Cambridge: Cambridge University Press, 2003), 649: R. G. Pettitt, East Africa Dep't C.O. to P. Gent, F.O., 19 June 1968, ONA, .

149. "Report" Department of External Affairs, Muscat and Oman, 20 May 1965, UNHCR, Box 280.

150. Erik Gilbert, *Dhows and the Colonial Economy of Zanzibar, 1860–1970* (Athens: Ohio University Press, 2005), 159; and Esmond Bradley Martin, "The Geography of Present-Day Smuggling in the Western Indian Ocean: The Case of the Dhow," *Great Circle* 1, no. 2 (October 1979): 27.

151. "Mackeja to Clutterbuck," 19 October 1966, ICRC, B AG 233 203-003, 06/08/1964-19/10/1970.

152. Judith Marshall, "(Im)mobility in a Sea of Migration: Race, Mobilities, and Transnational Families in Zanzibar and Oman, 1856–2019" (PhD diss., Michigan State University, 2021), 20–21.

153. Riikka Suhonen, "Mapinduzi Daima—Revolution Forever: Using the 1964 Revolution in Nationalistic Political Discourses in Zanzibar" (MA thesis, University of Helsinki, 2009), 47.

154. Hinai, *Ā'idūn Haythu al-Ḥulm*, 63; Eric Burton, "Diverging Visions in Revolutionary Spaces: East German Advisers and Revolution from Above in Zanzibar, 1964–1970," in *Between East and South: Spaces of Interaction in the Globalizing Economy of the Cold War*, ed. Anna Calori et al. (Berlin: De Gruyter, 2019), 101. About ten to fifteen thousand Asians left Zanzibar for India and Pakistan, and then often went on to Dubai, England, and Canada, for which see Dana April Seidenberg, *Mercantile Adventurers: The World of East African Asians* (New Delhi: New Age International, 1996), 203. A similar exodus of Asians from Kenya occurred from March 1968 to March 1969, during which approximately eighteen thousand Asians left the country. Cynthia Salvadori, *Through Open Doors: A View of Asian Cultures in Kenya* (Nairobi: Kenway Publishers, 1989), 11.

155. Wimmelbücker, "Aspekte eines gesellschaftlichen", 481. Karume initially treated this exodus dismissively, remarking, "let the educated flee!" Ghassany, *Kwa Heri Ukoloni*, 181, 259.

3. "ON BEHALF OF ZANZIBARIS ABROAD":
THE ZANZIBAR ORGANIZATION AND POSTCOLONIAL
TANZANIAN POLITICS, 1964–1985

1. Ludger Wimmelbücker, "Aspekte eines gesellschaftlichen Umbruchs: Die sansibarische Revolution von 1964," in *Unser Leben von der Revolution und*

danach—Maisha yetu kabla ya mapinduzi na baadaye, ed. Sauda Barwani et al. (Cologne: Rüdiger Köppe, 2003), 482.

2. James Mayall, "Nationalism," in *The Columbia History of the 20th Century*, ed. Richard Bulliet (New York: Columbia University Press, 1998), 196.

3. Wolfgang Schivelbusch, *The Culture of Defeat: On National Trauma, Mourning, and Recovery*, trans. Jefferson Chase (New York: Henry Holt, 2003).

4. Benedict Anderson, "Long-Distance Nationalism: World Capitalism and the Rise of Identity Politics" (The Wertheim Lecture, Centre for Asian Studies Amsterdam, 1992), 11. For an informative application of the concept, see Birgit Bock-Luna, *The Past in Exile: Serbian Long Distance Nationalism and Identity in the Wake of the Third Balkan War* (Berlin: Lit Verlag, 2007), 15–16.

5. "Let Us Be Consistent," by "Zanzibaris Abroad," undated typescript, KP no. 8. This statement repeats the phrase "we Africans," condemning apartheid alongside the revolution of 1964, and warning of the spread of communism.

6. Suleiman Shahbal, *Zanzibar: The Rise and Fall of an Independent State* (Dubai: Self-published, 2002), 455.

7. See, for instance, Jean P. Smith, *Settlers at the End of Empire: Race and the Politics of Migration in South Africa, Rhodesia, and the United Kingdom* (Manchester: Manchester University Press, 2022).

8. Abeid Awadh Abeid Ghania to Ahmed Seif Kharussy [*sic*], 6 May 1964, KP no. 1.

9. Aman Thani to Abdulrab Ali Said, August 2, 1973 and Aman Thani Bashir to Sk. Ahmed, December 7, 1973, KP no. 7; and "Iliyopinduliwa ni Serikali ya Wananchi," *FZV*, 12 January 1986. Indeed, according to Mzee Aboud, Eritrea was ready to offer support to a post-1964 exile movement for the liberation of Zanzibar. Harith Ghassany, *Kwa Heri Ukoloni, Kwa Heri Uhuru! Zanzibar na Mapinduzi ya Afrabia* (n.p.: Lulu Press, 2010), 196.

10. Like many nationalist exiles, the ZNP intelligentsia in exile held Zanzibar's people apart from their criticisms of the revolution and the postcolonial state. This extended to a stated belief that the Zanzibaris themselves were totally innocent of the deeds of the revolution. *FZV*, 16 January/February 1980; and Aman Thani to ASK, May 1972, KP no. 6.

11. John Armstrong, "Mobilized and Proletarian Diasporas," *American Political Science Review* 70, no. 2 (1976): 393–408.

12. Wimmelbücker, "Aspekte eines gesellschaftlichen Umbruchs," 482.

13. See, for instance, Leillah to ASK Majid, May 28, 1973, and Abdulla Ali to ASK, 1973, KP no. 7. Aman Thani seemed to be at the center of contention; some exiles contended that he opposed their plans and was spreading rumors about other members of the liberation front.

14. Ghassany, *Kwa Heri Ukoloni*, 196.

15. Ghassany, *Kwa Heri Ukoloni*, 194–195.

16. Juma Haji Kassim (Deira Dubai) to Bwana Muhariri, "Ukatili na Unyama wa Mreno Wafichuliwa," 30 July 1974, KP no. 7.

17. Riyami, *Pride and Joy*, 125.

18. Kharusi to Dr. Deltgen, 17 May 1971, and Letter to the Editor, *Daily Telegraph*, July 25, 1973, KP no. 7.

19. Suleiman Khatib to Sheikh Ahmed Seif, 25 August 1969, KP no. 3.

20. A sense of where the most active membership was located is offered by a petition calling for the release of Ali Muhsin, Juma Aley, and Maulid Mshangama. "The Zanzibar Organization," undated, KP no. 9. Signators come from the United Kingdom, Dubai, and Cairo.

21. Mohammed Abdulla to Jumuiya ya WaZanzibari, 1 August 1977, KP no. 3.

22. H. Marhuby, *My Zanzibar: From Idyllic to Upheaval* (n.p.: self-published, 2017), 526. Many Zanzibaris with one-way Zanzibar exit permits (called colloquially "mkeka") had emigrated to Egypt and Iraq, where they received asylum and pursued education.

23. Sauda Barwani, "Suleiman Malik," in *Unser Leben von der Revolution und danach*, ed. Barwani et al., 110.

24. Leillah to ASK Majid, May 28, 1973, and Aman Thani to Sk. Ahmed, 7 December 1973, KP no. 7. Apparently the Zanzibar Liberation Front had a bank account for the first time only after Karume's assassination.

25. "Zanzibar Organization Constitution," March 1968, KP no. 16.

26. Ali Muhsin al-Barwani admits as much in *Conflict and Harmony in Zanzibar* (Dubai: self-published, 1997), 287.

27. In March 1964, Sheikh Ali Riyami of the Zanzibar and Overseas Association wrote to the UNHCR headquarters in Geneva: "It appears that there is an acute refugee problem to the solution of which we need your humane and urgent cooperation." Sh. Ali Riyami, Zanzibar and Overseas Association in Southsea Hants, England to UNHCR Geneva, 22 March 1964 (stamp 25 March), UNHCR, Box 280; and Geneva to F. J. Homann Herimberg, 1 April 1964, UNHCR Box 280.

28. Barwani, "Suleiman Malik," 108–110.

29. A. Burdett, ed., *Records of Oman, 1961–1965*, de Burlet (N. Aspin) (CRO) to Crosthwait (BHC Zanzibar), 26 March 1964, ONA; and Geneva to F. J. Homann Herimberg, 1 April 1964, UNHCR, Box 280.

30. "Zanzibar Organization Press Release, 16 October 1968, KP no. 16.

31. Mohamed Bakari, *The Democratisation Process in Zanzibar: A Retarded Transition* (Hamburg: Institute of African Affairs, 2001), 199–200. Bakari notes that the exiles worked closely with Amnesty International and other NGOs to raise awareness of further human rights abuses in Zanzibar, that they formed the "Zanzibar Organization based in Britain" and that "their mode of operation was much more diplomatic oriented and not military." Bakari is keen to prove that CUF is a phenomenon separate from and not dependent on the exiles.

32. Salim Abdulla to Mr. A. Mohammed N. Lemky, 14 August 1964, KP no. 1.

33. Kharusi to *The News Portsmouth*, 20 September 1975, KP no. 6. By 1990 the name was changed to *Zanzibar Newsletter* after an editorial transition. These post-1990 issues are found in the Northwestern vertical file at Northwestern University's Herskovits Library.

34. Kharusi to Salim Rashid, 10 November 1981, KP no. 8.

35. Bakari, *Democratisation Process in Zanzibar*, 104; Ahmed Seif Kharusi, *Zanzibar: Africa's First Cuba* (Richmond, UK: Foreign Affairs Publishing, 1967); *The Agony of Zanzibar: A Victim of the New Colonialism* (Richmond, UK: Foreign Affairs Publishing, 1969); *Letters Smuggled Out of Zanzibar* (Portsmouth, UK: Portsmouth Printers Ltd., 1971); and *Zanzibar Cries for Help* (Hampshire, UK: The Zanzibar Organization), 1974.

36. Barwani, "Suleiman Malik," 100, 102. See also James Brennan, "Radio Cairo and the Decolonization of East Africa, 1953–1964," in *Making a World after Empire: The Bandung Moment and Its Political Afterlives*, ed. Christopher J. Lee (Athens: Ohio University Press, 2010), 173–195.

37. Barwani, "Suleiman Malik," 102. Malik denied being an official member of Z.O. and denied that the organization received support from any government.

38. Leonhard Harding, "Nyerere in neuem Licht: Interpretationen in den Lebensgeschichten von Sansibaris," in *Unser Leben von der Revolution und danach*, ed. Barwani et al., 557.

39. Said Hemed Mauly to Ahmed Seif, Dubai, 21 November 1974, KP no. 6. Mauly related an incident he had heard in Delhi in a meeting with the Tanzanian ambassador, where he opined about the Zanzibar Organization that they were "wananchi waliokimbia na kuishi uhamishioni." They were also "kikundi cha watu wabaya." See also comments of Salim Rashid about *FZV* in Barwani, "Suleiman Malik," 106.

40. Notable among those is Oscar Kambona, the most prominent Tanzanian dissident of the liberation generation.

41. Hamed Suleiman, Oman Police, Ruwi, Muscat to Ahmed Seif, 7 May 1973, KP no. 7.

42. Muscat to ASK, 29 October 1974, KP no. 6.

43. "Open Letter to the Sultan of Oman," *FZV*, November/December 1974, KP no. 7.

44. Salim Barwani to Kharusi, 14 April 1976, KP no. 3.

45. Ahmed Hamoud al-Harthi to Sultan Qaboos, October 1977, al-Rawahi Public Library in Mutrah. I thank Ahmed al-Maazmi for sending me this source.

46. A. Clayton to Sheikh Ahmed Seif, n.d., and Harold Soref to Kharusi, 10 July 1974, KP no. 7. Soref was chairman of the Africa Group at the Monday Club, a conservative group opposed to British decolonization policy in Rhodesia and South Africa. See also Brennan, "Nyerere,"153.

47. HM Othman to Kharusi, 14 June 1985, KP no. 8.

48. I.S. 26, 12/16/2012.

49. Kharusi to Acting Matron, Royal Alexandra Hospital for Sick Children, 12 February 1972, KP no. 7.

50. Salim Barwani to Kharusi, 14 April 1976, KP no. 3. Barwani was later brought to Oman with help from Kharusi and others. He turned in his Tanzanian passport at the London embassy and received an Omani passport.

51. Jeremy Jones and Nicholas Ridout, *Oman, Culture and Diplomacy* (Oxford: Oxford University Press, 2012), 184; Jeffrey James Byrne, "Africa's Cold War,"

in *The Cold War in the Third World*, ed. Robert J. McMahon (Oxford: Oxford University Press, 2013), 101–123; and Ethan R. Sanders, "A Small Stage for Global Conflicts: Decolonization, the Cold War, and Revolution in Zanzibar," *Canadian Journal of History* 55, no. 2 (December 2017): 479–508.

52. George Roberts, *Revolutionary State-Making in Dar-es-Salaam: African Liberation and the Global Cold War, 1961–1974* (Cambridge: Cambridge University Press, 2021); Ethan R. Sanders, "Conceiving the Tanganyika-Zanzibar Union in the Midst of the Cold War: Internal and International Factors," *African Review* 41, no. 1 (2014): 35–70; and Natalia Telepneva, "Our Sacred Duty: The Soviet Union, the Liberation Movements in the Portuguese Colonies, and the Cold War, 1961–1975" (PhD thesis, London School of Economics, 2014).

53. Ammar Ali Jan has recently argued that in India, political Islam and communism both trace their genealogy to the earlier Khilafat movement. Ammar Ali Jan, "Islam, Communism and the Search for a Fiction," in *Muslims Against the Muslim League: Critiques of the Idea of Pakistan*, ed. Ali Usman Qasmi and Megan Eaton Robb (Cambridge: Cambridge University Press, 2018), 255–284.

54. Kelly Askew, "Sung and Unsung: Musical Reflections on Tanzanian Postsocialisms," *Africa* 76, no. 1 (2006): 17. Abdulrazak Gurnah vividly evokes this sentiment among the exiles in his novel *Admiring Silence*, putting them into the words of "Uncle Hashim," who was imprisoned and had family members killed in 1964. For ASP anticommunism, see Jonathon Glassman, *War of Words, War of Stones: Racial Thought and Violence in Colonial Zanzibar* (Bloomington: Indiana University Press, 2011), 339n87. For ZNP's "Islamic socialism," see Shahbal, *Zanzibar*, 159–160. Suleiman Malik expressed contempt for "MaComrad," who called ZNP reactionary and themselves progressive, but according to Malik pursued individualist interests. Barwani, "Suleiman Malik," 112.

55. Ali Mazrui, "Tanzaphilia: A Diagnosis," *Transition* 6, no. 31 (1967): 20–26; and Seth Markle, *Motorcycle on Hell Run: Tanzania, Black Power, and the Uncertain Future of Pan-Africanism, 1964–1974* (East Lansing: Michigan State University Press, 2017).

56. David Westerlund, "Freedom of Religion Under Socialist Rule in Tanzania, 1961-1977" *Journal of Church and State* 24.1 (Winter 1982), 87-103.

57. Marie-Aude Fouéré, "Recasting Julius Nyerere in Zanzibar: The Revolution, the Union, and the Enemy of the Nation," in *Remembering Nyerere in Tanzania: History Memory Legacy*, ed. Marie-Aude Fouéré (Dar-es-Salaam: Mkuti wa Nyota Publishers, 2015).

58. Helen Louise Hunter, *The Hundred Days Revolution* (Santa Barbara, CA: ABC-CLIO, 2010), 96–98. See also Tity de Vries, "Not an 'Ugly American': Sal Tas, a Dutch Reporter as Agent of the West in Africa," in *Transnational Anti-Communism and the Cold War: Agents, Activities and Networks*, ed. Luc van Dongen, Stephanie Roulin, and Giles Scott-Smith (New York: Palgrave Macmillan, 2014), 75.

59. Marhuby, *My Zanzibar*, 438. For comments on the role of East German intelligence in Zanzibar, see Eric Burton, "Diverging Visions in Revolutionary Spaces: East German Advisers and Revolution from above in Zanzibar, 1964–1970," in *Between East and South: Spaces of Interaction in the Globalizing Economy*

of the Cold War, ed. Anna Calori et al. (Berlin: De Gruyter, 2019); and G. Thomas Burgess, "The Rise and Fall of a Socialist Future: Ambivalent Encounters Between Zanzibar and East Germany in the Cold War," in *Navigating Socialist Encounters: Moorings and (Dis)Entanglements between Africa and East Germany during the Cold War*, ed. Marcia Schenck, et al. (Berlin: De Gruyter Oldenbourg, 2021), 169–192. At least one Zanzibari was arrested by East German Police in Berlin and accused of helping an East German girl defect to West Berlin. Kharusi to Stephanie Grant, 22 July 1970, KP no. 6.

60. Haroub Othman, "Revolution: Class Struggle or Racial War?," in *Yes, in My Lifetime: Selected Works of Haroub Othman*, ed. Saida Yahya-Othman (Dar-es-Salaam: Mkuti wa Nyota, 2013), 194.

61. *FZV*, May/June 1978. For an accounting of these years through oral history, see Marie-Aude Fouéré, "Remembering the Dark Years (1964–1975) in Contemporary Zanzibar," *Encounters: The International Journal for the Study of Culture and Society* 5 (2012): 113–126.

62. Al-Barwani, *Conflict and Harmony*, 264.

63. Ariel Crozon, "Zanzibar en Tanzanie: Essai D'histoire Politique" (Science politique, Universite de Pau et des Pays de L'adour, 1992) 225, 302; and Roman Loimeier, *Between Social Skills and Marketable Skills: The Politics of Islamic Education in 20th Century Zanzibar* (Leiden: Brill, 2009). In 1965, religion as a school subject in Zanzibar was replaced by politics. For postrevolution education in Zanzibar, see Loiemeier, *Between Social Skills*, 461–508.

64. For instance, in a statement heavy on emphasis of a suffering ummah: "Draft Resolution on Zanzibar," *FZV*, March/April 1971, and "Memorandum of the Zanzibar Muslims to World Muslim Conference Held in Tripoli, Libya Shawwal 1390–December 1970," KP no. 6. Similar dynamics can be observed in Soviet exile discourse; see Violeta Davoliūtė and Tomas Balkelis, eds., *Narratives of Exile and Identity: Soviet Deportation Memoirs* (Budapest: Central European University Press, 2018).

65. It often inadvertently accomplished the opposite: embedding these distinctions into permanent majority-minority dynamics. Abdin Chande, "Muslim-State Relations in East Africa Under Conditions of Military and Civilian or One-Party Dictatorships," *Historia Actual Online* 17 (2008): 110; Kassim M. Kassim to "Alfred," 25 November 1974, KP no. 7. Kassim's letter discusses the interference of state socialist cadres with Muslims in Tanzania, including hassling people going on hajj and an alleged attempt by Tanzanian Youth League members to destroy a mosque.

66. Ahmed Idarus Baalawy, *Nyerere and Muslim Tanzania* (Portsmouth: The Zanzibar Organization, 1982/1983), 8. See also Hamza Mustafa Njozi, *Mwembechai Killings and the Political Future of Tanzania* (Ottawa: Globalink Communications, 2000), 90–91.

67. G. Thomas Burgess, "An Imagined Generation: Umma Youth in Nationalist Zanzibar," in *In Search of a Nation: Histories of Authority and Dissidence in Tanzania*, ed. Gregory Maddox and James Giblin (Dar-es-Salaam: Mkuti wa

Nyota 2005). See also Laura Fair, "'It's Just No Fun Anymore': Women's Experiences of Taarab before and after the 1964 Zanzibar Revolution," *International Journal of African Historical Studies* 35, no. 1 (2002): 61–81; and Kelly Askew, *Performing the Nation: Swahili Music and Cultural Politics in Tanzania* (Chicago: University of Chicago, 2002).

68. Crozon, "Zanzibar en Tanzanie," 181.

69. Esmond Bradley Martin, *Zanzibar: Tradition and Revolution* (London: Hamish Hamilton, 1978), 20–21; Don Petterson, *Revolution in Zanzibar: An American's Cold War Tale* (Boulder: Westview Press, 2002), 166; Anthony Clayton, *The Zanzibar Revolution and Its Aftermath* (London: C. Hurst, 1981), 149; Crozon, "Zanzibar en Tanzanie," 199; and Marcia Schenck et al., introduction to *Navigating Socialist Encounters: Moorings and (Dis)Entanglements between Africa and East Germany during the Cold War*, ed. Marcia Schenck et al. (Berlin: De Gruyter Oldenbourg, 2021), 9.

70. Crozon, "Zanzibar en Tanzanie," 275.

71. Paul Sprute, "Diaries of Solidarity in the Global Cold War: The East German Friendship Brigades and Their Experience in 'Modernizing Angola,'" in *Navigating Socialist Encounters: Moorings and (Dis)Entanglements between Africa and East Germany during the Cold War*, ed. Marcia Schenck et al. (Berlin: De Gruyter Oldenbourg, 2021), 305.

72. Crozon, "Zanzibar en Tanzanie," 125; and Cranford Pratt, *The Critical Phase in Tanzania, 1945–1968: Nyerere and the Emergence of a Socialist Strategy* (Cambridge: Cambridge University Press, 1976), 180. A relevant study that the author has not been able to consult is Saada Wahab, "Nationalization and Redistribution of Land in Zanzibar: The Case Study of Western District, 1965–2008" (MA thesis, University of Dar-es-Salaam, 2011).

73. Clayton, *Zanzibar Revolution and Its Aftermath*, 38; and Chris Jones, "Plus Ça Change, Plus Ça Reste Le Même? The New Zanzibar Land Law Project," *Journal of African Law* 40, no. 1 (1996): 19–42.

74. Ibrahim Shao, *The Political Economy of Land Reforms in Zanzibar: Before and after the Revolution* (Dar-es-Salaam: UDSM Press, 1992), 54; and "Watu Waliopewa Eka Tatu, Dole, A.S.P. Branch," ZNA, AK 17/20; see also "Nyarka za mashamba yalioshikwa na serikali," July–October 1964, ZNA, AKP 41/6.

75. Zuhura Yunus, *Bi Ubwa Amour Zahor: Mwanamke Mapinduzi* (Dar-es-Salaam: Vision Publishing Ltd., 2021), 189.

76. Including a belief by many of them in the "sinfulness" of land expropriation. Pragmatically, no doubt many saw that what the government gave, it could just as quickly take away. Shao, *Political Economy of Land Reforms*, 55.

77. Shao, *Political Economy of Land Reforms*, 53, 57–58.

78. Shao, *Political Economy of Land Reforms*, 49–50, 53; Burton, "Diverging Visions," 90n17; and K. I. Tambila, "Aspects of the Political Economy of Unguja and Pemba," in *The Political Plight of Zanzibar*, ed. Maliyamkono (Dar-es-Salaam: Tema Publishers, 2000), 81. The reforms were implemented eighteen months after

being announced in March 1964. In Unguja and Pemba, 28 percent and 29 percent, respectively, of arable land was recorded as redistributed.

79. Burton, "Diverging Visions," 89; Askew, "Sung and Unsung", 26; and G. Thomas Burgess, *Race, Revolution and the Struggle for Human Rights in Zanzibar: The Memoirs of Ali Sultan Issa and Seif Sharif Hamad* (Athens: Ohio University Press, 2009), 163.

80. For Nyerere's criticism of town life, see Emily Callaci, *Street Archives and City Life: Popular Intellectuals in Postcolonial Tanzania* (Durham, NC: Duke University Press, 2017). In his position as visiting professor of African Studies at Amherst College in 1981–1982, the former revolutionary minister Abdulrahman Babu criticized Nyerere's policies, arguing that the state should have focused more aggressively on industrialization instead of romanticizing traditional agriculture. A. M. Babu, "The Tanzania That Might Have Been," *Africa Now*, December 1981.

81. Burton, "Diverging Visions," 107. According to Ali Sultan Issa, this was the turning point for the corruption of the revolution, as Karume also took over the Ministry of Finance. Burgess, *Race, Revolution*, 167.

82. Crozon, "Zanzibar en Tanzanie," 264.

83. Crozon, "Zanzibar en Tanzanie," 307.

84. Shao, *Political Economy of Land Reforms*, 87.

85. Amir Mohamed, *A Guide to a History of Zanzibar* (New Delhi: Good Luck Publishers, 2006), 132.

86. Habiba al-Hinai, *'Āidūn Ḥaythu al-Ḥulm, Mashāhid wa-Dhikriyyāt 'awda min Zanjibār wa al-Jazīrah al-Khaḍrā' ila 'Uman* (Beirut: Beirut Bookshop, 2013), 63–64; Marhuby, *My Zanzibar*, 427–428; I.S. 1, 8/11/2011; I.S. 52, 6/23/2013; and "Letter Dated 1st May Smuggled Out of Zanzibar" (1971), KP no. 7.

87. Martin, *Tradition and Revolution*, 62.

88. Martin, *Tradition and Revolution*, 61; and Crozon, "Zanzibar en Tanzanie," 269.

89. Crozon, "Zanzibar en Tanzanie," 261.

90. Elizabeth McMahon, "Developing Workers: Coerced and 'Voluntary' Labor in Zanzibar, 1909–1970," *International Labor and Working Class History* 92 (Fall 2017): 128; Petterson, *Revolution in Zanzibar*, 166; and Burgess, "An Imagined Generation," 216–249.

91. "State of the Economy," Tanzania Supplement, *Africa Now*, January 1986, 51. For parallel struggles around students and national development in mainland Tanzania, see Andrew Ivaska, *Cultured States: Youth, Gender, and Modern Style in 1960s Dar-es-Salaam* (Durham, NC: Duke University Press, 2011).

92. Burgess, *Race, Revolution*, 22; and Burton, "Diverging Visions," 101–102. H. Marhuby makes a similar observation in *My Zanzibar*, 429.

93. "Encouraging Reports from Zanzibar" *FZV*, 14 July 1971, KP no. 6: "It has been reported to us that two large groups of people in Zanzibar broke into two State shops simultaneously although in each shop a Policeman was on a watch. These

people took away foodstuffs for their own consumption.... Two other groups invaded cultivated fields owned by Abeid Karume, the Zanzibar despot, and Edington Kisasi. According to the report after the incident about 40 people, once ardent supporters of the Afro-Shirazi Party, have been arrested and detained."

94. Shao, *Political Economy of Land Reforms*, 63. Primary and secondary school pupils were even ordered to go pick cloves in 1976.

95. Shao, *Political Economy of Land Reforms*, 63; and McMahon, "Developing Workers," 127–128.

96. Shao, *Political Economy of Land Reforms*, 63.

97. Shao, *Political Economy of Land Reforms*, 64.

98. Shao, *Political Economy of Land Reforms*, 69–70. Mainland migrant labor remained cheaper than local labor and thus attractive to Zanzibar farmers in this period. Ironically, it seems some mainlanders moved to Zanzibar in the 1970s to avoid being forcibly "villagized" by the implementation of ujamaa.

99. Crawford Young, "Nation, Ethnicity and Citizenship: Dilemmas of Democracy and Civil Order in Africa," in *Making Nations, Creating Strangers States and Citizenship in Africa*, ed. Paul Nugent, Daniel Hammett, and Sara Dorman (Leiden: Brill, 2007), 241–264.

100. Laurie Lambert, *Comrade Sister: Caribbean Feminist Revisions of the Grenadian Revolution* (Charlottesville: University of Virginia Press, 2020), 12.

101. Crozon, "Zanzibar en Tanzanie," 132.

102. Crozon, "Zanzibar en Tanzanie," 241. Nyerere balked at the suggestion, pointing out that the islands did not need a "new sultan."

103. Martin observed that he could make no friends during his time in Zanzibar because of the level of fear of being spied on or reported for even minor infractions. Martin, *Tradition and Revolution*, 16–17.

104. For the argument that a central role in the mass mobilizing of state building is played by a system of internal surveillance, see John Entelis, "Islamist Politics and the Democratic Imperative: Comparative Lessons from the Algerian Experience," *Journal of North African Studies* 9, no. 2 (2004): 205.

105. Crozon, "Zanzibar en Tanzanie," 128.

106. Crozon, "Zanzibar en Tanzanie," 134–135.

107. Martin, *Tradition and Revolution*, 12–13. Security services in 1975 left Martin alone but interrogated and harassed all those he talked to. See also Aman Thani, "My Ordeal and Escape," *FZV*, September–October 1972, KP no. 6; Ali Muhsin al-Barwani, *I Was Nyerere's Prisoner* (Portsmouth: Zanzibar Organization, 1975); and A. Burdett, ed., *Records of Oman, 1966–1971*, 646, R. H. Hobden, Canadian High Commission Dar-es-Salaam to P. R. H. Wright, Cairo, 24 May 1968, ONA.

108. According to Mzee Aboud, he was sent with others after the revolution to ask Jamshid to re-establish the overthrown government in Pemba. See Ghassany, *Kwa Heri Ukoloni*, 194.

109. In one case Zanzibaris were used as political pawns in a reconciliation between Nyerere and Kenyan president Daniel Moi. Al-Barwani, *Conflict and*

Harmony, 289. This story was also related to me by the family of one of those arrested by the Kenyan government in Nairobi.

110. Nasser al-Riyami, *Zanzibar: Personalities and Events*, trans. Ali Rashid al-Abri (Beirut: Beirut Bookshop, 2012), 274.

111. "Released Political Prisoners: Zanzibar" and "Some People Who are Still in Prison in Zanzibar," n.d., KP no. 7.

112. Muhamed Nassor Jahadhmy, "A Case History of My Imprisonment," n.d., KP no. 7.

113. Handwritten letter in Swahili from "Amani," n.d., KP 01.

114. "Revolution- Detainee Release Bonds," n.d., ZNA, AK 17/12. These files pertaining to the revolution in the Zanzibar archives appear to have been picked over and offending files removed. In one case, on a file labeled "Stolen Property at Raha Leo," the word "stolen" was crossed out and above it the word "lost" written.

115. Crozon, "Zanzibar en Tanzanie," 224.

116. Crozon, "Zanzibar en Tanzanie," 221.

117. Ronald Aminzade, *Race, Nation and Citizenship in Post-Colonial Africa: The Case of Tanzania* (Cambridge: Cambridge University Press, 2014), 202.

118. Iain Walker, "Identity and Citizenship among the Comorians of Zanzibar," In *The Indian Ocean: Oceanic Connections and the Creation of New Societies*, ed. Engseng Ho and Abdul Sheriff(London: Hurst, 2014), 239; and Ghassany, *Kwa Heri Ukoloni*, 277.

119. Aminzade, *Race, Nation and Citizenship*, 210. Karume also got involved in the mainland controversy against an Asian Muslim mutual aid organization, the East African Muslim Welfare Society. Abdin Chande, *Islam, Ulamaa and Community Development: A Case Study of Religious Currents in East Africa* (San Francisco: Austin and Winfield Publishers, 1998), 138; and Issa Ziddy, "Hasan b. Amir al-Shirazi (1880–1979)," *Sudanic Africa* 16 (2005): 9.

120. Bakari, *Democratisation Process in Zanzibar*, 76; and al-Hinai, *'Ā'idūn*, 66.

121. Parita Mukta, *Shards of Memory: Woven Lives in Four Generations* (London: Weidenfeld and Nicolson, 2002), 54.

122. Martin, *Tradition and Revolution*, 69–71; Amrit Wilson, *The Threat of Liberation: Imperialism and Revolution in Zanzibar* (London: Pluto Press, 2013), 55–56; Mohammed Makame Haji, "The Quick Sands of Law and Marriage in Zanzibar: Some Missing Footnotes," *Journal of Culture Society and Development* 15 (2016): 36–38; Akbar Keshodkar "Marriage as a Means to Preserve Asian-ness: The Post-Revolutionary Experience of the Asians of Zanzibar," *Journal of Asian and African Studies* 45, no. 2 (April 2010): 226–240; Richa Nagar, "The South Asian Diaspora in Tanzania: A History Retold," *Comparative Studies of South Asia, Africa and the Middle East* 16, no. 2 (Fall 1996): 62–80; Fidahussein A. Hameer, *Crying Out for Freedom: The Event of Forced Marriages in 1970s Zanzibar* (Birmingham: Sun Behind the Cloud Publishing, 2014); and S. Maoulidi, "Between Law and Culture: Contemplating Rights for Women in Zanzibar," in *Gender and Culture at the limit of rights*, ed. D. L. Hodgson (Philadelphia: University of Pennsylvania Press, 2011), 44.

123. I.S. 11, 8/24/2011.

124. Martin, *Tradition and Revolution*, 72. Karume was clearly acutely aware of colonial citizenship laws but interpreted them in often idiosyncratic ways. He insisted that Zanzibaris were British protected persons, because "the British had wanted to protect that people of Zanzibar from slavery." Like many postcolonial subjects, Karume continued to think of the relationship with the British in terms of protection. See Ahmed Hamoud Al-Maamiry, *Oman and East Africa* (New Delhi: Lancers Books, 1979), 96.

125. Askew, "Sung and Unsung," 24–25; Shao, *Political Economy of Land Reforms*, 87 notes that the government made a deliberate attempt to phase out the high school certificate along with all scholarships for further studies abroad immediately after the revolution.

126. Burton, "Diverging Visions," 105; Crozon, "Zanzibar en Tanzanie," 233; and Adrian Pyre, Amnesty International to Kharusi, 18 May 1973, KP no. 7. These and other suspected extrajudicial executions were not confirmed until the mid-1970s. Nyerere controversially allowed their extradition after Karume threatened to break the Union.

127. Letter to the Editor of the *Times* about Michael Wolfers's article, "New Island Puritanism," July 1970, KP no. 7. The letter asserts, "Last month 17 people, all leading members of the Afro-Shirazi Party, among them Said Kapapa and Bopa, had an interview with the Zanzibar president and told him bluntly that all the people in the islands demand elections for a representative government of their choice as soon as possible. 'The citizens do not want to remain a day longer under your rule.' Karume ordered all 17 delegates thrown into prison."

128. "Karume's Recent Barbaric and inhuman Act," *FZV*, 10 May 1971, KP no. 8.

129. Marhuby, *My Zanzibar*, 479; and Crozon, "Zanzibar en Tanzanie," 281.

130. George W. Triplett, "Zanzibar: The Politics of Revolutionary Inequality," *Journal of Modern African Studies* 9, no. 4 (December 1971): 614. al-Hinai, *Aʾidūn Ḥaythu al-Ḥulm* (64–65) writes that mothers wishing to leave Zanzibar would be forced to leave their children behind, as a guarantee they would return.

131. Crozon, "Zanzibar en Tanzanie," 218, 240.

132. Yunus, *Bi Ubwa*, 176.

133. Askew, "Sung and Unsung," 26; Martin, *Zanzibar*, 123; and Cranford Pratt, *The Critical Phase in Tanzania, 1945–1968: Nyerere and the Emergence of a Socialist Strategy* (Cambridge: Cambridge University Press, 1976), 180. Abdul Sheriff, who was studying in America at the time of the revolution, recognized that those living outside Zanzibar faced unique difficulties demonstrating their nationality to obtain a passport. Regina Feindt, "Abdul Sheriff," in *Unser Leben von der Revolution und danach*, ed. Barwani et al., 308.

134. Aminzade, *Race, Nation and Citizenship*, 201.

135. Crozon, "Zanzibar en Tanzanie," 218–219.

136. "The Tragic Story of Zanzibar," by A. S. Kharusi, n.d. [but after Hanga's execution], and "Zanzibar—Isle of Horrors," n.d., KP no. 6 (emphasis added). See

also "Ilitoweka ya Neema Ikapaa ya Nakama Januari 12, 1964," special issue, *FZV*, 12 January 1986, KP no. 10, which relates similar events in Swahili.

137. "Zanzibar's Detained Ex-Ministers," undated typescript, KP no. 7.

138. Lisa Wedeen, *Peripheral Visions: Publics, Power and Performance in Yemen* (Chicago: University of Chicago Press, 2008), 201.

139. "Cowboys and Indians," *FZV*, 11 July 1973, KP no. 9.

140. Aman Thani Fairooz, *Ukweli ni Huu (Kuusuta Uwongo)* (Dubai: self-published, 1994).

141. "The Ninth Anniversary of Zanzibar Independence," n.d., KP no. 7; and A.S. Kharusi, "The Tragic Story of Zanzibar," n.d., KP no. 9.

142. *FZV*, January–February 1978, KP. Subsequently repeated in Kharusi's political tracts, such as *Letters Smuggled Out of Zanzibar*, 17. Ahmed Seif Kharusi, "Zanzibar—Isles of Horror," KP no. 6.

143. *FZV*, January–February 1978, KP.

144. Al-Barwani, *Conflict and Harmony*, 272.

145. See also the definition of *political mythology* in Stuart Kaufman, *Nationalist Passions* (Ithaca, NY: Cornell University Press, 2015); and J. W. van Prooijen and K. M. Douglas, "Conspiracy Theories as Part of History: The Role of Societal Crisis Situations," *Memory Studies* 10, no. 3 (2017): 323–333.

146. Liisa Malkki, *Purity and Exile: Violence, Memory and National Cosmology among Hutu Refugees in Tanzania* (Chicago: University of Chicago Press, 1995), 102; and Paul Hockenos, *Homeland Calling: Exile Patriotism and the Balkan Wars* (Ithaca, NY: Cornell University Press, 2003).

147. A tendency noted at the time by one of Kharusi's supporters in Portsmouth. Peter Phelps to Kharusi, 8 May 1974, KP no. 7.

148. Issa Shivji, *Pan-Africanism or Pragmatism: Lessons of the Tanganyika-Zanzibar Union* (Dar-es-Salaam: Mkuti wa Nyota Publishers, 2008), 67. Shivji posits that Nyerere ignored the racial chauvinism of the ASP, contrary to his own "non-racial and pan-African principles." Pratt, *Critical Phase*, 139, argues that Nyerere declared the Union out of fear of communist subversion. In her most recent book, Amrit Wilson overestimates the coercive role of the United States in the Union as well as the importance of Zanzibar to US Cold War concerns, based on one telegram. She dismisses Nyerere as being a "liberal" who negotiated for independence instead of fighting. See Wilson, *The Threat of Liberation*, 62–63. This is likely a result of her reliance on Babu as a main source. See Glassman, *War of Words*, 292–293.

149. *FZV*, January–February 1978, and *FZV* 13, nos. 3/4 (March/April 1978), 4, KP no. 8: "Being mission trained he cannot divest himself of the medieval crusaders' mentality and fear of the 'heathen Saracens.' Nyerere's morbid fear is of Arabs." See Baalawy, *Nyerere and Muslim Tanzania*. Baalawy, like Ali Muhsin and others, was held in a Tanzanian prison for ten years. According to Muhammad Abdul-Muttalib Hashim, the idea of Nyerere as anti-Muslim originally came from Kambona, who alleged that the confiscation of urban property in Dar-es-Salaam was motivated by the desire to break the power of Swahili Muslims within the state.

Ghassany, *Kwa Heri Ukoloni*, 213. Kambona, though not Muslim, was both highly motivated and highly capable of appealing to the exiles in the language they had only recently been directing at him.

150. Mohammed Shamte, the exiled prime minister of the overthrown Zanzibar government, told Kharusi that when he met Nyerere in Lagos in the late 1950s, Nyerere told him, "Why don't you annex Zanzibar to Tanganyika, after all its [*sic*] no bigger than Moshi." *FZV*, 13, nos. 3/4 (March/April 1978). See also Mahmood Ntege-Lubwana, "Amin's Twin," *Africa Events*, June 1985, 14. The rhetoric about Nyerere as imperialist echoes right-wing rhetoric from prominent Britons like Harold Soref about Zanzibar, which he refers to as "part of President Nyerere's Empire." Soref to Editor, *Evening Standard*, 10 July 1974, KP no. 6. For Nyerere as "obsessed" with the union to the detriment of Tanganyika, see Barwani, "Suleiman Malik," 116.

151. *FZV* 13, nos. 3/4 (March/April 1978). Muhammad Abdul-Muttalib Hashim similarly claimed that the British created "African socialism" through the influence of a "British Jew," Joan Wickers, on Nyerere. Frankly, the accusations of Nyerere being Zionist are calumny. In 1967, according to Haroub Othman, Nyerere stated that "the establishment of the state of Israel was an act of aggression against the Arab people." Haroub Othman, "The Arusha Declaration and the Triangle Principles of Tanzanian Foreign Policy," in *Yes, in My Lifetime: Selected Works of Haroub Othman*, ed. Saida Yahya-Othman (Dar-es-Salaam: Mkuti wa Nyota, 2013), 13. See also Mzee Aboud's comments in Ghassany, *Kwa Heri Ukoloni*, 189. The related myth of the hidden hand of Israel in the revolution is echoed in many exile publications, for example, al-Maamiry, *Oman and East Africa*, 93–94; and Baalawy, *Nyerere and Muslim Tanzania*, 4–6.

152. *FZV* (January/February 1980), KP no. 16. See also Kharusi, *Zanzibar Cries for Help*, 5. See Harding, "Nyerere in neuem Licht," 508, for discussion of revolution as invasion.

153. *FZV* (January/February 1980), KP no. 16.

154. Al-Barwani, *Conflict and Harmony*, 185; and "Hands off Uganda and Zanzibar," *FZV* 13, nos. 11/12 (November/December 1978), 3. In his interview with Ghassany, Muhammad Abdul-Muttalib Hashim claims that Kambona asked Guinean president Ahmed Sekou Toure to protect Hanga (the Tanzanian ambassador to Guinea at that time) by not sending him to Zanzibar, but Nyerere allowed it, allegedly because Karume threatened to break the Union. Ghassany, *Kwa Heri Ukoloni*, 205. See also Ali Nabwa, "Nyerere si Malaika," *Dira*, 20–26 December 2002.

155. "Hands off Uganda and Zanzibar," *FZV* 13, nos. 11/12 (November/December 1978), 3. See also Aman Thani's comments in *Ukweli ni Huu*.

156. Baalawy, *Nyerere and Muslim Tanzania*, 10.

157. Baalawy, *Nyerere and Muslim Tanzania*, 9.

158. Ghassany, *Kwa Heri Ukoloni*, 211. Joshua Nkomo, the leader of the nationalist party ZAPU in Southern Rhodesia, confirmed that Nyerere uttered these words. Nkomo objected strongly to their implications at the time. Jeremiah Opira,

former deputy chief of intelligence under Milton Obote, who was imprisoned by Nyerere, similarly confirmed these words.

159. Baalawy, *Nyerere and Muslim Tanzania*, 10.

160. See Harding, "Nyerere in neuem Licht," 504 quoting Khatib M. Rajab al-Zinjibari, "Nyerere Against Islam in Zanzibar and Tanganyika," https://www.julius nyerere.org/resources/view/nyerere_against_islam_in_zanzibar_and_tanganyika#:~:text=Nyerere%2C%20a%20devout%20Catholic%20saw,a%20radical%20 Christian%20from%20Uganda. Nyerere was a strong supporter of the ASP and instrumental in its formation.

161. See, for instance, Juma Khamis Juma and Arshad Islam, *The East African Muslim Welfare Society (1945–1968): The Case of Tanzania* (Gombak: IIUM Press, 2017).

162. Wilson, *Threat of Liberation*, 80–86.

163. In an ironic twist, Humud's father Muhammad was the murderer of Sultan Ahmed in 1956 and had been released from prison by Umma Comrades. Ann Grimstad, "Zanzibar: The Nine-Hour Revolution" (PhD diss., University of Florida, 2018), 127.

164. Wilson, *Threat of Liberation*, 80, 82.

165. Ahmed Badawi Qullatein, Ali Sultan Issa, A. M. Babu, Hashil Seif Hashil, Salim Saleh Salim, and Salim Ahmed Rashid were all sentenced to eighteen years in prison. See Hashil's account in *Mimi, Umma Party na Mapinduzi ya Zanzibar* (Paris: DL$_2$A Buluu Publishing, 2018). H. Chase, "Zanzibar Treason Trial," *Review of African Political Economy* 6 (1976): 19–33; see also Barwani, "Suleiman Malik," 122–126. Some of the sentenced were released September 17, 1977; others were released on Union day the following year. Nyerere released thirteen Zanzibaris on April 26, 1978, after six years' detention, to mark the fourteenth anniversary of the Union.

166. Haroub Othman, "The Union with Zanzibar," in *Mwalimu: The Influence of Nyerere*, ed. Colin Legum and Geoffrey Mmari (Oxford: James Currey, 1995), 174.

167. Crozon, "Zanzibar en Tanzanie," 293–295; and Chase, "Zanzibar Treason Trial," 19–33. Jumbe continued the hardline approach of the "liberators" until deposed by Tanzania's ruling party in 1984, because of his increasing resistance to the Union. Max Mmuya and Amon Chaligha, *Towards Multiparty Politics in Tanzania* (Dar-es-Salaam: UDSM Press, 1992), 5, 93; Haroub Othman, "Succession Politics and the Union Presidential Elections," in *Yes, in My Lifetime: Selected Works of Haroub Othman*, edited by Saida Yahya-Othman (Dar-es-Salaam: Mkuti wa Nyota, 2013), 73; and Haroub Othman, "Nyerere's Political Legacy," Iin *Tanzania after Nyerere*, ed. Michael Dood (New York: Pinter Publishers, 1988), 90.

168. "Statement of the Zanzibar Liberation Front on Occasion of Karume's Assassination on Friday Evening 7th of April, 1972," KP no. 7 (emphasis added).

169. David Martin, "Despatch from Dar-es-Salaam," 6 May 1973, KP no. 9.

170. Martin, "Despatch" [written on the document: "trial will be in public, press allowed"], 7 May 1973, KP no. 9. A report from Graham Mytton claimed that

as many as twenty-three people were being held on the mainland in association with the plot. Graham Mytton, "Zanzibar Trials," *African Service News Talks*, KP no. 9.

171. Crozon, "Zanzibar en Tanzanie," 296.

172. Hashil, *Mimi, Umma Party, na Mapinduzi*; al-Barwani, *Conflict and Harmony*, 235–239; and Bakari, *Democratisation Process in Zanzibar*, 129. See "Nyerere's Hypocrisy," in *Habusu: Zanzibar Political Prisoners* no. 6 (1976), Herskovits Library, Vertical File Tanzania, Northwestern University (hereafter NU). Umma member Ali Sultan Issa was imprisoned from 1972 to 1978. Roman Loiemeier, "Memories of Revolution: Patterns of Interpretation," in *Social Memory, Silenced Voices, and Political Struggle: Remembering the Revolution in Zanzibar*, ed. Bill Bissell and Marie-Aude Fouéré (Dar-es-Salaam: Mkuti wa Nyota, 2018), 49. A fictional rendering of the conditions that facilitated this convergence is found in the travails of Adam Shafi's young protagonist Hamza in his novel *Haini*, jailed for his alleged role in the conspiracy that killed "Kigogo" (Karume). See Adam Shafi, *Haini* (Nairobi: Longhorn Publishers, 2003).

173. Crozon, "Zanzibar en Tanzanie," 298.

174. Crozon, "Zanzibar en Tanzanie," 300; Wilson, *Threat of Liberation*.

175. "Zanzibar Trial Fund—Zanzibar Trial: Urgent Appeal to Mwalimu Nyerere," 10 September 1973, KP no. 9.

176. For his part, Nyerere deliberately did not intervene in the island's internal affairs, in order to preserve the Union, which he had personally brokered, and which he regarded as important to regional security. Crozon, "Zanzibar en Tanzanie," 240.

177. Though the council retains legislative powers even after the 1977 merger of ASP and TANU into CCM.

178. Crozon, "Zanzibar en Tanzanie," 316–326, 328–336.

179. Crozon, "Zanzibar en Tanzanie," 349.

180. Dr. P.A.C. Isichei on behalf of Raph Uwechue Editor in Chief, AFRICA (international business, economic and political monthly), 22 May 1973, KP no. 9.

181. "Who Gets Libyan Aid?," *Africa*, no. 115 (March 1981). For the covert history of the WICS, see "Gaddafi's Secret Missionaries," www.reuters.com/article/us-libya-missionary/special-report-gaddafis-secret-missionaries-idUSBRE82S07T20120329.

182. Resolutions and Recommendations of the International Youth Conference of the Muslim Youth, Convening in Tripoli, 2–12 July 1973, KP no. 9.

183. Resolutions and Recommendations, KP no. 9. The delegates related a letter Ali Muhsin wrote to Gamel Abdel Nasser, asking him "to act with speed in trying to save Islam" and warning that "the history of Andalusia may be repeated in Zanzibar and East Africa." It references the 1969 banning of the East African Muslim Welfare Society (EAMWS).

184. Resolutions and Recommendations, KP no. 9.

185. "Resolutions on Zanzibar," Muslim Organizations Conference, 6–10 April 1974, KP no. 6.

186. For oil price trends in the 1970s and 1980s, see Dermot Gately, "Lessons from the 1986 Oil Price Collapse" (Brookings Papers on Economic Activity, 1986), 237. For the impact of oil price in Tanzania, see J. F. Shao, "Tanzania: A Blood-Sucking Government Running Down the National Economy" and "I Should Prefer to Cease Being President," submitted to NDP, June 1980, 5, KP.

187. Shao, "Tanzania." See also *Bulletin of Tanzanian Affairs* 10 (July 1, 1980).

188. Michael Lofchie, "Agrarian Crisis and Economic Liberalization in Tanzania," *Journal of Modern African Studies* 16, no. 3 (1978): 451–475.

189. Shao, "Tanzania," KP. This is followed by an undated letter to Oscar Kambona from John Shao, PO Box 1147, SUNY-Binghamton (the latter became vice chancellor at Tumaini University).

190. Bakari, *Democratisation Process in Zanzibar*, 112.

191. Tambila, "Aspects," 87, 89.

192. W. C. Bissell, "Engaging Colonial Nostalgia," *Cultural Anthropology* 20, no. 2 (May 2005): 219.

193. Julius Emeka Okolo, "Liberia: The Military Coup and Its Aftermath," *The World Today* 37, no. 4 (1981): 149–157. The instability ranged from an April coup in Liberia, an attempted coup in Turkey in September, an attempted coup in Zambia in October, and an attempted coup in Guinea-Bissau, and a coup in Bangladesh, to a coup in Mauritania.

194. "A Verbal Safety Valve," *Africa*, December 1982.

195. "Nyerere: The Man and the Challenge," *New African*, October 1980: "Mwanakwacha, a private company that was hired by parastatal NAFCO, to provide lorries for cement transport, was paid and got the lorries from another parastatal, the National Raod Haulage Company."

196. Colm Foy, "Tanzania Tackles Its Crisis," *Africa Asia*, December 1984.

197. "State of the Economy: Tanzania Supplement," *Africa Now*, January 1986.

198. "Tanzanian Push for Privatization," *Africa Now*, August 1986, 10.

199. Marie-Aude Fouéré, "The Revolution, the Union, and the Enemy of the Nation," in *Remembering Nyerere in Tanzania*, ed. Marie-Aude Fouéré (Dar-es-Salaam: Mkuti wa Nyota, 2015), 188.

200. Abdillatif Abdalla, *Sauti ya Dhiki* (Nairobi: Oxford University Press, 1973), was written while the author was serving a prison sentence in Kenya for sedition. See also Ann Biersteker, "The Significance of the Swahili Literary Tradition and Interpretation of Early Twentieth-Century Political Poetry" (Boston University African Studies Center, AH Number 6, 1990); and Jose Arturo Saavedra Casco, *Utenzi, War Poems, and the German Conquest of East Africa: Swahili Poetry as a Historical Source* (Trenton, NJ: Africa World Press, 2007).

201. Crozon, "Zanzibar en Tanzanie," 402–405.

202. Binti Zinjibari, "Ndio" Risala, "Toleo Maalum la Wazanzibari," 25 February 1984, 2–4, KP no. 10. According to Kharusi, "ndio" is "the symptoms of madness which befell Nyerere (Dalila za kichaa kilichompata Mwalimu) to speak and then respond to himself (akajiitikia mwenyewe)."

203. Kelly Askew, "Tanzanian Newspaper Poetry: Political Commentary in Verse," in *Remembering Nyerere in Tanzania: History, Memory, Legacy*, ed. Marie-Aude Fouéré (Dar-es-Salaam: Mkuti wa Nyota Publishers, 2015).
204. Crozon, "Zanzibar en Tanzanie," 413–414.
205. Crozon, "Zanzibar en Tanzanie," 542.
206. "Unguja ni Njema," *FZV*, February 1990 (Uhuru Freedom 1990), Herskovits Library, Vertical File Tanzania, NU.
207. Crozon, "Zanzibar en Tanzanie," 544.
208. Crozon, "Zanzibar en Tanzanie," 615, 619.
209. Crozon, "Zanzibar en Tanzanie," 535.
210. Al-Barwani, *Conflict and Harmony*, 271.

4. ZANZIBARI DIASPORA COMMUNITIES IN THE ARABIAN GULF, 1964–1977

1. HCR Geneva to HCR London, 1 May 1967, UNHCR, Fonds 11, Series 1, Box 32, 1 QAT ZAN. On 16 April 1967, Mohamed al-Mulla wrote a letter to UNHCR officials inquiring about returning to Zanzibar, an option not available to many politically active exiles until the 1990s.

2. Protection-Travel Documents-Dubai, "Extract from Mr. Goodyear's report on his visit to the Trucial States, Qatar, Kuwait and Saudi Arabia, 25 March 1970 to 5 April 1970," UNHCR, Fonds 11, Series 1, Box 182, 6/2/DUB. The reverse was also true; a passenger wishing to go from Oman to Zanzibar had to break their voyage at Mombasa. "Immigration," Ali Said Akbary, Regional Commissioner Zanzibar to Permanent Secretary, Ministry of Home Affairs, Nairobi, 3 September 1966, ZNA, AK 9/17.

3. Noora Lori, *Offshore Citizens: Permanent Temporary Status in the Gulf* (Cambridge: Cambridge University Press, 2019), 112.

4. Lori, *Offshore Citizens*.

5. Lori, *Offshore Citizens*, 86–88.

6. Muhammad Morsy Abdullah, *The United Arab Emirates: A Modern History* (London: Croom Helm, 1978), 138.

7. Abdullah, *United Arab Emirates*.

8. A 4.5 percent tax on all imports and exports, except gold, which was untaxed, leading to Dubai becoming the third largest gold importer in the world by the mid-1960s. See Goodyear, Report on Visit to Dubai, 14–20 May 1966, UNHCR, 15/DUB/ZAN, 1–2.

9. Abdullah, *United Arab Emirates*, 135.

10. Syed Ali, *Dubai: Gilded Cage* (New Haven, CT: Yale University Press, 2010), 28. Statistics from the Ministry of Labor indicated that in 1976, African countries were a tiny fraction of the total number of expatriates in the UAE issued work permits, with the majority issued to Indian nationals. Ali Mohamed Khalifa, *The United Arab Emirates: Unity in Fragmentation* (Boulder, CO: Westview Press, 1979), 111.

11. Sara Cosemans, "The Politics of Dispersal: Turning Ugandan Colonial Subjects into Postcolonial Refugees (1967–76)" *Migration Studies* 6, no. 1 (March 2018): 99–119.

12. The Representative, UNHCR Branch Office, London, "Zanzibar Refugees in Dubai," 12 May 1967, UNHCR, 6/2/DUB.

13. See Mahmood Mamdani, *From Citizen to Refugee. Ugandan Asians Come to Britain* (London: Frances Pinter, 1973).

14. Kharusi to J. D. R. Kelly, UNHCR London, 9 August 1970, KP no. 6.

15. Mr. Goodyear visit to Iran, Dubai and Qatar, November 1967–9 December 1967, UNHCR, 15/DUB/ZAN.

16. Saud Ahmed al-Busaidi, *Memoirs of an Omani Gentleman from Zanzibar* (Muscat: al-Roya Press, 2012); and "Mr. Goodyear visit," UNHCR, 15/DUB/ZAN.

17. The Representative, UNHCR Branch Office, London, "Zanzibar Refugees in Dubai," 12 May 1967, UNHCR, 6/2/DUB.

18. A. Burdett, ed., *Records of Oman, 1966–1971*, 642, Leslie Goodyear to David Roberts, 30 January 1968, ONA.

19. "Examples of Individual Hardship among Zanzibari Refugees Now in Dubai," 28 May 1966, UNHCR Archives, Fonds 11, Series 1, Box 256, 15/DUB/ZAN.

20. "Goodyear Report on Visit to Dubai in Connecting with Zanzibari Refugees, 2/2/67–10/2/67," UNHCR, 15/DUB/ZAN.

21. H. Marhuby, *My Zanzibar: From Idyllic to Upheaval* (n.p.: self-published, 2017), 511. For a fictional account of using a fake passport to escape Zanzibar, see Abdulrazak Gurnah, *By The Sea* (London: Bloomsbury, 2001).

22. Marhuby, *My Zanzibar*, 476.

23. "Mr. Goodyear visit to Trucial States, Qatar, Kuwait and Saudi Arabia," 25 March 1970–5 April 1970, UNHCR, 6/2/DUB. Goodyear's reports are a major source for understanding national and community dynamics, even though the files that contain them have been anonymized (and thus many interesting parts have been removed) according to UNHCR guidelines.

24. "Karume Hints: Don't come to Hell," KP no. 7.

25. "Note for the File," Carsten Brink-Petersen meeting with Z Kirui, Senior Assistant Secretary of the Ministry of Home Affairs, 6 June 1970, and summary of meeting, 9 June 1970, UNHCR, Fonds 11, Series 1, Box 184, 6/2/KENYA; I.S. 38, 4/13/13; and "Extract from Mr. Goodyear's Report on his visit to the Trucial States, Qatar, Kuwait and Saudi Arabia," 25 March 1970, UNHCR, 6/2/DUB.

26. "Extract from Mr. Goodyear's report on his visit to the Trucial States, Qatar, Kuwait and Saudi Arabia, 25 March 1970 to 5 April 1970," UNHCR, 6/2/DUB.

27. Goodyear, Report on Visit to Qatar, Dubai, Ras Al Khaima & Abu Dhabi, 23 November 1971–2 December 1971, UNHCR, 1/QAT.ZAN L.A.

28. "Goodyear Report 1971," UNHCR, 1/QAT/ZAN.

29. "Karume's Black Lies," undated typescript, KP no. 7.

30. The British Political Agent in Abu Dhabi called NCOs "the most important documents in the whole machinery for issuing visas." Quoted in Lori, *Offshore Citizens*, 80.

31. *FZV*, July 1975, KP; and Babakerim, *The Aftermath of the Zanzibar Revolution* (Muscat: self-published, 1994), 1, 13–14.

32. Ariel Crozon, "Zanzibar en Tanzanie: Essai D'histoire Politique" (Science politique, Universite de Pau et des Pays de L'adour, 1992), 131. The governments of Kenya, Tanzania, Uganda, and Zambia had met soon after the revolution to develop a joint policy for the treatment of prohibited immigrants in their territories. Nyerere was known to relax these policies to allow the free movement of those fleeing Zanzibar to the mainland.

33. Amrit Wilson, *The Threat of Liberation: Imperialism and Revolution in Zanzibar* (London: Pluto Press, 2013), 87.

34. Wilson, *Threat of Liberation*, 87; and Ahmed Seif Kharusi, *Letters Smuggled Out of Zanzibar* (Portsmouth: Portsmouth Printers Ltd., 1971).

35. Harith Ghassany, *Kwa Heri Ukoloni, Kwa Heri Uhuru! Zanzibar na Mapinduzi ya Afrabia* (n.p.: Lulu Press, 2010), 200, 202. Muhammad Abdul-Muttalib Hashim's father was killed in Zanzibar eight months after the revolution.

36. Aman Thani Fairooz, *Ukweli ni Huu (Kuusuta Uwongo)* (Dubai: self-published, 1994). Thani was joined by his family in Zanzibar in December 1976. Aman Thani to Kharusi, 13 April 1974, KP no. 6.

37. Al-Barwani, *Conflict and Harmony*, 248.

38. Al-Barwani, *Conflict and Harmony*, 249.

39. I.S. 30, 2/15/2013. Referring to the Shimba people, a clan of the Mijikenda. See Thomas T. Spear, "Traditional Myths and Historian's Myths: Variations on the Singwaya Theme of Mijikenda," *History in Africa* 1 (1974): 71.

40. I.S. 30.

41. I.S. 54, 8/1/2013.

42. I.S. 55, 3/3/2014.

43. The High Commissioner to Leslie A. Goodyear, "Zanzibari refugees in Dubai," 7 July 1967, and Mohamed al-Mulla to Leslie Goodyear, 29 June 1967, UNHCR, 6/2/DUB.

44. A. Burdett, ed., *Records of Oman*, 650–51, D. Pragnell, British Consul General, Muscat to P. Gent, FO, 7 July 1968, ONA.

45. Hassan Abdalla to British Red Cross Society, 23 January 1965, UNHCR, Box 280.

46. H. Abdulla to Sec Gen of Tanzanian Red Cross Society, 30 January 1965, UNHCR, Box 280.

47. H. Abdulla to Sec Gen of Tanzanian Red Cross Society, 30 January 1965, UNHCR, Box 280.

48. "The Zanzibari Community in Dubai," 29 December 1965, UNHCR, 15/DUB/ZAN.

49. Goodyear to The High Commissioner, 30 May 1966, UNHCR, 15/DUB/ZAN. These conditions help explain the motivation for Ali Muhsin al-Barwani to publish a short booklet in Swahili, *Jifunze Kusoma Kiarabu (Kwa Wiki Tatu)* (Dubai: self-published, n.d.) after his release from prison, teaching the recognition and pronunciation of Arabic letters.

50. UNHCR Geneva to UNHCR London, 13 October 1965, UNHCR, 15/DUB/ZAN.
51. See ZNA, DJ 4/1-7. See also Engseng Ho and Abdul Sheriff, eds., *The Indian Ocean: Oceanic Connections and the Creation of New Societies* (London: Hurst, 2014), 240n4.
52. "Janu Hassan's Statement," 14 June 1970, KP no. 6.
53. Untitled typescript in Swahili, n.d., KP no. 7 (emphasis added). A heavily edited version in English was published as "Escape to Freedom" in *FZV*, August/September 1974, KP no. 6.
54. Al-Barwani, *Conflict and Harmony*, 275.
55. "Resolutions on Zanzibar," Muslim Organizations Conference, 6-10 April 1974, KP no. 6. His son Maktoum was chosen in December 1971 as the first prime minister of the UAE. Abdallah Omran Taryam, *The Establishment of the United Arab Emirates, 1950-85* (London: Croom Helm, 1987), 208.
56. "Goodyear Report on Dubai, 1966," 1-2, UNHCR, 15/DUB/ZAN.
57. Peter Liendhardt, *Sheikhdoms of Eastern Arabia* (New York: Palgrave, 2001), 124.
58. Goodyear Report on Visit to Dubai in Connecting with Zanzibari Refugees, 2 February 1967–10 February 1967, UNHCR, 15/DUB/ZAN.
59. Taryam, *Establishment of the United Arab Emirates*, 54. Syed Ali has the population in 1968 at sixty-five thousand. Syed Ali, *Dubai: Gilded Cage* (New Haven, CT: Yale University Press, 2010).
60. Ali, *Dubai*, 80-81.
61. " Goodyear 1971," UNHCR, 1/QAT/ZAN.
62. Lori, *Offshore Citizens*, 91; and Manal Jamal, "The Tiering of Citizenship and Residency and the Hierarchization of Migrant Communities: The United Arab Emirates in Historical Context," *International Migration Review* 49, no. 3 (Fall 2015): 601-632.
63. Liendhardt, *Sheikhdoms of Eastern Arabia*, 119.
64. Ghassany, *Kwa Heri Ukoloni*, 203.
65. Lori, *Offshore Citizens*, 165; Noora Lori and Yoana Kuzmova, "Who Counts as 'People of the Gulf'? Disputes over the Arab Status of Zanzibaris in the United Arab Emirates," https://pomeps.org/who-counts-as-people-of-the-gulf-disputes-over-the-arab-status-of-zanzibaris-in-the-uae.
66. Muhammad Morsy Abdullah, *The United Arab Emirates: A Modern History* (London: Croom Helm, 1978), 138.
67. Lori, *Offshore Citizens*, 86-88.
68. Report H.B.M. Political Agency in Dubai, 29 December 1965, UNHCR, 15/DUB/ZAN.
69. Almulla to Goodyear, 29 June 1967, UNHCR, 6/2/DUB; and HCR Geneva to HCR London, "Zanzibar refugees in Dubai," 6 June 1967, UNHCR, 15/DUB/ZAN.
70. Annex to L. A. Goodyear, Report on Visit to Dubai, 14-20 May 1966, UNHCR, 15/DUB/ZAN.

71. Lori, *Offshore Citizens*.
72. Lori, *Offshore Citizens*, 180–181.
73. H. H. Schindler, Note for the File: Mr. Goodyear's mission to Trucial Coast of Oman and Muscat, 30 March 1966, UNHCR, 15/DUB/ZAN.
74. "Goodyear Report 1967," 25 November 1967–9 December 1967, UNHCR, 15/DUB/ZAN.
75. The High Commissioner to Leslie A. Goodyear, "Zanzibari refugees in Dubai," 7 July 1967, UNHCR, 6/2/DUBAI.
76. Report H.B.M. Political Agency in Trucial States, Dubai, 29 December 1965, UNHCR, 15/DUB/ZAN.
77. Report H.B.M. Political Agency in Dubai, 29 December 1965, UNHCR, 15/DUB/ZAN.
78. HCR London to UNHCR Geneva, "Zanzibar refugees in Dubai," 12 May 1967, UNHCR, 6/2/DUB.
79. Note for the File: Refugees from Zanzibar: Situation in Dubai, 18 November 1965, UNHCR, 15/DUB/ZAN.
80. Dubai-Protection-General-Dubai., Extract from Mr. Goodyear's report, 1970, UNHCR, Fonds 11, Series 1, Box 146, 6/1/DUB.
81. Extract from M. Goodyear's Report of his visit to Dubai from 24 April 68 to 3 May 1968, UNHCR, 6/1/DUB.
82. Ghassany, *Kwa Heri Ukoloni*, 198–199.
83. Ghassany, *Kwa Heri Ukoloni*, 204.
84. Ghassany, *Kwa Heri Ukoloni*, 207.
85. Ghassany, *Kwa Heri Ukoloni*, 206.
86. Ghassany, *Kwa Heri Ukoloni*, 202–203.
87. Goodyear to High Commissioner, 28 June 1966, UNHCR, 15/DUB/ZAN.
88. Jamieson to Goodyear, 17 June 1966, UNHCR, 15/DUB/ZAN.
89. Said Shaksy to Goodyear, 1 June 1967, UNHCR, 15/DUB/ZAN.
90. Aman Thani to Abdulrab Ali Said, 2 August 1973, KP.
91. Ahmed al-Riyami, *My Pride and Joy* (Muscat: self-published, 2007), 123.
92. UNHCR to HH Sheikh Rashid el-Sabaa, ruler of Dubai, 19 December 1967, UNHCR, 15/DUB/ZAN. The Dubai Minister of State, Mohamed Said al-Mulla, oversaw the disbursement of these funds.
93. Leslie Goodyear to H.H. Sh. Rashid al Sabaa, 19 December 1967, UNHCR, 15/DUB/ZAN .
94. "Goodyear's Report 1967," UNHCR, 15/DUB/ZAN.
95. "Goodyear Report 1971," "Refugees from Zanzibar," UNHCR, 1/QAT/ZAN.
96. Ghassany, *Kwa Heri Ukoloni*, 204. Zanzibaris also settled extensively in the neighborhood of Port Said.
97. Ghassan Arnaout to Said Mohamed Lemky, 22 January 1973, UNHCR, Fonds 11, Series 1, Box 46, 1/ZAN/GEN.
98. Ghassan Arnaout to Said Mohamed Lemky, 22 January 1973, UNHCR, Fonds 11, Series 1, Box 46, 1/ZAN/GEN.

99. Hassan M. Hassan to Goodyear, 24 June 1970, UNCHR, 1/SAU/ZAN.

100. Goodyear to High Commissioner, 2 August 1968, and Refugee Situations—Refugees from Saudi Arabia in Zanzibar, UNHCR, 1/SAU/ZAN; and Aide-memoire, 29 April 1970, 6/1/SAU/Protection-General-Saudi Arabia.

101. Barwani to Hassan Mohammed al-Hassan, 22 June 1970, UNHCR, 1/SAU/ZAN.

102. Ahmed al-Riyami, *Quite Another* (Muscat: self-published, 2010), 113–119, 156–158.

103. al-Riyami, *My Pride and Joy*, 15–16, 21. One of Ali Ahmed's daughters remained in Zanzibar.

104. al-Riyami, *My Pride and Joy*, 124–125.

105. al-Riyami, *My Pride and Joy*, 39.

106. al-Riyami, *My Pride and Joy*, 19.

107. al-Riyami, *My Pride and Joy*, 22–23.

108. al-Riyami, *My Pride and Joy*, 126.

109. al-Riyami, *My Pride and Joy*, 129.

110. Independence was gained (reluctantly in many respects) on September 3, 1971, and Britain's power over Qatar's foreign affairs and defense officially ended. Helga Graham, *Arabian Time Machine* (London: Heinemann, 1978), 13.

111. Ghassany, *Kwa Heri Ukoloni*, 204.

112. Qatar, which became independent in 1971, had a per capita income of over $17,000 in 1989 (compare to Oman's, $5,600 in the same year).

113. Hashim A. Hashim with Khalfan S. Rashid [unsigned but using his PO box as return address in Doha-Qatar, Arabian Gulf], addressed to Mr. Goodyear, 21 May 1967, UNHCR, 1/QAT.ZAN.

114. The lone exception was the Palestinian Liberation Organization, and that recognition was apparently only granted after "intolerable pressure."

115. "Report on Visit to Iran and to Trucial States of Dubai and Qatar," 25 November 1967–9 December 1967, UNHCR, 15/DUB/ZAAN.

116. "Report on Visit to Iran and to Trucial States of Dubai and Qatar," 25 November 1967–9 December 1967, UNHCR, 15/DUB/ZAAN.

117. "Refugees from Zanzibar in Dubai," 25 November 1967–9 December 1967, "Report on Visit to Iran and to Trucial States of Dubai and Qatar," 14, UNHCR, 15/DUB/ZAN.

118. L. A. Goodyear, Report on Visit to Qatar, Dubai, Ras Al Khaima & Abu Dhabi, 23 November 1971–2 December 1971, UNHCR, 1/QAT/ZAN.

119. L. A. Goodyear, Report on Visit to Qatar, Dubai, Ras Al Khaima & Abu Dhabi, 23 November 1971–2 December 1971, UNHCR, 1/QAT/ZAN.

120. L. A. Goodyear, Report on Visit to Qatar, Dubai, Ras Al Khaima & Abu Dhabi, 23 November 1971–2 December 1971, UNHCR, 1/QAT/ZAN. See also Extract from Mr. Goodyear, 1970, UNHCR, 6/1/DUB.

121. A. Burdett, ed., *Records of Oman*, 644–645, D. C. Carden HBM Consul-General to Goodyear, 24 March 1968, and P. R. H. Wright, British Embassy Cairo to P. Gentt, Arabian Dep't FO, 24 May 1968, ONA.

122. This may partially be due to Bahrain's and Doha's refusals to join the nascent UAE federation. A laissez-passer attached to an Imamate passport allowed Saud Ahmed to cross from Egypt to Libya. Busaidi, *Memoirs*, 155.

123. Memo to HC from Leslie A. Goodyear, 24 May 1968 and 26 May 1967, UNCHR, 1/QAT/ZAN.

124. Mr. Goodyear visit to Trucial States, Qatar, Kuwait and Saudi Arabia, 25 March 1970–5 April 1970, UNHCR, 6/2 DUB/ DUBAI.

125. UNCHR rep in Beirut to I. C. Jackson, UNHCR, 29 February 1968.

126. Lori, *Offshore Citizens*; and Aman Thani to Rashid Hamadi, 27 March 1974, KP no. 6.

127. 29 HBM Political Agency, Trucial States, Dubai, December 1965, UNHCR, 15/DUB/ZAN.

128. "Analysis of Requests for Education or Training Received from Zanzibar Refugee Youths in Dubai," Annex IV, UNHCR, 15/DUB/ZAN.

129. Burdett, *Records of Oman*, 642, Leslie Goodyear UNHCR to Mr. David Roberts, British Political Agent, Dubai, 30 January 1968, ONA.

130. "Report on Visit to Iran and to Trucial States of Dubai and Qatar," 25 November 1967–9 December 1967, UNHCR, 15/DUB/ZAN.

131. L. A. Goodyear, Report, UNHCR, 1/QAT/ZAN.

132. L. A. Goodyear Report, UNHCR, 1/QAT/ZAN.

133. John Duke Anthony, *Arab States of the Lower Gulf: People, Politics, Petroleum* (Washington, DC: The Middle East Institute, 1975), 211.

134. L. A. Goodyear, Report on Visit to Qatar, Dubai, Ras Al Khaima & Abu Dhabi, 23 November 1971–2 December 1971, UNHCR, 1/QAT/ZAN.

135. Al-Riyami, *My Pride and Joy*, 22–23.

136. Al-Riyami, *My Pride and Joy*, 22–23.

137. Burdett, *Records of Oman*, 641, T. J. Clark, HBM Political Agency Dubai to M. R. Melhuish, Esq, Political Residency Bahrain, 14 September 1967, "Zanzibari Refugees," ONA.

138. Burdett, *Records of Oman*, 641, ONA.

139. Zanzibar Women's Welfare Association Address Presented to Mr. Goodyear UNHCR on Sunday, 28 November 1971, UNHCR, 1/QAT/ZAN.

140. The ruler of Bahrain and Sh. Rashid and his son Muhammad in Dubai played key roles in offering asylum to the victims of marriage threats. Ghassany, *Kwa Heri Ukoloni*, 206.

141. "Zanzibar Women's Welfare Association Address," UNHCR, 1/QAT/ZAN.

142. F. M. S. al-Miskery to United Nations, 21 June 1970, UNHCR, 1/SAU/ZAN.

143. "Examples of Individual Hardship among Zanzibari Refugees Now in Dubai," 28 May 1966, UNHCR, 15/DUB/ZAN.

144. "Examples of Individual Hardship Among Zanzibari Refugees Now in Dubai," 28 May 1966, UNHCR, Fonds 11, Series 1, Box 256, 15/DUB/ZAN.

145. "Goodyear Report on Visit to Dubai in Connecting with Zanzibari Refugees, 2/2/67–10/2/67," UNHCR, 15/DUB/ZAN .

146. Husein M. Yahya, Sharjah to Aman Thani, Dubai, 28 September 1973, KP no. 7. See the contrast made by Harding in his analysis of Aisha Amour Zahor. Leonhard Harding, "Nyerere in neuem Licht: Interpretationen in den Lebensgeschichten von Sansibaris," in Unser Leben von der Revolution und danach, ed. Barwani et al., 530: "she . . . did not allow herself to be forced into an exile milieu or exile mentality . . ."

147. Wimmelbücker, "Aspekte eines gesellschaftlichen Umbruchs," 482.

148. "Refugees from Zanzibar in Qatar," Khalfan Salim Rashid to Mr. L. A. Goodyear, 22 April 1967, UNHCR, 1/QAT/ZAN.

149. Ahmed Hamoud al-Maamiry, *Islamism and Economic Prosperity in Third World Countries* (New Delhi: Lancers Press, 1983), 26–27, 86–87, 122.

150. Al-Maamiry, *Islamism and Economic Prosperity*, 86, 122.

151. Al-Maamiry, *Islamism and Economic Prosperity*, 103, 116. Al-Maamiry's perspective was one widely shared by the new technocratic classes running or involved in the new oil economies. Muhammad al-Buraey, *Administrative Development: An Islamic Perspective* (Kegan Paul International, 1985; London: Routledge, 2010). That "inward turn" is also evident from al-Maamiry's elder by a decade, Ali Muhsin. During his time in prison, where he dialogued with other prisoners of various nationalities and religions, engaged critically with the Bible, and undertook theological apologetics for Islam. See al-Barwani, *Conflict and Harmony*, 230–231. This literature shows the continuing influence of older nineteenth-century debates between Christians and Muslims in Zanzibar. See Valerie Hoffman, "Muslim-Christian Encounters in Late Nineteenth-Century Zanzibar," *MIT Electronic Journal of Middle East Studies* 5 (Fall 2005): 59–78.

152. "Viewpoint: Zanzibaris in Exile," *FZV*, September 1973, KP no. 11.

153. "Viewpoint." KP no. 11.

154. Husein M. Yahya to Aman Thani, 28 September 1973, KP no. 6. Husein, responding to a letter from Thani accusing him of engaging in secret and harmful activities, accuses Thani of, among other things, forcing members of the association to not publicly identify as Arab, of exorbitant requests for 5 percent tithing by refugees to support a counterrevolutionary force, and of a "cutthroat policy" of trying to squash all criticisms.

155. Nafla S. Kharusi, "Identity and Belonging among Ethnic Return Migrants of Oman," *Nationalism and Ethnic Politics* 19, no. 4 (2013): 424–446.

5. RETURN MIGRATION FROM EAST AFRICA AND THE POLITICS OF CITIZENSHIP IN OMAN, 1970–2020

1. François Constantin and François Le Guennec-Coppens, "Dubai Street: Zanzibar," *African Politics* 30 (1988): 13. For theorization of return migration, see David Cook-Martin. *Scramble for Citizens: Dual Nationality and State Competition for Immigrants* (Palo Alto, CA: Stanford University Press, 2013), 2; see also Eva

Østergaard-Nielsen, ed., *International Migration and Sending Countries: Perceptions, Policies, and Transnational Relations* (New York: Palgrave Macmillan, 2003). Rogaia AbuSharaf, "The Omani-Zanzibari Family: Between Politics and Pedigree in an Empire on the Rim," *Journal of the Women of the Middle East and the Islamic World* 16 (2018): 67; and J. E. Peterson, *Oman's Insurgencies: The Sultanate's Struggle for Supremacy* (London: Saqi Books, 2008), 420. Mayuko Okawa cites Oman's in-country population of citizens in 1970 as 660,000, with 10,000 Omani expats living in Kuwait. Mayuko Okawa, "Nationality Law and Concept of Nation in Oman: A Case Study of Omani Returnees from Africa," *Modern Middle East* 45 (2008): 22. John Peterson estimates the population to have been ~500,000. J. E. Peterson, "Oman Faces the Twenty-First Century," in *Political Change in the Arab Gulf States: Stuck in Transition*, ed. Mary Ann Tetreault, Gwenn Okruhlik, and Andrzej Kapiszewski (Boulder: Lynne Rienner, 2011), 100. Sulaiman al-Farsi, *Democracy and Youth in the Middle East: Islam, Tribalism and the Rentier State in Oman* (New York: Routledge, 2013), 9.

2. Takeyuki Tsuda, introduction to *Diasporic Homecomings: Ethnic Return Migration in Comparative Perspective*, ed. Takeyuki Tsuda (Stanford, CA: Stanford University Press, 2009), 7.

3. Ian Skeet, *Oman: Politics and Development* (New York: Palgrave Macmillan, 1992), 54. Skeet notes that the cultural disruption of this Zanzibari migration to Muscat was tempered by the fact that most commerce in the city was already in nonindigenous hands. See also Abdin Chande, *Islam, Ujamaa, and Community Development: A Case Study of Religious Currents in East Africa* (San Francisco: Austin and Winfield Publishers, 1998), 233n11; and Marc Valeri, *Oman: Politics and Society in the Qaboos State* (London: Hurst, 2009) 88.

4. Umi Wikan, *Behind the Veil Behind the Veil in Arabia: Women in Oman* (Baltimore, MD: Johns Hopkins University Press, 1982), 40.

5. A smaller number of these continue to preserve Swahili and to continue patterns of sociality and culture refined in East Africa; I.S. 13, 8/23/2011. One interviewee claimed that one out of every three households in Muscat speaks it; I.S. 48, 5/30/2013. Another claimed that 70 percent of people over age thirty-five in Sharqiya in the 1970s spoke Swahili; I.S. 35, 3/27/2013.

6. A. Burdett, ed., *Records of Oman*, Vol. 5, 1970, BCGM D. Crawford, 1 November 1970, ONA. "Qaboos said he had received several letters from Zanzibaris asking to settle in the Sultanate and he specifically mentioned one from the leaders of the Zanzibari community in East Africa, which had offered the services of qualified doctors, engineers, etc., to the sultan."

7. Calvin Allen Jr. and W. Lynn Rigsbee II, *Oman under Qaboos: From Coup to Constitution, 1970–1996* (London: Routledge, 2000), 78. Ahmed b. Hamoud Al-Maamiry saw Qaboos's response to the situation in the southern part of the Gulf as a progressive, pragmatic approach necessitated by communist subversion. al-Maamiry. *Whither Oman* (New Delhi: Lancers Publishers, 1981). Al-Azri, *Social and Gender Inequality in Oman: The Power of Religious and Political Tradition*.

(London: Routledge, 2013), 103–104, notes the anticommunism of Sheikh Ahmed Khalili, the mufti of Oman, and a Zanzibari.

8. Legislated, for example, by the British Labour government for East African Indians at roughly the same time. See Randall Hansen, "The Kenyan Asians, British Politics, and the Commonwealth Immigrants Acts, 1968," *Historical Journal* 42, no. 3 (1999): 809–834. The difference is that there had been no previous promise or guarantee of imperial citizenship for East African returnees.

9. Danielle Allen, *Talking to Strangers: Anxieties of Citizenship Since Brown v. Board of Education* (Chicago: University of Chicago Press, 2004), 12.

10. Liisa Malkki, *Purity and Exile: Violence, Memory and National Cosmology among Hutu Refugees in Tanzania* (Chicago: University of Chicago Press, 1995), 174.

11. Erica Benner, "Nationality without Nationalism," *Journal of Political Ideologies* 2, no. 2 (1997): 189–206; John Gillis, *Commemorations: The Politics of National Identity* (Princeton, NJ: Princeton University Press, 1994); and Cook-Martin. *Scramble for Citizens*, 6.

12. Miriam Cooke, *Tribal Modern: Branding New Nations in the* Arab Gulf (Berkeley: University of California Press, 2014), 31–49; Nadav Samin, *Of Sand or Soil: Genealogy and Tribal Belonging in Saudi Arabia* (Princeton, NJ: Princeton University Press, 2015), 2–10, 13; Madawi al-Rasheed, "Transnational Connections and National Identity Zanzibari Omanis in Muscat," in *Monarchies and Nations: Globalisation and Identity in the Arab States of the Gulf*, ed. Paul Dresch and James Piscatori (London: I. B. Tauris, 2005), 108; and Sulaiman al-Farsi, *Democracy and Youth in the Middle East: Islam, Tribalism and the Rentier State in Oman* (New York: Routledge, 2013), 53, 116.

13. Valeri, *Oman*, 157.

14. Harith Ghassany, *Kwa Heri Ukoloni, Kwa Heri Uhuru! Zanzibar na Mapinduzi ya Afrabia* (n.p.: Lulu Press, 2010), 207.

15. G. Thomas Burgess, *Race, Revolution and the Struggle for Human Rights in Zanzibar: The Memoirs of Ali Sultan Issa and Seif Sharif Hamad* (Athens: Ohio University Press, 2009), 253.

16. Valeri, *Oman*, 156.

17. Miriam Joyce, *The Sultanate of Oman: A Twentieth Century History* (London: Praeger, 1995), 104.

18. Ali Muhsin al-Barwani, *Conflict and Harmony in Zanzibar* (Dubai: self-published, 1997). See also Tsuda, introduction, 21–22.

19. S. G. Phillips and Jennifer Hunt, "'Without Sultan Qaboos, We Would Be Yemen': The Renaissance Narrative and the Political Settlement in Oman," *Journal of International Development* 29, no. 5 (July 2017): 653.

20. Through the facilities of Ahmed Sultan al-Miskery; see al-Barwani, *Conflict and Harmony*, 298.

21. Al-Barwani, *Conflict and Harmony*, 298.

22. I.S. 30, 2/15/2013.

23. Mohamed Musa al-Yousef, *Oil and the Transformation of Oman* (London: Stacey International, 1995), 62; and Saad Eddin Ibrahim, "Oil, Migration and the New Arab Social Order," in *Rich and Poor States in the Middle East: Egypt and the New Arab Order*, ed. Malcolm Kerr and El Sayed Yassin (Boulder: Westview Press, 1982), 17–70.

24. Valeri, *Oman*, 83; *Development in Oman, 1970–1974* (Muscat: Ministry of Development, National Statistical Department, 1975), 42; and John Townsend, *Oman: The Making of a Modern State* (London: Croom-Helm, 1977), 168.

25. Donald Hawley, *Oman and Its Renaissance* (London: Stacey International, 1977), 201.

26. Hawley, *Oman and Its Renaissance*, 216; and David Greenslade, *Ibtisam al-Habsi and Her Zanzibar Court* (Muscat: Ministry of Heritage and Culture, 2013), 53–54.

27. I.S. 1, 8/11/2011.

28. Elections 1963: Zanzibar Government General, "Application for appointment as staff for the General Election," June 1963, ZNA, AK 28/1.

29. Ahmed al-Riyami, *Quite Another* (Muscat: self-published, 2010), 121–125.

30. Terence Clark, *Underground to Overseas: The Story of Petroleum Development Oman* (London: Stacey International, 2007), 59, 62, 78. Clark thought the greatest difficulty encountered by PDO was the training and development of Omani personnel.

31. Valeri, *Oman*, 75; and Joseph Kechichian, *Oman and the World: The Emergence of an Independent Foreign Policy* (Santa Monica, CA: Rand Corp., 1995), 244. For a broader (if dated) discussion of social class and national development, see James Petras, *Critical Perspectives on Imperialism and Social Class in the Third World* (New York: Monthly Review Press, 1978).

32. Clark, *Underground to Overseas*, 76.

33. Asya al-Bualy and Fatima Jinja, *Dhikriyyāt min al-Māḍī al-Jamīd* (Muscat: Nahda Publishing, 2010), 22n2.

34. Hasan Kamoonpuri, *Oman Top Business Leaders* (Muscat: Oman Daily Observer, 2010), 140-147; and I.S. 26.

35. Kamoonpuri, *Top Business Leaders*, 354–356.

36. Valeri, *Oman*, 87; and Allen and Rigsbee, *Oman under Qaboos*, 42.

37. "Information Re: Students Abroad," ZNA, AK 29/40.

38. British Embassy Muscat to Robert McGregor, 2 May 1972, TNA, FCO 8/1845/157.

39. Juma Aley, *Zanzibar in the Context* (New Delhi: Lancers Books, 1988), 85.

40. Ahmed al-Riyami, *My Pride and Joy* (Muscat: Self-published, 2007), 46.

41. Allen and Rigsbee, *Oman under Qaboos*, 171.

42. I.S. 50, 6/18/2013. Shaksy also founded the Oman consul general in Karachi. The Ministry of Health started to function in August 1970. See *Development in Oman*, 8. Jamali was appointed in August 1970. Valeri, *Oman*, 86. For Jamali's role in Dubai, see Frauke Heard-Bey, *From Trucial States to United Arab Emirates* (London: Longman, 1996), 325.

43. Joyce, *Sultanate of Oman*, 110.

44. Nasser al-Riyami, *Zanzibar: Personalities and Events*, trans. Ali Rashid al-Abri (Beirut: Beirut Bookshop, 2012), 377; and *Diplomatic List: United States Department of State* (Washington, DC: US Government Printing Office, 1979), 50.

45. Saud's daughter was later appointed minister of higher education. Saud b. Ahmed al-Busaidi, *Memoirs of an Omani Gentleman from Zanzibar* (Muscat: al-Roya Press, 2012), 177–178.

46. Juma Aley, *Enduring Links* (Dubai: Union Printing Press, 1994).

47. Ali Mazrui, "On Ancestry, Descent, and Identity," *Mazrui Annual Newsletter*, no. 17, Eve of 1993.

48. Jonathon Glassman, *War of Words, War of Stones: Racial Thought and Violence in Colonial Zanzibar* (Bloomington: Indiana University Press, 2011), 60.

49. Dr. Salem al-Ismaily has also published a work of fiction about politics and the Zanzibar revolution, which is discussed in chapter 6.

50. Roman Loimeier, *Between Social Skills and Marketable Skills: The Politics of Islamic Education in 20th Century Zanzibar* (Leiden: Brill, 2009), 373. For the Jeanes schools and colonial education in East Africa, see Kenneth King, *Pan-Africanism and Education: A Study of Race, Philanthropy, and Education in the United States of America and East Africa* (New York: Diasporic Africa Press, 2016).

51. John Beasant and Christopher Ling, *Sultan in Arabia: A Private Life* (Edinburgh: Mainstream Publishing, 2004), 108; Valeri, *Oman*, 85; al-Bualy and Jinja, *Dhikriyyat*, 43n2; and Aley, *Zanzibar in the Context*, 85.

52. Allen and Rigsbee, *Oman under Qaboos*, 170.

53. *Jawharat Oman*, August 2012, https://issuu.com/oeronline/docs/jawahart-eng-aug-12.

54. Maulid Haj, *A Jail Tale: The Autobiography of an Omani in 1960s Tanzania* (Muscat: al-Roya Publishing, 2004). Portions of *A Jail Tale* were originally published in Swahili by Oxford University Press in 1990, as *Umleavyo*.

55. Al-Riyami, *My Pride and Joy*, 18.

56. Domenyk Eades and Zayana al-Badaei, *The Pioneer Professor Fatma Salem Seif Al-Maamary (1911–2002): A Historical, Documentary and Academic Study* (Muscat: The Ministry of Education, 2013), 36, 68.

57. Nathaniel Mathews, "Jumuiya ya Kiislamu ya Istiqaama Tanzania and Modern Ibādism in East Africa, 1985–2016," in *Oman, Ibadism and Modernity*, ed. Abdulrahman al-Salimi and Reinhard Eisener (Hildesheim: George Olms, 2017), 241.

58. Babakerim, *The Aftermath of the Zanzibar Revolution* (Muscat: Self-published, 1994), 1, 13–14.

59. Shaaban S. al-Farsy, *Mzanzibari Asimilia Hadithi Yake* (Muscat: self published, 1994) 4.

60. Said Abdulla Seif L-Hatimy, *Tunda Liliwalo Hadharani* (n.p.: self-published, 1995), i.

61. Issa Nasser al-Ismaily, *Will Zanzibar Regain Her Past Prosperity* (Muscat: self-published, 2015), xiii

62. I.S. 30, 2/15/13.
63. Al-Riyami, *My Pride and Joy*, 133–138.
64. Al-Riyami, *My Pride and Joy*, 130.
65. See, for instance, Dr. Khalid al-Balushi, *Istishrāf al-Tajribat-l-'Umaniyya fī "Gwādur": Naḥw Khiṭāb Insānī Muta'addad* (Nizwa: University of Nizwa/Al-Intishār al-'Arabi, 2013); and George Murer, "Baloch Mashkat (Muscat) and the Sultan Qaboos Era: Cultural Performance, Cosmopolitanism and Translocal Consciousness," *Arabian Humanities* 15 (2022).
66. See, for instance, Muḥsin Ḥamud al-Kindi, *Al-Ṣaḥāfa al-'Umāniyya al-Muhājira wa Shakhṣiyyāthā: Shaikh Hāshil bin Rāshid al-Maskarī numūdhajā* (Beirut: Riad al-Rayyes Books, 2009), 473.
67. Beginning in 1980, a series of increasing restrictions were implemented on marriage between Omanis and all foreigners, except for certain individuals who could obtain prior approval from the Ministry of Interior. These restrictions were in effect until 2005, when they were relaxed with respect to marrying other Gulf Cooperation Council (GCC) citizens. See Mandana Limbert, "Marriage Status and the Politics of Nationality," in *The Gulf Family: Kinship, Policies and Modernity*, ed. Alanoud Alsharekh (London: Saqi Books, 2007), 172; for parallel prohibitions see Paul Dresch, "Debates on Marriage and Nationality in UAE," in *Monarchies and Nations: Globalisation and Identity in the Arab States of the Gulf*, ed. Paul Dresch and James Piscatori (London: I. B. Tauris, 2005), 149–150. In an interview, it was stated that wealthy Omanis at the time were marrying and divorcing Egyptians, Moroccans, and Jordanians without taking full responsibility for the resulting children, resulting in complaints by these states to the Omani government.
68. Nafla Kharusi, "Identity and Belonging among Ethnic Return Migrants of Oman," *Nationalism and Ethnic Politics* 19, no. 4 (2013): 434–435.
69. See, for instance, Marc Valeri, "Identity Politics and Nation-Building under Sultan Qaboos," in *Sectarian Politics in the Persian Gulf*, ed. Lawrence Potter (London/New York: Hurst/Oxford University Press, 2013), 200. While al-Lawati is a distinct nisba within the tribal landscape of modern Oman, al-Zinjibari is not. The "Zanzibaris" are, practically speaking, not a separate ethnicity in Oman, contra Valeri, *Oman*, 20n29. Julia Verne and Detlef Müller-Mahn, "We Are Part of Zanzibar: Translocal Practices and Imaginative Geographies," in *Regionalizing Oman: Political, Economic and Social Dynamics*, ed. Steffen Wippel (Springer Link, 2013), 76.
70. Khalid al-Azri, "Change and Conflict in Contemporary Omani Society: The Case of Kafa'a in Marriage," *British Journal of Middle Eastern Studies* 37, no. 2 (August 2010): 128; and David Theo Goldberg, *The Racial State* (Oxford: Blackwell Publishers, 2002).
71. They offer an interesting contrast to Black Arabs in the Gulf, whose African ancestry remains evident but whose cultural roots have attenuated over many generations. See Paul Zeleza, *In Search of African Diasporas: Testimonies and Encounters* (Durham, NC: Carolina Academic Press, 2012), 507, 517. See also al-Azri, "Change and Conflict in Contemporary Omani Society," 127–128.

72. Valeri, *Oman*, 232–233; and Amal Sachedina, *Celebrating the Past, Living the Modern: The Politics of Time in the Sultanate of Oman* (New York: Cornell University Press, 2021), 177–184.

73. Valeri, *Oman*, 133.

74. Mandana Limbert, *In the Time of Oil: Piety, Memory and Social Life in an Omani Town* (Palo Alto, CA: Stanford University Press, 2010), 144–147; and Irtefa Binte-Farid, "'True' Sons of Oman: National Narratives, Genealogical Purity and Transnational Connections in Modern Oman," in *Gulfization of the Arab World*, ed. Marc Owen Jones, Ross Porter, and Marc Valeri (Berlin: Gerlach Press, 2018), 47.

75. Kharusi, "Identity and Belonging,"

76. Nathaniel Mathews, "The Zinjibari Diaspora, 1698–2014: Citizenship, Migration and Revolution in Zanzibar, Oman and the Post-War Indian Ocean" (PhD diss., Northwestern University, 2016), 224.

77. I.S. 5, 8/17/2011.

78. Cosmopolitanism and cultural intermixture has long been important to Swahili self-conceptions. Jeremy Prestholdt, *Domesticating the World: African Consumerisms and the Genealogy of Globalization* (Berkeley: University of California Press, 2008), 175. Many interviewees emphasized that the Swahili were historically "non-tribal" in orientation. I.S. 15, 8/26/2011. Compare to Latin American nationalists: Ana María Alonso, "Territorializing the Nation and 'Integrating the Indian': 'Mestizaje' in Mexican Official Discourses and Public Culture," in *Sovereign Bodies: Citizens, Migrants and States in the Postcolonial World*, ed. Thomas Blom Hansen, and Finn Stepputat (Princeton, NJ: Princeton University Press, 2005), 39–60.

79. This is also why Jamshid, was unable until recently to come to live permanently in the sultanate, even though his grandfather had been born in Oman. "Zanzibar's Former Sultan Arrives in Oman for Retirement," *The National*, September 16, 2020, www.thenationalnews.com/world/gcc/zanzibar-s-former-sultan-arrives-in-oman-for-retirement-1.1077596.

80. al-Busaidi, *Memoirs of an Omani Gentleman*, 165.

81. For how Kuwaitis similarly understand their nationality as allegiance to a sovereign, see Ahn Nga Longva, "Citizenship in the Gulf States: Conceptualization and Practice," in *Citizenship and State in the Middle East: Approaches and Applications*, ed. Nils Butenschon, Uri Davis, and Manuel Hassassian (Syracuse: Syracuse University Press, 2000), 192.

82. al-Riyami, *My Pride and Joy*, 134.

83. For comments on the appeal of monarchy to East African returnees, see Zulfikar Hirji, *Between Empires, Sheikh-Sir Mbarak al-Hinawy 1896–1959* (London: Azimuth Editions, 2012), 79.

84. Valeri, *Oman*, 95. As background, since 1970 there has been a distinction made between the royal family and descendants of the original "empire builder," "Seyyid" Said bin Sultan. However, to exclude members of the Zanzibar branch of al-Said from succeeding, the ruling family further redefined itself as descendants of Turki bin Said. J. E. Peterson, "Rulers, Merchants and Shaikhs in Gulf Politics," in

The Gulf Family: Kinship Policies and Modernity, ed. Alanoud Alsharekh (London: Middle East Institute SOAS, 2007), 28.

85. Mohammed Nasser Saeed al Kharusi, letters to the editor, *Oman Observer*, 29 October 1984, KP no. 1.

86. See Binte-Farid, "'True' Sons of Oman," 51.

87. I.S. 12, 8/24/2011.

88. Al-Kindi, *Al-Saḥafa al-'Umaniyya*, 486.

89. Limbert, *In the Time of Oil*, 161; and Dawn Chatty, "Women Working in Oman: Individual Choice and Cultural Constraints," *International Journal of Middle East Studies* 32, no. 2 (May 2000): 244. These transformations in women's dress had knock-on effects in Zanzibar, as the association of the abeya with Gulf wealth made them desirable and symbolically resonant of one's overseas connections. See Paola Ivanov, "Cosmopolitanism or Exclusion? Negotiating Identity in the Expressive Culture of Contemporary Zanzibar, in *The Indian Ocean: Oceanic Connections and the Creation of New Societies*, ed. Engseng Ho and Abdul Sheriff (London: Hurst and Co., 2014), 221.

90. Cooke, *Tribal Modern*, 27.

91. I.S. 11, 8/24/2011; Chatty, "Women Working in Oman", 243; al-Azri, *Social and Gender Inequality in Oman*, 94; and Mohamed Bakari, *The Democratisation Process in Zanzibar: A Retarded Transition* (Hamburg: Institute of African Affairs, 2001), 136. Zanzibari women were the first modern Omani nurses and the first Omani women in the police force.

92. Clark, *Underground to Overseas*, 61. The issue of dress is part of a large agenda pursued by Gulf monarchies in the name of heritage. Gregory Gause, *Oil Monarchies: Domestic and Security Challenges in the Arab Gulf States* (New York: Council on Foreign Relations, 1994), 20. Interestingly, the relatively open attitudes of women were condemned by the mufti of Oman, Ahmed Khalili, himself a returnee from Zanzibar. Al-Azri, *Social and Gender Inequality*, 121.

93. Marc Valeri, "Nation-Building and Communities in Oman Since 1970: The Swahili-Speaking Omanis in Search of Identity," *African Affairs* 106, no. 424 (2007): 489; Calvin Allen Jr., *The Modernization of the Sultanate* (Boulder: Westview Press, 1987), 103; Madawi al-Rasheed, "Transnational Connections," 103; and Paul Zeleza, *In Search of African Diasporas: Testimonies and Encounters* (Durham, NC: Carolina Academic Press, 2012), 516.

94. Dawn Chatty, "L'Activite Feminine en Oman: Entre choix individual et contraintes culturelles," in *L'Oman contemporain: Etat, territoire, identite*, ed. Marc Lavergne and Brigitte Dumortier (Paris: Editions Karthala, 2002), 264–265.

95. Chatty, "L'Activite Feminine en Oman," 265.

96. I.S. 56, 5/08/2013.

97. I.S. 8, 8/20/2011.

98. It is worth noting that although converting to Islam is not the same as "becoming Arab," the two processes were closely intertwined and speak to the difficulties of delineating a clear line between ethnic and religious belonging when ethnicity is defined broadly as a form of social imagination, and conversion is a

form of "new" personhood. See the revealing observations in Janet McIntosh, *The Edge of Islam: Power, Personhood, and Ethnoreligious Boundaries on the Kenya Coast* (Durham, NC: Duke University Press, 2009).

99. I.S. 1. An interviewee who grew up in colonial Zanzibar recalled her aunt, her mother's sister, as a rebel who had married a Shirazi: "In those days qabila was everything and marrying a pure African was unacceptable."

100. I.S. 12, 8/24/2011; I.S. 13, 8/25/2011; and I.S. 50.

101. I.S. 12. For cases of long-term residents in India without citizenship, a concept he calls "blurred membership," see Kamal Sadiq, *Paper Citizens: How Illegal Immigrants Acquire Citizenship in Developing Countries* (New York: Oxford University Press, 2009). For "permanent temporary status," see Noora Lori, *Offshore Citizens: Permanent Temporary Status in the Gulf* (Cambridge: Cambridge University Press, 2019).

102. I.S. 7, 8/19/2011.

103. J. R. H. Evans to H. T. Jamieson, 30 August 1966, UNHCR, 15/DUB/ZAN.

104. Will Hanley, *Identifying with Nationality: Europeans, Ottomans and Egyptians in Alexandria* (New York: Columbia University Press, 2017), 75.

105. I.S. 2, 8/13/2011.

106. I.S. 49, 6/10/2013.

107. As did South Asians; see Gijsbert Oonk, "Gujarati Asians in East Africa, 1880–2000: Colonization, De-colonization, and Complex Citizenship Issues," *Diaspora Studies* 8, no. 1 (2015): 66–79; and I.S. 28, 2/4/2013.

108. I.S. 9, 8/20/2011.

109. Al-Rasheed, "Transnational Connections," 100; and Mayuko Okawa, "Nationality Law and Concept of Nation in Oman: A Case Study of Omani Returnees from Africa," *Modern Middle East* 45 (2008): 22–35. , 25; and *Qanūn Tanthīm al-Jinsiya al-Omaniyya*, Ministry of Interior, 1972, article 3, 34.

110. Okawa, "Nationality," 28.

111. Cook-Martin, *Scramble for Citizens*, 55. This echoes the debates about "sufficiency" in marriage (kafa'a), in which women are expected to uphold the purity of the lineage by not "marrying down." Cooke, *Tribal Modern*, 39–41.

112. Al-Azri, *Social and Gender Inequality*, 133.

113. Okawa, "Nationality," 30.

114. Allen and Rigsbee, *Oman under Qaboos*, 126–127; al-Yousef, *Oil and the Transformation of Oman*, 45; and Dermot Gately, "Lessons from the 1986 Oil Price Collapse" (Brookings Papers on Economic Activity, 1986), 237–284. In response the government devalued the Omani riyal and reduced government spending, including a massive personnel reduction in the armed forces. Alan Hoskins, *A Contract Officer in Oman* (Kent: DJ Costello Publishers, 1988).

115. In the 2013 Oman TV series *Min al-Sawāhil*, one man in Fuoni, Zanzibar, refuses to be interviewed by show host Mohamed al-Murjebi and complains bitterly about the failure of the state to grant him Omani nationality. Episode 11, 19 July 2013, Oman TV, www.youtube.com/watch?v=zQ-X4x3Ks3E.

116. Saud Salim Al-Unsi, *Al-'Ādāt al-'Umanī* (Muscat: Ministry of Heritage and Culture Oman, 1991), 32. For Arab identity, Arab nationalism, and Arabic language, see Yasir Suleiman. *The Arabic Language and National Identity: A Study in Ideology* (Washington, DC: Georgetown University Press, 2003).

117. J. E. Peterson, "Oman's Diverse Society: Northern Oman," *Middle East Journal* 58, no. 1 (2004): 32–51; Aaron Rubin, *The Mehri Language of Oman* (Leiden: Brill 2010); and Aaron D. Rubin, *The Jibbali (Shahri) Language of Oman : Grammar and Texts* (Leiden: Brill, 2014).

118. Valeri, "Nation-Building," 479.

119. I am borrowing this model from M. H. Abdulaziz Mkilifi, "Triglossia and Swahili-English Bilingualism in Tanzania," *Language in Society* 1, no. 2 (October 1972): 197–213.

120. Jan Vansina, "New Linguistic Evidence and 'the Bantu Expansion,'" *The Journal of African History* 36, no. 2 (1995): 173–195. See Sarah Hillewaert, "The Ideological Motivations for Language Change: The Loss of Dialectical Variation and Identity among the Swahili Speaking People of the Kenya Coast," in *Kiswahili Research and Development in Eastern Africa*, ed. Rocha Chimera et al. (Mombasa: National Museum of Kenya, 2011), 131–151.

121. Kharusi, "Identity and Belonging."

122. Al-Rasheed, "Transnational Connections,"101.

123. I.S. 30; and Al-Rasheed, "Transnational Connections,"103. Eades and al-Badaei, *Pioneer Professor* also contains some accounts of language practice in linguistically mixed families.

124. I.S. 1.

125. I.S. 9.

126. I.S. 52.

127. I.S. 2; I.S. 13; and Limbert, *In the Time of Oil*, 156.

128. I.S. 9.

129. Ministry of Education, *Illiteracy Eradication Programs and Plans in Sultanate of Oman: Fruitful Efforts* (Muscat: Directorate General of Education Programs/Department of Continuing Education), 2010; and Okawa, "Nationality," 34n14.

130. Saida al-Farsy, "'Aina al-Muwāṭana yā Muwāṭin," *al-Shabeeba*, April 24, 2011. See also an earlier polemic by Anwār Muhammad al-Rawwas, "Al-Insilākh min Lughat-ul-Qurān al-Karīm," *Jarīda Oman*, 19 May 2004. The broader irony of such polemics in favor of Arabic is that the linguistic footprint of south Asian languages like Hindi and Gujarati on Eastern Gulf Arabic dialects is enormous. See Clive D. Holes, "Language and Identity in the Arabian Gulf," *Journal of Arabian Studies* 1, no. 2 (2011): 129–145. Moreover, several sultans, including Said bin Taimur, were reputed to be more fluent in Gujarati or Swahili than in Arabic.

131. Nafla Kharusi, "The Ethnic Label Zinjibari: Politics and Language Choice Implications among Swahili Speakers in Oman," *Ethnicities* 12, no. 3 (2012): 335–353.

132. Asya al-Bualy,"Rud ala Aina al-Muwātana ya Muwātin," *Shurfaat*, May 10, 2011.

133. To be clear, the Zanzibaris' Islamic religious education had in most cases enabled them to read the Quran, and thus they could not be said to be illiterate in Arabic script. But reading the Quran and speaking a colloquial Omani dialect of Arabic are two different things. After the revolution, the Zanzibaris had often been referred to by UNHCR officials as Manga Arabs, with officials commenting that almost none of them spoke Arabic. For more on Arabic language and Arabic literacy in Zanzibar, see Issa Ziddy, *Lugha ya Kiarabu Zanzibar: Historian a mbinu za usomeshaji* (Zanzibar: self-published, 2011).

134. This is also due to the "WhatsApp" culture of sending voice-notes. Franziska Fay, "'To Everyone Who Told Zanzis That They Are Not Omani': Young Swahili-speaking Omanis' Belonging in Postdiaspora Oman," *Arabian Humanities* 15 (2022).

135. Kharusi. "Identity and Belonging."

136. Kharusi, "The Ethnic Label Zinjibari," 339.

137. Abu Jahdham Nasser al-Jahdhamy, *Taalamu Kiomani* (Muscat: An-Naḥda Press, 2007), 4–5.

138. al-Jahdhamy, *Taalamu Kiomani*, 5.

139. Ghassany, *Kwa Heri Ukoloni*, 34.

140. The author once witnessed an elderly Swahili-speaking man from Kenya at the shops in the mall, unsuccessfully trying to find a shopkeeper to communicate with him in Swahili, even though he also spoke English.

141. See the case studies in Benjamin Lawrance and Jacqueline Stevens, eds., *Citizenship in Question: Evidentiary Birthright and Statelessness* (Durham, NC: Duke University Press, 2017).

6. TRANSREGIONAL RELATIONS, OMANI HERITAGE, AND A VERNACULAR HISTORIOGRAPHY OF ZANZIBAR, 1990–2020

1. "Zanzibar ni nchi kamili" or "Zanzibar ni mamlaka kamili." See essays in "50 Years of the Union between Tanganyika and Zanzibar," special issue, *African Review: A Journal of African Politics, Development and International Affairs* 41, no. 1 (2014).

2. Emma Hunter, introduction to *Citizenship, Belonging and Political Community in Africa: Dialogues Between Past and Present*, ed. Emma Hunter (Athens: Ohio University Press, 2016), 2; and John Coakley, *Nationalism, Ethnicity and the State: Making and Breaking Nations* (Los Angeles: Sage Publications, 2012), 95. As Marie-Aude Fouéré noted, the written word, printed images, and movies can all be appropriated to imagine community. Marie-Aude Fouéré, "Film as Archive: *Africa Addio* and the Ambiguities of Remembrance in Contemporary Zanzibar," *Social Anthropology* 24, no. 1 (February 2016): 82–96.

3. Michel-Rolph Trouillot, *Silencing the Past: Power and the Production of History* (Boston: Beacon Press, 1997), 21; Axel Harnet Sievers, ed., *A Place in the World: New Local Historiographies in Africa and South Asia* (Leiden: Brill, 2001); Karin Barber, ed., *Africa's Hidden Histories: Everyday Literacy and Making the Self* (Bloomington: Indiana University Press, 2006); and Derek Peterson and Giacomo Macola, eds., *Recasting the Past: African History Writing and Political Work in Modern Africa* (Athens: Ohio University Press, 2009).

4. Gerd Nonneman and Marc Valeri, "The 'Heritage' Boom in the Gulf: Critical and Interdisciplinary Perspectives," *Journal of Arabian Studies* 7, no. 2 (2017): 155–156.

5. Michael Rothberg, *Multi-directional Memories: Remembering the Holocaust in the Age of Decolonization* (Palo Alto, CA: Stanford University Press, 2009); and Maurice Halbwachs, ed., *On Collective Memory*, trans. Lewis A. Coser (Chicago: Chicago University Press, 1992), 42.

6. Takeyuka Tsuda, "Why Does the Diaspora Return Home? The Causes of Ethnic Return Migration," in *Diasporic Homecomings: Ethnic Return Migration in Comparative Perspective*, ed. Takeyuki Tsuda (Stanford, CA: Stanford University Press, 2009), 25.

7. Jan Assman, "Communicative and Cultural Memory," in *Cultural Memories: The Geographical Point of View*, ed. Peter Meusburger, Michael Heffernan, and Edgar Wunder (Heidelberg: Dordrecht, 2011), 15–27.

8. F. R. Ankersmit, *Historical Representation* (Stanford, CA: Stanford University Press, 2002).

9. Dr. Mouza Abid Ghubash, "Mafhūm al-Mawrūth al-Shaʻabī wa ʻAlāqatihi bi-l-ʻUmuq al-Nafsī wa al-Ijtimāʻī," in *Faʻāliyyāt wa Nāshiṭ: Ḥiṣād Anshiṭat al-Muntadā al-Adabī, 1991–1992*, ed. Salim Muhammad al-Ghailānī and Muhammad Ali al-Sulaibi (Muscat: Ministry of Heritage and Culture, 1993), 37.

10. Miriam Cooke, *Tribal Modern: Branding New Nations in the Arab Gulf* (Berkeley: University of California Press, 2014), 171.

11. Rosie Bsheer, *Archive Wars: The Politics of History in Saudi Arabia* (Stanford, CA: Stanford University Press, 2020).

12. Marc Valeri, *Oman: Politics and Society in the Qaboos State* (London: Hurst, 2009), 143–146. Other authors note the "nostalgia" inherent in the heritage concept. See Cooke, *Tribal Modern*, ch. 6; and Edward Simpson, *Muslim Society and the Western Indian Ocean: Seafarers of Kacch* (New York: Routledge, 2006), 37, 45.

13. Valeri, *Oman*, 140–146. For an intriguing parallel approach to memory, see essays in Alon Confino and Peter Fritzsche, eds., *The Work of Memory: New Directions in Study of German Society and Culture* (Urbana: University of Illinois Press, 2002).

14. Jeffrey Barash, *Collective Memory and the Historical Past* (Chicago: University of Chicago Press, 2016), 171.

15. For an influential work discussing these dynamics for Germans after World War II, see Andrew Demshuk, *The Lost German East: Forced Migration and the*

Politics of Memory (Cambridge: Cambridge University Press, 2012). See also the essays in Peter Mandaville and Terrence Lyons, eds., *Politics from Afar: Transnational Diasporas and Networks* (London: Hurst Publishers, 2012).

16. Ben Rawlence, "Briefing: The Zanzibar Election," *African Affairs* 104, no. 416 (July 2005): 516.

17. Mohamed Bakari, *The Democratisation Process in Zanzibar: A Retarded Transition* (Hamburg: Institute of African Affairs, 2001), 193. Between 1976 and 1985, the economic performance of Zanzibar's economy declined by 27 percent. W. C. Bissell, "Engaging Colonial Nostalgia," *Cultural Anthropology* 20, no. 2 (May 2005): 217.

18. Robtel Pailey, *Development, Dual Citizenship and Its Discontents in Africa: The Political Economy of Belonging to Liberia* (Cambridge: Cambridge University Press, 2021), 16. See also Morten Jerven, *Africa: Why Economists Get It Wrong* (London: Zed Books, 2015).

19. Stephane Dufoix, *Diasporas*, trans. William Rodamor and Roger Waldinger (Berkeley: University of California Press, 2008), 29; Timothy Ranja, *Success under Duress: A Comparison of the Indigenous African and East Africa Asian Entrepreneurs* (Dar-es-Salaam: Economic and Social Research Foundation, 2003); and Aneeth Kaur Hundle, "Insecurities of Expulsion: Emergent Citizenship Formations and Political Practices in Postcolonial Uganda," *Comparative Studies of South Asia, Africa, and the Middle East* 39, no. 1 (2019): 8–23.

20. Simon Turner, "Suspended Spaces—Contesting Sovereignties in a Refugee Camp," in *Sovereign Bodies: Citizens, Migrants and States in the Postcolonial World Bodies*, ed. Thomas Blom Hansen and Finn Stepputat (Princeton, NJ: Princeton University Press, 2005), 316–317.

21. *FZV* 13, nos. 7 and 8 (July/August 1978), KP no. 8.

22. Ahmed Hamoud al-Maamiry, *Oman and East Africa* (New Delhi: Lancers Books, 1979), 102–103. The work was translated into Arabic by Muhammad Amin Abdullah for the Omani Ministry of Heritage and Culture. *'Uman wa Sharq Ifriqiyya*, 3rd ed., trans. Muhammad Amin Abdullah (Muscat: Ministry of Heritage and Culture, 2016).

23. Ahmed Idarus Baalawy, *Nyerere and Muslim Tanzania* (Portsmouth: The Zanzibar Organization, 1982/1983), 1–2.

24. Baalawy, *Nyerere and Muslim Tanzania*, 2.

25. A. S. Kharusi, "Statement on the Tanzanian Goodwill Mission to Arab States," *FZV*, 10 April 1978, KP no. 8.

26. "Zanzibar: The Lion Awakes" and "the Gathering Storm," *FZV* 15, nos. 1/2 (January/February 1980), KP no. 8.

27. "Zimbabwe or Liberia—A Choice for Nyerere," *FZV* 15, nos. 5 and 6 (May/June 1980), KP no. 8.

28. Greg Cameron, "Political Violence, Ethnicity and the Agrarian Question in Zanzibar," in *Swahili Modernities: Identity, Development and Power on the Coast of East Africa*, ed. Pat Caplan and Farouk Topan (Trenton, NJ: Africa World Press, 2004), 107.

29. Ariel Crozon, "Zanzibar en Tanzanie: Essai D'histoire Politique" (Science politique, Universite de Pau et des Pays de L'adour, 1992), 474.

30. Baalawy, *Nyerere and Muslim Tanzania*, 1.

31. Crozon, "Zanzibar en Tanzanie," 440; and Songe Mbele, "Tanzania: Union at the Ballot Box," *AfricaAsia*, May 1984.

32. Bakari, *Democratisation Process in Zanzibar*, 193. Not until Ali Hassan Mwinyi's presidency was a full reset of relations accomplished.

33. Crozon, "Zanzibar en Tanzanie," 501–506.

34. David Brewin, "Zanzibar Government- Changes," *Bulletin of Tanzanian Affairs*, no. 30 (May 1988), www.tzaffairs.org/category/issue-number/issue-30/.

35. G. Thomas Burgess, *Race, Revolution and the Struggle for Human Rights in Zanzibar: The Memoirs of Ali Sultan Issa and Seif Sharif Hamad* (Athens: Ohio University Press, 2009), 286.

36. Crozon, "Zanzibar en Tanzanie," 439.

37. *FZV*, September 1984, KP no. 8. Muhammad A. Hashim Azzinjibari to Ali Hassan Mwinyi, 30 April 1984, KP no. 10. See also Ali Muhsin al-Barwani, *Conflict and Harmony in Zanzibar* (Dubai: self-published, 1997), 275.

38. Bakari, *Democratisation Process in Zanzibar*, 115, 194; Julia Verne and Detlef Müller-Mahn, "We Are Part of Zanzibar: Translocal Practices and Imaginative Geographies," in *Regionalizing Oman: Political, Economic and Social Dynamics*, ed. Steffen Wippel (Dordrecht: Springer Link, 2013), 82; and Michael Lofchie, *The Political Economy of Tanzania: Decline and Recovery* (Philadelphia: University of Pennsylvania Press, 2014), 11. François Constantin observes that shortly after this, Nyerere received the Aga Khan in Dar-es-Salaam, for the first time in twenty years. François Constantin, "Sur les modes populaires d'action diplomatique: Affaires de famille et affaires d'État en Afrique orientale," *Revue française de science politique* 36, no. 5 (1986): 672–694.

39. Ali Ahmed Saleh, interview with author, May 30, 2013.

40. Roman Loimeier, *Between Social Skills and Marketable Skills: The Politics of Islamic Education in 20th Century Zanzibar* (Leiden: Brill, 2009), 55; Zanzibar Government, *Investment Act 1986 and Guidelines for Investors* (Government of Zanzibar, 1989), ZNA, BA 13/37; K. I. Tambila, "Aspects of the Political Economy of Unguja and Pemba." In *The Political Plight of Zanzibar*, ed. Maliyamkono (Dar-es-Salaam: Tema Publishers, 2000), 84; and Kjersti Larsen, "Translocal Experiences and Intersecting Mobilities: Reflections on Motility and Actual and Imagined Movability in Contemporary Zanzibar," in *Translocal Connections across the Indian Ocean*, ed. Francesca Declich (Leiden: Brill, 2018), 236n26.

41. Burgess, *Race*, 234; Mbele, "Tanzania"; Ahmed Rajab, "A Tale of Two Presidents," *Africa Events*, November 1986; and Ibrahim Shao, *Political Economy of Land Reforms in Zanzibar: Before and after the Revolution* (Dar-es-Salaam: UDSM Press, 1992), 94–95. In 1987 Hamad was removed from CCM's Central Committee and thrown out of the government of Zanzibar. Burgess, *Race*.

42. Suleiman Shahbal, *Zanzibar: The Rise and Fall of an Independent State* (Dubai: Self-published, 2002), 455.

43. Ahmed Issa Omar al-Mazrui, "Zanzibar-Oman Relations: A Historical Perspective" (MA thesis, University of Dar-es-Salaam, 1996), 88; Crozon, "Zanzibar en Tanzanie," 515; and Joseph Kechician, *Oman and the World: The Emergence of an Independent Foreign Policy* (Santa Monica, CA: Rand Corporation, 1995), 246.

44. Orne Westad, *The Global Cold War: Third World Interventions and the Making of Our Times* (Cambridge: Cambridge University Press, 2006), 387.

45. Loiemeier, *Between Social Skills*, 123; Mara Leichtman, "Daʿwa as Development: Kuwaiti Islamic charity in East and West Africa," *Muslim World* 112 (Winter 2022): 100–129; Chanfi Ahmed, "Networks of Islamic NGOs in Sub-Saharan Africa: Bilal Muslim Mission, African Muslim Agency (Direct Aid), and al Haramayn," *Journal of Eastern African Studies* 3, no. 3 (2009): 426–437; and Kimberly Wortmann, "Omani Religious Networks in Contemporary Tanzania and Beyond" (PhD Committee on the Study of Religion, Harvard University, 2018), 84–91. The Aga Khan has also been very involved in education and other charitable initiatives.

46. Kimberly Wortmann, "Reading Ibāḍī Women's Legacies through Stone Town's Built Environment," *Islamic Africa* 12 (2021): 23–24.

47. Abdin Chande, *Islam, Ujamaa, and Community Development: A Case Study of Religious Currents in East Africa* (San Francisco: Austin and Winfield Publishers, 1998), 258; and Simon Turner, "'These Young Men Show No Respect for Local Customs'—Globalisation and Islamic Revival in Zanzibar," *Journal of Religion in Africa* 39, no. 3 (2009): 237–261.

48. Westad, *Global Cold War*, 387.

49. Goran Hyden and Bo Karlstrom, "Structural Adjustment as a Policy Process: The Case of Tanzania," *World Development* 21, no. 9 (1993): 1395–1404.

50. Max Mmuya and Amon Chaligha, *Towards Multiparty Politics in Tanzania* (Dar-es-Salaam: UDSM Press, 1992), 7; and Robert Gilpin, *The Challenge of Global Capitalism: The World Economy in the 21st Century* (Princeton, NJ: Princeton University Press, 2000), 7.

51. Bakari, *Democratisation Process in Zanzibar*, 153.

52. Mmuya and Chaligha, *Towards Multiparty Politics*, 10.

53. Jeremy Prestholdt, "Locating the Indian Ocean: Notes on the Postcolonial Reconstitution of Space," *Journal of Eastern African Studies* 9, no. 3 (2015): 440–467.

54. Barash, *Collective Memory and the Historical Past*, 69; Paul Connerton, "Seven Types of Forgetting," *Memory Studies* 1, no. 59 (2008): 59–71; Gina Sanchez Gibau, "Cyber Cvs: Online Conversations on Cape Verdean Diaspora Identities," in *Diasporas in the New Media Age: Identity, Politics, and Community*, ed. Pedro Oiarzabal and Andoni Alonso (Reno: University of Nevada Press, 2010), 119.

55. Arjun Appadurai, *Modernity at Large: Cultural Dimensions of Globalization* (Minneapolis: University of Minnesota Press, 1996), 1–10.

56. Martin Gurri, *The Revolt of the Public and the Crisis of Authority in the New Millennium* (San Francisco: Stripe Press, 2018).

57. Michael Peter Smith and Luis Eduardo Guarnizo, eds., *Transnationalism from Below: Comparative Urban and Community Research* (London: Routledge, 1998).

58. Meg Arenberg, "Swahili Poetry's Digital Geographies: WhatsApp and the Forming of Cultural Space," *Postcolonial Text* 15, nos. 3 and 4 (2020): 2.

59. Irene Brunotti, "From Baraza to Cyberbaraza: Interrogating Publics in the Context of the 2015 Zanzibar Electoral Impasse," *Journal of Eastern African Studies* 13, no. 1 (2019): 18–34. See also Kai Kresse, *Swahili Muslim Publics and Postcolonial Experience* (Bloomington: Indiana University Press, 2018).

60. Shireen Mirza, "Muslims, Media and Mobility in the Indian Ocean Region," in *The Shi'a in Modern South Asia: Religion, History and Politics*, ed. Justin Jones and Ali Usman Qasmi (Cambridge: Cambridge University Press, 2015), 131–158; and Valeri, *Oman*, 143. The *Oman National Plan for the Alliance of Civilizations* (Muscat: n.p., 2011) lays out both a record of and a vision toward the conscious and humane exercise of Omani soft power since the 1970s, involving conferences, cultural exchanges, exhibitions and publications. There is a notable maritime emphasis, with discussion of the donation of the royal yacht to the UN Educational, Scientific and Cultural Organization (UNESCO) Silk Route Project, the Shahab Oman ship, which makes voyages of international goodwill, symbolizing Oman's ancient maritime presence, and the 2010 voyage of the *Jewel of Muscat*, a ship built in the traditional style dating to the ninth century, which sailed to India, Sri Lanka, and Malaysia.

61. Al-Mazrui, "Zanzibar-Oman Relations," 70.

62. Al-Mazrui, "Zanzibar-Oman Relations," 73; Erik Gilbert, *Dhows and the Colonial Economy of Zanzibar, 1860–1970* (Athens: Ohio University Press, 2005), 166–167. Bwejuu is the town in Unguja where most shoreline property is now owned by Zanzibari Omanis. Verne and Müller-Mahn, "We Are Part of Zanzibar," 85.

63. Mayuko Okawa, "Nationality Law and Concept of Nation in Oman: A Case Study of Omani Returnees from Africa," *Modern Middle East* 45 (2008): 29.

64. Crozon, "Zanzibar en Tanzanie," 456; and al-Mazrui, "Zanzibar-Oman Relations," 85.

65. Kimberly Wortmann, "Ibadi Muslim Schools in Post-Revolutionary Zanzibar," *Africa* 92, no. 2 (February 2022): 249–264.

66. Dufoix, *Diasporas*, 32.

67. Abdul Sheriff, *The History and Conservation of Zanzibar Stone Town* (Athens: Ohio University Press, 1995); Inger Lise Syversen, "Intentions and Reality in Architectural Heritage Management: In Search of the Influence of International Policy Documents on Contemporary Sustainable Local Heritage Management" (PhD diss., Chalmers University of Technology, Sweden, 2007). Ali Muhsin al-Barwani also visited his ancestral home in Ibra, Oman in this period. al-Barwani, *Conflict and Harmony in Zanzibar* (Dubai: Self-published, 1997), 298.

68. Mahmoud Khalifa al-Bimani, "Duwwar Wasā'il al-'I'lām al-'Umaniyya al-Ḥukūmiyya Ibrāz Munjazāt al-Wujūd al-'Umanī fi Sharq Afrīqiyā: Dirāsa

Istiṭlāʿiyya Taḥlīliyya" (paper presented at the International Conference on the Omani Role in East Africa, 11–13 December 2012, Sultan Qaboos University).

69. Hamad Muhammad al-Murjebi, *Mughāmir ʿUmānī fī Adghāl Ifriqiyyā: Ḥayā Hamad bin Muhammad bin Jumaʿal-Murjibi (Al-Maʿrūf bi-Tībūu Tīb), 1840–1905*, trans. Muhammad al-Mahrooqi (Cologne: Kamel/Verlag, 2006); and Al-Seyyid Al-Amjad Hamoud Ahmed Seif al-Busaidi, *Al-Dar al-Manẓūm fī Dhikr Mahāsin al-ʾAmṣār al-Rūsūm*, ed. Muhammad al-Mahrooqi (Muscat: Ministry of Heritage and Culture, 2006).

70. I.S., 8/18/2011. Mohamed al-Maḥrooqi, *Min Forodhani: Youmiyāt Riḥla ila Zanjibār wa Mumbāsā wa al-Barr al-ʾIfrīqiya* (Muscat: Beit Ghushām, 2013).

71. Nasr Ghalib Khalifa al-Busaidi, *Riḥlāt ʿUmāni ila al-Sharq al-ʾIfriqiyya: al-Wujūd al-ʿUmani wa Atharihi fī Bilād al-Sharq al-ʾIfrīqi Jamāl al-Ṭabīʿiyya wa ʾAthar al-Ḥiḍāra* (Muscat: Beirut Bookshop, 2017).

72. Salha Bint Seif Sulaiman al-Miskery, "Aḍwāʾ Jadīda ala al-Muʾatharāt al-Ḥaḍāriyya al-ʿUmāniyya fī Zanjibār wa al-Jazīra al-Khuẓrāʾ," in *Namādhij min al-Buḥūth al-Tārīkhiyya al-Fāʾiza fī musābiq-l-Muntadā al-Adabī, 1996–97* (Muscat: Ministry of Heritage and Culture Oman, 2001), 73–116.

73. Ali A. Mazrui, "Mazrui Annual Newsletter No. 17: On Ancestry, Descent and Identity", Eve of 1993.

74. Sultan Muhammad al-Qasimi, *Taqsīm al-Imbrāṭūriyyat-l-ʿUmāniyya: 1856–1862* (Sharjah: Al-Qasimi Publications, 2012).

75. Mazrui, "Annual Newsletter No. 17." Al-Maamiry passed away in July 1992. See Juma Aley, *Enduring Links* (Dubai: Union Printing Press, 1994).

76. Zuhura Yunus, *Biubwa Amour Zahor: Mwanamke Mapinduzi* (Dar-es-Salaam: Vision Publishing Ltd., 2021), 140.

77. Marie-Aude Fouéré, "Reinterpreting Revolutionary Zanzibar in the Media Today: The Case of Dira Newspaper," *Journal of Eastern African Studies* 6, no. 4 (2012): 672–689.

78. Nasser Abdullah al-Riyami, *Zanjibār: Shaksiyāt wa Aḥdāth* (Cairo: Maktab Beirut, 2009). This source is explored in Nathaniel Mathews, "Memory, History, Heritage: Omani-Zanzibaris Remember the Zanzibar Revolution, 1964–present," in *Social Memory and the 1964 Zanzibar Revolution*, ed. Garth Myers and Marie-Aude Fouéré (Dar-es-Salaam: Mkuti wa Nyota, 2017), 279–310.

79. Habiba al-Hinai, *ʾĀʾidūn Ḥaythu al-Ḥulm: Mashāhid wa-Dhikriyyāt ʿauda min Zanjibār wa al-Jazīrat-l-Khaḍrāʾ ʿUman* (Beirut: Beirut Bookshop, 2013), 43.

80. Sheikha al-Ghonaimi, *Zanjibār: Wa Akfān min Rahim Al-ʾAlam* (Muscat: Maktabat-l-Ḍāmri li-l-Nashr wa al-Tawzīʿ, 2012).

81. Muhammad Seif al-Rahbi, *al-Seyyid Marra min Hunā* (Beirut: al-Intishār al-ʿArabi, 2011). The novel is also informed by its author's reading of historical works like Abdullah Saleh al-Farsy's *Al-Busaʿidiyyun Hukkam Zanjibar* and al-Mugheiry's *Juhaynat al-Akhbar*.

82. Huda Hamed, *I Saw Her in My Dreams*, trans. Nadine Sino (Austin: University of Texas Press, 2023).

83. Mathews, "Memory," 294–298; I.S. 34, 3/3/2013; Ahmed al-Khalili, "al-ʿUmāniyyūn wa Atharahum fī al-Jawānab al-ʿIlmiyya wa al-Maʿarfiyya bi-Sharq Ifrīqīyya," in *Faʿāliyyāt wa Nāshiṭ: Ḥiṣād: Anshiṭat al-Muntadā*, ed. Salim Muhammad al-Ghailani and Muhammad Ali al-Sulaibi (Muscat: Ministry of Heritage and Culture, 1994), 180; and Mayuko Okawa, "The Empire of Oman in the Formation of Oman's National History: An Analysis of School Social Studies Textbooks and Teachers' Guidelines," *Research Note*, nos. 31–32 (2015): 95–120, www.jstage.jst.go.jp/article/ajames/31/1/31_KJ00010032648/_pdf/-char/en.

84. Harith Ghassany, *Kwa Heri Ukoloni, Kwa Heri Uhuru! Zanzibar na Mapinduzi ya Afrabia* (n.p.: Lulu Press, 2010), 242.

85. "Sheikh Ali Bin Muhsin al-Barwani na Siasa za Zanzibar," interview with Professor Ibrahim Noor, posted February 8, 2016, www.youtube.com/watch?v=sdUqIOYPzE8. .

86. Madawi al-Rasheed, "Transnational Connections and National Identity Zanzibari Omanis in Muscat," in *Monarchies and Nations: Globalisation and Identity in the Arab States of the Gulf*, ed. Paul Dresch and James Piscatori (London: I. B. Tauris, 2005), 100.

87. One is reminded of Lauren Benton's observation on sovereignty's ambition to control inherently porous boundaries: "Mere patches of regulated land may appear to signify claims to vast holdings." Lauren Benton, *Law and Geography in European Empires, 1400–1900* (Cambridge: Cambridge University Press, 2009), 279.

88. Hamud Muhammad Ruzaiq, *Fatḥ al-Mubīn fī Sīrat-l-Sādat-l-Busaʿidīn* (Muscat: Ministry of Heritage and Culture, 1977); Abdalla Saleh al-Farsy, *Seyyid Said bin Sultan* (Zanzibar: Mwongozi Printing Press, 1947), translated into Arabic as *Al-Busaʿidiyyun Hukkam Zanjibar* (Muscat: Ministry of Heritage and Culture, 2005), reprinted by Sultan Qaboos University in 2005; Zahir Said, *Tanzih al-Abṣār fī Riḥla Sultān Zanjibār* (Muscat: Ministry of Heritage and Culture, 2008); and *al-ʿUmāniyyūn wa qalʿa Mombāsā*, no. 9 (Muscat: Ministry of National Heritage and Culture, 1994).

89. Said Ali al-Mugheiry, *Juhaynat-l-Akhbār fī tārīkh Zanjibār*, ed. Muḥammad Ali al-Sulaibi (Muscat: Ministry of Heritage and Culture Oman, 2001). The history of this text is explained in a series of documents in the Zanzibar archives, which reveal Zanzibar officials' reluctance to publish or get involved with the work, as its emphasis on tribes was deemed out of step with the move toward representative democracy and the universal franchise.

90. *Oman in History* (Muscat, Oman: Ministry of Information, 1995). In a volume introduced by Zanzibar-born Ahmed al-Khalili, Soghayrun emphasized the connection between Omani activities in the interior during the nineteenth century, and the Omani role in the spread of Swahili as lingua franca. Ibrahim Zein Soghayrun, "Al-Ishām al-ʿUmāni fī al-Majālāt al-Thaqāfiyya wa al-Fikriyya wa al-Kashf ʿAn Majāhil al-Qārat-l-Ifrīqīyya fī al-ʿAhd al-Busaʿīdī," in *Faʿāliyyāt wa Nāshiṭ: Ḥiṣād Anshiṭat al-Muntadā al-Adabī, 1991–1992*, ed. Salim Muhammad al-Ghailani and Muhammad Ali al-Sulaibi (Muscat: Ministry of Heritage and Culture, 1993), 214.

91. Saud Salim al-Unsi, *al-'Ādāt al-'Umaniyya* (Muscat: Ministry of Heritage and Culture Oman, 1991), 23.

92. Al-Unsi, *al-'Ādāt al-'Umaniyya*, 23.

93. Al-Unsi, *al-'Ādāt al-'Umaniyya*, 24.

94. Okawa, "Empire of Oman," 103–109. See also Mandana Limbert, "Oman: Cultivating Good Citizens and Religious Virtue," in *Teaching Islam: Textbooks and Religion in the Middle East*, ed. Eleanor Doumato and Gregory Starrett (Boulder: Lynne Rienner, 2006), 159–191.

95. *Al-Dirāsāt al-Ijtimā'iyya: Level No. 8* (Muscat: Ministry of Education, 2007), 76.

96. *Al-Dirāsāt al-Ijtimā'iyya*, 20–21. A map of the "Omani empire" is on page 61. A similar map is reproduced in an earlier published textbook for the ninth-grade level: *Al-Dirāsāt al-Ijtimā'iyya: Level No. 9* (Muscat: Ministry of Education, 2004).

97. *Al-Dirāsāt al-Ijtimā'iyya: Level No. 8*, 75.

98. Saud Salim al-Balushi, *Hadha Watani fi al-Sīrat-l-Ḥiḍāriyya* (Muscat: Ministry of Education, 2006), 130.

99. al-Balushi, *Hadha*, 131. A similar phrasing is found in Soghayrun, "Al-Ishām al-'Umāni fi al-Majālāt," 204.

100. Ibrahim al-Shaarawi, *al-'Umāniyyun fī Sharq Afrīqiyā* (Muscat: Ministry of Education, 2005), 15.

101. Al-Shaarawi, *al-'Umāniyyun fī Sharq Afrīqiyā*, 30.

102. Al-Shaarāwi, *al-'Umāniyyun fī Sharq Afrīqiyā*, 31.

103. Al-Shaarawi, *al-'Umāniyyun fī Sharq Afrīqiyā*, 38–39.

104. Loimeier, *Between Social Skills*, 562; al-Barwani, *Conflict and Harmony*, 153; Juma Aley, *Zanzibar in the Context* (New Delhi: Lancers Books, 1988), 19; and Aley, *Enduring Links*.

105. See Hussein Bashir Abdallah, *Dola Kongwe ya Zanzibar: Kutoka Oman hadi Kongo* (Dar-es-Salaam: Katambi Enterprises, 2013).

106. Hussein Bashir Abdallah, *Utukufu wa Zanzibar* (Dar-es-Salaam: Kauthar Printers, 2010).

107. Abdallah, *Dola Kongwe*, 79–80.

108. Said Salim al-Naamani, *Al-Hijrāt al-'Umaniyya ila Sharq Ifriqiyyā: ma bain al-Qarnain al-Awal wa al-Sāb'a al-Hijraīn, Dirāsa Siyāsa wa Haḍāriyya* (Damascus: Dār al-Farqad, 2012).

109. The Omani government has donated to the upkeep of the Zanzibar Archives. Ahmed Issa Omar Al-Mazrui, "Zanzibar-Oman Relations: A Historical Perspective" (MA thesis, University of Dar-es-Salaam, 1996), 70. Several Omani intellectuals interviewed bemoaned the tepid interest of the Omani government in historical preservation initiatives for Omani history in East Africa.

110. "Early Notification of Collapse of House of Wonders in Zanzibar," 25 December 2020, UNESCO, https://whc.unesco.org/en/news/2233.

111. The House of Wonders thus exemplifies the notion of ambivalent heritage. See Peter Probst, "Iconoclash in the Age of Heritage," *African Arts* 45, no. 3 (2012):

10–13; and Ashish Chadha, "Ambivalent Heritage: Between Affect and Ideology in a Colonial Cemetery," *Journal of Material Culture* 11, no. 3 (2006): 339–363.

112. Bissell, "Engaging Colonial Nostalgia," 226; Paola Ivanov, "Cosmopolitanism or Exclusion? Negotiating Identity in the Expressive Culture of Contemporary Zanzibar," in *The Indian Ocean: Oceanic Connections and the Creation of New Societies*, ed. Engseng Ho and Abdul Sheriff (London: Hurst, 2014), 218.

113. In her study conducted in the mid-1980s, Grandmaison estimated the community in Burundi to be about thirty-five hundred. Collete Grandmaison, *Turāthna: Hijrāt al-Ḥarth ila Awāsiṭ al-Qārat-l-'Afriqiyya* (Muscat: Ministry of Heritage and Culture Oman, 1984), 6. See also "Stateless in Burundi: Omanis Search for a Nationality," December 3, 2012, https://english.alarabiya.net/articles/2012/12/03/253074.

114. I.S. 10, 8/23/11. See also "Rāshid al-ʿAbri: Yaʾūd li-ahlihi baʿad sitīn ʿāmā min inqiṭāʾ akhbārihi," *al-Watan*, March 20, 2013.

115. Sheikh Saleh Hashil al-Miskery, "Ālāf min Ahlna Yantadhirūn Iʿtirāfna bihim," *Al-Watan*, May 9, 2013.

116. Christian Joppke, *Selecting by Origin: Ethnic Migration and the Liberal State* (Boston: Harvard University Press, 2005), 2. In 1992 the Yemeni government actually airlifted many Yemeni-descended Somalis back to Yemen. See Alessandra Vianello, "One Hundred Years in Brava: The Migration of Umar Ba Umar from Hadhramaut to East Africa and Back, c. 1890–1990," *Journal of Eastern African Studies* 6, no. 4 (2012): 655–671.

117. Ghassany, *Kwa Heri Ukoloni*, xii.

118. The bibliography on the subject could easily double the length of this book. A good recent treatment is Gunja SenGupta and Awam Amkpa, *Sojourners, Sultans, and Slaves: American and the Indian Ocean in the Age of Abolition and Empire* (Berkeley: University of California Press, 2023). See also Jonathon Glassman, "Racial Violence, Universal History, and Echoes of Abolition in Twentieth-Century Zanzibar," in *Abolition and Imperialism in Britain, Africa and the Atlantic*, ed. Derek Peterson (Athens: Ohio University/Swallow Press, 2010). In Zanzibar in 2014 a neighbor, a Swahili-speaking Zanzibari of South Asian ancestry, discussed slavery in Zanzibar. He repeated the common trope that Arabs used to keep the slaves down in chambers beneath the church, a building only built after the abolition of slavery.

119. In the context of the Time of Politics, the Zanzibar intelligentsia defended itself against vigorous charges of slaveholding from the intellectuals of the Afro-Shirazi Party, who celebrated abolition and abolitionists. Jonathon Glassman, *War of Words, War of Stones: Racial Thought and Violence in Colonial Zanzibar* (Bloomington: Indiana University Press, 2011), 159; and Glassman, "Racial Violence," 186–191.

120. Ghassany, *Kwa Heri Ukoloni*, 324.

121. A theme also taken up in Western historiography. For a classic work of criticism see Robert Phillipson, "Slaves and Saviours: Images of Arabs and Englishmen in *Uhuru wa Watumwa*," *Ba Shiru* 13, no. 1 (1989): 40–49. See also Nathaniel

Mathews, "'Arab-Islamic Slavery': A Problematic Term for a Complex Reality," *Research Africa Reviews* 4, no. 2 (August 2020), https://sites.duke.edu/research africa/files/2020/08/1-4-Arab-Islamic-Slavery-2020.pdf.

122. Al-Barwani, *Conflict and Harmony*, 184.

123. Issa Nasser al-Ismaily, *Will Zanzibar Regain Her Past Prosperity* (Muscat: self-published, 2015), 304.

124. Glassman, "Racial Violence," 188; Melvin Page, "Tippu Tip and the Arab 'Defense' of the East African Slave Trade," *Etudes D'histoire Africaine* 6 (1974): 111; and John Iliffe, *A Modern History of Tanganyika* (New York: Cambridge University Press, 1979), 46–47.

125. Ahmed Hamoud al-Maamiry, *Omani Sultans in Zanzibar (1832–1964)* (New Delhi: Lancers Books, 1988), 77; and Michael Lofchie, *Zanzibar: Background to Revolution* (Princeton, NJ: Princeton University Press, 1965), 209–210.

126. Issa Nasser al-Ismaily, *Kinyanganyiro na Utumwa* (Muscat, Oman: self published, 1999), 187.

127. Issa Nasser al-Ismaily, *Uzanzibari na Usultani* (Muscat, Oman: self-published, 1996). 23.

128. Seyyid Hamad Ahmad al-Ḥaddad, *Dirāsat al-'Arab wa al-Islam fī Sharq 'Afrīqiyā* (Beirut: Dar al-Minhaj, 2007), 320–321.

129. Babakerim, *The Aftermath of the Zanzibar Revolution* (Muscat: self-published, 1994), 9.

130. Al-Ismaily, *Kinyanganyiro*; L. W. Hollingsworth, *A Short History of the East Coast of Africa* (London: Macmillan, 1956), 129; al-Maamiry, *Oman and East Africa*, 28; al-Maamiry, *Omani Sultans*, 20, 79, 81; al-Riyami, *Zanzibar*, 239–250; al-Ḥaddad, *Dirāsat al-'Arab*, 312; and al-Ismaily, *Will Zanzibar*, 229–230.

131. Emily Jane O'Dell, "Yesterday Is Not Gone: Memories of Slavery in Zanzibar and Oman in Memoirs, Fiction, and Film," *Journal of Global Slavery* 5, no. 3 (2020): 357–401.

132. al-Rahbi, *al-Seyyid Marra min Hunā*.

133. Shariff, *Tanzania*, 88–91.

134. Shariff, *Tanzania*, 107–144, esp. 134–135.

135. Ibrahim Noor Shariff, *Tanzania na Propaganda za Udini* (Muscat: self published, 2014), 23–24.

136. Shariff, *Tanzania*, 40–44.

137. Riikka Suhonen, "Mapinduzi Daima—Revolution Forever: Using the 1964 Revolution in Nationalistic Political Discourses in Zanzibar" (MA thesis, University of Helsinki, 2009), 71; and Blamuel Njururi, "Saudi Work for Kenyans—New Slave Trade, or Job Creation?," *New African Development*, September 1977.

138. See for instance the YouTube video testimonies of Nigerian, Zimbabwean, Liberian, and Tanzanian women who claim they were treated as "slaves" there.

139. See al-Haddad, *Dirāsat al-'Arab* for the recapitulation of these themes in Arabic language historiography.

140. Marie-Aude Fouéré, "Recasting Julius Nyerere in Zanzibar: The Revolution, the Union and the Enemy of the Nation," in *Remembering Nyerere in*

Tanzania: History Memory Legacy, ed. Marie-Aude Fouéré, 171–196 (Dar-es-Salaam: Mkuti wa Nyota Publishers), 2015), 78.

141. See, for instance, Imad Jasim al-Bahrani, *Zanjibār bi-Mulāmiḥ ʿUmāniyya* (Beirut: Dar Soual, 2017), 23.

142. Al-Ismaily, *Will Zanzibar,* 307. Maulid M. Haj dedicated his short account of politics in Zanzibar to "those who strove for and won independence from British Rule in December 1963." Maulid M. Haj, *Zanzibar: The Last Years of the Protectorate; A Constitutional and Political Account* (Muscat: al Roya Publishing, 2006).

143. Arif Dirlik, *Postmodernity's Histories: The Past as Legacy and Project* (Lanham, MD: Rowman & Littlefield, 2000), 19. The central problem stems from how the meaning of a successful revolution is interpreted by individuals through the lens of their personal experience, which is often at odds with the official state narrative.

144. Fouéré, "Reinterpreting Revolutionary Zanzibar," 672–689.

145. Al-Ismaily, *Uzanzibari,* 16; and Shaaban S. al-Farsy, *Mzanzibari Asimilia Hadithi Yake* (Muscat: self published, 1994), 16–17.

146. Al-Busaidi, Saud Ahmed. *Memoirs of an Omani Gentleman from Zanzibar* (Muscat: al-Roya Press, 2012).

147. Al-Busaidi, *Memoirs,* 98.

148. Al-Busaidi, *Memoirs,* 99, 101.

149. Al-Maamiry, *Oman and East Africa,* 91.

150. Al-Maamiry, *Oman and East Africa,* 295.

151. Ghassany, *Kwa Heri Ukoloni,* 235.

152. Al-Barwani, *Conflict and Harmony,* 152; Ghassany, *Kwa Heri Ukoloni,* 236–237; and al-Ismaily, *Will Zanzibar,* 275.

153. Al-Maamiry, *Oman and East Africa,* 96–99, 102. The discourse is also picked up by Zanzibaris. Issa Ziddy, *Lugha ya Kiarabu Zanzibar: Historia na Mbinu za Usomeshaji* (Zanzibar: self-published, 2011), 56. For the theme of decolonization as the "giving up" of Arab privileges, see also Aley, *Zanzibar in the Context,* 52.

154. Al-Ismaily, *Will Zanzibar,* 250.

155. Maulid Haj, *Sowing the Wind: Zanzibar and Pemba before the Revolution* (Zanzibar: Gallery Publications, 2001), 18, 79; and al-Maamiry, *Oman and East Africa,* 101

156. Haj, *Sowing the Wind,* 28.

157. Al-Farsi, *Mzanzibari,* 8, 69.

158. Even the late Seif Sharif Hamad gave credence to this theory. Burgess, *Race,* 190.

159. Fouéré, "Recasting Julius Nyerere," 179.

160. Al-Ismaily, *Will Zanzibar,* 273–275, 299–300.

161. Shariff, *Tanzania,* 58

162. Dr. Saleh Mahrus Muhammad Muhammad, *Zanjibār: Al-Ayām al-Akhīra li-l-Hukm al-ʿUmāni fī Sharq Afrīqiyyā* (Cairo: Al-Maktāb al-ʿArabi li-l-Muʿārif, 2019).

163. Ghassany, *Kwa Heri Ukoloni*, 199.

164. Al-Ismaily, *Will Zanzibar*; and Timothy Parsons, *The 1964 Army Mutinies and the Making of Modern East Africa* (Westport, CT: Praeger, 2003).

165. Ghassany, *Kwa Heri Ukoloni*, 185–186.

166. Al-Riyami, *Zanzibar*, 159.

167. Al-Ismaily, *Will Zanzibar*, 301; and al-Riyami, *Zanzibar*, 269.

168. Al-Maamiry, *Oman and East Africa*, 102. This overestimates their role; Umma cadres did not plan the military action that facilitated the revolution.

169. Al-Busaidi, *Memoirs*, 135.

170. Shahbal, *Zanzibar*, 443. Drawing on Helene Louise Hunter, *The Hundred Days Revolution* (Santa Barbara, CA: ABC-CLIO, 2010). Parsons repeats a less conspiratorial version of this view that Nyerere formed the Union to limit Communist influence in Zanzibar. Parsons, *1964 Army Mutinies* (Westport, CT: Praeger, 2003), 164. Issa Nasser al-Ismaily stresses the role of Nyerere as the power behind the Union. Al-Ismaily, *Will Zanzibar*, 313–317. Tanzanian intellectuals have also advanced al-Ismaily's view, downplaying the pressure of the British and the Americans and stressing that Nyerere acted for his own independent reasons. See Godfrey Mwakikagile, *The Union of Tanganyika and Zanzibar: Product of the Cold War?* (Washington, DC: New Africa Press, 2008).

171. Al-Farsi, *Mzanzibari*, 71-75.

172. Shariff, *Tanzania*, 35. Other exile sources claim Nyasaland.

173. Al-Haddād, *Dirāsat al-'Arab*, 294.

174. Al-Baḥrānī, *Zanjibār*, 23.

175. Fouéré, "Recasting Julius Nyerere," 184.

176. Al-Ismaily, *Will Zanzibar*, 278. This is largely borne out in in the oral histories presented in chapter 2.

177. Yunus, *Biubwa Amour Zahor*, 147.

178. "Majzurah Zanjibār al-Juz'a al-Thāni," 2020. www.youtube.com/watch?v=UQoSOrHcExY.

179. "The Mass Graves of Zanzibar," https://zanzibarhistory.org/mass_graves.htm.

180. For more on the politics of the film, see Fouéré, "Film as Archive."

181. For example, Mwinjilisti Kusupa published a memoir of the 1,888 days he spent as a political detainee in a Tanzanian prison. Mwinjilisti K. Kusupa, *Maisha Yangu Gerezani (2001–2007) au Simulizi la Siku elfu moja mia nane themanini na nane za Mateso* (Dar-es-Salaam: Karljamer Print Technology, 2011). Kusupa as a Christian was later active in the same Christian-Muslim polemics engaged in by Ali Muhsin in *Let the Bible Speak (Wacha Biblia Hukumu)*.

182. Shahbal, *Zanzibar*.

183. Salem ben Nasser al Ismaily, *The Sultanate of Zanzibar* (Indianapolis: Dog Ear Publishing, 2014), 19, 369–370.

184. Hashil S. Hashil, *Mimi, Umma Party na Mapinduzi ya Zanzibar* (Paris: DL₂A Buluu Publishing, 2018).

185. Ally Saleh, "Matatizo ya Kisiasa ya Zanzibar: Mgororo au Hasara ya Mfumo wa Vyama Vingi?," in *Siasa katika Tanzania na uchaguzi mkuu wa 1995*, ed. D. Mukangara and R. Mukandala (Dar-es-Salaam: Interpress Tanzania Ltd., 1998).

186. Garth Andrew Myers, "Isle of Cloves, Sea of Discourses: Writing about Zanzibar," *Ecumene* 3, no. 4 (1996): 408–426; and Jeffrey Blustein, *The Moral Demands of Memory* (Cambridge: Cambridge University Press, 2012), 19.

187. Adam Shafi, *Kasri ya Mwinyi Fuad* (Dar-es-Salaam: Tanzanian Publishing House, 1978); Adam Shafi, *Kuli* (Nairobi: Longhorn Publishers, 2005 (1979); and Adam Shafi, *Haini* (Nairobi: Longhorn Publishers, 2003).

188. Naila Barwani, *Imepita Jana* (Bedfordshire: Bright Pen Publishing, 2010), 94. In descriptions clearly picked from a mix of personal experience and stories told to her, she describes the disappearance of Warda and her mother, who were returning from a wedding in rural Zanzibar (Burudika), "when a group of revolutionaries saw them and hacked them to death with knives and machetes."

189. Hashil S. Hashil and Ahmed Faris, *Living under the Shadow of Terror: Zanzibar Caught Off Guard* (n.p.: CreateSpace Independent Publishing, 2015), 10–11.

190. Hashil and Faris, *Living under the Shadow*, 6. Mention should also be made of the daughter of the late Mervyn Smithyman, Anne Chappel, who in 2015 published a novel based on the Zanzibar revolution, *Zanzibar Uhuru: Revolution, Two Women and the Challenge of Survival* (2015).

191. Al-Ghonaimi, *Zanjibār*, 90–101, 113.

192. Niklas Olsen, *History in the Plural: An Introduction to the Work of Reinhart Koselleck* (New York: Berghahn Books, 2012), 294. Reinhart Kosselleck calls this "secondary memory," generated in schools, by families, and by historians. To Jan Assman cultural memory is a static residual memory that continues after the death of the living communicative memory. See Marianne Hirsch, *The Generation of Postmemory: Writing and Visual Culture after the Holocaust* (New York: Columbia University Press, 2012).

193. Michael Lambek, "The Past Imperfect: Remembering as Moral Practice," in *Tense Past: Cultural Essays in Trauma and Memory*, ed. Paul Antze and Michael Lambek (New York: Routledge, 1996), 241.

194. Ali Ahmed Saleh, interview with author, May 30, 2013.

195. Tony Judt, "The Past Is Another Country: Myth and Memory in Postwar Europe," *Daedalus* 121, no. 4 (Fall 1992): 83–118; M. G. Vassanji carefully captures this dynamic among East African Indians in *The Gunny Sack* (London: Heinemann, 1989): the impetus toward memory as an act of self-restitution from the shameful moments of the past.

196. A central aim of Judith Marshall's work. See Marshall, "(Im)mobility in a Sea of Migration: Race, Mobilities, and Transnational Families in Zanzibar and Oman, 1856–2019" (PhD diss., Michigan State University, 2021). Omani returnees have also been active in this field. See Mohamed Nasser al-Sinawi al-Harthi, *Understanding Uganda's Historic Relationship with Oman since 1844* (Muscat: self-published, 2022).

197. See, for instance, James Giblin and David Anthony, "Book Forum: Current Zanzibar commentators and War of Words, War of Stones," *Cultural Dynamics* 28, no. 3 (2016): 320–331.

198. The seizure of power through violent force appears to have embedded a deep paranoia of losing power among certain sections of CCM in Zanzibar. "Averting Violence in Zanzibar's Knife Edge Election" (International Crisis Group, Briefing no. 144, June 11, 2019), www.crisisgroup.org/africa/horn-africa/tanzania/b144-averting-violence-zanzibars-knife-edge-election.

199. Nathalie Arnold Koenings, "'For Us It's What Came After': Locating Pemba in Revolutionary Zanzibar," in *Social Memory, Silenced Voices, and Political Struggle: Remembering the Revolution in Zanzibar*, ed. William Cunningham Bissell and Marie-Aude Fouéré (Dar-es-Salaam: Mkuti wa Nyota, 2018), 145–190.

CONCLUSION

1. Lupa Ramadhani, "Identity Politics and Conflicts in Zanzibar," *African Review: A Journal of African Politics, Development and International Affairs* 44, no. 2 (2017): 172–202.

2. Greg Cameron, "Zanzibar's Turbulent Transition," *Review of African Political Economy* 29, no. 92 (2002): 313–330.

3. "Zanzibar Wave of Violence: A Fact Finding Report on Police Brutality and Election Mismanagement in Zanzibar" (International Federation for Human Rights/Legal and Human Rights Center, no. 307, 2001), /www.refworld.org/pdfid/46f146f10.pdf; and "The Bullets Were Raining: The January 2001 Attack on Peaceful Demonstrators in Zanzibar," *Human Rights Watch Tanzania* 14, no. 3 (April 2002), www.hrw.org/reports/2002/tanzania/zanz0402.pdf.

4. "Kenya: 100 New Refugees Arriving Daily from Zanzibar and Pemba," UNHCR Briefing Notes, February 20, 2001, www.unhcr.org/news/briefing-notes/kenya-100-new-refugees-arriving-daily-zanzibar-and-pemba.

5. Sigrun Ross and Kjetil Tronvoll, "'We Are All Zanzibari!': Identity Formation and Political Reconciliation in Zanzibar," *Journal of Eastern African Studies* 9, no. 1 (2015): 91–109; and Sterling Roop and Kjetil Tronvoll, "Constitutional Discord and Division in Tanzania: The Breakdown of the Government of National Unity in Zanzibar," *Africa Today* 68, no. 2 (2021): 123–140.

6. Marie-Aude Fouéré, "Zanzibariness in the Shadow of an Ambiguous Documentary State," in *Across the Waves: Strategies of Belonging in Indian Ocean Island Societies*, ed. Iain Walker and Marie-Aude Fouéré (Leiden: Brill, 2022), 40–41.

7. Frederick Jjuuko and Godfrey Muriuki, eds., *Shirikisho Ndani ya Shirikisho: Uzoefu wa Muungano wa Tanzania na Mchakato wa Kuiunganisha Afrika Mashariki* (Kampala: Fountain Publishers, 2010), 67; and Suhonen, "Mapinduzi Daima," 71 Such anti-Arab prejudice possibly contributed to the forced resignation of Seif Sharif Hamad in 1988. Cameron, "Zanzibar's Turbulent Transition," 318.

8. Marie-Aude Fouéré argued that they have been replaced by mainland-islander tensions. Fouéré, "Zanzibariness in the Shadow," 23. The 1950s and 1960s were *also* fundamentally about tensions between mainlanders and islanders, which was mapped by most mainlanders onto an Arab-African binary.

9. Based on proven reserves of some twenty-eight trillion cubic feet of gas. Amrit Wilson, *The Threat of Liberation: Imperialism and Revolution in Zanzibar* (London: Pluto Press, 2013), 107–108.

10. "Gingerly Coming Back: After Decades of Silence, Oman Re-establishes Links with East Africa," *The Economist*, April 22, 2014, www.economist.com/baobab/2014/04/22/gingerly-coming-back.

11. "Rais Magfuli akutana na Waziri wa Mafuta na Gesi wa Oman," MaElezo TV, October 18, 2017, www.youtube.com/watch?v=N8MLxQA35KU.

12. The rhetoric of "blood mixture" is ubiquitous in the vernacular historiography as well as in the discourse of Zanzibari intellectuals: Issa Nasser al-Ismaily, *Uzanzibari na Usultani* (Muscat: self-published, 1996), 24; Shaaban al-Farsi, *Zanzibar Historical Accounts* (n.p.: n.d.), 8; and Othman Khamis, "Kwa Ukweli na Uwazi," *Zanzibar Leo*, May 3, 2014.

13. Arif Dirlik, "Race Talk, Race, and Contemporary Racism," *PMLA* 123, no. 5 (October 2008): 1363–1379.

14. Jon Soske, *Internal Frontier: African Nationalism and the Indian Diaspora in Twentieth-Century South Africa* (Athens: Ohio University Press, 2017); Fahad al-Mukrashi, "Oman's Nationality Law Forces Bright Students Abroad," *Gulf News*, April 22, 2016; and Zahra Babar, "The 'Enemy Within': Citizenship Stripping in the Post-Arab Spring GCC," *Middle East Journal* 71, no. 4 (Autumn 2017): 525–543.

15. Nelly Mtema, "Dual Citizenship Now on Horizon," *Tanzania Daily News*, May 28, 2014. For dual citizenship as a theme in African politics, see Robtel Pailey, *Development, Dual Citizenship and Its Discontents in Africa: The Political Economy of Belonging to Liberia* (Cambridge: Cambridge University Press, 2021), 15; and Yossi Harpaz, *Citizenship 2.0: Dual Nationality as a Global Asset* (Princeton, NJ: Princeton University Press, 2019).

16. Ariel Crozon, "Zanzibar en Tanzanie: Essai D'histoire Politique" (Science politique, Universite de Pau et des Pays de L'adour, 1992), 445–446.

17. Marie-Aude Fouéré, "Zanzibaris in the Shadow of an Ambiguous Documentary State," in *Across the Waves: Strategies of Belonging in Indian Ocean Island Societies*, ed. Iain Walker and Marie-Aude Fouéré (Leiden: Brill 2022), 21–48.

18. Mohamed Bakari, *The Democratisation Process in Zanzibar: A Retarded Transition* (Hamburg: Institute of African Affairs, 2001), 122–123; and Haroub Othman, "Tanzania Foreign Policy and Some International Legal Problems," in *Yes, in My Lifetime: Selected Works of Haroub Othman*, ed. Saida Yahya-Othman (Dar-es-Salaam: Mkuti wa Nyota, 2013), 42.

19. As Crozon noted, the Omani government had no real interest in supporting the political opposition in Zanzibar and steered clear of overt commentary on the issue. Crozon, "Zanzibar en Tanzanie," 540.

20. In contrast, low-wage migrant labor is subject to the whims and control of state authorities. Economically, the Omani state benefits from having fewer citizens and more migrant labor. Citizen laborers make claims on rights, they organize and unionize, and the state would be responsible for their long-term care. See K. C. Das and Nilambari Gokhale, "Omanization and Policy and International Migration in Oman," Middle East Institute, February 2, 2010, www.mei.edu/publications/omanization-policy-and-international-migration-oman; Françoise De Bel-Air, "Demography, Migration, and the Labour Market in Oman" (Gulf Labour Markets, Migration and Population [GLMM] Programme of the Migration Policy Center [MPC] and the Gulf Research Center [GRC], Explanatory Note no. 7/2018), http://gulfmigration.org.

21. "Stateless in Burundi: Omanis Search for a Nationality," http://english.alarabiya.net/articles/2012/12/03/253074.html.

22. "Stateless in Burundi."

23. Sana Aiyar, "Anticolonial Homelands across the Indian Ocean: The Politics of the Indian Diaspora in Kenya, ca. 1930–1950," *American Historical Review* 116, no. 4 (October 2011): 987; and Frederick Cooper, "Possibility and Constraint: African Independence in Historical Perspective," *The Journal of African History* 49 no. 2 (2008): 195.

24. Pat Caplan, "'But the Coast, of Course, Is Quite Different': Academic and Local Ideas about the East African Littoral," *Journal of Eastern African studies* 1, no. 2 (2007): 312.

25. Isabel Hofmeyer"The Black Atlantic Meets the Indian Ocean: Forging New Paradigms of Transnationalism for the Global South—Literary and Cultural Perspectives," *Social Dynamics* 33, no. 2 (2007): 3 32. See also similar calls in Pier Larsen, *Ocean of Letters: Language and Creolization in an Indian Ocean Diaspora* (Cambridge: Cambridge University Press, 2009), 9–10.

BIBLIOGRAPHY

Because of the wide range of different kinds of sources I have used, the bibliography is organized by genre and language. Arabic published sources and Swahili published sources are kept distinct, and there are separate sections for published interviews, archives, published primary sources, government and NGO reports, theses and dissertations, websites, journal articles, and books.

INTERVIEWS

The author conducted research interviews with nearly sixty people born in Oman and Zanzibar. All interviews were conducted in Muscat, Oman, unless otherwise noted. Due to IRB restrictions, and to protect my research subjects' identity, interviews (with a couple exceptions noted in the text) have been anonymized and numbered according to a list in the possession of the author. I.S. stands for interview subject, and the number matches a name on the complete list of interviewees held by the author. In parentheses is the birthplace of the interviewee.

I.S. 1, 8/11/2011 (Zanzibar)
I.S. 2, 8/13/2011 (Tanzania)
I.S. 3, 8/14/2011 (Zanzibar)
I.S. 4, 8/14/2011 (Zanzibar)
I.S. 5, 8/17/2011 (Tanzania)
I.S. 6, 8/18/2011 (Oman)
I.S. 7, 8/19/2011 (Oman)
I.S. 8, 8/20/2011 (Kenya)
I.S. 9, 8/20/2011 (Tanzania)
I.S. 10, 8/23/2011 (Oman)
I.S. 11, 8/24/2011 (Zanzibar, Burundi)
I.S. 12, 8/24/2011 (Tanzania)

I.S. 13, 8/25/2011 (Tanzania)
I.S. 14, 8/25/2011 (Burundi)
I.S. 15, 8/26/2011 (Zanzibar)
I.S. 16, 8/29/2011 (Oman)
I.S. 17, 10/30/2012 (Tanzania)
I.S. 18, 11/10/2012 (Tanzania)
I.S. 19, 11/23/2012 (Zanzibar)
I.S. 20, 12/3/2012, (Zanzibar)
I.S. 21, 12/3/2012 (Zanzibar)
I.S. 22, 12/6/2012 (Tanzania)
I.S. 23, 12/6/2012 (Tanzania)
I.S. 24, 12/8/2012 (Zanzibar)
I.S. 24, 12/13/2012 (Tanzania)
I.S. 25, 12/13/2012 (Pemba)
I.S. 26, 12/16/2012 (Zanzibar)
I.S. 27, 1/19/2013 (Tanzania)
I.S. 28, 2/4/2013 (Tanzania)
I.S. 29, 2/12/2013 (Burundi)
I.S. 30, 2/15/2013 (Zanzibar)
I.S. 31, 2/19/2013 (Zanzibar, Rwanda/Burundi)
I.S. 32, 2/20/2013 (Zanzibar)
I.S. 33, 3/1/2013 (Zanzibar)
I.S. 34, 3/3/2013 (Tanzania)
I.S. 35, 3/27/2013 (Zanzibar)
I.S. 36, 4/6/2013 (Tanzania)
I.S. 37, 4/9/2013 (Tanzania)
I.S. 38, 4/13/2013 (Zanzibar)
I.S. 39, 4/16/2013 (Zanzibar)
I.S. 40, 4/18/2013 (Kenya/Ethiopia)
I.S. 41, 4/18/2013 (Zanzibar)
I.S. 42, 5/8/2013 (Uganda)
I.S. 43, 5/13/2013 (Uganda)
I.S. 44, 5/15/2013 (Kenya)
I.S. 45, 5/28/2013 (Zanzibar)
I.S. 46, 5/29/2013 (Uganda)
I.S. 47, 5/29/2013 (Oman)
I.S. 48, 5/30/2013 (Zanzibar)
I.S. 49, 6/10/2013 (Zanzibar)
I.S. 50, 6/18/2013 (Zanzibar)
I.S. 51, 6/22/2013 (Zanzibar)
I.S. 52, 6/23/2013 (Zanzibar)
I.S. 53, 7/26/2013 (Kenya)
I.S. 54 8/1/2013 (Pemba)
I.S. 55, 3/3/2014 (Zanzibar) [conducted in Zanzibar]

I.S. 56, 5/8/2013 (Zanzibar) [conducted in Zanzibar]
I.S. 57, 5/16/2014 (Zanzibar) [conducted in Zanzibar]
I.S. 58, 5/23/2014 (Zanzibar) [conducted in Zanzibar]
I.S. 59, 6/6/2014 (Zanzibar) [conducted in Zanzibar]

ARCHIVES

British Red Cross (BRC), London, United Kingdom
    RCC 1/12/4/190
    RCC 1/12/4/191
    RCC 1/12/4/192
    British Red Cross Annual Report 1964
Charles Young Research Library, Michael Lofchie Collection (MLC), University of California Los Angeles (UCLA)
    Newspapers
        The Adal Insaf
        Mwongozi
        Afrika Kwetu
        Sauti ya Afro-Shirazi
    General publications
        Report of a Commission of Inquiry into Disturbances in Zanzibar during June 1961 (London: Her Majesty's Stationery Office, 1961)
Herskovits Library, Vertical File Tanzania, Northwestern University (NU), Evanston, Illinois
    Habusu
    Free Zanzibar Voice, 1990
International Committee of the Red Cross (ICRC) Archives, Geneva
    B AG 233 203
    B AG 209 203-002
    B AG 225 203-002
    B AG 225 203-004
    B AG 233 203-001
    B AG 233 203-002
    B AG 233 203-003
    B AG 234 203-002
Kharusi Papers (KP). Photographs by James Brennan. Documents in possession of the author. Cited with permission of Sauda Barwani.
The National Archives (TNA), London
    ADM 1/20963
    DO 185/60–61 "Casualties and Refugees of the Zanzibar Revolution"
    FCO 8 "Foreign Office and Foreign and Commonwealth Office: Arabian Department and Middle East Department"
    FO 371 "General Correspondence from 1906–1955"

Oman National Archives (ONA), Muscat
  Records of Oman, 1961–1965, 1966–1971
Qatar Digital Library
  Affairs of the Persian Gulf, Vol. I, British Library: India Office Records and Private Papers
UN High Commission on Refugees (UNHCR)Archives, Geneva
  Classified Subject Files, 1951–1970, Fonds 11, Series 1
    Box 7, 1/BDI/TAN
    Box 32, 1/0/QAT/ZAN
    Box 34, 1/0/SAU/ZAN
    Box 35, 100/GEN/ZAN
    Box 36, 100/ABU/ZAN
    Box 45, 1/ZRE/ZAN
    Box 46, 1/ZAN/GEN, 1/ZAN/BAH, 1/ZAN/ABU, 1/ZAN/KUW, 1/ZAN/DUB
    Box 47, 100/ARE/ZAN, 1/ZAN/SAU
    Box 79, 100/DUB/ZAN
    Box 146, 6/1/DUB
    Box 165, 6/1/SAU
    Box 175, 6/1/ZAN
    Box 182, 6/2/DUB
    Box 184, 6/2/KENYA
    Box 187, 6/2/ZAN
    Box 196, 6/6/ZAN
    Box 256, 15/0/DUB/ZAN
    Box 280, "Manga Arabs—evacuation out from Zanzibar"
    Box 322, 1/GEN/ZAN
Zanzibar National Archives Kilimani, Unguja, Tanzania (ZNA)
  General publications
    James W. Robertson, *The Kenya Coastal Strip : Report of the Commissioner* (London: H. M. Stationery Office, 1961)
    Zanzibar Census, March 1958 (Government of Zanzibar)
    Zanzibar Protectorate, *List of Electors, Constituency: Ngambo* (Zanzibar: The Legislative Council [Elections] Decree, 1957)
  Newspapers
    Al-Falaq
    Mwongozi
  Files
    AB 1/147
    AB 5/20
    AB 26/11, 13, 16, 24, 40, 43, 47, 50, 57, 63, 65, 72, 79
    AK 28/1, 82
    AB 28/82
    AB 45/44

AB 45/45
AK 9/17, 20
AK 14/8
AK 15/1
AK 16/48
AK 17/10, 12, 20
BA 13/37
BA 14/43
DC 8/4-15
DJ 4/1-7
DD 1/6
DO 40/52

NEWSPAPERS AND MAGAZINES

Africa
"A Verbal Safety Valve." *Africa*, December 1982.
Africa Asia
Foy, Colm. "Tanzania Tackles Its Crisis," *Africa Asia*, December 1984.
Africa Events
Rajab, Ahmed. "A Tale of Two Presidents." *Africa Events*, November 1986.
Africa Now
Babu, A. M. "The Tanzania That Might Have Been." *Africa Now*, December 1981.
"State of the Economy: Tanzania Supplement." *Africa Now*, January 1986.
"Tanzanian Push for Privatization." *Africa Now*, August 1986.
Al-Arabiya
"Stateless in Burundi: Omanis Search for a Nationality," December 3, 2012. https://english.alarabiya.net/articles/2012/12/03/253074.
Al-Nuur (Tanzania)
Al-Shabība (Oman)
Saida al-Farsy. "Aina al-Muwāṭana yā Muwāṭin." *al-Shabeeba*, April 24, 2011.
Al-Watan (Oman)
al-Miskery, Sheikh Saleh Hashil. "Ālāf min 'Ahlna Yantadhirūn I'tirāfna bihim." *Al-Watan*, May 9, 2013.
"Rāshid al-'Abri: Ya'ūd li-'Ahlihi ba'd Sitīn 'Āmā min Inqiṭā' akhbārihi," *al-Watan*, March 20, 2013.
Bulletin of Tanzanian Affairs
The Citizen (Tanzania)
Daily Telegraph (UK)
Daima
The East African
The Economist
Free Zanzibar Voice, 1971–1986

Gulf News (Dubai)
Jarīda Oman
 al-Rawwas, Anwār Muhammad. "Al-Insilākh min Lughat-l-Qurān al-Karīm," *Jarīda Oman*, May 19, 2004.
Jawharat Oman
Mawio
Mazrui Annual Newsletter
 Mazrui, Ali A. "Mazrui Annual Newsletter No. 17: On Ancestry, Descent and Identity." Eve of 1993.
Muscat Daily
Mwananchi (Tanzania)
New African
 "Nyerere: The Man and the Challenge." *New African*, October 1980.
New African Development
The New York Times
Oman Daily Observer
Reuters
Shurfaat (Oman)
 al-Bualy, Asya. "Rud ala Aina al-Muwātana ya Muwātin." *Shurfaat*, May 10, 2011.
Tanzania Daily News
Times of Oman
Zanzibar Leo (Zanzibar)
Zanzibar Newsletter

ARABIC PUBLISHED SOURCES

al-Baḥrāni, ʿImād Jāsim. *Zanjibār bi-Mulāmiḥ ʿUmāniyya*. Beirut: Dar Soual, 2017.
al-Balushi, Dr. Khalid. *Istishrāf al-Tajribat-l-ʿUmaniyya fī "Gwādur": Naḥw Khiṭāb Insānī Mutaʿaddad*. Nizwa: University of Nizwa/al-Intishār al-ʿArabi, 2013.
al-Balushi, Saud Salim. *Hadha Watani fī al-Sīrat-l-Ḥiḍāriyya*. Muscat: Ministry of Education, 2006.
al-Barwani, Ali Muhsin. *Al-Ṣirāʿāt wa Al-Wiʾām fī Zanjibār: Dhikriyyāt Ali Muhsin al-Barwani*. Translated by Said Amir. Beirut: Dar al-Gharīr, 2010.
al-Barwani, Muhammad Ali Khamis. *Riḥla Abī al-Ḥārith*. Muscat: Ministry of Heritage and Culture, 2010.
al-Bualy, Asya and Fatma Jinja. *Dhikriyyāt min al-Māḍī al-Jamīd*. Muscat: al-Nahda Publishing, 2010.
al-Busaidi, Al-Seyyid Al-Amjad Hamoud Ahmed Seif. *Al-Dar al-Manẓūm fī Dhikr Mahāsin al-ʾAmṣār al-Rusūm*. edited by Muhammad al-Maḥrūqi. Muscat: Ministry of Heritage and Culture, 2006.

al-Busaidi, Jumm'a Khalifa. *Dirāsāt fī Ma'ālim al-Dawlat-l-Busa'idiyya: al-Ḥaditha min al-Imāma ilā al-Sultana*. Seeb: Maktabat-l-Ḍāmri li-l-Nashr wa al-Tawzī', 2015.

al-Busaidi, Nasr. Ghalib Khalifa. *Riḥlāt 'Umāni ila al-Sharq al-'Ifrīqiyya: al-Wujūd al-'Umani wa Atharihi fī Bilād al-Sharq al-'Ifrīqi Jamāl al-Ṭabī'iyya wa Athar al-Ḥiḍāra*. Muscat: Beirut Bookshop, 2017.

Al-Dirāsāt al- Ijtimā'iyya: Level No. 8. Muscat: Ministry of Education, 2007.

Al-Dirāsāt al-Ijtimā'iyya: Level No. 9. Muscat: Ministry of Education, 2004.

al-Farsy, Sheikh Abdullah Salih. *Al-Busa'idiyyun Hukkam Zanjibar*. (4th edition) Muscat: Ministry of Heritage and Culture, 2005.

al-Ghonaimi. Sheikha. *Zanjibār: Wa Akfān min Rahim Al-'Alam*. Muscat: Maktabat-l-Ḍāmri li-l-Nashr wa al-Tawzī', 2012.

al-Ḥaddad, Seyyid Hamad Ahmad. *Dirāsat al-'Arab wa al-Islam fī Sharq Afrīqiyā*. Beirut: Dar al-Minhaj, 2007.

al-Hinai, Habiba. *'Ā'idūn Ḥaythu al-Ḥulm:, Mashāhid wa-Dhikriyyāt 'auda min Zanjibār wa al-Jazīrat-l-Khaḍrā' ilā 'Uman*. Beirut: Beirut Bookshop, 2013.

al-Ismaily, Issa Nasser. *Zanjibār: Al-Takālib al-Istī'mārī wa Tijārat-l-Riqq*. Translated by Mubarak Khalfan Najim al-Subāhī. Dubai: Dar al-Gharīr, 2012.

al-Khalili, Ahmed. "al-'Umāniyyūn wa Atharahum fi al-Jawānab al-'Ilmiyya wa al-Ma'arfiyya bi-Sharq Ifrīqīyya." In *Fa'āliyyāt wa Nāshiṭ: Ḥiṣād: Anshiṭat al-Muntadā al-Adabī, 1991–1992*, edited by Salim Muhammad al-Ghailānī and Muhammad Ali al-Sulaibi, 177–191. Muscat: Ministry of Heritage and Culture, 1994.

al-Kindi, Muḥsin Ḥamūd. *al-Ṣaḥāfat-l-'Umāniyyat-l-Muhājira wa Shakhṣiyyāthā: Shaikh Hāshil bin Rāshid al-Miskirī Numūdhajā*. Beirut: Riad al-Rayyes Books, 2009.

al-Maamiry, Ahmed Hamoud. *'Uman wa Sharq Ifriqiyya*. 3rd ed. Translated by Muhammad Amin 'Abd Allah. Muscat: Ministry of Heritage and Culture, 2016.

al-Mahrooqi, Mohamed. *Min Forodhani: Youmiyāt Riḥla ilā Zanjibār wa Mumbāsā wa al-Barr al-'Ifrīqiya*. Muscat: Beit Ghushām, 2013.

al-Miskery, Salha Bint Seif Sulaiman. "Aḍwā' Jadīda 'alā al-Mu'atharāt al-Ḥaḍāriyya al-'Umāniyya fi Zanjibār wa al-Jazīra al-Khuẓrā'." In *Namādhij min al-Buḥūth al-Tārīkhiyya al-Fā'iza fī musābiq-l-Muntadā al-Adabī, 1996–97*, 73–116. Muscat: Ministry of Heritage and Culture Oman, 2001.

al-Mugheiry. Saīd Ali. *Juhaynat-l-Akhbār fī tārīkh Zanjibār*. Edited by Muḥammad Alil al-Sulaibi. Muscat: Ministry of Heritage and Culture Oman, 2001.

al-Murjebi, Hamad Muhammad. *Mughāmir 'Umānī fī 'Adghāl 'Ifriqiyyā: Ḥayā Hamad bin Muhammad bin Juma'at-l-Murjibi (Al-Ma'rūf bi-Tībūu Tīb), 1840–1905*. Translated by Muhammad al-Mahrūqi. Cologne: Kamel/Verlag, 2006.

al-Naamani, Said Salim. *Al-Hijrāt al-'Umaniyya ilā Sharq Ifriqiyyā: ma bain al-Qarnain al-Awal wa al-Sāb'a al-Hijrain, Dirāsa Siyāsa wa Haḍāriyya*. Damascus: Dār al-Farqad, 2012.

al-Qasimi, Sultan Muhammad. *Taqsīm al-Imbrāṭūriyyat-l-ʿUmāniyya: 1856–1862*. Sharjah: Al-Qasimi Publications, 2012.

al-Rahbi, Muhammad Seif. *al-Seyyid Marra min Hunā*. Beirut: al-Intishār al-ʿArabi, 2011.

al-Riyami, Nasser Abdullah. *Zanjibār: Shaksiyāt wa Aḥdāth*. Cairo: Maktab Beirut, 2009.

al-Saifi, Muhammad Abdullah Said Nasir. *Ḥikāyāt wa Riwāyāt al-Ibāḍiyya fī Zanjibār wa ma Jāwaruhā min Duwwal Sharq Ifriqiyā*. Muscat: al-Numair, 2013.

al-Shaarawi, Ibrahim. *al-ʿUmāniyyun fī Sharq Afrīqiyā*. Muscat: Ministry of Education, 2005.

al-Ṭaee, Abdullah Muhammad. *Tārikh ʿUmān Al-Siyāsī*. Kuwait: Maktabat-al-Kuwait al-Waṭaniyya, 2008.

al-ʿUmāniyyūn wa qalʿa Mombāsā, no. 9. Muscat: Ministry of National Heritage and Culture, 1994.

al-Unsi, Saud Salim. *al-ʿĀdāt al-ʿUmaniyya*. Muscat: Ministry of Heritage and Culture Oman, 1991.

Ghubash, Dr. Mouza Abid. "Mafhūm al-Mawrūth al-Shaʿabī wa ʿAlāqatihi bi-l-ʿUmuq al-Nafsī wa al-Ijtimāʿī." In in *Faʿāliyyāt wa Nāshiṭ: Ḥiṣād Anshiṭat al-Muntadā al-Adabī, 1991–1992*. edited by Salim Muhammad al-Ghailānī and Muhammad Ali al-Sulaibi, 37–74. Muscat: Ministry of Heritage and Culture, 1993.

Grandmaison, Collete. *Turāthna: Hijrāt al-Ḥarth ila Awāsiṭ al-Qārat-l-'Afriqiyya*. Muscat: Ministry of Heritage and Culture Oman, 1984.

Muhammad, Abdullah Najib. *Dirāsāt fī-l-Adab al-Sawāḥilī: al-Qiṣaṣ al-Shaʿbī*. Cairo: Maktaba al-Nahḍa al-Misriyya, 1987.

Muhammad, Dr. Saleh Maḥrus Muhammad. *Zanjibār: al-Ayām al-Akhīra li-l-Hukm al-ʿUmāni fī Sharq Afrīqiyyā*. Cairo: Al-Maktāb al-ʿArabi li-l-Muʿārif, 2019.

Qirāʾāt wa Dirāsāt wa Buḥūth fī al-Fikr wa al-Adab wa al-Turāth al-ʿUmanī. Muscat: Ministry of Heritage and Culture, 1994.

Ruzaiq, Hamud Muhammad. *Fatḥ al-Mubīn fī Sīrat-l-Sādat-l-Busaʿidīn*. Muscat: Ministry of Heritage and Culture, 1977.

Said, Zāhir. *Tanzih al-Abṣār fī Riḥla Sultān Zanjibār*. Muscat: Ministry of Heritage and Culture, 2008.

Soghayrun, Ibrahim Zein. "Al-Ishām al-ʿUmāni fī al-Majālāt al-Thaqāfiyya wa al-Fikriyya wa al-Kashf an Majāhil al-Qārat-l-Ifrīqīyya fī Al-ʿAhd al-Busaʿīdī." In *Faʿāliyyāt wa Nāshiṭ: Ḥiṣād Anshiṭat al-Muntadā al-Adabī, 1991–1992*, edited by Salim Muhammad al-Ghailānī and Muhammad Ali al-Sulaibi, 73–116. Muscat: Ministry of Heritage and Culture, 1993.

SWAHILI PUBLISHED SOURCES

Abdallah, Hussein Bashir. *Dola Kongwe ya Zanzibar: Kutoka Oman hadi Kongo*. Dar-es-Salaam: Katambi Enterprises, 2013.

———. *Utukufu wa Zanzibar*. Dar-es-Salaam: Kauthar Printers, 2010.
al-Barwani, Ali Muhsin. *Jifunze Kusoma Kiarabu (Kwa Wiki Tatu)*. Dubai: self-published, n.d.
———. *Kujenga na Kubomolewa Zanzibar (Kumbukumbu)*. N.p.: Self-published, 2004.
al-Farsy, Shaaban S. *Mzanzibari Asimilia Hadithi Yake*. Muscat: Self published, 1994.
al-Ismaily, Issa Nasser. *Kinyanganyiro na Utumwa*. Muscat, Oman: Self published, 1999.
———. *Uzanzibari na Usultani*. Muscat: Self-published, 1996.
al-Jahdhamy, Abu Jahdham Nasser. *Taalamu Kiomani*. Muscat: Al-Naḥda Press, 2007.
Barwani, Naila. *Imepita Jana*. Bedfordshire: Bright Pen Publishing, 2010.
el-Murjebi, Hamed Muhammad. *Maisha Ya Hamed Bin Muhammed El Murjebi Yaani Tippu Tip Kwa Maneno Yake Mwenyewe*. Nairobi: East African Literature Bureau, 1958.
Fairooz, Aman Thani. *Ukweli ni Huu (Kuusuta Uwongo)*. Dubai: Self-published, 1994.
Ghassany, Harith. *Kwa Heri Ukoloni, Kwa Heri Uhuru! Zanzibar na Mapinduzi ya Afrabia*. N.p.: Lulu Press, 2010.
Haj, Maulid. *Umleavyo*. Nairobi: Oxford University Press, 1990.
Hashil, Hashil S. *Mimi, Umma Party na Mapinduzi ya Zanzibar*. Paris: DL2A Buluu Publishing, 2018.
Jjuuko, Frederick, and Godfrey Muriuki, eds. *Shirikisho Ndani ya Shirikisho: Uzoefu wa Muungano wa Tanzania na Mchakato wa Kuiunganisha Afrika Mashariki*. Kampala: Fountain Publishers, 2010.
Juma, Ali Shaaban. *Abeid Karume, 1905–1972*. Zanzibar: Rafiki Publishers, 2013.
Kusupa, Mwinjilisti K. *Maisha Yangu Gerezani (2001–2007) au Simulizi la Siku elfu moja mia nane themanini na nane za Mateso*. Dar-es-Salaam: Karljamer Print Technology, 2011.
L-Hatimy, Said Abdulla Seif. *Tunda Liliwalo Hadharani*. N.p.: Self-published, 1995.
Mdundo, Minael-Hosanna O. *Masimulizi ya Sheikh Thabit Kombo Jecha*. Dar-es-Salaam: Dar es Salaam University Press, 1995.
Mrina, B. F., and W. T. Mattoke. *Mapambano ya Ukombozi Zanzibar*. Dar-es-Salaam: Tanzania Publishing House, 1980.
Saleh, Ally. "Matatizo ya Kisiasa ya Zanzibar: Mgororo au Hasara ya Mfumo wa Vyama Vingi?" In *Siasa katika Tanzania na uchaguzi mkuu wa 1995*, edited by D. Mukangara and R. Mukandala. Dar-es-Salaam: Interpress Tanzania Ltd., 1998.
Shafi, Adam. *Kasri ya Mwinyi Fuad*. Dar-es-Salaam: Tanzanian Publishing House, 1978.
———. *Haini*. Nairobi: Longhorn Publishers, 2003.
———. *Kuli*. Nairobi: Longhorn Publishers, 2005.

Shariff, Ibrahim Noor. *Tanzania na Propaganda za Udini*. Muscat: Self published, 2014.

———. *Tungo Zetu*. Trenton, NJ: Red Sea Press, 1988.

Yunus, Zuhura. *Biubwa Amour Zahor: Mwanamke Mapinduzi*. Dar-es-Salaam: Vision Publishing Ltd., 2021.

Ziddy, Issa. *Lugha ya Kiarabu Zanzibar: Historia na Mbinu za Usomeshaji*. Zanzibar: Self-published, 2011.

OTHER PUBLISHED PRIMARY SOURCES

al-Mazrui, al-Amin Ali. *The History of the Mazru'i Dynasty of Mombasa*. Oxford: Oxford University Press, 1996.

Barwani, Sauda, R. Feindt, L. Gerhardt, L. Harding, and L. Wimmelbücker, eds. *Unser Leben von der Revolution und danach—Maisha yetu kabla ya mapinduzi na baadaye*. Cologne: Rüdiger Köppe, 2003.

Barwani, Sauda, and Ludwig Gerhart, eds. *Life and Poems of Bi Zainab Himid, 1920–2002*. Berlin: Rudiger Koppe, 2012.

Casson, Lionel, ed. *The Periplus Maris Erythraei: Text with Introduction, Translation, and Commentary*. Princeton, NJ: Princeton University Press, 1989.

Kresse, Kai, and Hassan Mwakimako, eds. *Guidance (Uwongozi) by Sheikh al-Amin Mazrui: Selections from the First Swahili Islamic Newspaper*. Leiden: Brill, 2016.

McRitchie, James, and Sigvard von Sicard. *An Azanian Trio: Three East African Arabic Historical Documents*. Leiden: Brill, 2020.

GOVERNMENT AND NGO REPORTS

"Averting Violence in Zanzibar's Knife Edge Election." International Crisis Group, Briefing no. 144, June 11, 2019. www.crisisgroup.org/africa/horn-africa/tanzania/b144-averting-violence-zanzibars-knife-edge-election.

"The Bullets Were Raining: The January 2001 Attack on Peaceful Demonstrators in Zanzibar." *Human Rights Watch Tanzania* 14, no. 3 (April 2002). www.hrw.org/reports/2002/tanzania/zanzo402.pdf.

De Bel-Air, Françoise. "Demography, Migration, and the Labour Market in Oman." Gulf Labour Markets, Migration and Population (GLMM) program of the Migration Policy Center (MPC) and the Gulf Research Center (GRC), Explanatory Note no. 7/2018, http://gulfmigration.org.

Diplomatic List: United States Department of State. Washington, DC: US Government Printing Office, 1979.

Gately, Dermot. "Lessons from the 1986 Oil Price Collapse." Brookings Papers on Economic Activity, 1986. www.brookings.edu/wp-content/uploads/1986/06/1986b_bpea_gately_adelman_griffin.pdf, 237–284.

"Kenya: 100 New Refugees Arriving Daily from Zanzibar and Pemba." UNHCR Briefing Notes, February 20, 2001. www.unhcr.org/news/briefing-notes/kenya-100-new-refugees-arriving-daily-zanzibar-and-pemba.

Ministry of Education. *Illiteracy Eradication Programs and Plans in Sultanate of Oman: Fruitful Efforts*. Muscat: Directorate General of Education Programs/Department of Continuing Education, 2010.

Oman National Plan for the Alliance of Civilizations. Muscat: n.p., 2011.

Qanūn Tandhīm al-Jinsiya al-Omaniyya. Muscat: Ministry of Interior, 1972.

Wilson, F. B. *A Note on Adult Literacy amongst the Rural Population of the Zanzibar Protectorate*. Zanzibar: Government Printer, 1939.

"Zanzibar Wave of Violence: A Fact Finding Report on Police Brutality and Election Mismanagement in Zanzibar." International Federation for Human Rights/Legal and Human Rights Center no. 307, 2001. www.refworld.org/pdfid/46f146f10.pdf.

DISSERTATIONS AND THESES, CONFERENCE PAPERS, PROCEEDINGS, AND LECTURES

al-Bīmāni, Mahmoud Khalifa. "Duwwar Wasā'il al-'I'lām al-'Umaniyya al-Ḥukūmiyya Ibrāz Munjazāt al-Wujūd al-'Umanī fi Sharq 'Afrīqiyā: Dirāsa Istiṭlā'iyya Taḥlīliyya." Paper presented at the International Conference on the Omani Role in East Africa 11–13 December 2012, Sultan Qaboos University.

Alem, Fehmi. "The Question of Oman in the United Nations." MA thesis, The American University, 1967.

al-Hassen, Maha Yassine Ziad. "To Tell What the Eye Beholds: A Post 1945 Transnational History of Afro-Arab 'Solidarity Politics.'" PhD diss., University of Southern California, 2017.

al-Khalili, Majid. "Oman's Foreign Policy: Foundations and Practice." PhD diss., Florida International University, 2005.

al-Mazrui, Ahmed Issa Omar. "Zanzibar-Oman Relations: A Historical Perspective." MA thesis, University of Dar-es-Salaam, 1996.

Anderson, Benedict. "Long-Distance Nationalism: World Capitalism and the Rise of Identity Politics." The Wertheim Lecture, Centre for Asian Studies Amsterdam, 1992.

Biersteker, Ann. "The Significance of the Swahili Literary Tradition and Interpretation of Early Twentieth-Century Political Poetry." Boston University African Studies Center, AH no. 6, 1990.

Brass, Paul. "On the Study of Riots, Pogroms, and Genocide." Prepared for the Sawyer Seminar session "Processes of Mass Killing" at the Center for Advanced Study in the Behavioral Sciences, Stanford University, December 6–7, 2002. www.anveshi.org.in/wp-content/uploads/2017/04/Ripogen.pdf.

Crozon, Ariel. "Zanzibar en Tanzanie: Essai D'histoire Politique." Science politique, Universite de Pau et des Pays de L'adour, 1992.

Daly, Samuel. "Our Mother Is Afro-Shirazi, Our Father Is the Revolution: The 1964 Zanzibar Revolution in Tanzanian History." Senior thesis, Columbia University, 2009.

El Sheikh, Mahmoud Abel Rahman. "State, Cloves, and Planters: A Reappraisal of British Colonialism in Zanzibar, 1890–1934." PhD diss., University of California Los Angeles, 1986.

Grimstad, Ann. "Zanzibar: The Nine-Hour Revolution." PhD diss., University of Florida, 2018.

Issa, Amina Ameir. "'From Stinkibar to Zanzibar': Disease, Medicine, and Public Health in Colonial Urban Zanzibar, 1870–1963." PhD diss., University of KwaZulu Natal, 2009.

Khoury, Nabeel A. "The Politics of Intra-Regional Migration." In *International Migration in the Arab World: Proceedings of an ECWA Population Conference, Nicosia, Cyprus, 11–16 May 1981*, 753–776. Beirut: UNECWA, 1982.

Marshall, Judith. "(Im)mobility in a Sea of Migration: Race, Mobilities, and Transnational Families in Zanzibar and Oman, 1856–2019." PhD diss., Michigan State University, 2021.

Mathews, Nathaniel. "The Zinjibari Diaspora, 1698–2014: Citizenship, Migration and Revolution in Zanzibar, Oman and the Post-War Indian Ocean." PhD diss., Northwestern University, 2016.

Suhonen, Riikka. "Mapinduzi Daima—Revolution Forever: Using the 1964 Revolution in Nationalistic Political Discourses in Zanzibar." MA thesis, University of Helsinki, 2009.

Syversen, Inger Lise. "Intentions and Reality in Architectural Heritage Management: In Search of the Influence of International Policy Documents on Contemporary Sustainable Local Heritage Management." PhD diss., Chalmers University of Technology, Sweden, 2007.

Telepneva, Natalia. "Our Sacred Duty: The Soviet Union, the Liberation Movements in the Portuguese Colonies, and the Cold War, 1961–1975." PhD diss., London School of Economics, 2014.

Wahab, Saada. "Nationalization and Re-distribution of Land in Zanzibar: The Case Study of Western District, 1965–2008." MA thesis, University of Dar-es-Salaam, 2011.

Wortmann, Kimberly. "Omani Religious Networks in Contemporary Tanzania and Beyond." PhD diss., Harvard University, 2018.

WEBSITES AND ONLINE AUDIOVISUAL MATERIALS

al-Bahry. "Death in Zanzibar 1964." August 18, 2009. http://zanzibarwebsite.com/m/discussion?id=2712669%3ATopic%3A59773.

al-Murjebi, Muhammad. "Min as-Sawāhil." Episode 11, July 19, 2013. Oman TV. www.youtube.com/watch?v=zQ-X4x3Ks3E.

al-Zinjibari, Khatib M. Rajab. "Nyerere against Islam in Zanzibar and Tanganyika." n.d. https://www.juliusnyerere.org/resources/view/nyerere_against_islam_in_zanzibar_and_tanganyika#:~:text=Nyerere%2C%20a%20devout%20Catholic%20saw,a%20radical%20Christian%20from%20Uganda.

Chachage, Chambi. "Dispensing Survivor's Justice in Zanzibar." *Pambazuka News*, April 15, 2010. www.pambazuka.org/governance/dispensing-survivors-justice-zanzibar.

Das, K. C., and Nilambari Gokhale. "Omanization and Policy and International Migration in Oman." Middle East Institute. February 2, 2010. www.mei.edu/publications/omanization-policy-and-international-migration-oman.

Lori, Noora, and Yoana Kuzmova. "Who Counts as 'People of the Gulf'? Disputes over the Arab Status of Zanzibaris in the United Arab Emirates." *POMEPS: Racial Formations in Africa and the Middle East: A Transregional Approach*, n.d. https://pomeps.org/who-counts-as-people-of-the-gulf-disputes-over-the-arab-status-of-zanzibaris-in-the-uae.

"Majzurah Zanjibār al-Juz'a al-Thānī." 2020. www.youtube.com/watch?v=UQoSOrHcExY.

"The Mass Graves of Zanzibar." https://zanzibarhistory.org/mass_graves.htm.

"Rais Magfuli akutana na Waziri wa Mafuta na Gesi wa Oman." October 18, 2017. MaElezo TV. www.youtube.com/watch?v=N8MLxQA35KU.

"Sheikh Ali Bin Muhsin al-Barwani na Siasa za Zanzibar." Interview by Professor Ibrahim Noor, 1996. Posted February 8, 2016, www.youtube.com/watch?v=sdUqIOYPzE8.

JOURNAL ARTICLES

AbuSharaf, Rogaia. "The Omani-Zanzibari Family: Between Politics and Pedigree in an Empire on the Rim." *Journal of the Women of the Middle East and the Islamic World* 16 (2018): 60–89.

Ahmed, Chanfi. "Networks of Islamic NGOs in sub-Saharan Africa: Bilal Muslim Mission, African Muslim Agency (Direct Aid), and al Haramayn." *Journal of Eastern African Studies* 3, no. 3 (2009): 426–437.

Aiyar, Sana. "Anticolonial Homelands across the Indian Ocean: The Politics of the Indian Diaspora in Kenya, ca. 1930–1950." *American Historical Review* 116, no. 4 (October 2011): 987–1013.

al-Azri, Khalid. "Change and Conflict in Contemporary Omani Society: The Case of Kafa'a in Marriage." *British Journal of Middle Eastern Studies* 37, no. 2 (August 2010): 121–137.

al-Mahrouqi, Mohammad. "Religious Discourse in the Poetry of Abū Muslim al-Bahlānī." *Journal of African Cultural Studies* 14, no. 1 (June 2001): 89–106.

al-Rashoud, Talal. "From Muscat to the Maghreb: Pan-Arab Networks, Anticolonial Groups, and Kuwait's Arab Scholarships (1953–1961)." *Arabian Humanities* 12 (2019). https://doi.org/10.4000/cy.5004.

Ankersmit, S. N. "The Sublime Dissociation of the Past: Or How to Be(come) What One Is No Longer." *History and Theory* 40, no. 3 (2001): 295–323.

Arenberg, Meg. "Swahili Poetry's Digital Geographies: WhatsApp and the Forming of Cultural Space." *Postcolonial Text* 15, nos. 3 and 4 (2020): 1–24.

Armstrong, John. "Mobilized and Proletarian Diasporas." *American Political Science Review* 70, no. 2 (1976): 393–408.

Askew, Kelly. "Sung and Unsung: Musical Reflections on Tanzanian Postsocialisms." *Africa* 76, no. 1 (2006): 15–43.

Babar, Zahra. "'The "Enemy Within': Citizenship Stripping in the Post-Arab Spring GCC." *Middle East Journal* 71, no. 4 (Autumn 2017): 525–543.

Bang, Anne. "Authority, Piety, Writing and Print: A Preliminary Study of the Circulation of Islamic Texts in Late Nineteenth and Early Twentieth-Century Zanzibar." *Africa: Journal of the International African Institute* 81, no. 1 (2011): 89–107.

Baynham, Mark ."The East African mutinies of 1964." *Journal of Contemporary African Studies* 8, no. 1 (1989): 153–180.

Becker, Sascha O., Sharun Mukand, and Ivan Yotzov. "Persecution, Pogroms and Genocide: A Conceptual Framework and New Evidence." *Explorations in Economic History* 86 (2022): 1–18.

Beckingham, C. F. "The Reign of Aḥmad Ibn Saʿīd, Imam of Oman." *Journal of the Royal Asiatic Society of Great Britain and Ireland* 3 (1941): 257–260.

Benner, Erica. "Nationality without Nationalism." *Journal of Political Ideologies* 2, no. 2 (1997): 189–206.

Bentley, Jerry. "A New Forum for Global History." *Journal of World History* 1, no. 1 (1990): iii–v.

Bhacker, Reda M. "Family Strife and Foreign Intervention: Causes in the Separation of Zanzibar from Oman: a Reappraisal." *Bulletin of the School of Oriental and African Studies* 54, no. 2 (1991): 269–280.

Bishara, Fahad. "The Many Voyages of Fateh Al-Khayr: Unfurling the Gulf in the Age of Oceanic History." *International Journal of Middle East Studies* 52, no. 3 (2020): 397–412.

Bissell, W. C. "Engaging Colonial Nostalgia." *Cultural Anthropology* 20, no. 2 (May 2005): 215–248.

Bjerk, Paul K. "Sovereignty and Socialism in Tanzania: The Historiography of an African State." *History in Africa* 37 (2010): 275–319.

Brennan, James. "Lowering the Sultan's Flag: Sovereignty and Decolonization in Coastal Kenya." *Comparative Studies in Society and History* 50, no. 4 (2008): 831–861.

Brewin, David. "Zanzibar Government-Changes." *Bulletin of Tanzanian Affairs*, no. 30 (May 1988). www.tzaffairs.org/category/issue-number/issue-30/.

Brielle, E. S., J. Fleisher, and S. Wynne-Jones, K. Sirak, N. Broomandkhosbacht, K. Callan, E. Curtis, et al. "Entwined African and Asian Genetic Roots of Medieval Peoples of the Swahili Coast." *Nature* 615 (2023): 866–873.

Brunotti, Irene. "From Baraza to Cyberbaraza: Interrogating Publics in the Context of the 2015 Zanzibar Electoral Impasse." *Journal of Eastern African Studies* 13, no. 1 (2019): 18–34.

Cameron, Greg. "Zanzibar's Turbulent Transition." *Review of African Political Economy* 29, no. 92 (2002): 313–330.

Caplan, Pat. "'But the Coast, of Course, Is Quite Different': Academic and Local Ideas about the East African Littoral." *Journal of Eastern African Studies* 1, no. 2 (2007): 305–320.

Chadha, Ashish. "Ambivalent Heritage: Between Affect and Ideology in a Colonial Cemetery." *Journal of Material Culture* 11, no. 3 (2006): 339–363.

Chande, Abdin. "Muslim-State Relations in East Africa Under Conditions of Military and Civilian or One-Party Dictatorships." *Historia Actual Online* 17 (2008): 97–111.

Chase, H. "Zanzibar Treason Trial." *Review of African Political Economy* 6 (1976): 19–33.

Chatty, Dawn. "Women Working in Oman: Individual Choice and Cultural Constraints." *International Journal of Middle East Studies* 32, no. 2 (May 2000): 241–254.

Chittick, Neville. "A New Look at the History of Pate." *The Journal of African History* 10, no. 3 (1969): 375–391.

Clayton, Anthony. "The General Strike in Zanzibar, 1948." *The Journal of African History* 17, no. 3 (1976): 417–434.

Constantin, François. "Sur les modes populaires d'action diplomatique: Affaires de famille et affaires d'État en Afrique orientale." *Revue française de science politique* 36, no. 5 (1986): 672–694.

Cosemans, Sara. "The Politics of Dispersal: Turning Ugandan Colonial Subjects into Postcolonial Refugees (1967–76)." *Migration Studies* 6, no. 1 (March 2018): 99–119.

Crane, Susan. "Writing the Individual Back into Collective Memory." *American Historical Review* 102, no. 5 (December 1997): 1372–1385.

Crystal, Jill. "Coalitions in Oil Monarchies: Kuwait and Qatar." *Comparative Politics* 21, no. 4 (1989): 427–443.

Connerton, Paul. "Seven Types of Forgetting." *Memory Studies* 1, no. 1 (2008): 59–71.

Constantin, François, and François Le Guennec-Coppens. "Dubai Street: Zanzibar." *African Politics* 30 (1988): 7–21.

Cooper, Fred. "Africa and the World Economy." *African Studies Review* 24, nos. 2/3 (June–September 1981): 1–86.

———. "Possibility and Constraint: African Independence in Historical Perspective." *The Journal of African History* 49 no. 2 (2008): 167–196.

Dirlik, Arif. "Race Talk, Race, and Contemporary Racism." *PMLA* 123, no. 5 (October 2008): 1363–1379.

Duara, Prasenjit. "Transnationalism and the Predicament of Sovereignty: China, 1900–1945." *American Historical Review* 102, no. 4 (October 1997): 1030–1051.

Dutkiewicz, Piotr, and Gavin Williams. "'All the King's Horses and All the King's Men Couldn't Put Humpty Dumpty Together.'" *IDS Bulletin* 18, no. 3 (1987): 1–6.

Eickelman, Dale F. "From Theocracy to Monarchy: Authority and Legitimacy in Inner Oman, 1935–1957." *International Journal of Middle East Studies* 17, no. 1 (1985): 3–24.

Eken, Sena. "Breakup of the East African Community." *Finance and Development* (December 1979): 36–40. www.elibrary.imf.org/view/journals/022/0016/004/article-A010-en.xml.

El Shakry, Omnia. "History without Documents: The Vexed Archives of Decolonization in the Middle East." *American Historical Review* 120, no. 3 (2015): 920–934.

Elkins, Caroline. "Looking beyond Mau Mau: Archiving Violence in the Era of Decolonization." *American Historical Review* 120, no. 3 (June 2015): 852–868.

Entelis, John. "Islamist Politics and the Democratic Imperative: Comparative Lessons from the Algerian Experience." *Journal of North African Studies* 9, no. 2 (2004): 202–215.

Fair, Laura. "'It's Just No Fun Anymore': Women's Experiences of Taarab before and after the 1964 Zanzibar Revolution." *International Journal of African Historical Studies* 35, no. 1 (2002): 61–81.

Fay, Franziska. "'Kuishi Ughaibuni': Emplaced Absence, the Zanzibar Diaspora Policy, and Young Men's Experiences of Belonging in Zanzibar and Oman." *Journal of Indian Ocean World Studies* 6, no. 1 (2022): 10–37.

———. "'To Everyone Who Told Zanzis That They Are Not Omani': Young Swahili-speaking Omanis' Belonging in Postdiaspora Oman." *Arabian Humanities* 15 (2022). https://doi.org/10.4000/cy.7304.

"50 Years of the Union Between Tanganyika and Zanzibar." Special issue, *African Review: A Journal of African Politics, Development and International Affairs* 41, no. 1 (2014).

Fouéré, Marie-Aude. "Film as Archive: *Africa Addio* and the Ambiguities of Remembrance in Contemporary Zanzibar." *Social Anthropology* 24, no. 1 (February 2016): 82–96.

———. "Recasting Julius Nyerere in Zanzibar: The Revolution, the Union and the Enemy of the Nation." *Journal of Eastern African Studies* 8, no. 3 (April 2014): 478–496.

———. "Reinterpreting Revolutionary Zanzibar in the Media Today: The Case of Dira Newspaper." *Journal of Eastern African Studies* 6, no. 4 (2012): 672–689.

———. "Remembering the Dark Years (1964–1975) in Contemporary Zanzibar." *Encounters: The International Journal for the Study of Culture and Society* 5 (2012): 113–126.

Ghazal, Amal. "Omani Fatwas and Zanzibari Cosmopolitanism: Modernity and Religious Authority in the Indian Ocean." *Muslim World* 105, no. 2 (April 2015): 236–250.

———. "The Other Frontiers of Arab Nationalism: Ibadis, Berbers, and the Arabist-Salafi Press in the Interwar Period." *International Journal of Middle East Studies* 42, no. 1 (2010): 105–122.

Giblin, James, and David Anthony. "Book Forum: Current Zanzibar commentators and War of Words, War of Stones." *Cultural Dynamics* 28, no. 3 (2016): 320–331.

Glassman, Jonathon. "Creole Nationalists and the Search for Nativist Authenticity in Twentieth-Century Zanzibar: The Limits of Cosmopolitanism." *The Journal of African History* 55, no. 2 (July 2014): 229–247.

———. "Slower Than a Massacre: The Multiple Sources of Racial Thought in Colonial Africa." *American Historical Review* 109, no. 3 (June 2004): 720–754.

———. "Sorting Out the Tribes: The Creation of Racial Identities in Colonial Zanzibar's Newspaper Wars." *The Journal of African History* 41, no. 3 (2000): 395–428.

Goswami, Manu "Rethinking the Modular Nation Form." *Comparative Studies of Society and History* 44, no. 4 (2002): 770–799.

Grandmaison, Colette Le Cour. "Rich Cousins, Poor Cousins: Hidden Stratification among the Omani Arabs in Eastern Africa." *Africa* 59, no. 2 (1989): 176–184.

Gurnah, Abdulrazak. *Admiring Silence*. New York: New Press, 1996.

———. *By The Sea*. London: Bloomsbury, 2001.

———. *Memory of Departure*. London: Jonathan Cape, 1987.

———. *Pilgrims Way*. London: Jonathan Cape, 1988.

Haji, Mohammed Makame. "The Quick Sands of Law and Marriage in Zanzibar: Some Missing Footnotes." *Journal of Culture Society and Development* 15 (2016): 31–41.

Hansen, Randall. "The Kenyan Asians, British Politics, and the Commonwealth Immigrants Acts, 1968." *Historical Journal* 42, no. 3 (1999): 809–834.

Hardinge, Arthur H. "Legislative Methods in the Zanzibar and East Africa Protectorates." *Journal of the Society of Comparative Legislation* 1, no. 1 (March 1899): 1–10.

Hasan, Mushirul. "Partition Narratives." *Social Scientist* 30 (2002): 24–53.

Hirji, Zulfikar. "Relating Muscat to Mombasa: Spatial Tropes in the Kinship Narratives of an Extended Family Network in Oman." *Anthropology of the Middle East* 2, no. 1 (Spring 2007): 55–69.

Ho, Engseng. "Empire through Diasporic Eyes: A View from the Other Boat." *Comparative Studies in Society and History* 46, no. 2 (2004): 210–246.

Hoffman, Valerie. "Muslim-Christian Encounters in Late Nineteenth-Century Zanzibar." *MIT Electronic Journal of Middle East Studies* 5 (Fall 2005): 59–78.

Hofmeyer, Isabel. "The Black Atlantic Meets the Indian Ocean: Forging New Paradigms of Transnationalism for the Global South—Literary and Cultural Perspectives." *Social Dynamics* 33, no. 2 (2007): 3–32.

Holes, Clive D. "Language and Identity in the Arabian Gulf." *Journal of Arabian Studies* 1, no. 2 (2011): 129–145.

Hopkins, A. G. "Rethinking Decolonization." *Past and Present* 200, no. 1 (2008): 211–247.

Hundle, Aneeth Kaur. "Insecurities of Expulsion: Emergent Citizenship Formations and Political Practices in Postcolonial Uganda." *Comparative Studies of South Asia, Africa, and the Middle East* 39, no. 1 (2019): 8–23.

Hyden, Goran, and Bo Karlstrom. "Structural Adjustment as a Policy Process: The Case of Tanzania." *World Development* 21, no. 9 (1993): 1395–1404.

Jamal, Manal. "The Tiering of Citizenship and Residency and the 'Hierarchization' of Migrant Communities: The United Arab Emirates in Historical Context." *International Migration Review* 49, no. 3 (Fall 2015): 601–632.

Jansen, Stef. "The Violence of Memories: Local Narratives of the Past after Ethnic Cleansing in Croatia." *Rethinking History: The Journal of Theory and Practice* 6, no. 1 (2002): 77–93.

Jones, Chris. "Plus Ça Change, Plus Ça Reste Le Même? The New Zanzibar Land Law Project." *Journal of African Law* 40, no. 1 (1996): 19–42.

Judt, Tony. "The Past Is Another Country: Myth and Memory in Postwar Europe." *Daedalus* 121, no. 4 (Fall 1992): 83–118.

Kara, Taushif. "Provincializing Mecca? (1924–1969)." *Global Intellectual History* 7, no. 6 (2022): 1037–1057.

Kelly, John D., and Martha Kaplan, "Nation and Decolonization: Toward a New Anthropology of Nationalism." *Anthropological Theory* 1, no. 4 (2001): 419–437.

Keshodkar, Akbar. "Marriage as a Means to Preserve Asian-ness: The Post-Revolutionary Experience of the Asians of Zanzibar." *Journal of Asian and African Studies* 45, no. 2 (April 2010): 226–240.

Kharusi, Nafla. "The Ethnic Label Zinjibari: Politics and Language Choice Implications among Swahili Speakers in Oman." *Ethnicities* 12, no. 3 (2012): 335–353.

———. "Identity and Belonging among Ethnic Return Migrants of Oman." *Nationalism and Ethnic Politics* 19, no. 4 (2013): 424–446.

Lee, Christopher. "The Indian Ocean during the Cold War: Thinking through a Critical Geography." *History Compass* 11, no. 7 (2013): 524–530.

Leichtman, Mara. "Da 'wa as Development: Kuwaiti Islamic Charity in East and West Africa." *Muslim World* 112 (Winter 2022): 100–129.

Lewis, Earl. "'To Turn as on a Pivot': Writing African Americans into a History of Overlapping Diasporas." *American Historical Review* 100, no. 3 (1995): 765–787.

Limbert, Mandana. "Caste, Ethnicity, and the Politics of Arabness in Southern Arabia." *Comparative Studies of South Asia, Africa, and the Middle East* 34, no. 3 (2014): 590–598.

———. "Escape from Zanzibar: Refugees, Documents, and the Indian Ocean Shipping Regime." *International Journal Of Middle East Studies* 54 (2022): 753–757.

Lofchie, Michael. "Agrarian Crisis and Economic Liberalization in Tanzania." *Journal of Modern African Studies* 16, no. 3 (1978): 451–475.

———. "Was Okello's Revolution a Conspiracy?" *Transition* 33 (1967): 36–42.

Markle, Seth. "'Brother Malcom, Comrade Babu': Black Internationalism and the Politics of Friendship." *Biography* 36, no. 3 (Summer 2013): 540–567.

Martin, B. G. "Arab Migrations to East Africa in Medieval Times." *International Journal of African Historical Studies* 7, no. 3 (1974): 367–390.

Martin, Esmond Bradley. "The Geography of Present-Day Smuggling in the Western Indian Ocean: The Case of the Dhow." *Great Circle* 1, no. 2 (October 1979): 18–35.

Martin, Peter J. "The Zanzibar Clove Industry" *Economic Botany* 45, no. 4 (October–December 1991): 450–459.

Mathews, Nathaniel. "'Arab-Islamic Slavery': A Problematic Term for a Complex Reality." *Research Africa Reviews* 4, no. 2 (August 2020). https://sites.duke.edu/researchafrica/files/2020/08/1-4-Arab-Islamic-Slavery-2020.pdf.

Matory, J. Lorand. "The English Professors of Brazil: On the Diasporic Roots of the Yoruba Nation." *Comparative Studies in Society and History* 41, no. 1 (January 1999): 72–103.

Mazrui, Ali. "Tanzaphilia: A Diagnosis." *Transition* 6, no. 31 (1967): 20–26.

McCurdy, Sheryl. "Fashioning Sexuality: Desire, Manyema Ethnicity, and the Creation of the Kanga, 1880–1900." *International Journal of African Historical Studies* 39, no. 3 (2006): 441–469.

McMahon, Elizabeth. "Developing Workers: Coerced and 'Voluntary' Labor in Zanzibar, 1909–1970." *International Labor and Working Class History* 92 (Fall 2017): 114–133.

———. "'A Solitary Tree Builds Not': Heshima, Community, and Shifting Identity in Postemancipation Pemba Island." *International Journal of African Historical Studies* 39, no. 2 (2006): 197–219.

Meyer, John, John Boli, George M. Thomas, and Francisco O. Ramirez. "World Society and the Nation-State." *American Journal of Sociology* 103, no. 1 (1997): 144–181.

Milford, Ismay, Gerard McCann, Emma Hunter, and Daniel Branch. "Another World? East Africa, Decolonisation, and the Global History of the Mid-Twentieth Century." *The Journal of African History* 62, no. 3 (2021): 394–410.

Mkilifi, M. H. Abdulaziz. "Triglossia and Swahili-English Bilingualism in Tanzania." *Language in Society* 1, no. 2 (October 1972): 197–213.

Murer, George "Baloch Mashkat (Muscat) and the Sultan Qaboos Era: Cultural Performance, Cosmopolitanism and Translocal Consciousness" *Arabian Humanities* 15 (2022). https://doi.org/10.4000/cy.7146.

Myers, Garth. "Narrative Representations of Revolutionary Zanzibar." *Journal of Historical Geography* 26, no. 3 (July 2000): 429–448.

Myers, Garth Andrew. "Isle of Cloves, Sea of Discourses: Writing about Zanzibar." *Ecumene* 3, no. 4 (1996): 408–426.

Nagar, Richa. "The South Asian Diaspora in Tanzania: A History Retold." *Comparative Studies of South Asia, Africa and the Middle East* 16, no. 2 (Fall 1996): 62–80.

Nonneman, Gerd, and Marc Valeri. "The 'Heritage' Boom in the Gulf: Critical and Interdisciplinary Perspectives." *Journal of Arabian Studies* 7, no. 2 (2017): 155–156.

Nora, Pierre. "Between Memory and History: Les Lieux de Memoire." *Representations* 26 (Spring 1989): 7–24.
Nyberg-Sorensen Ninna, Nicholas Van Hear, and Poul Engberg-Pedersen. "The Migration-Development Nexus: Evidence and Policy Options State-of-the-Art Overview." *International Migration* 3, no. 4 (2002): 49–73.
Oberst, Timothy. "Transport Workers, Strikes and the 'Imperial Response': Africa and the Post World War II Conjuncture." *African Studies Review* 31, no. 1 (1988): 117–33.
O'Dell, Emily Jane. "Yesterday Is Not Gone: Memories of Slavery in Zanzibar and Oman in Memoirs, Fiction, and Film." *Journal of Global Slavery* 5, no. 3 (2020): 357–401.
Oishi, Takashi. "Indian Muslim Merchants in Mozambique and South Africa: Intra-Regional Networks in Strategic Association with State Institutions, 1870s–1930s." *Journal of the Economic and Social History of the Orient* 50, nos. 2/3 (2007): 287–324.
Okawa, Mayuko. "The Empire of Oman in the Formation of Oman's National History: An Analysis of School Social Studies Textbooks and Teachers' Guidelines." *Research Note*, nos. 31–32 (2015): 95–120. www.jstage.jst.go.jp/article/ajames/31/1/31_KJ00010032648/_pdf/-char/en.
———. "Nationality Law and Concept of Nation in Oman: A Case Study of Omani Returnees from Africa." *Modern Middle East* 45 (2008): 22–35.
Okolo, Julius Emeka "Liberia: The Military Coup and Its Aftermath." *World Today* 37 no. 4 (1981): 149–157.
Ongkili, James P. "The British and Malayan Nationalism, 1946–1957." *Journal of Southeast Asian Studies* 5, no. 2 (1974): 255–277.
Oonk, Gijsbert. "Gujarati Asians in East Africa, 1880–2000: Colonization, Decolonization, and Complex Citizenship Issues." *Diaspora Studies* 8, no. 1 (2015): 66–79.
Page, Melvin. "Tippu Tip and the Arab 'Defense' of the East African Slave Trade." *Etudes d'histoire africaine* 6 (1974): 105–117.
Peterson, J. E. "Oman's Diverse Society: Northern Oman." *Middle East Journal* 58, no. 1 (2004): 32–51.
Phillips, S. G., and Jennifer Hunt. "'Without Sultan Qaboos, We Would Be Yemen': The Renaissance Narrative and the Political Settlement in Oman." *Journal of International Development* 29, no. 5 (July 2017): 645–660.
Phillipson, Robert. "Slaves and Saviours: Images of Arabs and Englishmen in *Uhuru wa Watumwa*." *Ba Shiru* 13, no. 1 (1989): 40–49.
Pouwels, Randall. "Eastern Africa and the Indian Ocean to 1800: Reviewing Relations in Historical Perspective." *International Journal of African Historical Studies* 35 (2002): 385–425.
Pouwels, Randall L. "The Medieval Foundations of East African Islam." *International Journal of African Historical Studies* 11, no. 3 (1978): 201–226.
Prestholdt, Jeremy. "Locating the Indian Ocean: Notes on the Postcolonial Reconstitution of Space." *Journal of Eastern African Studies* 9, no. 3 (2015): 440–467.

———. "Politics of the Soil: Separatism, Autochthony, and Decolonization at the Kenyan Coast." *The Journal of African History* 55, no. 2 (2014): 249–270.

Probst, Peter. "Iconoclash in the Age of Heritage." *African Arts* 45, no. 3 (2012): 10–13.

Rabi, Uzi. "The Ibadhi Imamate of Muhammad Bin 'Abdallah al-Khalili (1920–54): The Last Chapter of a Lost and Forgotten Legacy." *Middle Eastern Studies* 44, no. 2 (2008): 169–188.

Ramadhani, Lupa. "Identity Politics and Conflicts in Zanzibar." *African Review: A Journal of African Politics, Development and International Affairs* 44, no. 2 (2017): 172–202.

Rawlence, Ben. "Briefing: The Zanzibar Election." *African Affairs* 104, no. 416 (July 2005): 515–523.

Roberts, George. "MOLINACO, the Comorian Diaspora, and Decolonisation in East Africa's Indian Ocean." *The Journal of African History* 62, no. 3 (2021): 411–429.

Robertson, P. A. "Zanzibar—Crossroads of East Africa." *Journal of the Royal Society for the Encouragement of Arts, Manufactures and Commerce* 112, no. 5096 (July 1964): 607–614.

Romero, Patricia. "Seyyid Said bin Sultan buSaid of Oman and Zanzibar: Women in the Life of this Arab Patriarch." *British Journal of Middle East Studies* 39, no. 3 (December 2012): 372–391.

Roop, Sterling, and Kjetil Tronvoll. "Constitutional Discord and Division in Tanzania: The Breakdown of the Government of National Unity in Zanzibar." *Africa Today* 68, no. 2 (2021): 123–140.

Ross, Sigrun, and Kjetil Tronvoll. "'We Are All Zanzibari!': Identity Formation and Political Reconciliation in Zanzibar." *Journal of Eastern African Studies* 9, no. 1 (2015): 91–109.

Ruggie, John Gerard. "Territoriality and Beyond: Problematizing Modernity in International Relations." *International Organization* 47, no. 1 (Winter 1993): 139–174.

Safran, William. "Diasporas in Modern Societies: Myths of Homeland and Return." *Diaspora* 1, no. 1 (Spring 1991): 83–99.

Sanders, E. R. "A Small Stage for Global Conflicts: Decolonization, the Cold War, and Revolution in Zanzibar." *Canadian Journal of History* 55, no. 2 (December 2017): 479–508.

Sanders, Ethan R. "Conceiving the Tanganyika-Zanzibar Union in the Midst of the Cold War: Internal and International Factors." *African Review* 41, no. 1 (2014): 35–70.

Sheriff, Abdul. "Race and Class in the Politics of Zanzibar." *Afrika Spectrum* 36, no. 3 (2001): 301–318.

Sinha, Subir. "Lineages of the Developmentalist State: Transnationality and Village India." *Comparative Studies in Society and History* 50, no. 1 (2008): 57–90.

Spear, Thomas T. "Traditional Myths and Historian's Myths: Variations on the Singwaya Theme of Mijikenda." *History in Africa* 1 (1974): 67–84.

Staudacher, Sandra. "Shifting Urban Margins: Accessing Unequal Spaces of Ageing and Care in Zanzibar and Muscat." *Anthropological Forum* 29, no. 1 (2019): 77–94.

Strauss, Scott. "Contested Meanings and Conflicting Imperatives: A Conceptual Analysis of Genocide." *Journal of Genocide Research* 3, no. 3 (2001): 349–375.

Tanner, R. E. S. "Cousin Marriage in the Afro-Arab Community of Mombasa, Kenya." *Africa: Journal of the International African Institute* 34, no. 2 (April 1964): 127–138.

Tarrow, Sidney. "Social Movements in Contentious Politics: A Review Article." *American Political Science Review* 90, no. 4 (December 1996): 874–883.

Turner, Simon. "'These Young Men Show No Respect for Local Customs'—Globalisation and Islamic Revival in Zanzibar." *Journal of Religion in Africa* 39, no. 3 (2009): 237–261.

Valeri, Marc. "Nation-Building and Communities in Oman Since 1970: The Swahili-Speaking Omanis in Search of Identity." *African Affairs* 106, no. 424 (2007): 479–496.

van Prooijen, J. W., and K. M. Douglas. "Conspiracy Theories as Part of History: The Role of Societal Crisis Situations." *Memory Studies* 10, no. 3 (2017): 323–333.

Vansina, Jan. "New Linguistic Evidence and 'the Bantu Expansion.'" *The Journal of African History* 36, no. 2 (1995): 173–195.

Vaughan, C. M. "The Politics of Regionalism and Federation in East Africa, 1958–1964." *Historical Journal* 62, no. 2 (2018): 519–540.

Vianello, Alessandra. "One Hundred Years in Brava: The Migration of Umar Ba Umar from Hadhramaut to East Africa and Back, c. 1890–1990." *Journal of Eastern African Studies* 6, no. 4 (2012): 655–671.

Walker, Lydia. "Decolonization in the 1960s: On Legitimate and Illegitimate Nationalist Claims-Making." *Past & Present* 242, no. 1 (February 2019): 227–264.

Westerlund, David. "Freedom of Religion under Socialist Rule in Tanzania, 1961–1977." *Journal of Church and State* 24, no. 1 (Winter 1982): 87–103.

Wilkinson, John. "Oman and East Africa: New Light on Early Kilwan History from the Omani Sources." *International Journal of African Historical Studies* 14, no. 2 (1981): 272–305.

Willis, Justin, and George Gona. "Tradition, Tribe and State in Kenya: The Mijikenda Union, 1945–1980." *Comparative Studies in Society and History* 55, no. 2 (2013): 448–473.

Wortmann, Kimberly. "Ibadi Muslim Schools in Post-Revolutionary Zanzibar." *Africa* 92, no. 2 (March 2022): 249–264.

———. "Reading Ibāḍī Women's Legacies through Stone Town's Built Environment." *Islamic Africa* 12 (2021): 1–26.

Yahya-Othman, Saida, ed. *Yes, in My Lifetime: Selected Works of Haroub Othman.* Dar-es-Salaam: Mkuti wa Nyota, 2013.

Żbik, Sebastian. "The Omani Prince in the Search for Protectors: Abdulaziz bin Said's Struggle for Power and Money in the Time of Growing British Dominance in the Indian Ocean Region." *Journal of Colonialism and Colonial History* 23, no. 1 (2022). https://doi.org/10.1353/cch.2022.0010.

Zenker, Olaf. "Autochthony, Ethnicity, Indigeneity and Nationalism: Time-Honouring and State-Oriented Modes of Rooting Individual–Territory-

Group Triads in a Globalizing World." *Critical Anthropology* 31, no. 1 (2011): 63–81.

Ziddy, Issa. "Hasan b. Amir al-Shirazi (1880–1979)." *Sudanic Africa* 16 (2005): 1–26.

BOOKS AND BOOK CHAPTERS

Abblas, Shiblak. "Arabia's Bidoon." In *Statelessness and Citizenship: A Comparative Study on the Benefits of Nationality*, edited by Brad Blitz and Maureen Lynch, 174–186. Cheltenham: Edward Elgar, 2011.

Abdalla, Abdillatif. *Sauti ya Dhiki*. Nairobi: Oxford University Press, 1973.

Abdulla, Abdulkhaleq. "The Impact of Globalization on Arab Gulf States." In *Globalization and the Gulf*, edited by John W. Fox, Nada Mourtada-Sabbah, and Mohammed Al Mutawa. New York: Routledge, 2006.

Abdullah, Muhammad Morsy. *The United Arab Emirates: A Modern History*. London: Croom Helm, 1978.

Aiyar, Sana. *Indians in Kenya: The Politics of Diaspora*. Boston: Harvard University Press, 2015.

Al Ismaily, Salem Ben Nasser. *The Sultanate of Zanzibar*. Indianapolis: Dog Ear Publishing, 2014.

al-Azri, Khalid. *Social and Gender Inequality in Oman: The Power of Religious and Political Tradition*. London: Routledge, 2013.

al-Barwani, Ali Muhsin. *Conflict and Harmony in Zanzibar*. Dubai: Self-published, 1997.

al-Buraey, Muhammad. *Administrative Development: An Islamic Perspective*. London: Routledge, 2010. First published by Kegan Paul International, 1985.

al-Busaidi, Saud Ahmed. *Memoirs of an Omani Gentleman from Zanzibar*. Muscat: al-Roya Press, 2012.

Alexander, Jeffrey C., Ron Eyerman, Bernhard Giesen, Neil J. Smelser, and Piotr Sztompka. *Cultural Trauma and Collective Identity*. Berkeley: University of California Press, 2004.

Aley, Juma. *Enduring Links*. Dubai: Union Printing Press, 1994.

———. *Zanzibar in the Context*. New Delhi: Lancers Books, 1988.

al-Fahim, Mohammed. *From Rags to Riches: A Story of Abu Dhabi*. London: London Centre of Arab Studies, 1995.

al-Farsi, Shaaban. *Zanzibar Historical Accounts*. n.p., n.d.

al-Farsi, Sulaiman. *Democracy and Youth in the Middle East: Islam, Tribalism and the Rentier State in Oman*. New York: Routledge, 2013.

al-Farsy, Abdalla Saleh. *Seyyid Said bin Sultan*. Zanzibar: Mwongozi Printing Press, 1947.

al-Harthi, Muhammad Nasser al Sinawi. *Understanding Uganda's Historic Relationship with Oman since 1844*. Muscat: Self-published, 2022.

Ali, Syed. *Dubai: Gilded Cage*. New Haven, CT: Yale University Press, 2010.

al-Ismailiya, Shahira. *The Story of Our Father*. Muscat: Self-published, 2014.

al-Ismaily, Issa Nasser. *Will Zanzibar Regain Her Past Prosperity*. Muscat: Self-published, 2015.
Allen, Calvin, Jr. *The Modernization of the Sultanate*. Boulder, CO: Westview Press, 1987.
Allen, Calvin, and W. Lynn Rigsbee II. *Oman under Qaboos: From Coup to Constitution, 1970–1996*. London: Routledge, 2000.
Allen, Danielle. *Talking to Strangers: Anxieties of Citizenship Since Brown v. Board of Education*. Chicago: University of Chicago Press, 2004.
al-Maamiry, Ahmed Hamoud. *Islamism and Economic Prosperity in Third World Countries*. New Delhi: Lancers Press, 1983.
———. *Oman and East Africa*. New Delhi: Lancers Books, 1979.
———. *Omani Sultans in Zanzibar (1832–1964)*. New Delhi: Lancers Books, 1988.
———. *Whither Oman*. New Delhi: Lancers Publishers, 1981.
al-Nakib, Farah. *Kuwait Transformed: A History of Oil and Urban Life*. Stanford, CA: Stanford University Press, 2016.
Alonso, Ana María. "'Territorializing the Nation' and 'Integrating the Indian': 'Mestizaje' in Mexican Official Discourses and Public Culture." In *Sovereign Bodies: Citizens, Migrants and States in the Postcolonial World*, edited by Thomas Blom Hansen, and Finn Stepputat, 39–60. Princeton, NJ: Princeton University Press, 2005.
al-Rasheed, Madawi. "Transnational Connections and National Identity Zanzibari Omanis in Muscat." In *Monarchies and Nations: Globalisation and Identity in the Arab States of the Gulf*, edited by Paul Dresch and James Piscatori, 96–113. London: I. B. Tauris, 2005.
al-Riyami, Ahmed. *My Pride and Joy*. Muscat: Self-published, 2007.
———. *Quite Another*. Muscat: Self-published, 2010.
———. *Saluting My Hero*. Muscat: Self published, 2006.
al-Riyami, Nasser. *Zanzibar: Personalities and Events*. Translated by Ali Rashid al-Abri. Beirut: Beirut Bookshop, 2012.
alShehabi, Omar. "Histories of Migration in the Gulf." in Abdulhadi Khalaf, et al. (eds.) *Transit States: Labour, Migration and Citizenship in the Gulf*. London: Pluto Press, 2015.
al-Tawqi, Habiba. *Diamond Life: Autobiography of Habiba al-Tawqi*. Dubai: Index Media, 2008.
al-Yousef, Mohamed Musa. *Oil and the Transformation of Oman*. London: Stacey International, 1995.
Aminzade, Ronald. *Race, Nation and Citizenship in Post-Colonial Africa: The Case of Tanzania*. Cambridge: Cambridge University Press, 2014.
Anderson, Benedict. *Imagined Communities*. London: Verso, 2006.
Anghie, Anthony. *Imperialism, Sovereignty and the Making of International Law*. Cambridge: Cambridge University Press, 2004.
Ankersmit, F. R. *Historical Representation*. Stanford, CA: Stanford University Press, 2002.

Anthony, John Duke. *Arab States of the Lower Gulf: People, Politics, Petroleum*. Washington, DC: The Middle East Institute, 1975.
Appadurai, Arjun. *Modernity at Large: Cultural Dimensions of Globalization*. Minneapolis: University of Minnesota Press, 1996.
Arsan, Andrew. *Interlopers of Empire: The Lebanese Diaspora in Colonial French West Africa*. Oxford: Oxford University Press, 2014.
Askew, Kelly. *Performing the Nation: Swahili Music and Cultural Politics in Tanzania*. Chicago: University of Chicago, 2002.
———. "Tanzanian Newspaper Poetry: Political Commentary in Verse." In *Remembering Nyerere in Tanzania: History, Memory, Legacy*, edited by Marie-Aude Fouéré, 213–250. Dar-es-Salaam: Mkuti wa Nyota Publishers, 2015.
Assman, Jan. "Communicative and Cultural Memory." In *Cultural Memories: The Geographical Point of View*, edited by Peter Meusburger, Michael Heffernan, and Edgar Wunder, 15–27. Heidelberg: Dordrecth, 2011.
Ayany, Samuel G. *A History of Zanzibar: A Study in Constitutional Development*. Nairobi: East African Literature Bureau, 1970.
Baalawy, Ahmed Idarus. *Nyerere and Muslim Tanzania*. Portsmouth: The Zanzibar Organization, 1982/1983.
Babakerim. *The Aftermath of the Zanzibar Revolution*. Muscat: Self-published, 1994.
Bakari, Mohamed. *The Democratisation Process in Zanzibar: A Retarded Transition*. Hamburg: Institute of African Affairs, 2001.
Baldacchino, Godfrey. "Displaced Passengers: States, Movements, and Disappearances in the Indian Ocean." In *Connectivity in Motion: Island Hubs in the Indian Ocean World*, edited by Burkhard Schnepel and Ed Alpers, 93–110. New York: Palgrave-Macmillan, 2018.
Bang, Anne. "Cosmopolitanism Colonised? Three Cases from Zanzibar, 1890–1920." In *Struggling with History: Islam and Cosmopolitanism in the Western Indian Ocean*, edited by Kai Kresse and Ed Simpson, 167–188. New York: Columbia University Press, 2008.
Barash, Jeffrey. *Collective Memory and the Historical Past*. Chicago: University of Chicago Press, 2016.
Barber, Karin, ed. *Africa's Hidden Histories: Everyday Literacy and Making the Self*. Bloomington: Indiana University Press, 2006.
Barraclough, Geoffrey. *An Introduction to Contemporary History*. New York: Penguin, 1967.
Bates, Robert H. *Markets and States in Tropical Africa*. Berkeley: University of California Press, 1981.
Beasant, John, and Christopher Ling. *Sultan in Arabia: A Private Life*. Edinburgh: Mainstream Publishing, 2004.
Bell, Duncan, ed. *Memory, Trauma and World Politics: Reflections on the Relationship between Past and Present*. New York: Palgrave Macmillan, 2006.
Bennett, Norman. *A History of the Arab State of Zanzibar*. London: Methuen, 1978.

Benton, Lauren. *Law and Geography in European Empires, 1400–1900*. Cambridge: Cambridge University Press, 2009.

Bertz, Ned. *Diaspora and Nation in the Indian Ocean: Transnational Histories of Race and Urban Space in Tanzania*. Honolulu: University of Hawai'i Press, 2015.

Bhacker, Reda. *Trade and Empire in Muscat and Zanzibar: Roots of British Domination*. New York: Routledge, 1992.

Binte-Farid, Irtefa. "'True' Sons of Oman: National Narratives, Genealogical Purity and Transnational Connections in Modern Oman." In *Gulfization of the Arab World*, edited by Marc Owen Jones, Ross Porter, and Marc Valeri, 41–56. Berlin, Germany: Gerlach Press, 2018.

Bishara, Fahad. *Sea of Debt: Law and Economic Life in the Western Indian Ocean, 1780–1950*. Cambridge: Cambridge University Press, 2017.

Bissell, William Cunningham. *Urban Design, Chaos, and Colonial Power in Zanzibar*. Bloomington: Indiana University Press, 2011.

Bjerk, Paul. *Building a Peaceful Nation: Julius Nyerere and the Establishment of Sovereignty in Tanzania*. Rochester, NY: University of Rochester, 2015.

Blustein, Jeffrey. *The Moral Demands of Memory*. Cambridge: Cambridge University Press, 2012.

Bock-Luna, Birgit. *The Past in Exile: Serbian Long Distance Nationalism and Identity in the Wake of the Third Balkan War*. Berlin: Lit Verlag, 2007.

Boer, Nienke. *The Briny South: Displacement and Sentiment in the Indian Ocean World*. Durham, NC: Duke University Press, 2023.

Bose, Sugata. *A Hundred Horizons: The Indian Ocean in the Age of Global Empire*. Cambridge, MA: Harvard University Press, 2006.

Bosniak, Linda. *The Citizen and the Alien: Dilemmas of Contemporary Membership*. Princeton, NJ: Princeton University Press, 2008.

Brass, Paul. *Theft of an Idol: Text and Context in the Representation of Collective Violence*. Princeton, NJ: Princeton University Press, 1997.

Breckenridge, Keith. Introduction to *Registration and Recognition: Documenting the Person in World History*, edited by Keith Breckenridge and Simon Szreter, 1–36. London: British Academy, 2012.

Brennan, James. "Radio Cairo and the Decolonization of East Africa, 1953–1964." In *Making a World after Empire: The Bandung Moment and Its Political Afterlives*, edited by Christopher J. Lee, 173–195. Athens: Ohio University Press, 2010.

Brennan, James R. "Julius Rex: Nyerere through the Eyes of His Critics, 1953–2013." In *Remembering Nyerere in Tanzania: History, Memory and Legacy*, edited by Marie-Aude Fouéré, 143–169. Dar-es-Salaam: Mkuti wa Nyota, 2015.

———. *Taifa: Making Nation and Race in Urban Tanzania*. Athens: Ohio University Press, 2012.

Breuilly, John. *Nationalism and the State*. Manchester: Manchester University Press, 1993.

Bromber, Katrin. "Working with 'Translocality': Conceptual Implications and Analytical Consequences." In *Regionalizing Oman: Political, Economic, and Social Dynamics*, 63–72. New York: Springer, 2013.

Bsheer, Rosie. *Archive Wars: The Politics of History in Saudi Arabia*. Stanford, CA: Stanford University Press, 2020.

Burgess, G. Thomas. "An Imagined Generation: Umma Youth in Nationalist Zanzibar." In *In Search of a Nation: Histories of Authority and Dissidence in Tanzania*, edited by Gregory Maddox and James Giblin, 216–249. Dar-es-Salaam: Mkuti wa Nyota 2005.

———. "Mao in Zanzibar: Nationalism, Discipline, and the (De)Construction of Afro-Asian Solidarities." In *Making a World After Empire: The Bandung Movement and Its Political Afterlives*, edited by Christopher Lee, 196–234. Athens: Ohio University Press, 2010.

———. "Memories, Myths, and Meanings of the Zanzibar Revolution." In *War and Peace in Africa*, edited by Toyin Falola and Raphael Chijioke Njoku, 429–450. Durham, NC: Carolina Academic Press, 2010.

———. *Race, Revolution and the Struggle for Human Rights in Zanzibar: The Memoirs of Ali Sultan Issa and Seif Sharif Hamad*. Athens: Ohio University Press, 2009.

———. "The Rise and Fall of a Socialist Future: Ambivalent Encounters between Zanzibar and East Germany in the Cold War." In *Navigating Socialist Encounters: Moorings and (Dis)Entanglements between Africa and East Germany during the Cold War*, edited by Marcia Schenck, Immanuel R. Harisch, Anne Dietrich, and Eric Burton, 169–192. Berlin: De Gruyter Oldenbourg, 2021.

Burke, Roland. *Decolonization and the Evolution of International Human Rights*. Philadelphia: University of Pennsylvania Press, 2010.

Burton, Andrew, and Helene Charton-Bigot, eds. *Generations Past: Youth in East African History*. Athens: Ohio University Press, 2010.

Burton, Eric. "Diverging Visions in Revolutionary Spaces: East German Advisers and Revolution from Above in Zanzibar, 1964–1970." In *Between East and South: Spaces of Interaction in the Globalizing Economy of the Cold War*, edited by Anna Calori, Anne-Kristin Hartmetz, Bence Kocsev, James Mark, and Jan Zofka, 85–116. Berlin: De Gruyter, 2019.

Byrne, Jeffrey James. "Africa's Cold War." In *The Cold War in the Third World*, edited by Robert J. McMahon, 101–123. Oxford: Oxford University Press, 2013.

Callaci, Emily. *Street Archives and City Life: Popular Intellectuals in Postcolonial Tanzania*. Durham, NC: Duke University Press, 2017.

Cameron, Greg. "Political Violence, Ethnicity and the Agrarian Question in Zanzibar." In *Swahili Modernities: Identity, Development and Power on the Coast of East Africa*, edited by Pat Caplan and Farouk Topan, 103–119. Trenton, NJ: Africa World Press, 2004.

Carter, John R. L. *Tribes in Oman*. London: Peninsular Publishing, 1982.

Casco, Jose Arturo Saavedra. *Utenzi, War Poems, and the German Conquest of East Africa: Swahili Poetry as a Historical Source*. Trenton, NJ: Africa World Press, 2007.

Chande, Abdin. *Islam, Ujamaa, and Community Development: A Case Study of Religious Currents in East Africa*. San Francisco: Austin and Winfield Publishers, 1998.

Chappel, Anne. *Zanzibar Uhuru: Revolution, Two Women and the Challenge of Survival*. N.p.: CreateSpace Independent Publishing, 2015.

Chatty, Dawn. "L'activite feminine en Oman: Entre choix individual et contraintes culturelles." In *L'Oman contemporain: Etat, territoire, identite*, edited by Marc Lavergne and Brigitte Dumortier, 261–277. Paris: Editions Karthala, 2002.

Cheyette, Bryan. *Diasporas of the Mind Jewish and Postcolonial Writing and the Nightmare of History*. New Haven, CT: Yale University Press, 2013.

Clark, Terence. *Underground to Overseas: The Story of Petroleum Development Oman*. London: Stacey International, 2007.

Clayton, Anthony. *The Zanzibar Revolution and Its Aftermath*. London: C. Hurst, 1981.

Coakley, John. *Nationalism, Ethnicity and the State: Making and Breaking Nations*. Los Angeles: Sage Publications, 2012.

Cohen, Dennis L. "Class and the Analysis of African Politics." In *The Political Economy of Africa: Problems and Prospects*, edited by D. Cohen and J. Daniel, 85–111. London: Longman, 1981.

Cohen, Robin. *Global Diasporas*. New York: Routledge, 2008.

Confino, Alon. *The Nation as a Local Metaphor: Wurtemberg, Imperial Germany, and National Memory, 1871–1918*. Chapel Hill: University of North Carolina Press, 1997.

Confino, Alon, and Peter Fritzsche, eds. *The Work of Memory: New Directions in Study of German Society and Culture*. Urbana: University of Illinois Press, 2002.

Connah, Graham. *African Civilizations: An Archaeological Perspective*. New York: Cambridge University Press, 2001.

Cook-Martin, David. *Scramble for Citizens: Dual Nationality and State Competition for Immigrants*. Palo Alto, CA: Stanford University Press, 2013.

Cooke, Miriam. *Tribal Modern: Branding New Nations in the Arab Gulf*. Berkeley: University of California Press, 2014.

Cooper, Fred. *Africa since 1940*. Cambridge: Cambridge University Press, 2002.

———. *Colonialism in Question: Theory, Knowledge, History*. Berkeley: University of California Press, 2005.

Cooper, Frederick. *From Slaves to Squatters: Plantation Labor and Agriculture in Zanzibar and Coastal Kenya*. Portsmouth, NH: Heinemann, 1997.

Craggs, Ruth, and Claire Wintle, eds. *Cultures of decolonization: Transnational Productions and Practices, 1945–1970*. Manchester: Manchester University Press, 2016.

Creet, Julia. Introduction to *Memory and Migration: Multidisciplinary Approaches to Memory Studies*, edited by Andrea Klitzmann and Julia Creet, 3–28. Toronto: University of Toronto Press, 2011.

Davis, Eric, and Nicolas Gavrielides, eds. *Statecraft in the Middle East: Oil, Historical Memory, and Popular Culture*. Gainesville: University of Florida Press, 1991.

Davoliūtė, Violeta, and Tomas Balkelis, eds. *Narratives of Exile and Identity: Soviet Deportation Memoirs*. Budapest: Central European University Press, 2018.

de la Cadena, Marisol. *Indigenous Mestizos: The Politics of Race and Culture in Cuzco, Peru, 1910–1991*. Durham, NC: Duke University Press, 2000.

de Vries, Tity. "Not an 'Ugly American': Sal Tas, a Dutch Reporter as Agent of the West in Africa." In *Transnational Anti-Communism and the Cold War: Agents, Activities and Networks*, edited by Luc van Dongen, Stephanie Roulin, and Giles Scott-Smith, 64–78. New York: Palgrave Macmillan, 2014.

Decker, Corrie. *Mobilizing Zanzibari Women: The Struggle for Respectability and Self-Reliance in Colonial East Africa*. New York: Palgrave Macmillan, 2014.

Demshuk, Andrew. *The Lost German East: Forced Migration and the Politics of Memory*. Cambridge: Cambridge University Press, 2012.

Development in Oman, 1970–1974. Muscat: Ministry of Development, National Statistical Department, 1975.

Dietrich, Christopher R. W. *Oil Revolution: Anticolonial Elites, Sovereign Rights, and the Economic Culture of Decolonization*. Cambridge: Cambridge University Press, 2017.

Dirlik, Arif. "It Is Not Where You Are from, It is Where You Are At: Place-Based Alternatives to Diaspora Discourse." In *World on the Move: Globalization, Migration and Cultural Security*, edited by Jonathan Friedman and Shalini Randeria, 141–165. London: I. B. Tauris, 2004.

———. *Postmodernity's Histories: The Past as Legacy and Project*. Lanham. MD: Rowman & Littlefield, 2000.

Dresch, Paul. "Debates on Marriage and Nationality in UAE." In *Monarchies and Nations: Globalisation and Identity in the Arab States of the Gulf*, edited by Paul Dresch and James Piscatori, 149–150. London: I. B. Tauris, 2005.

Dufoix, Stephane. *Diasporas*. Translated by William Rodamor and Roger Waldinger. Berkeley: University of California Press, 2008.

Dunn, Kevin C., and Martin Boas. *Politics of Origin in Africa: Autochthony, Citizenship and Conflict*. London: Zed Books, 2013.

Eades, Domenyk, ed., and Zayana al-Badaei, trans. *The Pioneer Professor Fatma Salem Seif Al-Maamary (1911–2002): A Historical, Documentary and Academic Study*. Muscat: The Ministry of Education, 2013.

Earle, Jonathon. *Colonial Buganda and the End of Empire: Political Thought and Historical Imagination in Africa*. New York: Cambridge University Press, 2017.

Eickelman, Christine. *Women and Community in Oman*. New York: New York University Press, 1984.

Eisenstadt, S. N. *Paradoxes of Democracy: Fragility, Continuity, and Change*. Baltimore, MD: Johns Hopkins University Press, 1999.

El Mallakh, Ragaei. *Kuwait: Economic Development and Regional Cooperation*. Chicago: University of Chicago Press, 1968.

Embree, Ainslee. "Imperialism and Decolonization." In *The Columbia History of the Twentieth Century*, edited by Richard Bulliet, 147–171. New York: Columbia University Press, 1998.

Esedebe, P. Olisanwuche. *Pan-Africanism: The Idea and the Movement*. Washington, DC: Howard University Press, 1982.

Eyerman, Ron. "The Past in the Present: Culture and the Transmission of Memory." In *The Collective Memory Reader*, edited by Jeffrey Olick, Vered Vinitzky Seroussi, and Daniel Levy, 304–306. Oxford: Oxford University Press, 2011.

Eyerman, Ron, and Giuseppe Sciortino. Introduction to *The Cultural Trauma of Decolonization: Colonial Returnees in the National Imagination*, edited by Ron Eyerman and Giuseppe Sciortino, 1–25. New York: Palgrave Macmillan, 2020.

Fabian, Steven. *Making Identity on the Swahili Coast: Urban Life, Community, and Belonging in Bagamoyo*. Cambridge: Cambridge University Press, 2019.

Fair, Laura. *Pastimes and Politics: Culture, Community, and Identity in Post-Abolition Urban Zanzibar, 1890–1945*. Athens: Ohio University Press, 2001.

Falola, Toyin. *Nationalism and African Intellectuals*. Rochester, NY: Boydell and Brewer, 2004.

Fouéré, Marie-Aude. "Recasting Julius Nyerere in Zanzibar: The Revolution, the Union, and the Enemy of the Nation." In *Remembering Nyerere in Tanzania: History Memory Legacy*, edited by Marie-Aude Fouéré, 171–196. Dar-es-Salaam: Mkuti wa Nyota Publishers, 2015.

———. "Zanzibariness in the Shadow of an Ambiguous Documentary State." In *Across the Waves: Strategies of Belonging in Indian Ocean Island Societies*, edited by Iain Walker and Marie-Aude Fouéré, 21–48. Leiden: Brill, 2022.

Freeman, Christopher. "Technology and Invention." In *The Columbia History of the 20th Century*, edited by Richard Bulliet, 314–344. New York: Columbia University Press, 1998.

Freitag, Ulrike. *Indian Ocean Migrations and State Formation in Hadhramaut*. Leiden: Brill, 2003.

Fuccaro, Nelida. *Histories of City and State in the Persian Gulf: Manama since 1800*. New York: Cambridge University Press, 2009.

Gause, F. Gregory. "Gulf Regional Politics: Revolution, War and Rivalry." In *Dynamics of Regional Politics: Four Systems on the Indian Ocean Rim*, edited by W. Howard Wriggins, 23–88. New York: Columbia University Press, 1992.

Gause, Gregory. *Oil Monarchies: Domestic and Security Challenges in the Arab Gulf States*. New York: Council on Foreign Relations, 1994.

Gelvin, James, and Nile Green, eds. *Global Muslims in the Age of Steam and Print*. Berkeley: University of California Press, 2014.

Ghazal, Amal. *Islamic Reform and Arab Nationalism: Expanding the Crescent from the Mediterranean to the Indian Ocean, 1880s–1930s*. New York: Routledge, 2010.
Gibau, Gina Sanchez. "Cyber CVs: Online Conversations on Cape Verdean Diaspora Identities." In *Diasporas in the New Media Age: Identity, Politics, and Community*, edited by Pedro Oiarzabal and Andoni Alonso, 110–121. Reno: University of Nevada Press, 2010.
Gilbert, Erik. *Dhows and the Colonial Economy of Zanzibar, 1860–1970*. Athens: Ohio University Press, 2005.
———. "Oman and Zanzibar: The Historical Roots of a Global Community." In *Cross Currents and Community Networks: The History of the Indian Ocean World*, edited by Himanshu Prabha Ray and Edward A. Alpers, 163–178. Oxford: Oxford University Press, 2007.
Gillis, John. *Commemorations: The Politics of National Identity*. Princeton, NJ: Princeton University Press, 1994.
Gilpin, Robert. *The Challenge of Global Capitalism: The World Economy in the 21st Century*. Princeton, NJ: Princeton University Press, 2000.
Glassman, Jonathon. "Racial Violence, Universal History, and Echoes of Abolition in Twentieth-Century Zanzibar." In *Abolition and Imperialism in Britain, Africa and the Atlantic*, edited by Derek Peterson, 175–206. Athens: Ohio University/Swallow Press, 2010.
———. *War of Words, War of Stones: Racial Thought and Violence in Colonial Zanzibar*. Bloomington: Indiana University Press, 2011.
Goldberg, David Theo. *The Racial State*. Oxford: Blackwell Publishers, 2002.
Gomez, Michael. *Exchanging Our Country Marks: The Transformation of African Identities in the Colonial and Antebellum South*. Chapel Hill: University of North Carolina Press, 1998.
Goswami, Chhaya. *The Call of the Sea: Kachhhi Traders in Muscat and Zanzibar*. New Delhi: Orient Blackswan, 2011.
Goswami, Manu. *Producing India: From Colonial Economy to National Space*. Chicago: University of Chicago Press, 2004.
Graham, Helga. *Arabian Time Machine*. London: Heinemann, 1978.
Greenslade, David. *Ibtisam al-Habsi and Her Zanzibar Court*. Muscat: Ministry of Heritage and Culture, 2013.
Grimstad, Ann Lee. "The Voice of the Revolution: Remembering and Re-Envisioning Field Marshal John Okello." In *Social Memory, Silenced Voices, and Political Struggle*, edited by W. C. Bissell and Marie-Aude Fouéré, 79–107. Dar-es-Salaam: Mkuti wa Nyota, 2018.
Gupta, Pamila. *Portuguese Decolonization in the Indian Ocean World: History and Ethnography*. London: Bloomsbury, 2018.
Gurri, Martin. *The Revolt of the Public and the Crisis of Authority in the New Millennium*. San Francisco: Stripe Press, 2018.
Guyot, Laurenn. "Locked in a Memory Ghetto: A Case Study of a Kurdish Community in France." In *Memory and Migration: Multidisciplinary Approaches to*

Memory Studies, edited by Andrea Klitzmann and Julia Creet, 135–155. Toronto: University of Toronto Press, 2014.

Haj, Maulid. *A Jail Tale: The Autobiography of an Omani in 1960s Tanzania*. Muscat: AlRoya Publishing, 2004.

———. *Sowing the Wind: Zanzibar and Pemba before the Revolution*. Zanzibar: Gallery Publications, 2001.

———. *Zanzibar: The Last Years of the Protectorate; A Constitutional and Political Account*. Muscat: Al Roya Publishing, 2006.

Halbwachs, Maurice, trans. *On Collective Memory*. Edited and translated by Lewis A. Coser. Chicago: Chicago University Press, 1992.

Hamed, Huda. *I Saw Her in My Dreams*. Translated by Nadine Sino. Austin: University of Texas Press, 2023.

Hameer, Fidahussein A. *Crying Out for Freedom: The Event of Forced Marriages in 1970s Zanzibar*. Birmingham: Sun Behind the Cloud Publishing, 2014.

Hanley, Will. *Identifying with Nationality: Europeans, Ottomans and Egyptians in Alexandria*. New York: Columbia University Press, 2017.

Hansen, Thomas Blom, and Finn Stepputat, eds. *Sovereign Bodies: Citizens, Migrants and States in the Postcolonial World*. Princeton, NJ: Princeton University Press, 2005.

Harpaz, Yossi. *Citizenship 2.0: Dual Nationality as a Global Asset*. Princeton, NJ: Princeton University Press, 2019.

Harris, Joseph. *Repatriates and Refugees in a Colonial Society: The Case of Kenya*. Washington, DC: Howard University Press, 1987.

Hartwig, Friedhelm. "The Segmentation of the Indian Ocean Region: Arabs and the Implementation of Immigration Regulations in Zanzibar and British East Africa." In *Space on the Move: Transformations of the Indian Ocean Seascape in the Nineteenth and Twentieth Century*, edited by Jan-Georg Deutsch and Brigitte Reinwald, 21–38. Berlin: Klaus Schwarz Verlag, 2002.

Hashil, Hashil S., and Ahmed Faris. *Living under the Shadow of Terror: Zanzibar Caught Off Guard*. N.p.: CreateSpace Independent Publishing, 2015.

Hawley, Donald. *Oman and Its Renaissance*. London: Stacey International, 1977.

Heard-Bey, Frauke. *From Trucial States to United Arab Emirates*. London: Longman, 1996. First published 1982.

Herb, Michael. *All in the Family: Absolutism, Revolution and Democracy in Middle East Monarchies*. Albany: State University of New York Press, 1999.

Hillewaert, Sarah. "The Ideological Motivations for Language Change: The Loss of Dialectical Variation and Identity among the Swahili Speaking People of the Kenya Coast." In *Kiswahili Research and Development in Eastern Africa*, edited by Rocha Chimera, Mohamed Karama, Ahmed Hussein, and Khalid Omar, 131–151. Mombasa: National Museum of Kenya, 2011.

Hindess, Barry. "Citizenship and Empire." In *Sovereign Bodies: Citizens, Migrants, and States in the Postcolonial World*, edited by Thomas Blom Hansen, and Finn Stepputat, 241–256. Princeton, NJ: Princeton University Press, 2005.

Hirji, Zulfikar. *Between Empires, Sheikh-Sir Mbarak al-Hinawy 1896–1959*. London: Azimuth Editions, 2012.

Hirsch, Marianne. *The Generation of Postmemory: Writing and Visual Culture after the Holocaust*. New York: Columbia University Press, 2012.

Ho, Engseng. *Graves of Tarim: Genealogy and Mobility across the Indian Ocean*. Berkeley: University of California Press, 2006.

———. "Hadhramis Abroad in Hadhramaut: The Muwalladīn." In *Hadhrami Traders, Scholars and Statesmen in the Indian Ocean, 1750s–1960s*, edited by Ulrike Freitag and W. G. Clarence-Smith, 131–146. Leiden: Brill, 1997.

Ho, Engseng, and Abdul Sheriff, eds. *The Indian Ocean: Oceanic Connections and the Creation of New Societies*. London: Hurst, 2014.

Hockenos, Paul. *Homeland Calling: Exile Patriotism and the Balkan Wars*. Ithaca, NY: Cornell University Press, 2003.

Hodge, Joseph M., and Gerard Hodl. Introduction to *Developing Africa: Concepts and Practices in Twentieth-Century Colonialism*, edited by Joseph M. Hodge, Gerard Hodl, and Martina Kopf, 1–34. Manchester: Manchester University Press, 2014.

Hoffman, Valerie J. "Ibāḍīs in Zanzibar and the Nahḍa." In *Oman, Ibadism and Modernity*, edited by A. Al-Salimi and R. Eisener, 129–144. Studies on Ibadism and Oman, vol. 12. Hildesheim: Georg Olms Verlag, 2018.

Hollingsworth, L. W. *A Short History of the East Coast of Africa*. London: Macmillan, 1956. First published 1929.

Hosking, Geoffrey, and George Schopflin, eds. *Myths and Nationhood*. New York: Routledge, 1997.

Hoskins, Alan. *A Contract Officer in Oman*. Kent: DJ Costello Publishers, 1988.

Hunter, Emma. Introduction to *Citizenship, Belonging and Political Community in Africa: Dialogues between Past and Present*, edited by Emma Hunter, 1–16. Athens: Ohio University Press, 2016.

———. *Political Thought and the Public Sphere in Tanzania: Freedom, Democracy, and Citizenship in the Age of Decolonization*. Cambridge: Cambridge University Press, 2015.

Hunter, Helen Louise. *The Hundred Days Revolution*. Santa Barbara, CA: ABC-CLIO, 2010.

Huysmans, Jef. "Discussing Sovereignty and Transnational Politics." In *Sovereignty in Transition*, edited by Neil Walker, 209–228. London: Bloomsbury, 2010.

Ibrahim, Abdullahi Ali. "The 1964 Zanzibar Genocide: The Politics of Denial." In *Africa and the Gulf Region: Blurred Boundaries and Shifting Ties*, edited by Dale Eickelman and Rogaia Abusharaf, 55–73. Berlin: Gerlach Press, 2015.

Ibrahim, Saad Eddin. "Oil, Migration and the New Arab Social Order." In *Rich and Poor States in the Middle East: Egypt and the New Arab Order*, edited by Malcolm Kerr and El Sayed Yassin, 17–70. Boulder: Westview Press, 1982.

Iliffe, John. *A Modern History of Tanganyika*. New York: Cambridge University Press, 1979.

Ingrams, W. H. *Zanzibar: Its History and Its People*. London: Stacey International, 2007. First published 1931.
Ivanov, Paola. "Cosmopolitanism or Exclusion? Negotiating Identity in the Expressive Culture of Contemporary Zanzibar." In *The Indian Ocean: Oceanic Connections and the Creation of New Societies*, edited by Engseng Ho and Abdul Sheriff, 209–238. London: Hurst, 2014.
Ivaska, Andrew. *Cultured States: Youth, Gender, and Modern Style in 1960s Dar-es-Salaam*. Durham, NC: Duke University Press, 2011.
Jackson, Robert. *Sovereignty: The Evolution of the Idea*. Cambridge, UK: Polity, 2007.
Jan, Ammar Ali. "Islam, Communism and the Search for a Fiction." In *Muslims against the Muslim League: Critiques of the Idea of Pakistan*, edited by Ali Usman Qasmi and Megan Eaton Robb, 255–284. Cambridge: Cambridge University Press, 2018.
Jerven, Morten. *Africa: Why Economists Get It Wrong*. London: Zed Books, 2015.
Johnson, Paul. *Diaspora Conversions: Black Carib Religion and the Recovery of Africa*. Berkeley: University of California Press, 2007.
Jones, Jeremy, and Nicholas Ridout. *Oman, Culture and Diplomacy*. Oxford: Oxford University Press, 2012.
Joppke, Christian. *Selecting by Origin: Ethnic Migration and the Liberal State*. Boston: Harvard University Press, 2005.
Joseph, May. "Indian Ocean Ontology: Nyerere, Memory and Place." In *Reimagining Indian Ocean Worlds*, edited by Smriti Srinivas, Bettina Ng'weno, and Neelima Jeychandran, 42–57. London: Routledge, 2020.
———. *Nomadic Identities: The Performance of Citizenship*. Minneapolis: University of Minnesota Press, 1999.
Joyce, Miriam. *The Sultanate of Oman: A Twentieth Century History*. London: Praeger, 1995.
Juma, Juma Khamis, and Arshad Islam. *The East African Muslim Welfare Society (1945–1968): The Case of Tanzania*. Gombak: IIUM Press, 2017.
Kalter, Christopher. *Postcolonial People: The Return from Africa and the Remaking of Portugal*. Cambridge: Cambridge University Press, 2022.
Kamoonpuri, Hasan. *Oman Top Business Leaders*. Muscat: Oman Daily Observer, 2010.
Kaplan, Robert. *Monsoon: The Indian Ocean and the Future of American Power*. New York: Random House, 2010.
Kattan, Naim. *Farewell Babylon: Coming of Age in Jewish Baghdad*. Translated by Sheila Fischman. Vancouver: Raincoat Books, 2005.
Kaufman, Stuart. *Nationalist Passions*. Ithaca, NY: Cornell University Press, 2015.
Kechichian, Joseph. *Oman and the World: The Emergence of an Independent Foreign Policy*. Santa Monica, CA: Rand Corporation, 1995.
Kedourie, Elie. *Nationalism in Asia and Africa*. New York: World Publishing, 1970.
Khalifa, Al Mohamed. *The United Arab Emirates: Unity in Fragmentation*. Boulder: Westview Press, 1979.

Kharusi, Ahmed Seif. *The Agony of Zanzibar: A Victim of the New Colonialism.* Richmond, UK: Foreign Affairs Publishing, 1969.
———. *Letters Smuggled Out of Zanzibar.* Portsmouth, UK: Portsmouth Printers Ltd., 1971.
———. *Zanzibar: Africa's First Cuba.* Richmond, UK: Foreign Affairs Publishing, 1967.
———. *Zanzibar Cries for Help.* Hampshire, UK: The Zanzibar Organization, 1974.
King, Kenneth. *Pan-Africanism and Education: A Study of Race, Philanthropy, and Education in the United States of America and East Africa.* New York: Diasporic Africa Press, 2016. First published 1971.
Kleinman, Arthur, Veena Das, Mamphela Ramphele, and Pamela Reynolds, eds. *Violence and Subjectivity.* Berkeley: University of California Press, 1997.
Koenings, Nathalie Arnold. "'For Us It's What Came After': Locating Pemba in Revolutionary Zanzibar." In *Social Memory, Silenced Voices, and Political Struggle: Remembering the Revolution in Zanzibar*, edited by William Cunningham Bissell and Marie-Aude Fouéré, 145–190. Dar-es-Salaam: Mkuti wa Nyota, 2018.
Kohn, Margaret, and Keally McBride. *Political Theories of Decolonization: Postcolonialism and the Problem of Foundations.* Oxford: Oxford University Press, 2011.
Kresse, Kai. *Swahili Muslim Publics and Postcolonial Experience.* Bloomington: Indiana University Press, 2018.
Kuper, Leo. *Race, Class, and Power: Ideology and Revolutionary Change in Plural Societies.* London: Duckworth, 1974.
Kusimba, Chapurukha. *The Rise and Fall of Swahili States.* Lanham, MD: AltaMira Press, 1999.
Lambek, Michael. "The Past Imperfect: Remembering as Moral Practice." In *Tense Past: Cultural Essays in Trauma and Memory*, edited by Paul Antze and Michael Lambek, 235–254. New York: Routledge, 1996.
Lambert, Laurie. *Comrade Sister: Caribbean Feminist Revisions of the Grenadian Revolution.* Charlottesville: University of Virginia Press, 2020.
Larsen, Kjersti. "Silenced Voices, Recaptured Memories: Historical Imprints within a Zanzibari Life-World." In *Social Memory, Silenced Voices, Political Struggle: Remembering the Revolution in Zanzibar*, edited by W. C. Marie-Aude Fouéré, 251–278. Dar-es-Salaam: Mkuti wa Nyota, 2018.
———. "Translocal Experiences and Intersecting Mobilities: Reflections on Motility and Actual and Imagined Movability in Contemporary Zanzibar." In *Translocal Connections across the Indian Ocean*, edited by Francesca Declich, 227–255. Leiden: Brill, 2018.
Larsen, Pier. *Ocean of Letters: Language and Creolization in an Indian Ocean Diaspora.* Cambridge: Cambridge University Press, 2009.
Lawrance, Benjamin, and Jacqueline Stevens, eds. *Citizenship in Question: Evidentiary Birthright and Statelessness.* Durham, NC: Duke University Press, 2017.
Lee, Christopher. "Between a Moment and an Era: The Origins and Afterlives of Bandung." In *Making a World after Empire: Bandung and its Afterlives*, edited by Christopher Lee, 1–44. Athens: Ohio University Press, 2010.

Lehmann, Harmut, and James J. Sheehan. *An Interrupted Past: German-Speaking Refugee Historians in the United States after 1933*. Cambridge: Cambridge University Press, 2002.

Li, Tania Murray. *The Will to Improve: Governmentality, Development and the Practice of Politics*. Durham, NC: Duke University Press, 2007.

Liendhardt, Peter. *Shaikhdoms of Eastern Arabia*. New York: Palgrave, 2001.

Limbert, Mandana. *In the Time of Oil: Piety, Memory and Social Life in an Omani Town*. Palo Alto, CA: Stanford University Press, 2010.

———. "Marriage Status and the Politics of Nationality." In *The Gulf Family: Kinship, Policies and Modernity*, edited by Alanoud Alsharekh, 167–180. London: Saqi Books, 2007.

———. "Oman: Cultivating Good Citizens and Religious Virtue." In *Teaching Islam: Textbooks and Religion in the Middle East*, edited by Eleanor Doumato and Gregory Starrett, 159–191. Boulder: Lynne Rienner, 2006.

Lockwood, Sandra. "Nightmare in Paradise: The 1964 Zanzibar Revolution and Genocide." In *Hushed Voices: Unacknowledged Atrocities of the 20th Century*, edited by Heribert Adam, 13–26. Berkshire: Berkshire Academic Press, 2011.

Lofchie, Michael. *The Political Economy of Tanzania: Decline and Recovery*. Philadelphia: University of Pennsylvania Press, 2014.

———. *Zanzibar: Background to Revolution*. Princeton, NJ: Princeton University Press, 1965.

Loimeier, Roman. *Between Social Skills and Marketable Skills: The Politics of Islamic Education in 20th Century Zanzibar*. Leiden: Brill, 2009.

———. "Memories of Revolution: Patterns of Interpretation." In *Social Memory, Silenced Voices, and Political Struggle: Remembering the Revolution in Zanzibar*, edited by Bill Bissell and Marie-Aude Fouéré. Dar-es-Salaam: Mkuki wa Nyota, 2018.

Longva, Anh Nga. "Citizenship in the Gulf States: Conceptualization and Practice." In *Citizenship and State in the Middle East: Approaches and Applications*, edited by Nils Butenschon, Uri Davis, and Manuel Hassassian, 179–200. Syracuse: Syracuse University Press, 2000.

Lori, Noora. *Offshore Citizens: Permanent Temporary Status in the Gulf*. Cambridge: Cambridge University Press, 2019.

Machado, Pedro. *Ocean of Trade: South Asian Merchants, Africa and the Indian Ocean, c. 1750–1850*. Cambridge: Cambridge University Press, 2014.

Malkki, Liisa. *Purity and Exile: Violence, Memory and National Cosmology among Hutu Refugees in Tanzania*. Chicago: University of Chicago Press, 1995.

Mamdani, Mahmood. *Citizen and Subject: Contemporary Africa and the Legacy of Late Colonialism*. Princeton, NJ: Princeton University Press, 1997.

———. *Define and Rule: Native as Political Identity*. Boston: Harvard University Press, 2012.

———. *From Citizen to Refugee. Ugandan Asians Come to Britain*. London: Frances Pinter, 1973.

Mandal, Sumit. *Becoming Arab: Creole histories and Modern Identity in the Malay World*. Cambridge: Cambridge University Press, 2018.
Mandaville, Peter, and Terrence Lyons, eds. *Politics from Afar: Transnational Diasporas and Networks*. London: Hurst Publishers, 2012.
Manger, Leif O. *The Hadrami Diaspora: Community-building on the Indian Ocean Rim*. New York: Berghahn Books, 2010.
Mann, Greg. *From Empires to NGOs in the West African Sahel: The Road to Nongovernmentality*. Cambridge: Cambridge University Press, 2015.
Mann, Michael. *The Dark Side of Democracy: Explaining Ethnic Cleansing*. New York: Cambridge University Press, 2005.
Mapuri, Omar. *The 1964 Revolution: Achievements and Prospects*. Dar-es-Salaam: Tema Publishers, 1996.
Marashi, Afshin. *Exile and the Nation: The Parsi Community of India and the Making of Modern Iran*. Austin: University of Texas, 2020.
Marhuby, H. *My Zanzibar: From Idyllic to Upheaval*. N.p.: Self-published, 2017.
Markle, Seth. *Motorcycle on Hell Run: Tanzania, Black Power, and the Uncertain Future of Pan-Africanism, 1964–1974*. East Lansing: Michigan State University Press, 2017.
Martin, Esmond Bradley. *Zanzibar: Tradition and Revolution*. London: Hamish Hamilton, 1978.
Martin, J. Paul. "Ethnicity and Racism." In *The Columbia History of the 20th Century*, edited by Richard Bulliet, 172–202. New York: Columbia University Press, 1998.
Marx, Anthony. *Faith in Nation: Exclusionary Origins of Nationalism*. Oxford: Oxford University Press, 2003.
Mathews, Nathaniel. "Jumuiya ya Kiislamu ya Istiqaama Tanzania and Modern Ibādism in East Africa, 1985–2016." In *Oman, Ibadism and Modernity*, edited by Abdulrahman al-Salimi and Reinhard Eisener, 235–246. Hildesheim: George Olms, 2017.
———. "Memory, History, and Heritage among the Grieving Cosmopolitans: Omani-Zanzibaris Remember the Zanzibar Revolution, 1964–present." In *Social Memory and the 1964 Zanzibar Revolution*, edited by Garth Myers and Marie-Aude Fouéré, 279–310. Dar-es-Salaam: Mkuti wa Nyota, 2017.
Mauolidi, S. "Between Law and Culture: Contemplating Rights for Women in Zanzibar." In *Gender and Culture at the Limit of Rights*, edited by D. L. Hodgson, 32–54 Philadelphia: University of Pennsylvania Press, 2011.
Mayall, James. "Nationalism." In *The Columbia History of the 20th Century*, edited by Richard Bulliet, 172–202. New York: Columbia University Press, 1998.
Mbembe, Achille. *On the Postcolony*. Berkeley: University of California Press, 2001.
McDow, Thomas F. *Buying Time: Debt and Mobility in the Western Indian Ocean*. Athens: Ohio University Press, 2018.
McIntosh, Janet. *The Edge of Islam: Power, Personhood, and Ethnoreligious Boundaries on the Kenya Coast*. Durham, NC: Duke University Press, 2009.

McMahon, Elizabeth, and Corrie Decker. *The Idea of Development in Africa: A History*. Cambridge: Cambridge University Press, 2020.
McNeill, William. "Money and Economic Change." In *The Columbia History of the 20th Century*, edited by Richard Bulliet, 283–313. New York: Columbia University Press, 1998.
McPhee, Graham, and Prem Poddar. Introduction to *Empire and After: Englishness in Post-Colonial Perspective*, edited by Graham McPhee and Prem Poddar, 1–4. New York: Bergahn Books, 2007.
Medved, M., and J. Brockmeier. "When Memory Goes Awry." In *outledge International Handbook of Memory Studies*, edited by Anna Lisa Tota and Trever Hagen, 445–457. London: Routledge, 2016.
Middleton, John, and Jane Campbell. *Zanzibar: Its Society and Its Politics*. London: Oxford University Press, 1965.
Mirza, Shireen. "Muslims, Media and Mobility in the Indian Ocean Region." In *The Shi'a in Modern South Asia: Religion, History and Politics*, edited by Justin Jones and Ali Usman Qasmi, 131–158. Cambridge: Cambridge University Press, 2015.
Mitchell, Timothy. *Carbon Democracy: Political Power in the Age of Oil*. New York: Verso Books, 2011.
Mmuya, Max, and Amon Chaligha. *Towards Multiparty Politics in Tanzania*. Dar-es-Salaam: UDSM Press, 1992.
Mohamed, Amir. *A Guide to a History of Zanzibar*. New Delhi: Good Luck Publishers, 2006.
Moore, Barrington. *Social Origins of Dictatorship and Democracy: Lord and Peasant in the Making of the Modern World*. Boston: Beacon Press, 1966.
Moore, Margaret. *A Political Theory of Territory*. Oxford: Oxford University Press, 2015.
Mudimbe, Valentin. *The Invention of Africa: Gnosis, Philosophy, and the Order of Knowledge*. Bloomington: Indiana University Press, 1988.
Mukta, Parita. *Shards of Memory: Woven Lives in Four Generations*. London: Weidenfeld and Nicolson, 2002.
Mwakikagile, Godfrey. *The Union of Tanganyika and Zanzibar: Product of the Cold War?* Washington, DC: New Africa Press, 2008.
Myers, Garth. *Verandahs of Power: Colonialism and Space in Urban Africa*. Syracuse, NY: Syracuse University Press, 2003.
Njozi, Hamza Mustafa. *Mwembechai Killings and the Political Future of Tanzania*. Ottawa: Globalink Communications, 2000.
Nohlen, Dieter, Michael Krennerich, and Bernard Thibaut, eds. *Elections in Africa: A Data Handbook*. Oxford: Oxford University Press, 1999.
Okello, John. *Revolution in Zanzibar*. Nairobi: East African Publishing House, 1973.
Olsen, Niklas. *History in the Plural: An Introduction to the Work of Reinhart Koselleck*. New York: Berghahn Books, 2012.
Oman in History. Muscat, Oman: Ministry of Information, 1995.

Onley, James. *The Arabian Frontier of the British Raj: Merchants, Rulers, and the British in the Nineteenth Century Gulf*. Oxford: Oxford University Press, 2007.

Østergaard-Nielsen, Eva, ed. *International Migration and Sending Countries: Perceptions, Policies, and Transnational Relations*. New York: Palgrave Macmillan, 2003.

Osterhammel, Jurgen. "Epilogue: From Civilizing Missions to the Defence of Civility." In *Civilizing Missions in the Twentieth Century*, edited by Boris Barth and Rolf Hobson, 209–228. Leiden: Brill, 2020.

Othman, Haroub. "The Arusha Declaration and the Triangle Principles of Tanzanian Foreign Policy." In *Yes, in My Lifetime: Selected Works of Haroub Othman*, edited by Saida Yahya-Othman. Dar-es-Salaam: Mkuti wa Nyota, 2013.

———. "Nyerere's Political Legacy." In *Tanzania After Nyerere*, edited by Michael Dood, 158–164. New York: Pinter Publishers, 1988.

———. "Revolution: Class Struggle or Racial War?" In *Yes, in My Lifetime: Selected Works of Haroub Othman*, edited by Saida Yahya-Othman. Dar-es-Salaam: Mkuti wa Nyota, 2013.

———. "Succession Politics and the Union Presidential Elections." In *Yes, in My Lifetime: Selected Works of Haroub Othman*, edited by Saida Yahya-Othman. Dar-es-Salaam: Mkuti wa Nyota, 2013.

———. "Tanzania Foreign Policy and Some International Legal Problems." In *Yes, in My Lifetime: Selected Works of Haroub Othman*, edited by Saida Yahya-Othman. Dar-es-Salaam: Mkuti wa Nyota, 2013.

———. "The Union with Zanzibar." In *Mwalimu: The Influence of Nyerere*, edited by Colin Legum and Geoffrey Mmari, 170–175. Oxford: James Currey, 1995.

Pailey, Robtel. *Development, Dual Citizenship and Its Discontents in Africa: The Political Economy of Belonging to Liberia*. Cambridge: Cambridge University Press, 2021.

Parsons, Timothy. *The 1964 Army Mutinies and the Making of Modern East Africa*. Westport, CT: Praeger, 2003.

Perret, Françoise, and François Bugnion. *From Budapest to Saigon: History of the ICRC, 1956–1965*. Geneva: ICRC, 2018.

Peterson, Derek, and Giacomo Macola, eds. *Recasting the Past: African History Writing and Political Work in Modern Africa*. Athens: Ohio University Press, 2009.

Peterson, J. E. *Historical Muscat: An Illustrated Guide and Gazetteer*. Leiden: Brill, 2007.

———. "L'Odyssee de l'Oman: De l'Imamat au Sultanat." In *L'Oman Contemporain: État, territoire, identité*, edited by Marc Lavergne and Brigitte Dumortier, 29–41. Paris: Karthala, 2003.

———. *Oman: Political Foundations of an Emerging State*. London: Croom Helm, 1978.

———. "Oman Faces the Twenty-First Century." In *Political Change in the Arab Gulf States: Stuck in Transition*, edited by Mary Ann Tetreault, Gwenn Okruhlik and Andrzej Kapiszewski, 99–118. Boulder: Lynne Rienner, 2011.

———. *Oman's Insurgencies: The Sultanate's Struggle for Supremacy*. London: Saqi Books, 2008.

———. "Rulers, Merchants and Shaikhs in Gulf Politics." In *The Gulf Family: Kinship Policies and Modernity*, edited by Alanoud Alsharekh, 21–36. London: Middle East Institute SOAS, 2007.

Petras, James. *Critical Perspectives on Imperialism and Social Class in the Third World*. New York: Monthly Review Press, 1978.

Petterson, Don. *Revolution in Zanzibar: An American's Cold War Tale*. Boulder: Westview Press, 2002.

Pouwels, Randall. *Horn and Crescent: Cultural Change and Traditional Islam on the East African Coast, 800–1900*. Cambridge: Cambridge University Press, 2002. First published 1987.

Pratt, Cranford. *The Critical Phase in Tanzania, 1945–1968: Nyerere and the Emergence of a Socialist Strategy*. Cambridge: Cambridge University Press, 1976.

Prestholdt, Jeremy. *Domesticating the World: African Consumerisms and the Genealogy of Globalization*. Berkeley: University of California Press, 2008.

Prins, A. H. J. *The Swahili-Speaking Peoples of Zanzibar and the East African Coast, Arabs, Shirazi, and Swahili*. London: International African Institute, 1967.

Rabi, Uzi. *The Emergence of States in a Tribal Society: Oman Under Sa'id bin Taymur, 1932–1970*. Liverpool: Liverpool University Press, 2011.

Rajab, Ahmed. "Healing the Past, Reinventing the Present: From the Revolution to Maridhiano." In *Social Memory, Silenced Voices, and Political Struggle: Remembering the Revolution in Zanzibar*, edited by Bill Bissell and Marie-Aude Fouéré, 335–355. Dar-es-Salaam: Mkuti wa Nyota, 2018.

Ranja, Timothy. *Success under Duress: A Comparison of the Indigenous African and East Africa Asian Entrepreneurs*. Dar-es-Salaam: Economic and Social Research Foundation, 2003.

Ray, Darren. "Defining the Swahili." In *The Swahili World*, edited by S. Wynne-Jones and A. LaViolette, 66–80. New York: Routledge, 2017.

Reese, Scott. "'The Ink of Excellence': Print and Islamic Written Tradition of East Africa." In *Manuscript and Print in the Islamic Tradition*, edited by Scott Reese, 217–242. Berlin: De Gruyter, 2022.

Roberts, George. *Revolutionary State-Making in Dar-es-Salaam: African Liberation and the Global Cold War, 1961–1974*. Cambridge: Cambridge University Press, 2021.

Rockel, Stephen. *Carriers of Culture: Labor on the Road in Nineteenth Century East Africa*. Portsmouth, NH: Heinemann, 2006.

Rothberg, Michael. *Multi-directional Memories: Remembering the Holocaust in the Age of Decolonization*. Palo Alto, CA: Stanford University Press, 2009.

Rothchild, Donald. *Racial Bargaining in Independent Kenya: A Study of Minorities and Decolonization*. New York: Oxford University Press, 1973.

Rubin, Aaron. *The Mehri Language of Oman*. Leiden, Netherlands: Brill 2010.

Rubin, Aaron D. *The Jibbali (Shahri) Language of Oman: Grammar and Texts*. Leiden,: Brill, 2014.
Sachedina, Amal. *Celebrating the Past, Living the Modern: The Politics of Time in the Sultanate of Oman*. New York: Cornell University Press, 2021.
Sadgrove, Philip. "The Press: Engine of a Mini-renaissance in Zanzibar (1860–1920)." In *History of Printing and Publishing in the Languages and Countries of the Middle East*, edited by Philip Sadgrove, 151–178. Oxford: Oxford University Press, 2009.
Sadiq, Kamal. *Paper Citizens: How Illegal Immigrants Acquire Citizenship in Developing Countries*. New York: Oxford University Press, 2009.
Saleh, Mohamed Ahmed. "Swahili Elites and the Concept of Long-Distance Nationalism within the Diaspora." In *Translocal Connections across the Indian Ocean: Swahili Speaking Networks on the Move*, edited by Francesca Declich, 296–314. Leiden: Brill, 2018.
Salim, A. I. "The Movement for 'Mwambao' or Coastal Autonomy in Kenya, 1956–63." In *Hadith 2*, edited by B. A. Ogot, 212–228. Nairobi: East African Publishing House, 1970.
———. "'Native or Non-native?' The Problem of Identity and the Social Stratification of the Arab-Swahili of Kenya." In *Hadith 6: History and Social Change in East Africa*, 65–85. Nairobi: East African Literature Bureau, 1976.
———. *The Swahili-Speaking Peoples of Kenya's Coast, 1895–1965*. Nairobi: East African Publishing House, 1973.
Salvadori, Cynthia. *Through Open Doors: A View of Asian Cultures in Kenya*. Nairobi: Kenway Publishers, 1989.
Samin, Nadav. *Of Sand or Soil: Genealogy and Tribal Belonging in Saudi Arabia*. Princeton, NJ: Princeton University Press, 2015.
Schenck, Marcia, Immanuel R. Harisch, Anne Dietrich, and Eric Burton. Introduction to *Navigating Socialist Encounters: Moorings and (Dis)Entanglements between Africa and East Germany during the Cold War*, edited by Marcia Schenck, Immanuel R. Harisch, Anne Dietrich, and Eric Burton, 1–58. Berlin: De Gruyter Oldenbourg, 2021.
Schivelbusch, Wolfgang. *The Culture of Defeat: On National Trauma, Mourning, and Recovery*. Translated by Jefferson Chase. New York: Henry Holt, 2003.
Seidenberg, Dana April. *Mercantile Adventurers: The World of East African Asians*. New Delhi: New Age International, 1996.
Seigelberg, Mira. *Statelessness: A Modern History*. Cambridge, MA: Harvard University Press, 2020.
SenGupta, Gunja, and Awam Amkpa. *Sojourners, Sultans, and Slaves: American and the Indian Ocean in the Age of Abolition and Empire*. Berkeley: University of California Press, 2023.
Shafi, Adam. *Haini*. Nairobi: Longhorn Publishers, 2003.
Shahabuddin, Mohammad. *Minorities and the Making of Postcolonial States in International Laws*. Cambridge: Cambridge University Press, 2021.

Shahbal, Suleiman. *Zanzibar: The Rise and Fall of an Independent State*. Dubai: Self-published, 2002.
Shao, Ibrahim. *The Political Economy of Land Reforms in Zanzibar: Before and after the Revolution*. Dar-es-Salaam: UDSM Press, 1992.
Sharkey, Heather. *Living with Colonialism: Nationalism and Culture in the Anglo-Egyptian Sudan*. Berkeley: University of California Press, 2003.
Sheffer, Gabriel. *Diaspora Politics: At Home Abroad*. Cambridge: Cambridge University Press, 2009.
Sheriff, Abdul. *The History and Conservation of Zanzibar Stone Town*. Athens: Ohio University Press, 1995.
———. *Slaves, Spices, & Ivory in Zanzibar: Integration of an East African Commercial Empire into the World Economy, 1770–1873*. London: J. Currey, 1987.
Shipway, Martin. *Decolonization and Its Impact: A Comparative Approach to the End of Colonial Empires*. New York: Wiley-Blackwell, 2008.
Shivji, Issa. *Pan-Africanism or Pragmatism: Lessons of the Tanganyika-Zanzibar Union*. Dar-es-Salaam: Mkuti wa Nyota Publishers, 2008.
Shryrock, Andrew. *Nationalism and the Genealogical Imagination: Oral History and Textual Authority in Tribal Jordan*. Berkeley: University of California Press, 1997.
Sievers, Axel Harnet, ed. *A Place in the World: New Local Historiographies in Africa and South Asia*. Leiden: Brill, 2001.
Simpson, Edward. *Muslim Society and the Western Indian Ocean: Seafarers of Kacch*. New York: Routledge, 2006.
Skeet, Ian. *Oman: Politics and Development*. New York: Palgrave Macmillan, 1992.
Skinner, Quentin, and Bo Strath, eds. *States and Citizens: History, Theory, Prospects*. Cambridge: Cambridge University Press, 2003.
Smith, Alison. "The End of the Arab Sultanate: Zanzibar, 1945–1964." In *History of East Africa*, edited by D. A. Low and Alison Smith, 3:196–211. Oxford: Clarendon Press, 1976.
Smith, Anthony. *Nationalism: Theory, Ideology, History*. London: Polity Press, 2010.
Smith, Jean P. *Settlers at the End of Empire: Race and the Politics of Migration in South Africa, Rhodesia, and the United Kingdom*. Manchester: Manchester University Press, 2022.
Smith, Michael Peter, and Luis Eduardo Guarnizo, eds. *Transnationalism from Below: Comparative Urban and Community Research*. London: Routledge, 1998.
Soske, Jon. *Internal Frontiers: African Nationalism and the Indian Diaspora in Twentieth-Century South Africa*. Athens: Ohio University Press, 2017.
Sprute, Paul. "Diaries of Solidarity in the Global Cold War: The East German Friendship Brigades and their Experience in 'Modernizing Angola.'" In *Navigating Socialist Encounters: Moorings and (Dis)Entanglements between Africa and East Germany during the Cold War*, edited by Marcia Schenck, Immanuel R. Harisch, Anne Dietrich and Eric Burton, 293–318. Berlin: De Gruyter Oldenbourg, 2021.
Stockreiter, Elke. *Islamic Law, Gender, and Social Change in Post-Abolition Zanzibar*. Cambridge: Cambridge University Press, 2015.

Suleiman, Yasir. *The Arabic Language and National Identity: A Study in Ideology*. Washington, DC: Georgetown University Press, 2003.
Taiwo, Olufemi. *How Colonialism Preempted Modernity in Africa*. Bloomington: Indiana University Press, 2010.
Takriti, Abdel Razzaq. *Monsoon Revolution: Republicans, Sultans and Empire in Oman, 1965–1976*. Oxford: Oxford University Press, 2013.
Tambila, K. I. "Aspects of the Political Economy of Unguja and Pemba." In *The Political Plight of Zanzibar*, edited by T.L. Maliyamkono, 71–103. Dar-es-Salaam: Tema Publishers, 2000.
Taryam, Abdallah Omran. *The Establishment of the United Arab Emirates, 1950–85*. London: Croom Helm, 1987.
Taylor, Charles. "Nationalism and Modernity." In *Theorizing Nationalism*, edited by Ronald Beiner, 219–245. Albany: State University of New York Press, 1999.
Tilly, Charles. *Big Structures, Large Processes, Huge Comparisons*. New York: Russell Sage Foundation, 1984.
Topan, Farouk. "Polemics and Language in Swahili Translations of the Quran." In *The Quran and Its Readers Worldwide*, edited by Suha Taji-Farouki, 473–497. Oxford: Oxford University Press, 2016.
Torpey, John. *The Invention of the Passport: Surveillance, Citizenship, and the State*. Cambridge: Cambridge University Press, 1999.
Torpey, John, and Jane Caplan, eds. *The Development of State Practices in the Modern World*. Princeton, NJ: Princeton University Press, 2001.
Townsend, John. *Oman: The Making of a Modern State*. London: Croom-Helm, 1977.
Trouillot, Michel-Rolph. *Silencing the Past: Power and the Production of History*. Boston: Beacon Press, 1997.
Tsuda, Takeyuki. Introduction to *Diasporic Homecomings: Ethnic Return Migration in Comparative Perspective*, edited by Takeyuki Tsuda, 1–20. Stanford, CA: Stanford University Press, 2009.
———. "Why Does the Diaspora Return Home? The Causes of Ethnic Return Migration." In *Diasporic Homecomings: Ethnic Return Migration in Comparative Perspective*, edited by Takeyuki Tsuda, 21–43 (Stanford, CA: Stanford University Press, 2009).
Turner, Simon. "Suspended Spaces—Contesting Sovereignties in a Refugee Camp." In *Sovereign Bodies: Citizens, Migrants and States in the Postcolonial World Bodies*, edited by Thomas Blom Hansen and Finn Stepputat, 312–332. Princeton, NJ: Princeton University Press, 2005.
Valeri, Marc. "Identity Politics and Nation-Building under Sultan Qaboos." In *Sectarian Politics in the Persian Gulf*, edited by Lawrence Potter, 179–206. London/New York: Hurst/Oxford University Press, 2013.
———. *Oman: Politics and Society in the Qaboos State*. London: Hurst, 2009.
Vali, Ferenc A. *Politics of the Indian Ocean Region: The Balances of Power*. New York: Free Press, 1976.
Vassanji, M. G. *The Gunny Sack*. London: Heinemann, 1989.

Verne, Julia. *Living Translocality: Space, Culture, and Economy in Contemporary Swahili Trade*. Stuttgart: Franz Steiner Verlag, 2012.

Verne, Julia, and Detlef Müller-Mahn "We Are Part of Zanzibar: Translocal Practices and Imaginative Geographies." In *Regionalizing Oman: Political, Economic and Social Dynamics*, edited by Steffen Wippel, 75–89. Dordrecht: Springer Link, 2013.

von Joeden-Forgey, Elisa. "Life Force Atrocities Are Early Indicators of Genocide." In *At Issue: Genocide*, edited by Barbara Krasner, 47–54. New York: Greenhaven Publishing, 2021.

Wahab, Saada. *The History of Indians in Zanzibar from the 1870s to 1963*. Gottingen: Gottingen University Press, 2022.

Walker, Iain. "Identity and Citizenship among the Comorians of Zanzibar." In *The Indian Ocean: Oceanic Connections and the Creation of New Societies*, edited by Engseng Ho and Abdul Sheriff, 239–266. London: Hurst, 2014.

Walker, Iain, and Marie-Aude Fouéré, eds. *Across the Waves: Strategies of Belonging in Indian Ocean Island Societies*. Leiden: Brill, 2022.

Wedeen, Lisa. *Peripheral Visions: Publics, Power and Performance in Yemen*. Chicago: University of Chicago Press, 2008.

Weitzberg, Keren. *We Do Not Have Borders: Greater Somalia and the Predicaments of Belonging in Kenya*. Athens: Ohio University Press, 2017.

Werbner, Richard. "Introduction: Multiple Identities, Plural Arenas." In *Postcolonial Identities in Africa*, edited by Richard Werbner and Terence Ranger, 1–28. London: Zed Books, 1996.

West, Michael O. *The Rise of an African Middle Class Colonial Zimbabwe, 1898–1965*. Bloomington: Indiana University Press, 2002.

Westad, Orne. *The Global Cold War: Third World Interventions and the Making of Our Times*. Cambridge: Cambridge University Press, 2006.

Wikan, Umi. *Behind the Veil in Arabia: Women in Oman*. Baltimore, MD: Johns Hopkins University Press, 1982.

Wilkinson, John. *The Arabs and the Scramble for Africa*. Bristol, CT: Equinox Publishing Ltd., 2015.

———. *The Imamate Tradition of Oman*. Cambridge: Cambridge University Press, 1987.

Wilson, Amrit. *The Threat of Liberation: Imperialism and Revolution in Zanzibar*. London: Pluto Press, 2013.

Wriggins, W. Howard, ed. *Dynamics of Regional Politics: 4 Systems on the Indian Ocean Rim*. New York: Columbia University Press, 1992.

Young, Crawford. *The African Colonial State in Comparative Perspective*. New Haven, CT: Yale University Press, 1994.

———. "Nation, Ethnicity and Citizenship: Dilemmas of Democracy and Civil Order in Africa." In *Making Nations, Creating Strangers States and Citizenship in Africa*, edited by Paul Nugent, Daniel Hammett, and Sara Dorman, 241–264. Leiden: Brill, 2007.

Yuval-Davis, Nira. *Gender and Nation*. Los Angeles: Sage Publications, 1997.

Zahlan, Rosemarie Said. *The Origins of the United Arab Emirates: A Political and Social History of the Trucial States*. London: Macmillan, 1978.

Zeleza, Paul. *In Search of African Diasporas: Testimonies and Encounters*. Durham, NC: Carolina Academic Press, 2012.

Ziai, Aram. *Development Discourse and Global History: From Colonialism to the Sustainable Development Goals*. New York: Routledge, 2016.

INDEX

Note: Personal names have been alphabetized under first name.

1948 dockworkers strike, Zanzibar, 17, 181
1962 Commonwealth Immigration Act, 105
1986 oil price slump, 23, 152, 211n187, 247n186, 263n114

Abdullah Kassim Hanga, 47, 54; killing of, 71, 90, 93, 244n154; and the Red Cross, 72; role in revolution, 56, 71 220n106
Abdullah Salih al-Farsy (also Abdalla Salih and Abdullah Saleh Farsy), 168, 172n88
Abdulrahman Mohamed Babu, 15, 17, 72; arrests of, 47, 95; criticism of Nyerere, 239n80; electoral mobilization, 44–45; exile criticisms of, 179; resignation from ZNP, 47; and the revolution, 54, 71, 82;
Abeid Karume: assassination of, 94–96; birthplace controversy, 42–43, 49, 219n84; and colonial citizenship laws, 241n124; portrayal by exiles, 175, 179–180, 219n83; portrayal in oral histories, 62; posthumous mythologization, 96, 101; in the revolution, 54–58, 65, 73; as ruler of Zanzibar, 69–72, 84–91, 112;
Aboud Jumbe, 54, 71, 94, 97, 108, 161, 205n117
Abu Dhabi, 80, 101, 103, 110, 122, 124, 148 economic policies of, 104; residence policies of, 113–115; ruler of, 114 Zanzibari community in, 118
Abu Muslim al-Bahlani, 203n106

Adal Insaf, 40
Africa Addio, 92, 180, 222n6, 265n2
African Association, 16, 34–35, 41, 203n107
Africanity, 35, 77, 144
Africans, 7, 16, 18, 34–35, 41, 62–63, 72, 83; migration to Zanzibar, 36, 38–40; perception of returnees as, 143; protecting Arabs, 64–65; tensions with Arabs, 41, 43, 49, 93; victims in the revolution, 55, 92
Afrika Kwetu, 17, 34, 40
Afro-Arabs: definition of, 13; emigration from Zanzibar, 19, 73, 107; formation of, 14–18; memories of, 159, 183; and nationalism in Zanzibar, 16–17, 42, 188; relation to muwalladūn, 14; return to Zanzibar, 164–65; as returnees to Oman, 24, 134, 157; transformation in exile, 21, 77, 81; writing about slavery, 173–176; writing about the revolution, 176–182. *See also* muwalladūn
Afro-Asian Peoples Solidarity Conference, 16
Afro-Shirazi Party (ASP): anticommunism of, 218m71, 236n54; divisions within, 44–45, 47, 71, 180; election performances, 43–44, 46–48; exile views of, 91, 178; formation of, 35, 41; ideology of, 41; involvement in the revolution, 50, 54, 56; merger with TANU, 81, 96; nativism of, 219n81; and

329

Afro-Shirazi Party (ASP) (*continued*)
    the Revolutionary Council, 96; views on the monarchy, 45, 220n106
Afro-Shirazi Union. *See* Afro-Shirazi Party
Afro-Shirazi Youth League, 71
Aga Khan, 67
Agozi, 40
Ahmed Ali al-Riyami, 64, 124
Ahmed al-Khalili (mufti of Oman), 140, 167, 272n90
Ahmed Baalawy, 85, 93, 161
Ahmed Badawi Quallatein (Qulatein), 95
Ahmed bin Ibrahim al-Amiri, 169
Ahmed Hamoud al-Maamiry, 15, 119, 161, 174, 205n117; in exile, 78; and inward turn of exiles, 127; as Omani returnee, 139; return to Zanzibar, 166; as teacher in Zanzibar, 16
Ahmed Lamky, 16, 47, 78–79, 97, 111, 119, 205n118
Ahmed Mahmoud al-Harthi, 82
Ahmed Seif al-Kharusi, 16, 47, 78–79, 81, 92–93; correspondence of, 82–83; criticism of exiles, 127–28; criticism of Nyerere, 91–92; and democracy in Zanzibar, 80, 94–95; and *Free Zanzibar Voice*, 20, 77, 80; and Muammar Qaddafi, 96–97; reception by Omanis, 81–82; skepticism of Tanzanian diplomacy, 161; struggles for citizenship, 105, 208n152; and the Union, 96, 99–100; and the Zanzibar Organization, 80
Al-Amin al-Mazrui, 203n106
al-Busaidi dynasty, 10, 42 and the politics of decolonization, 220n106; in Oman, 168, 261n84; in Zanzibar, 10–12, 45
al-Falaq, 14, 16, 33, 39, 206n133
Algeria, 47, 78; and support for the revolution, 178–179
al-Hirth (tribal confederation), 11, 149
Ali Ahmed al-Riyami, 42, 47, 119
Ali Ahmed Saleh, 162
Ali Hassan Mwinyi, 98, 101, 162, 268n32
Ali Mazrui, 7, 166
Ali Muhammad al-Barwani, 137
Ali Muhsin al-Barwani, 14, 47, 56, 78, 80, 94, 97, 163, 170, 180; criticism of Nyerere, 84, 93–94; and definition of Zanzibar, 167; and Gamel Abdel Nasser, 180, 246n183; imprisonment and release, 78, 101, 109; inward turn of, 101, 255n151; memoir, 25; and nationalism in Zanzibar, 20, and Oman, 136, 270n67; praise of UAE, 113; return to Zanzibar, 165
Ali Sultan Issa al-Ismaily, 26, 53, 55, 223
Al-Jam'iyya al-Istiqāma al-Khayriyya al-Islāmiyya al-'ālamiyya. *See* Istiqāma
al-Nahda, 14
al-Najah, 14
al-Rawahi brothers, 60–63, 65
al-Ya'araba dynasty, 9, 159, 169
Aman Thani Fairooz, 14, 80, 88, 91, 108, 165, 179
Amnesty International, 80, 82, 234n31
Amour Ali Ameir al-Marhuby, 139
Anthony Ashworth, 141
Anthony Clayton, 82
anticolonial nationalism, 34, 43, 46–47, 49; Arab embrace of, 13–15, 139; divisive visions of, 44; elite criticism of, 33, 214n18; exile criticism of, 21, 177; and insurgency, 47; and Omani heritage, 160
Arab Association, 14, 16, 33–34, 88,
Arabian Gulf, 103, 107, 169; Zanzibaris in, 113–129
Arabic: fluency in, 265n133. *See also* Kiswahili; literacy
Arabism, 142, 144; and Swahili, 152–156
Arab League, 121
Arabs: demographics of in Zanzibar, 13; generations of, 13–18; returnee conception as, 144–146; Zanzibaris status as in the Gulf, 114. *See also* Afro-Arabs; Arabism; muwalladūn
"Arab slavery", 41, 160–161, 173–175
Asians: attitudes to nationalism, 3–4 ; emigration from East Africa, 232n154; in post–revolution Zanzibar, 89–90
Asim Jamali, 138
Asya al-Bualy, 26, 154, 212n191
asylum: in Bahrain, 254n140; in Dubai, 104, 110–114, 254n140; in Egypt, 234n22; in Great Britain, 81, 105; in Kenya, 67; in Oman, 68, 73, 110; for

Omanis in East Africa, 173; in Saudi Arabia, 24, 63; ZA facilitation of, 117

Bagamoyo, 11, 109,
Bahrain, 79, 80, 120, 122, 124, 162
Baluchi, 11, 152, 154
Basra, 168
belonging, 7, 26–27, 176; citizenship as, 5; and community, 185–189; Islam as resource for, 91, 159; and memory, 4; and migration, 38; and the nation-state, 15, 24, 67, 88, 134, 144, 146, 156; and the past, 158; transnationally, 157
birth certificate, 39–40, 43
Bi Ubwa Amour Zahour al-Ismaily, 17, 26, 66, 90, 180, 221n119
Blood report, 45
British Nationality Act, 1948, 38
British Red Cross (BRC), 52; estimates of revolution casualties, 225; expulsion from Zanzibar, 111
bureaucratic registration, 193n15
Burundi, 59–60, 168, 170, 188, 197, 274n113

Cairo, 72, 80, 96, 122; exiles in, 78, 79, 95, 101, 109, 111; muwalladūn education in, 15–17, 139, 140, 141, 153, 205n118, 211–212n191
Canning Award, 12
capitalism, 6, 127
certificate of identity, 120, 121
Chama Cha Mapinduzi (CCM), 81, 96, 98, 99, 162, 172, 185
Christianity, 42, 101, 174, 277n181
citizenship: and ancestry, 24, 89, 134; as birthright, 38; defined, 192n11; and development, 5–7, 187; and marriage, 148; and women, 147, 262n89. *See also* belonging; nation-state
Civic United Front (CUF), 185, 234n31
civil service: in Oman, 138, 141; in Zanzibar, 15, 41, 42, 176, 206n126;
Clove Growers Association, 36–37
cloves, 6, 32, 36–37, 48, 57, 86–87, 202n92
Cold War, 83, 163
Committee of ZNP and ZPPP in Exile, 78
Commonwealth Immigration Act of 1962

communism, 6, 84, 96, 209n160
Communist Party of Great Britain, 205n123
Comorians, 39, 64, 89, 94, 171
Conflict and Harmony in Zanzibar, 25
coup, 88, 247n193; in Oman, 23, 121–123, 129; revolution as, 62, 92, 101, 179

Dammam (Saudi Arabia), 24, 103, 119–120
Dar-es-Salaam, 1, 2, 11, 41, 88, 98, 105, 122, 139; escape to, 107–110,
David Roberts, 105, 115
"Dawlat Zanjibar," 167. *See also* Omani empire; Sultanate of Zanzibar and Pemba
decolonization, 5; and citizenship, 87; and the Cold War, 83; and conflict, 20, 52, 92, 105, 176; and development, 5, 85; and nation-building; and personal subjectivities, 4; and refugees; and transregional relations, 2. *See also* citizenship; nation state
Deira (neighborhood in Dubai), 112
democracy: and development, 23, 48–49, 196n39; and elections in Zanzibar, 16, 47, 163; and immigration, 38–45, 49; and monarchy, 6, 50; in Oman, 22; after the revolution, 79–80, 88, 101, 183. *See also* elections
development: economics of, 6, 22, 86–87; 97–98, 133, 160, 189; as ideology, 14–15, 31; mass expectations of, 5, 32, 163; in Oman, 23; in Zanzibar, 85, 207n136
developmental state: after the revolution, 85–87; in colonial Zanzibar, 13–18; expectations of, 5–7; failures of, 22, 87, 97; in Oman, 21–24, 136–141; religious tensions in, 83, 92–94, 98–100, 101
Dhofar, 23
dhows, 18, 37, 53, 62, 69, 70, 73, 106–107, 112, 126, 216–217n43–44
diaspora: after the revolution, 107–110; and citizenship, 3, 5–7 and decolonization, 1–4; and displacement, 18–21, 66–73; and generation; 92; tensions within, 21, 81, 125, 127–129; types of, 2–3. *See also* exile; refugee(s)
displacement. *See* diaspora; refugee(s)

Dubai, 2, 27, 78, 79, 80, 81, 88, 100, 108, 119, 120, 126; asylum in, 108–109, 110–113; economic policies, 248n8; education in, 123–124; naturalization policies of, 122–123; residence policies of, 113–118; ruler of, 104, 113–115, 117–118, 129 ; working in, 123–126

East African Airways, 137
East African Federation, 19
East African Muslim Welfare Society (EAMWS), 241n119
East Germany, 236–237n59
education: and colonialism, 204–205n114, 205n117–121
election(s): of 1957, 41, 43–44; of 1963, 47; enfranchisement of women in, 213n1; of January and June 1961, 45–47; and naturalization, 35–45
Erik Bennett (General Bennett), 141
Euan Smith Madrasa, 67
Executive Council, 34
exile, 1, 24; and counter-revolution, 78–79, 96; and generation, 20, 126–128; and Islam, 83–85, 255n151; journalism, 77, 80–81, 91–94; and long-distance nationalism, 77; and politics in diaspora, 18, 21; and relations with Tanzania, 72, 78; and representation of the nation, 77–78; and shifting nationality, 24. *See also* asylum; diaspora
exogenous origins, 33, 36, 45, 52. *See also* indigeneity; nativism

Faleh bin Nasser al-Thani, 121
Fareed al-Hinai, 138
Fatma bint Saada Nassor al-Lamky, 15
Fatma Jinja, 26, 185
Fatma Salem al-Maamiry, 140
Federation of Progressive Trade Unions, 17
Foreign Office (FO), 68
Free Zanzibar Voice (FZV), 20, 26, 77, 80
Fujairah, 124

Gamal Abdel Nasser, 231n144, 246n183
Gary Thomas Burgess, 55, 58, 86
generation(s): of Arabs in Zanzibar, 13–18, 47, 139, 142–143, 151; and language shift in Oman, 152–154; and memory transmission, 25, 159, 165, 169, 173, 176–177, 182–183, 187–188; in exile, 108–110, 126–129, 166
genocide, 55–56, 180, 222n6
George Mooring, 60
Georges Hoffman, 69
Ghana, 14, 32
Great Britain, 17, 88, 104, 157, 210n176
Gujarat, 10–11
Gulf Cooperation Council (GCC), 260n67
Gulf Technical College, 124

Habiba al-Hinai, 1, 19, 65, 91, 109, 166, 188
Hadhramaut, 11, 13, 68, 119
Hamaki (Harakati za Mabadaliko ya Kidemokrasia Zanzibar), 100
Hamed al-Harassy, 137
Hamed bin Muhammad al-Murjebi (Tippu Tip), 11
Hamoud Marhuby, 25, 65
Harith Ghassany, 50, 54, 155, 173, 178, 192n7
Harold Soref, 82
Haroub Othman, 82
Hashil bin Rashid al-Miskery, 14, 214n18
Hashil Seif Hashil, 25, 180
Hassan Abdulla, 111
Hassan Nassor Moyo, 108
heritage: ambivalent, 273–274n111; definition of, 159; and the Indian Ocean, 164; limitations of, 182–184, 266n12; of Oman in Zanzibar, 171–173; and Omani empire, 167–171; Omani national, 24–25, 142, 152, 158–160, 270n60; of returnees, 24, 154, 187; of slavery, 173–176
Hilal Muhammad Ali al-Barwani, 14
history: and memory, 4, 183; oral, 52, 60, 144, 150; writing, 158, 195n29. *See also* vernacular historiography
Horn of Africa, 169
Hunaina Sultan al-Mugheiry, 139

Ibadis. *See* Ibadism
Ibadism, 9, 12, 60, 140, 142, 228n91
Ibrahim Noor Shariff, 25, 174, 178, 219n83, 225n34
Ibtisam al-Habsi, 136

Ibuni Saleh, 94,
Idris Wakil, 162, 205n117
Imam Ahmed bin Said al-Busaidi, 10
Imamate of Oman, 9–10, 23, 200n68, 210n174, 229n104
Imamate passports, 68, 116, 119, 121–122, 229n104, 254n122
Imamate uprising, 23
Imam Nasir bin Murshid al-Ya'araba, 9
Imam Saif bin Sultan I al-Ya'araba, 9
Imam Saif bin Sultan II al-Ya'araba, 9
Imam Sultan bin Saif I al-Ya'araba, 9
immigration: and citizenship, 38, 42; in colonial Zanzibar; to Dubai, 113–114; and elections, 44; to the Gulf, 103; to Oman, 110–111, 148, to Qatar, 121; undocumented, 107–108, 148; to the United Kingdom, 105. *See also* asylum; migration; naturalization
independence. *See* decolonization; nation-state
India, 3, 7, 9, 12, 22, 37, 38, 104, 139, 141
Indian Association: founding of, 203n107
Indian Ocean: in decolonization, 5; dhows in, 36–37; diaspora(s), 2–4, 8; economic shifts in, 6–7, 163–164; as motif of cosmopolitanism, 142, 158. *See also* exile(s)
indigeneity, 3–4, 7, 20, 33, 35. *See also* belonging; nativism
intermarriage, 24, 42, 143, 198n62, 218–219n77, 261n78; Omani prohibitions on, 260n67
International Committee of the Red Cross (ICRC), 52, 69, 73
International Muslim Youth Conference, 96
Iran, 7, 35, 104, 139
Islam: as belonging, 4, 163, 262n98; in East Africa, 8, 11, 142, 169; and European colonialism, 174; and the exiles, 177–178, 219n81, 255n151; and the inward turn, 127–128; in Oman, 10, 159; and slavery, 174; as social critique, 83–85, 91, 96–99; in Zanzibar, 97, 170–171 246n183. *See also* Ibadism; Muslims in Tanzania
Issa Nasser al-Ismaily, 14, 16, 60, 141, 165, 171, 174, 176, 178, 206n126

Issa Salim Muhammad al-Rawahi, 61, 82
Istiqāma, 163

Jakaya Kikwete, 54, 172, 186
Juhaynat-l-Akhbār fī tārīkh Zanjibār, 272n89
Julius Nyerere: allegation of being pro-Israel, 244n151; allegations of religious bias, 98; attitude to Zanzibar, 240n102, 242n126, 244n150, 244n154; 47; exile criticism of, 92–94; 98–99; role in the revolution, 58; and the Tanzanian Union, 18–19, 243n148, 246n176, 277n170; views of Arabs, 93; visit to the Gulf, 162. *See also* Abdulrahman Mohamed Babu; Ahmed Seif Kharusi; Ali Muhsin al-Barwani; Oscar Kambona; Tanzanian Union; Zanzibar Revolution
Juma Aley, 170, 205n117, 221n135, 234n20

Kachchh, 11
Kenya: and Zanzibar refugees, 107–110, 117, 121, 128, 138, 148, 168, 189, 232n154, 247n200. *See also* Mombasa
Kenya coast, 46–47, 185
khādim, 143. *See also* slave descent
Kiinua Miguu (Central) prison, 64
killings, 55–58, 65. *See also* pogrom
Kinganganyiro na Utumwa, 171, 174
Kiswahili, 4, 8, 24–26; education in, 14–15; language of Zanzibar refugees, 67, 83; in Oman, 152, 155; and poetry, 98–99; and triglossia, 154. *See also* Arabic; literacy
Kuwait, 5
Kwa Heri Ukoloni, Kwa Heri Uhuru!, 25, 178

L. W. Hollingsworth, 82, 170
land re-distribution, 85–86
language shift, 152
Legislative Council, 16, 34–35, 41, 47
Leslie Goodyear, 103
Levant, 14
Libya, 2, 81, 96, 111, 113, 197n51
literacy: in Arabic, 13, 123, 199n65, 265n133; in English, 123, 152–153; in Swahili, 14–15, 152–153

long-distance nationalism, 77, 195n130
Lyutha Sultan al-Mugheiry, 139

Maendeleo Zanzibar, 100
Mainlanders, 10; as clove pickers, 12, 240n98; in electoral politics, 41, 42–43, 44; migration to Zanzibar, 36–37, 38–40; role in revolution, 224n23; as working class in Zanzibar, 17, 34. *See also* Africans
Majlis al-Dawla, 136
Makerere University, 16, 170, 205n117
Manga Arab: as refugees, 66–70, 73; definition of, 18; killings of, 63–64; migration to Zanzibar, 36–37, 216n43
Maulid Mshangama Haj, 94, 140, 165, 181
Mauritius, 10, 183
May Day Eve amnesties, 62, 65
Mayo College, 22
Mayuko Okawa, 256n
Medinat al-Naḥda, 136, 143
Medinat al-Qaboos, 136
memory: communicative, 159; multi-directional, 25–26, 158; transmission of, 169–170, 182; and the Zanzibar revolution, 176–181. *See also* history
Michael Lofchie, 32
migration, 8, 53, 73, 83, 86, 104, 105, 108, 115, 164, 186, 188; regulation of in colonial Zanzibar, 35–40, 216n43. *See also* asylum; exile; immigration; return migration
Mina al-Fahal, 136
Ministry of Heritage and Culture. *See* Omani Ministry of Heritage and Culture
mob violence. *See* pogrom
Mohamed Nassor Lamky, 206–207n133
Mohamed Said Al-Mulla, 116, 118, 248n1, 252n92
Mombasa, 9–10, 17, 67, 73, 79, 88, 103 148, 155, 168; migration to from Zanzibar, 62, 107–109, 112, 119, 121, 136, 140
monarchy. *See* al-Busaidi dynasty
Mozambique, 20, 79, 169
Mshashi, 200n67
Muhammad Abdul-Muttalib Hashim, 108, 114, 117, 119, 162, 178, 243, 244, 250

Muhammad al-Barwani, author, 14
Muhammad al-Barwani, chair of MB Holdings, 137
Muhammad Ali al-Barwani, 14
Muhammad Ali al-Hinawy, 138
Muhammad Ali Muhsin al-Barwani, 166
Muhammad al-Mawaly, 137
Muhammad al-Rumhi, 137
Muhammad Salim al-Barwani (Jinja), 47, 66
Muhammad Seif al-Rahbi, 166, 174, 271n81
Muhammad Shamte, 82, 244n150
Mukallah, 119
Muscat, 2, 9, 10, 18, 36, 38, 44, 79, 115, 122; development and expansion of, 23; migration to, 68, 69, 106, 110–113, 121; Zanzibaris in, 24
Muslims in Tanzania, 84–85, 91, 93, 94, 163, 237n65. *See also* Islam
Mutta. *See* Muhammad Abdul-Muttalib Hashim
muwalladūn, 11, 23, 26, 159, 172, 176; and belonging, 15, 189; definition of, 8–9; education of in Zanzibar, 13–15; history writing of, 182, 188; perception of in Oman, 143; wealth of, 186; as wealthy elites, 13–14, 34, 128, 186
mwambao, 46
Mwinyi Mkuu, 35
Mwongozi, 47
Mzee Aboud, 179, 233n9, 240n108

Nafla Kharusi, 152
Naila Barwani, 144, 155, 278n188
Nairobi, 2, 88,
Nasser al-Riyami, 25, 166, 172, 211–212n191
Nasser Seif al-Bualy, 154
nationalism: defined, 203n103
nationality decrees: in Oman; in Zanzibar, 217n50
nation-state: and belonging, 192n11; and decolonization, 5, 32; and diaspora, 2; and migration, 164; and the passport, 36; Swahili coast as, 4; Zanzibar as, 25. *See also* belonging; citizenship; naturalization; sovereignty
nativism: challenges to, 189; and the nation-state, 3–4; in the politics of Zanzibar, 33, 35, 42, 52, 219n81

naturalization: in Dubai, 118, 121–122; in Oman, 115, 134–136; in United Kingdom, 104–105; in Zanzibar, 38–40, 44, 45, 61, 67–68. *See also* citizenship; elections; exogenous origins; immigration
Nick Phillips, 72, 111
Nienke Boer, 2
Nigeria, 14
No Objection Certificate (NOC), 106, 108, 118, 122

Obed Seif al-Hatmi, 138
Okello, John, 223n16
Oman: and East Africa, 8–12; changing value of citizenship, 23–24, 120, 134–135; coup in, 23, 121–123; heritage of, 165, 167–173; and petroleum, 23; population of, 255–256n1; and Zanzibar refugees, 66–69. *See also* Omani empire; Seyyid Said; Said bin Taimur; Sultan Qaboos
Omani empire, 167–170, 171–173, 273n96
Omani Ministry of Heritage and Culture, 158, 159, 168
Omani National Archives, 172
Omani-Zanzibaris, 24–25, 152, 164, 166, 172
Oman State Council. *See* Majlis al-Dawla
Organization of Petroleum Exporting Countries (OPEC), 22, 23
Oscar Kambona, 54, 82; fallout with Nyerere, 81, 92; rapprochement with exiles, 243–44; role in revolution, 54, 56, 178, 244n23
Othman Sharif, 71, 90, 93

Pan African Freedom Movement of East and Central Africa (PAFMECA), 44–45
pan-Africanism, 13, 44, 83, 243n148; and the Union, 19
pan-Arabism, 13
passports: Abu Dhabi, 118; confiscation of, 90, 142, 151; Dubai, 114–115, 124; fraudulent use of, 148–150; Imamate, 116, 119–122; loss of in revolution; Muscat, 107, 111, 115, 120, 122; and Omani citizenship, 134–135, 189
Pemba, 10, 13, 19, 37, 39, 40, 52, 57, 59, 65, 109, 110, 140; in Zanzibar elections, 44–47

petroleum, 104, 120; and development, 6–7; discovery in Oman, 22–23, 210n174; price increase, 97. *See also* 1986 oil price slump
Petroleum Development Oman (PDO), 137, 141, 150, 210n174, 258n30
pogrom, 52, 61, 67, 92, 182; casualties of, 18, 55; character of, 57; contrasted with genocide, 56; mob in, 57–64, 66; of 1961, 46
Portsmouth, 2, 19, 20, 77, 78–79, 80
Portugal, 78
Prison Island, 18, 67, 69, 90, 223n11

Qatar, 80, 120–121, 122, 139; Zanzibaris in; per capita income, 253n112
Qurum, 136

Raha Leo, 56, 57, 59, 60, 61, 64, 65, 89,
Ras al-Khaymah, 109, 119–120, 124, 141,
Rashid Hamadi, 79, 91, 108, 109
Rashidiya (Dubai neighborhood), 118
Rashid Said al-Maktoum, 104, 113–115, 117
Red Cross, 18, 20, 52–53, 66–72, 111; revolutionary attitudes to, 71–72, 231n137
refugee(s), 8, 24, 46, 53, 62, 81–82, 88; in the Gulf, 104, 106, 114–125; as Manga, 67–73, 110–112; in Oman, 146. *See also* asylum; exile; migration
returnee(s), 27, 133; conceptions of Omani belonging, 144–147; and gender, 147–148; and language, 152–156; and Omani nationality law, 150–152; process of migration, 134–136; role in Omani development, 136–141; state attitudes towards, 142–144. *See also* Omani-Zanzibaris
return migration. *See* returnees
Reunion, 10
revolution. *See* Zanzibar revolution
Revolutionary Council, 1, 50, 70–71, 85, 108, 110, 161; excess of, 88, 90, 93–96, 180; factions within, 71
Robert Shaaban, 174
Ruwi, 112, 136

Sabaki, 8
Said Abdulla Seif al-Hatimy, 140

Said Seif al-Riyami, 108
Said Shaksy, 16, 138, 141, 258n42
Saif Hamed al-Hinai, 137
Salafism, 13
Salem ben Nasser al-Ismaily, 26, 138–39
Salim Ahmed Salim (al-Riyami), 17, 162
Salim Hamdan, 17
Salim Rashid, 17, 54, 235n39
Salma al-Kindy, 139
Samir al-Adawi, 139
Samira Salim Seif al-Maamiry, 15–16, 140, 192n10
Saqr Muhammad Salim al-Qasimi, 120
Saud Ahmed al-Busaidi, 14–16, 105, 139, 145, 177
Saudi Arabia, 24, 63, 80, 88, 119, 122, 124, 125, 159. *See also* Dammam
Sauti ya Afro Shirazi, 40
Sauti ya Cairo, 82
Sauti ya Unguja, 17
Sawt 'Uman, 23
Sayyida Matuka School, 66–67
secularism, 7, 15, 83–84, 91, 101
Seif Hamoud al-Bahlani, 138
Seif Sharif Hamad, 17, 26, 162
Seyyid Abdullah bin Khalifa, 48
Seyyid Ahmed Thabit, 117–18
Seyyid Bargash bin Said, 12, 167
Seyyid Hamad bin Ahmed al-Haddad, 179
Seyyidie Province, 46
Seyyid Jamshid bin Abdullah, 48, 50, 79, 80, 88, 117, 121, 240n108; migration to Oman, 186, 261n79; migration to Portsmouth, 19; and the politics of decolonization, 50, 220n106
Seyyid Jamshid Group, 80
Seyyid Khalifa bin Harub, 50; birth in Muscat, 220n104; death in Zanzibar, 45
Seyyid Said bin Sultan, 10, 12, 167–71, 174, 261n84
Shaaban Saleh al-Farsy (also al-Farsi), 14, 25, 140, 178, 228n86
Sharifa Lamky, 211–212n191
Sharjah, 79, 124, 146, 166
sheha, 39, 65, 228,

Shihr, 112
Shiism, 12
Shirazi, 64, 144; meaning of term, 55; 199n65; migration from Zanzibar, 89, 112–113; in Zanzibar politics, 47–48
Shirazi Association, 41, 203n107
slave descent, 43, 143, 219n84
slavery: abolition of in Zanzibar, 12; as heritage of Zanzibar, 173, 274n118; and Islam, 174; in political rhetoric, 41, 161, 242n124; in the vernacular historiography, 174–176; and Zanzibar economy, 49, 171; and the Zanzibar Revolution, 31, 89, 160, 173
sovereignty: and citizenship, 15; horizontal versus vertical, 32–33, 48–50, 145–146; of Zanzibar 12, 36, 42, 46, 84, 96, 160, 176, 187–188. *See also* anticolonial nationalism; Omani empire; Tanzania Union
stateless. *See* refugees
State University of Zanzibar, 171
Stone Town, 14, 26, 37, 57, 61, 66, 165, 166, 172
Suad Lamky, 211–212n191
Suleiman Malik, 80, 88
Sultan Ahmed al-Mugheiry, 16, 139, 245n163
Sultanate of Zanzibar and Pemba, 2, 31, 173
Sultan Qaboos, 27, 81, 104, 114, 129, 135, 145, 162–163
Sultan Qaboos University (SQU), 139, 172
Sultan Said bin Taimur, 22–23, 122, 210n176, 211n183, 264n130
Sunnism, 12
Swahili. *See* Kiswahili
Swahili Coast, 8, 10, 24–25, 37, 155, 169, 187
Swahili diaspora, 195n30
Swahili Muslim public sphere, 164, 189

Tanganyikan African National Union (TANU), 81, 96
Tanzania na Propaganda za Udini, 174, 180
Tanzania Union, 19, 70, 90, 160, 162, 180, 183; and Afro-Arab relations, 72; criticism of, 84, 94, 95–97, 99–100; Nyerere's interest in, 79, 92, 243n148,

244n150, 244n154, 245n165, 246n176, 277n170; and pan-Africanism, 83; ratification of, 207–208n148; 242n126; and Zanzibar sovereignty, 19, 101, 187. *See also* East African Federation
Timothy Landon, 141
translocal, 37–38, 150, 165
tribe, 9, 36, 40, 135, 142, 143, 149
triglossia, 154
Trucial States. *See* Abu Dhabi; Dubai; Fujairah; Ras al-Khaymah; Sharjah; UAE

Uganda, 15, 18, 19, 36, 54, 93, 96, 97, 115, 168, 169, 170
Umma Party: role in revolution, 223n15, 225n30
Unguja, 1, 10, 13, 14, 17, 18, 35, 37, 40, 43, 53, 55, 57, 58, 59, 70, 85, 89, 99, 101, 167, 179, 183, 185, 202n92, 238–239n78
Union (of Tanganyika and Zanzibar). *See* Tanzania Union
United Arab Emirates (UAE), 73, 103, 113, 117, 127, 165; nationality of, 122–123; work permits for, 248n10. *See also* Abu Dhabi, Dubai
United Kingdom, 19, 21, 38, 73, 88, 92, 116, 117, 141, 182; exiles in, 77–81, 83, 104–105, 124, 136, 137; higher education in, 137, 205n123
United Nations, 5, 125
United Nations High Commission on Refugees (UNHCR), 18, 52–53, 66–70, 72–73, 80, 103, 106, 108, 111, 115–118, 121, 123–126, 188
Unyamwezi, 11
urbanization, 198n54
ustaaarabu: and uungwana, 201n85. *See also* Arabism

van Riebeeck, 67–68, 111
vernacular historiography, 24, 26, 158–160, 170, 173–183
Vietnam, 47
violence. *See* killings; pogrom
visas: Omani; Tanzania; UAE; Zanzibar
voter registration, 213n2

Wahid al-Kharusi, 138
wali, 135, 149
Warith al-Kharusi, 137
Wattayah, 136
Wolfgang Dourado, 95
World Islamic Call, 96–97
World War I, 14, 34, 36, 182, 216n41
World War II, 3, 6, 15–16, 34, 38, 40, 177, 189

Yao-land, 11
Yemen, 112,
Young African Social Union, 17
Youth's Own Union, 17

Zainab Himid, 66
Zanjibar: Shakhshsiyāt wa Aḥdāth, 25
Zanzibar Affairs Office, 79
Zanzibar and Overseas Association, 234n27
Zanzibar and Pemba People's Party (ZPPP), 40, 45, 46, 48, 78, 82, 181, 218n59
Zanzibar Association (ZA), 21, 100, 106, 108, 115, 120; in Dubai and Abu Dhabi, 116–118, 123, 125, 127, 139, 161,162
Zanzibar Liberation Front, 79, 95, 234n24
Zanzibar National Archives (ZNA), 112, 171, 216n43, 273n109
Zanzibar Nationalist Party (ZNP): allegations of British hostility to, 177–178; ASP perception of, 41; election performance of, 43, 45; formation of, 16; leadership in exile, 73, 78–80, 95–100; naturalization drives of, 44; role in Zanzibar's independence, 47–48; socialist sympathies within, 17, 42, 83; splits within, 47, 49, 179; supporters targeted in revolution, 52–55, 65, 67, 87–88. *See also* democracy; elections; exiles
Zanzibar nationality, 16, 38, 40, 187. *See also* citizenship; naturalization
Zanzibar Organization (ZO), 26, 78–79, 80; founding of, 79; tactics of, 234n31; Tanzanian government view of, 235n39
Zanzibar protectorate, 12, 14, 37, 139

Zanzibar Revolution, 25, 53, 78, 83, 197n51; casualties of, 55, 224–5n28; counterhistory of, 91–94; as genocide, 225n35; as invasion, 54–55, 57, 91, 178, 244n152; memories of, 1–2, 24–25, 58–66, 176–183; refugees from, 70–73; and the Union as cultural trauma, 2

Zanzibar treason trial, 245n165
Zanzibar Youth and Students Union, 17
Zanzibar Youth Union, 17
Zayed bin Sultan al-Nehayan, 104, 114, 124
Ziwani, 18
Zuhura Yunus, 26

THE CALIFORNIA WORLD HISTORY LIBRARY

Edited by Edmund Burke III, Kenneth Pomeranz, and Patricia Seed

1. *The Unending Frontier: Environmental History of the Early Modern World,* by John F. Richards

2. *Maps of Time: An Introduction to Big History,* by David Christian

3. *The Graves of Tarim: Genealogy and Mobility across the Indian Ocean,* by Engseng Ho

4. *Imperial Connections: India in the Indian Ocean Arena, 1860–1920,* by Thomas R. Metcalf

5. *Many Middle Passages: Forced Migration and the Making of the Modern World,* edited by Emma Christopher, Cassandra Pybus, and Marcus Rediker

6. *Domesticating the World: African Consumerism and the Genealogies of Globalization,* by Jeremy Prestholdt

7. *Servants of the Dynasty: Palace Women in World History,* edited by Anne Walthall

8. *Island World: A History of Hawai'i and the United States,* by Gary Y. Okihiro

9. *The Environment and World History,* edited by Edmund Burke III and Kenneth Pomeranz

10. *Pineapple Culture: A History of the Tropical and Temperate Zones,* by Gary Y. Okihiro

11. *The Pilgrim Art: Cultures of Porcelain in World History,* by Robert Finlay

12. *The Quest for the Lost Nation: Writing History in Germany and Japan in the American Century,* by Sebastian Conrad; translated by Alan Nothnagle

13. *The Eastern Mediterranean and the Making of Global Radicalism, 1860–1914,* by Ilham Khuri-Makdisi

14. *The Other West: Latin America from Invasion to Globalization,* by Marcello Carmagnani

15. *Mediterraneans: North Africa and Europe in an Age of Migration, c. 1800–1900,* by Julia A. Clancy-Smith

16. *History and the Testimony of Language,* by Christopher Ehret

17. *From the Indian Ocean to the Mediterranean: The Global Trade Networks of Armenian Merchants from New Julfa,* by Sebouh David Aslanian
18. *Berenike and the Ancient Maritime Spice Route,* by Steven E. Sidebotham
19. *The Haj to Utopia: The Ghadar Movement and Its Transnational Connections, 1905–1930,* by Maia Ramnath
20. *Sky Blue Stone: The Turquoise Trade in World History,* by Arash Khazeni
21. *Pirates, Merchants, Settlers, and Slaves: Colonial America and the Indo-Atlantic World,* by Kevin P. McDonald
22. *Black London: The Imperial Metropolis and Decolonization in the Twentieth Century,* by Marc Matera
23. *The New World History: A Field Guide for Teachers and Researchers,* edited by Ross E. Dunn, Laura J. Mitchell, and Kerry Ward
24. *Margins of the Market: Trafficking and Capitalism across the Arabian Sea,* by Johan Mathew
25. *A Global History of Gold Rushes,* edited by Benjamin Mountford and Stephen Tuffnell
26. *A Global History of Sexual Science, 1880–1960,* edited by Veronika Fuechtner, Douglas E. Haynes, and Ryan M. Jones
27. *Potosí: The Silver City That Changed the World,* by Kris Lane
28. *A Global History of Runaways,* edited by Marcus Rediker, Titas Chakraborty, and Matthias van Rossum
29. *The City and the Wilderness: Indo-Persian Encounters on the Burmese Frontier,* by Arash Khazeni
30. *The Bloody Flag: Mutiny in the Age of Atlantic Revolution,* by Niklas Frykman
31. *Empire of Convicts: Indian Penal Labor in Colonial Southeast Asia,* by Anand A. Yang
32. *Zanzibar Was a Country: Exile and Citizenship between East Africa and the Gulf,* by Nathaniel Mathews

Founded in 1893,
UNIVERSITY OF CALIFORNIA PRESS
publishes bold, progressive books and journals
on topics in the arts, humanities, social sciences,
and natural sciences—with a focus on social
justice issues—that inspire thought and action
among readers worldwide.

The UC PRESS FOUNDATION
raises funds to uphold the press's vital role
as an independent, nonprofit publisher, and
receives philanthropic support from a wide
range of individuals and institutions—and from
committed readers like you. To learn more, visit
ucpress.edu/supportus.

www.ingramcontent.com/pod-product-compliance
Lightning Source LLC
Chambersburg PA
CBHW021335230426
43666CB00006B/300